INDONESIA
IN THE NEW WORLD

The **ANU Indonesia Project**, a leading international centre of research and graduate training on the Indonesian economy and society, is housed in the **Crawford School of Public Policy's Arndt-Corden Department of Economics**. The Crawford School is part of **ANU College of Asia and the Pacific** at **The Australian National University (ANU)**. Established in 1965 in response to profound changes in the Indonesian economic and political landscapes, the ANU Indonesia Project has grown from a small group of Indonesia-focused economists into an interdisciplinary research centre well known and respected across the world. Funded by ANU and the Australian Department of Foreign Affairs and Trade, the ANU Indonesia Project monitors and analyses recent developments in Indonesia; informs the Australian and Indonesian governments, business and the wider community about those developments and about future prospects; stimulates research on the Indonesian economy; and publishes the respected *Bulletin of Indonesian Economic Studies*.

ANU College of Asia and the Pacific's **Department of Political and Social Change** focuses on domestic politics, social processes and state–society relationships in Asia and the Pacific, and has a long-established interest in Indonesia.

Together with the Department of Political and Social Change, the ANU Indonesia Project holds the annual Indonesia Update conference, which offers an overview of recent economic and political developments and devotes attention to a significant theme in Indonesia's development. The *Bulletin of Indonesian Economic Studies* publishes the conference's economic and political overviews, while the edited papers related to the conference theme are published in the Indonesia Update Series.

The **ISEAS – Yusof Ishak Institute** (formerly Institute of Southeast Asian Studies) was established as an autonomous organization in 1968. It is a regional centre dedicated to the study of socio-political, security and economic trends and developments in Southeast Asia and its wider geostrategic and economic environment. The Institute's research programmes are the Regional Economic Studies (RES, including ASEAN and APEC), Regional Strategic and Political Studies (RSPS), and Regional Social and Cultural Studies (RSCS).

ISEAS Publishing, an established academic press, has issued more than 2,000 books and journals. It is the largest scholarly publisher of research about Southeast Asia from within the region. ISEAS Publishing works with many other academic and trade publishers and distributors to disseminate important research and analyses from and about Southeast Asia to the rest of the world.

Indonesia Update Series

INDONESIA IN THE NEW WORLD

Globalisation, Nationalism and Sovereignty

EDITED BY
ARIANTO A. PATUNRU
MARI PANGESTU
M. CHATIB BASRI

First published in Singapore in 2018 by
ISEAS Publishing
30 Heng Mui Keng Terrace
Singapore 119614

E-mail: publish@iseas.edu.sg
Website: http://bookshop.iseas.edu.sg

All rights reserved. No part of this publication may be reproduced, translated, stored in a retrieval system, or transmitted in any form or by any means, electronic, mechanical, photocopying, recording or otherwise, without the prior permission of the ISEAS – Yusof Ishak Institute.

© 2018 ISEAS – Yusof Ishak Institute, Singapore

The responsibility for facts and opinions in this publication rests exclusively with the authors and their interpretations do not necessarily reflect the views or the policy of the Institute or its supporters.

ISEAS Library Cataloguing-in-Publication Data

Indonesia in the New World : Globalisation, Nationalism and Sovereignty edited by Arianto A. Patunru, Mari Pangestu and M Chatib Basri.
"... an outcome of the Indonesia Update Conference held in Canberra on 15–16 September 2017."
1. Globalization – Economic aspects – Indonesia.
2. Nationalism – Indonesia.
3. Indonesia – Foreign relations.
4. Sovereignty.
I. Patunru, Arianto A., editor.
II. Pangestu, Mari, editor.
III. Basri, M. Chatib, editor.
IV. Indonesia Update Conference (35th : 2017 : Australian National University)
V. Title: Globalisation, Nationalism and Sovereignty.
DS644.4 I41 2017   2018

ISBN 978-981-4818-22-3 (soft cover)
ISBN 978-981-4818-28-5 (hard cover)
ISBN 978-981-4818-23-0 (e-book, PDF)

Cover photo: President Joko Widodo visits the remote Natuna Islands on board navy warship *KRI Imam Bonjol 383* in June 2016, a few days after the same vessel was involved in an altercation with a Chinese fishing boat.
Photo by Krishadiyanto. Reproduced with permission from Kantor Sekretariat Presiden, Republic of Indonesia.

Edited and typeset by Beth Thomson, Japan Online, Canberra
Indexed by Angela Grant, Sydney
Printed in Singapore by Markono Print Media Pte Ltd

Contents

Tables	vii
Figures	ix
Contributors	xi
Acknowledgments	xiii
Glossary	xv

1 Challenges for Indonesia in the new world 1
   Arianto A. Patunru, Mari E. Pangestu and M. Chatib Basri

PART 1 GLOBALISATION, NATIONALISM AND SOVEREIGNTY: THE INDONESIAN EXPERIENCE

2 Challenging geography: asserting economic sovereignty in a porous archipelago 17
   Anthony Reid

3 The new nationalism in Indonesia 35
   Edward Aspinall

4 Nationalism, sovereignty and foreign policy: Indonesia and the disputes over the South China Sea 52
   Shafiah F. Muhibat

PART 2 NATIONALISM IN PRACTICE

5 Feeding the *bangsa*: food sovereignty and the state in Indonesia 73
   Jeff Neilson

6 Nationalism, developmentalism and politics in Indonesia's mining sector 90
   Eve Warburton

| 7 | Who is afraid of economic openness? People's perceptions of globalisation in Indonesia
Yose Rizal Damuri and Mari Pangestu | 109 |

PART 3 IMPACT OF AND RESPONSE TO GLOBALISATION

8	Anti-globalisation, poverty and inequality in Indonesia *Arief Anshory Yusuf and Peter Warr*	133
9	Gender, labour markets and trade liberalisation in Indonesia *Krisztina Kis-Katos, Janneke Pieters and Robert Sparrow*	157
10	The good, the bad and the promise of globalisation: a private sector perspective *Manggi Habir*	180

PART 4 THE HUMAN FACE OF GLOBALISATION

11	Globalisation and labour: the Indonesian experience *T. Yudo Wicaksono and Chris Manning*	201
12	Restoring the rights of Indonesian migrant workers through the Village of Care (Desbumi) program *Anis Hidayah*	225
13	Globalisation, the role of the state and the rule of law: human trafficking in eastern Indonesia *Dominggus Elcid Li*	243

PART 5 NAVIGATING THE NEW GLOBALISATION

| 14 | Indonesia and the global economy: missed opportunities?
Hal Hill and Deasy Pane | 267 |
| 15 | International cooperation and the management of globalisation: the Indonesian experience
Titik Anas and Dionisius Narjoko | 294 |

Index   317

Tables

7.1	Selected indicators of openness, 2015–16	113
7.2	Characteristics of the sample	115
7.3	Summary of independent variables and the expected signs	120
7.4	Marginal effect of statistically significant variables for the response '3 = beneficial'	121
8.1	Change in poverty incidence and inequality, 1976–96, 2000–08 and 2008–16	135
8.2	Nominal rates of protection by sector, 2008 and 2015	139
8.3	Impact of global protectionism on output by sector	146
8.4	Impact of Indonesia's protectionism on nominal return to factors of production	148
8.5	Impact of Indonesia's protectionism on poverty incidence	149
8.6	Impact of Indonesia's protectionism on inequality	150
9.1	Labour force participation rate among people aged 16–64 by gender, 1999–2011	162
9.2	Summary statistics at the sectoral level, 2000 and 2010	166
9.3	Female labour intensity of international trade, 2000 and 2010	168
11.1	Service sector jobs in selected industries, 2011–15	208
11.2	Impact of technological change on employment	218
12.1	Number of new Indonesian migrant workers, 2011–16	228
12.2	Number of cases of human rights violations experienced by Indonesian migrant workers, 2011–16	230
12.3	Major migration policies in Indonesia	231
12.4	The three pillars of the Desbumi program	236

12.5	Location and funding of Desbumi projects in five provinces	238
12.6	Summary of progress of Desbumi projects in villages	239
13.1	Palm oil companies that have recruited East Nusa Tenggara workers without following proper procedures, 2014–16	255
14.1	Attitudes towards globalisation in selected countries, 2014	273
14.2	Comparative indicators of economic openness	279
14.3	Global market shares in electronics, 1990–2015	284
14.4	Global market shares in garments, 1976–2015	285
14.5	Global market shares in footwear, 1976–2015	285
14.6	Comparative rankings on Ease of Doing Business Index and Logistics Performance Index, 2006–17	289
14.7	Comparative performance on PISA maths and science tests, 2003–15	289
14.8	Comparative rankings on Corruption Perceptions Index, 2000–16	290
15.1	GDP by country group, 2016	311

Figures

7.1	Survey results: perceptions of the impact of economic openness on the economy	116
7.2	Survey results: perceptions of international economic cooperation and globalisation	117
8.1	Poverty incidence, 1970–2016	134
8.2	Gini coefficient of inequality, 1976–2016	136
8.3	Growth in world trade and GDP, 1990–2016	137
8.4	Trade-to-GDP ratio, Indonesia and the world, 1990–2016	137
8.5	Trade restrictions in G20 countries since October 2008	138
8.6	Impact of global protectionism on real expenditure per capita	144
8.7	Impact of global protectionism on real return to factors of production	145
8.8	Impact of Indonesia's protectionism in the food sector on real expenditure per capita	148
8.9	Impact of Indonesia's protectionism in the mineral sector on real expenditure per capita	151
8.10	Impact of Indonesia's protectionism in the food and mineral sectors on real expenditure per capita	152
9.1	Female labour force participation by age group, 1999–2011	163
9.2	Female labour force participation by sector, 1999–2011	163
9.3	Female share of workers and export share, 2000–10	170
9.4	Female share of workers and imported input share, 2000–10	172
9.5	Female share of workers and import penetration, 2000–10	174

11.1	Share of jobs by major sector, and unemployment rate, 1989–2016	204
11.2	Number of jobs in large and medium manufacturing firms by main industry group, 1989–2013	205
11.3	Share of service sector employment by major subsector, 1989–2016	207
11.4	Ratio of wages by firm ownership and trade orientation, 2014	210
11.5	Wage growth among production workers in selected industries by ownership and trade orientation, 2005–14	211
11.6	Share of firms using email and websites in their daily operations by sector, 2009 and 2015	215
11.7	Share of firms undertaking automation or adopting new technology in the previous three years, by sector, 2015	216
13.1	Number of passengers using East Nusa Tenggara airports, 1984–2016	253
13.2	Number and type of perpetrators of human trafficking in East Nusa Tenggara, 2014–16	256
14.1	Economic openness and inequality in Indonesia, 1976–2015	275
15.1	MFN and applied tariff rates in Indonesia, 1989–2016	296
15.2	Relationship between value of trade and applied tariff rates in Indonesia, 1989–2016	297
15.3	Average tariff rates under Indonesia's MFN and FTA commitments, 2017	301
15.4	Indonesian exports using the FTA concession, 2013–15	303
15.5	Indonesian imports using the FTA concession, 2016	304
15.6	Indonesia's score on the Logistics Performance Index, 2010–16	308
15.7	Intra-ASEAN and extra-ASEAN visitor arrivals in the ASEAN region and Indonesia, 1995–2015	309

Contributors

Titik Anas, Founder of Presisi Indonesia; and Lecturer, Padjadjaran University, Bandung

Edward Aspinall, Professor of Politics, Department of Political and Social Change, Coral Bell School of Asia Pacific Affairs, Australian National University, Canberra

M. Chatib Basri, Senior Lecturer, Department of Economics, University of Indonesia, Jakarta; former Indonesian Minister of Finance (2013–14); and former Chair of the Investment Coordinating Board (BKPM) (2012–13)

Yose Rizal Damuri, Head, Department of Economics, Center for Strategic and International Studies (CSIS), Jakarta

Manggi Habir, Independent Commissioner, PT Bank Danamon Indonesia Tbk, Jakarta

Hal Hill, HW Arndt Professor Emeritus of Southeast Asian Economies, Arndt-Corden Department of Economics, Crawford School of Public Policy, ANU College of Asia and the Pacific, Australian National University, Canberra

Krisztina Kis-Katos, Professor of International Economic Policy, Department of Economics, University of Göttingen, Göttingen

Chris Manning, Honorary Associate Professor, Arndt-Corden Department of Economics, Crawford School of Public Policy, ANU College of Asia and the Pacific, Australian National University, Canberra

Shafiah F. Muhibat, Senior Researcher and Head of Department of International Relations, Centre for Strategic and International Studies (CSIS), Jakarta

Dionisius Narjoko, Senior Economist, Economic Research Institute for ASEAN and East Asia (ERIA), Jakarta

Jeff Neilson, Senior Lecturer in Geography, School of Geosciences, University of Sydney, Sydney

Deasy Pane, PhD Candidate, Arndt-Corden Department of Economics, Crawford School of Public Policy, ANU College of Asia and the Pacific, Australian National University, Canberra

Mari Pangestu, Professor of International Economics, Faculty of Economics, University of Indonesia, Jakarta; former Indonesian Minister of Trade (2004–11); and former Indonesian Minister of Tourism and Creative Economy (2011–14)

Arianto A. Patunru, Fellow, Arndt-Corden Department of Economics, and Policy Engagement Coordinator, ANU Indonesia Project, Crawford School of Public Policy, ANU College of Asia and the Pacific, Australian National University, Canberra

Janneke Pieters, Assistant Professor, Development Economics Group, Department of Social Sciences, Wageningen University, Wageningen; and Research Fellow, Institute of Labor Economics (IZA), Bonn

Anthony Reid, Former Professor of Southeast Asian History, Australian National University, Canberra; University of California, Los Angeles; and National University of Singapore, Singapore

Robert Sparrow, Assistant Professor, Development Economics Group, Department of Social Sciences, Wageningen University, Wageningen; and Associate Professor, International Institute of Social Studies (ISS), Erasmus University Rotterdam

Eve Warburton, PhD Candidate, Department of Political and Social Change, Coral Bell School of Asia Pacific Affairs, Australian National University, Canberra

Peter Warr, John Crawford Professor of Agricultural Economics, Emeritus, and Director, Poverty Research Centre, Australian National University, Canberra

T. Yudo Wicaksono, Lead Data Analyst, Palladium, Jakarta; and Research Associate, Presisi Indonesia, Jakarta

Arief Anshory Yusuf, Professor of Economics, Department of Economics, Padjadjaran University, Bandung; Visiting Fellow, Australian National University, Canberra; and Visiting Professor, King's College London

Acknowledgments

All the papers in this volume, except Chapter 11 by T. Yudo Wicaksono and Chris Manning, were presented during the thirty-fifth Indonesia Update Conference at the Australian National University (ANU), Canberra, on 15–16 September 2017. Our greatest thanks go to the authors, without whom this book would not exist.

The Indonesia Update Conference is organised jointly by the ANU Indonesia Project and the Department of Political and Social Change, and has been conducted annually since 1983. In preparing for the 2017 conference, we were greatly supported by Budy Resosudarmo, who was then the head of the ANU Indonesia Project. We thank both Budy and his successor, Blane Lewis, for their support and guidance. We also acknowledge the helpful suggestions and feedback from all Indonesianists at the ANU.

We thank the core team of the 2017 Indonesia Update Conference for making the conference run smoothly: Nurkemala Muliani, Kate McLinton, Bayu Tegar Perkasa, Maxine McArthur and Thuy Thu Pham. We would also like to thank Rus'an Nasrudin, Donny Pasaribu and all the student volunteers for their assistance during the conference, and the speakers, chairs and discussants for their valuable contributions. We are grateful to Liam Gammon and his team at *New Mandala* for helping to promote the event.

We acknowledge the continuing support of the ANU College of Asia and the Pacific. The Australian Department of Foreign Affairs and Trade (DFAT), through its grant to the ANU Indonesia Project, has been a long-term supporter of the Update conferences and the associated series of books. We thank Allaster Cox from DFAT for his opening remarks to the conference. After the Update we held two follow-up events in Sydney and Adelaide (the 'Mini Updates'). For these, we thank the Lowy Institute (especially Aaron Connelly) in Sydney and the Institute for International Trade (especially Chris Findlay and Lisa Hunt) at the University of Adelaide.

The Indonesia Update series of books has been published since 1989. Once again, we would like to thank our publisher, ISEAS – Yusof Ishak Institute, especially Ng Kok Kiong and Rahilah Yusuf, for their excellent work. We are indebted to Beth Thomson for her superb editorial work; she has been involved in the Update book series since 1994. We also thank Angela Grant for assistance with indexing, and Kantor Sekretariat Presiden, Republic of Indonesia, for giving us permission to use the photo on the cover of President Joko Widodo.

Arianto A. Patunru, Mari Pangestu and M. Chatib Basri
Canberra, April 2018

Glossary

ABRI	Angkatan Bersenjata Republik Indonesia (Armed Forces of the Republic of Indonesia)
ADB	Asian Development Bank
AFAS	ASEAN Framework Agreement on Services
AFTA	ASEAN Free Trade Area
AIFTA	ASEAN–India FTA
AIIB	Asian Infrastructure Investment Bank
AIPEG	Australia Indonesia Partnership for Economic Governance
AKAN	Antar Kerja Antar Negara (International Labour Placement Program)
Ampera	Aliansi Melawan Perdagangan Orang (Alliance Against Human Trafficking)
ANI	Asosiasi Nikel Indonesia (Indonesian Nickel Association)
Antam	PT Aneka Tambang
APEC	Asia-Pacific Economic Cooperation
Apkasi	Asosiasi Pemerintah Kabupaten Seluruh Indonesia (Association of Indonesian District Governments)
APRIL	Asia Pacific Resources International Holdings Ltd
ASEAN	Association of Southeast Asian Nations
ATIGA	ASEAN Trade in Goods Agreement
ATM	automated teller machine
bangsa	the nation
Bank Indonesia	Indonesia's central bank
Banser	Barisan Ansor Serbaguna (Ansor Multipurpose Front), paramilitary organisation of Nahdlatul Ulama
banteng	'fortress' program/policy
Bapindo	Bank Pembangunan Indonesia (Indonesian Development Bank)

Bareskrim	Badan Reserse Kriminal (Criminal Investigation Agency)
berdikari	*berdiri di atas kaki sendiri* ('to stand on one's own two feet'), a program of economic self-reliance during the Sukarno era
Binapenta	Direktorat Jenderal Pembinaan Penempatan Tenaga Kerja dan Perluasan Kesempatan Kerja (Directorate General of Labour Force Placement and Expansion of Employment Opportunities)
BNI	Bank Negara Indonesia (State Bank of Indonesia)
BNI 1946	Bank Negara Indonesia 1946 (State Bank of Indonesia 1946)
BNP2TKI	Badan Nasional Penempatan dan Perlindungan Tenaga Kerja Indonesia (National Agency for the Placement and Protection of Indonesian Migrant Workers)
BP3TKI	Balai Pelayanan Penempatan dan Perlindungan Tenaga Kerja Indonesia (Service Centre for the Placement and Protection of Indonesian Migrant Workers)
BPJS	Badan Penyelenggara Jaminan Sosial (Social Security Administration Agency)
BPS	Badan Pusat Statistik (Statistics Indonesia), the central statistics agency
BRI	Bank Rakyat Indonesia (Indonesian People's Bank)
Bulog	Badan Urusan Logistik (the national food logistics agency)
CGE	computable general equilibrium (model)
COO	certificate of origin
CoW	Contract of Work
CPTPP	Comprehensive and Progressive Agreement for Trans-Pacific Partnership
CSIS	Centre for Strategic and International Studies
cultuurstelsel	Cultivation System (a nineteenth-century Dutch colonial policy of forced crop deliveries)
Darul Islam	Abode of Islam (name of an Islamic-state movement that rebelled against the central government in the 1950s, and remains active in a largely non-violent form)
Desbumi	Desa Peduli Buruh Migran (Village of Care for Migrant Workers)
Doi Moi	'renovation', 'reconstruction'; program of political and economic reforms initiated in Vietnam in 1986 with the goal of creating a socialist market economy
DPD	Dewan Perwakilan Daerah (Regional Representative Council)

Glossary xvii

DPR	Dewan Perwakilan Rakyat (People's Representative Council), Indonesia's parliament
dwifungsi	dual function (usually referring to the dual political and military functions of the Indonesian Armed Forces)
e-KTP	*kartu tanda penduduk elektronik* (electronic resident's identity card)
ERP	effective rate of protection
FDI	foreign direct investment
fintech	financial technology, and the businesses providing such technology
FTA	free trade agreement
G7	Group of Seven large economies (Canada, France, Germany, Italy, Japan, the United Kingdom and the United States)
GATS	General Agreement on Trade in Services
GATT	General Agreement on Trade and Tariffs
GDP	gross domestic product
Golkar	Golongan Karya (the state political party under the New Order, and a major post-New Order party)
Guided Democracy	the Sukarno era (1957–66)
haj	annual pilgrimage to Mecca
HKTI	Himpunan Kerukunan Tani Indonesia (Indonesian Farmers Association)
HSBC	Hongkong and Shanghai Banking Corporation
IJEPA	Indonesia–Japan Economic Partnership Agreement
IMF	International Monetary Fund
IRGSC	Institute of Resource Governance and Social Change
ITA	Information Technology Agreement
IUP	Izin Usaha Pertambangan (Mining Business Permit)
Jokowi	(President) Joko Widodo
kedaulatan pangan	food sovereignty
ketahanan pangan	food security
Komnas Perempuan	Komisi Nasional Anti Kekerasan Terhadap Perempuan (National Commission on Violence Against Women)
Konfrontasi	policy of confrontation against Malaysia during the Sukarno era
KORUS	Korea–US Free Trade Agreement
KPK	Komisi Pemberantasan Korupsi (Corruption Eradication Commission)
KPM	Koninklijke Paketvaart Maatschappij (Royal Steam Packet Company)
LNG	liquefied natural gas

LOI	Letter of Intent
Malari affair	Malapetaka 15 Januari (15 January disaster), riots of 15 January 1974 against the visit of Japanese prime minister Kakuei Tanaka
Maybank	Malayan Banking Berhad
MFA	Multi Fibre Arrangement
MP3EI	Masterplan Percepatan dan Perluasan Pembangunan Ekonomi Indonesia (Master Plan for the Acceleration and Expansion of Indonesia's Economic Development)
musrenbang	*musyawarah perencanaan pembangunan* (development planning meeting)
NAFTA	North American Free Trade Area (or Agreement)
Nahdlatul Ulama	traditionalist Islamic organisation founded in 1926
Nawacita	nine-point policy statement issued by Joko Widodo and Jusuf Kalla during the presidential election campaign in 2014
NEFOs	New Emerging Forces
negara	state
New Order	the Suharto era (1966–98)
NHM	Nederlandsche Handel-Maatschappij (Netherlands Trading Society)
NISM	Nederlandsch-Indische Stoomvaart Maatschappij (Netherlands Indies Steamship Company)
NRP	nominal rate of protection
NTB	non-tariff barrier
OCBC Bank	Oversea-Chinese Banking Corporation
OJK	Otoritas Jasa Keuangan (Financial Services Authority)
OLDEFOs	Old Established Forces
OLS	ordinary least squares
Pancasila	the five guiding principles of the Indonesian state (belief in God, humanitarianism, nationalism, democracy and social justice)
PDI	Partai Demokrasi Indonesia (Indonesian Democracy Party)
PDIP	Partai Demokrasi Indonesia-Perjuangan (Indonesian Democratic Party of Struggle)
Pelni	Pelayaran Nasional Indonesia (Indonesia's state-owned shipping company)
peranakan	descendants of fifteenth and sixteenth century Chinese immigrants to the Netherlands Indies, who adopted many local customs and were largely assimilated into local communities
Permesta rebellion	Perjuangan Semesta (uprising in Sulawesi in the late 1950s)

Pertamina	Perusahaan Pertambangan Minyak dan Gas Bumi Negara (Indonesia's state-owned oil and gas company)
PKS	Partai Keadilan Sejahtera (Prosperous Justice Party)
PPIT	Pusat Pelayanan Informasi Terpadu (Integrated Information Service Centre)
PPP	Partai Persatuan Pembangunan (United Development Party)
pribumi	indigenous Indonesian, not of immigrant stock
PRRI	Pemerintah Revolusioner Republik Indonesia (rebel movement in Sumatra in the late 1950s)
RCEP	Regional Comprehensive Economic Partnership
reformasi	'reform' (used to characterise post-New Order Indonesian society and politics)
Sakernas	Survei Angkatan Kerja Nasional (National Labour Force Survey)
SAM	social accounting matrix
SKA	Surat Keterangan Asal (certificate of origin)
SOE	state-owned enterprise
SPI	Serikat Petani Indonesia (Indonesian Peasants Union)
Susenas	Survei Sosio-Ekonomi Nasional (National Socio-Economic Survey)
TKA	*tenaga kerja asing* (foreign workers)
TKI	*tenaga kerja Indonesia* (Indonesian migrant worker)
TNI	Tentara Nasional Indonesia (Indonesian National Army)
totok	China-born or pure Chinese in Indonesia, as distinct from locally born or culturally hybridised *peranakan*
TPP	Trans-Pacific Partnership
TRIMs	Trade-Related Investment Measures
umroh	pilgrimage to Mecca that can be performed at any time of the year, other than the time specified for the *haj*
UNCTAD	United Nations Conference on Trade and Development
UOB	United Overseas Bank (Singapore)
VOC	Vereenigde Oost-Indische Compagnie (United East India Company/Dutch East India Company)
WTO	World Trade Organization

Currencies

$	US dollar
Rp	Indonesian rupiah

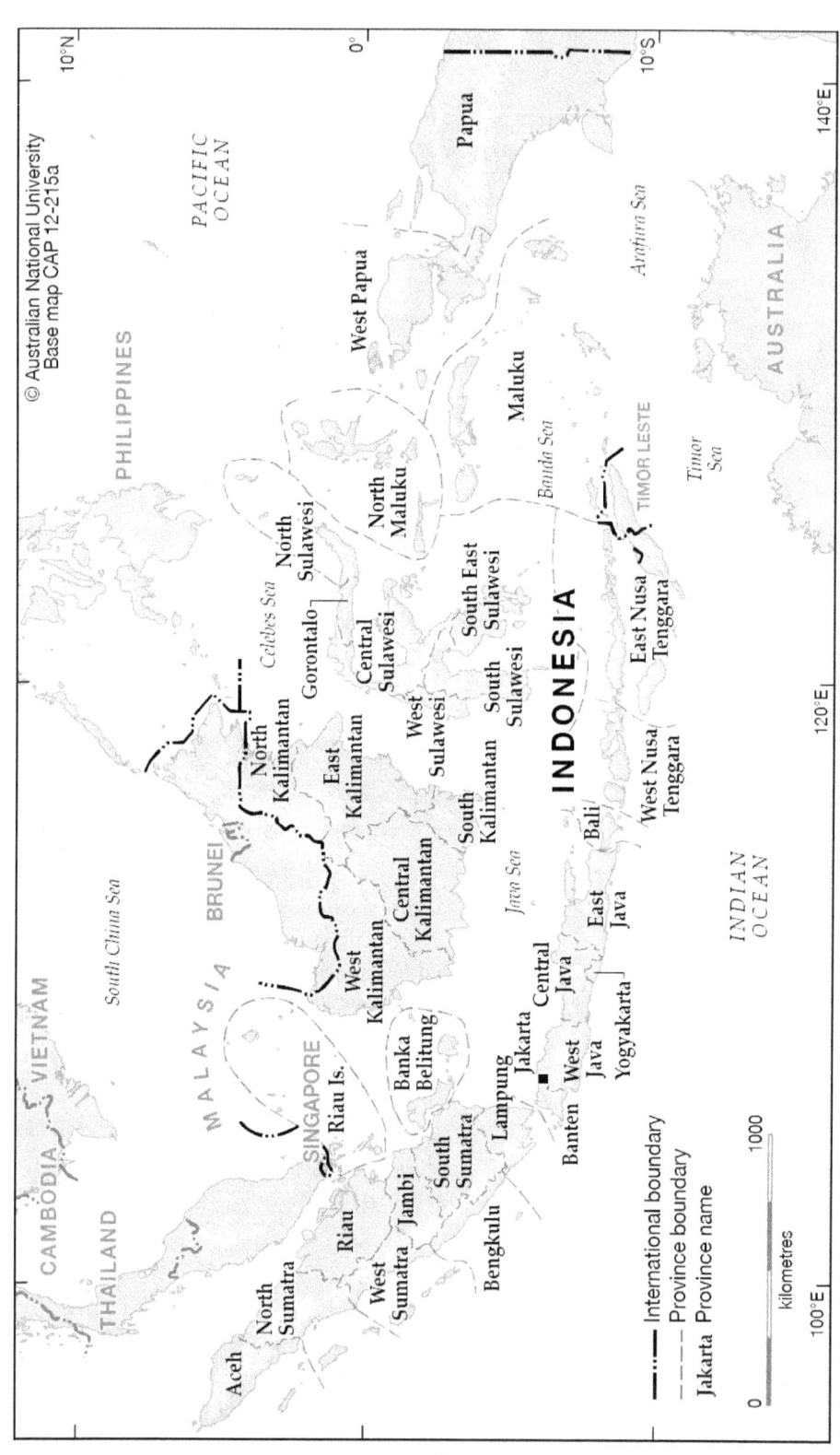

1 Challenges for Indonesia in the new world

*Arianto A. Patunru, Mari E. Pangestu and M. Chatib Basri**

The world is finally recovering from the 2007–08 global financial crisis. After contracting sharply in 2009 and increasing slowly in the subsequent years, world real GDP growth returned to 3 per cent in 2017. Ten years after the crisis, it appears that growth is at last showing sustainable signs of recovery. Other challenges remain, however. Trade growth has slowed and, despite an improvement in 2017, remains lower than before the global financial crisis. The slowdown in trade growth has been attributed to cyclical factors and to structural factors such as a lack of productivity growth and the maturation of global value chains. Protectionism is another factor, although, to date, it is not so much the increase in protectionist measures as the high level of uncertainty about trade policy that is affecting trade.

The policy uncertainty stems primarily from the perceived lack of benefits from globalisation. Almost half the world's population—that is, more than 3 billion people—have to survive on $2.50 or less every day. The richest 10 per cent of the global population owns more than 85 per cent of the global wealth. Inequality has increased even in the countries where poverty has declined. These factors are widely seen as the main causes of the re-emergence of anti-globalisation sentiment around the world, prompting leaders to adopt populist and inward-looking policies. The electoral consequences have been surprising; they include the election of Rodrigo Duterte in the Philippines, the success of the 'leave' campaign in

---

* A small part of this chapter is drawn from Patunru's opinion column as published in the *Jakarta Post*, 11 September 2017.

the Brexit referendum in the United Kingdom and the election of Donald Trump in the United States. Meanwhile, those in power show an increasingly authoritarian inclination—Erdoğan in Turkey, Putin in Russia and Xi in China, to name a few—often by exploiting the public's misgivings about globalisation.

In Indonesia, the discontent with globalisation is apparent in rising nationalism, a rejection of foreign interference and a distrust of democracy that is reminiscent of the New Order. The disappointment with globalisation is not entirely unjustified. In Indonesia as in many other countries, globalisation has had both good and bad results. Trade always creates both winners and losers, and in the absence of a well-functioning compensation mechanism and the free movement of labour across sectors, the winners appear to be concentrated disproportionately among a small number of elites. Corruption has only worsened this situation, allowing the dark side of globalisation to dominate. International networks of criminals, for example, have taken advantage of the easy access to digital technology and cheap flights to engage in human trafficking or to abuse the rights of migrant workers (see Chapter 12 of this volume by Hidayah and Chapter 13 by Li). Advances in digital technology (often aided by naiveté on the part of internet and social media users) have encouraged the spread of financial and banking fraud. Fake news is very easy to produce. Enter the double-edged sword of globalisation: improved access to better livelihoods *and* increased vulnerability. Politicians have been quick to take advantage of this chimera, leading to a rise in identity and populist politics, sometimes on the back of globalisation. Calls for nationalism of all sorts are ubiquitous across social media and chat groups, which are themselves almost costless, thanks to globalisation.

ECONOMIC NATIONALISM IN INDONESIA

Nationalism in the economic sphere takes the form of trade protectionism. It manifests mainly in economic policies that aim for self-sufficiency in an array of commodities, including those in which Indonesia is a natural net importer. Economic protectionism in Indonesia tends to come in waves; the most recent one emerged in the early 2000s and, despite some reform initiatives, has gathered strength under the current administration. It can be expected to persist for some time to come, given the coming general and presidential elections in 2019 as well as the worldwide trend towards protectionism.

After the fall of President Sukarno's ultra-nationalist regime, the New Order government of President Suharto instituted a series of market-friendly reforms, supported by able technocrats under the leadership of

Widjojo Nitisastro. These reforms included opening up the capital market, welcoming foreign investment and relaxing trade policies. But this period did not last long. The windfall revenues from the commodity boom of the early 1970s and the two oil booms in 1973–74 and 1979–80 allowed the government to entertain calls for protection in the form of import substitution, local content requirements, import licensing and export bans. When the oil price plunged in the 1980s, the oil revenue bonanza also disappeared.

Constrained budgets coupled with a global recession forced the government to change tack. From the mid-1980s to mid-1990s Indonesia experienced bold deregulation, export promotion and currency devaluation. However, the business groups that had prospered during the previous protectionist era still had the ear of government, and were now joined by new cronies (see Chapter 2 by Reid for a long-term view of protectionism in Indonesia). The New Order government granted import monopolies and other preferential treatment to these groups, especially those closest to President Suharto. Then the Asian financial crisis hit the region in 1997, pushing the Indonesian economy into an abyss. Once again bad times forced the government to adopt more liberal policies: import restrictions were removed, tariffs were cut and Indonesia's involvement in international trade agreements increased (see Chapter 15 by Anas and Narjoko).

But the interest in free trade again proved to be short-lived. Protectionism started to creep back in, beginning with restrictive measures on imported agricultural products in the early 2000s, followed by trade regulations and licensing requirements for imported textiles, steel, sugar and cloves. After the global financial crisis, the second Susilo Bambang Yudhoyono administration (2009–14) passed new laws on mining, farming and horticulture, all of which had a serious impact on the openness to trade and investment (see Chapter 5 by Neilson for the case of food and Chapter 6 by Warburton for the case of mining). The Yudhoyono government reinstated many import licensing procedures, tightened restrictions on the distribution of imported goods and banned the export of raw minerals.

Under the current president, Joko Widodo (2014–), the trend towards nationalism has strengthened. The president's own stance, however, appears to be a mixture of pragmatism and ambivalence. Addressing the Leaders Summit of the Indian Ocean Rim Association in March 2017, Jokowi embraced both nationalism and internationalism. Quoting President Sukarno, he stated that 'internationalism cannot live without nationalism' and vice versa — rhetoric that sounds impressive but whose exact meaning is unclear. At events such as the APEC CEO Summit (November 2014 in Beijing), the ASEAN Summit (April 2017 in Manila) and the G20 Summit (July 2017 in Hamburg), Jokowi has been eager to extend an invitation to foreign investors to come to Indonesia. At other times, however, he has criticised the existing international order. At the Asian–African Summit in Jakarta in April 2015, for example, he argued that the current global economic system—dominated by the World Bank, the IMF and the ADB—was obsolete and it was therefore imperative to build a new international economic order. During a state visit to the United States in October 2015, he said he wanted Indonesia to join the Trans-Pacific Partnership (TPP). He also supports the China-led Asian Infrastructure Investment Bank (AIIB). But he has openly criticised China for its position on the South China Sea dispute. In response to a statement by Beijing in June 2017 that implicitly included part of Indonesia's exclusive economic zone among the territories subject to 'overlapping claims', the president made a practical and widely reported demonstration of Indonesia's intention to uphold its own claim by holding a cabinet meeting on board a warship in the Natuna Islands (as shown on the cover of this book).

On economic policy, the president's stance leans clearly towards protectionism. During the presidential campaign, Jokowi's promises contained a lower dose of nationalism than those of his rival, General Prabowo Subianto. Yet he started his presidency with a heavy use of protectionist measures, mostly through the Ministry of Trade, the Ministry of Agriculture and the Ministry of Industry. It is true that tariffs have remained low under Jokowi, but protectionism in the form of non-tariff barriers has escalated. The Ministry of Trade calculates that the proportion of product lines subject to some form of import restriction rose from 9 per cent in 2011 to 35 per cent in 2016. Studies have shown that non-tariff barriers such as quotas, import licences and export bans are prone to corruption. In democratic polities such as Indonesia, import restrictions can lead to 'protection for sale', whereby protection is given to the highest bidders (cronies) or is granted to certain sectors (generally small business or agriculture) in order to gain a political advantage with the public (see Chapter 7 by Damuri and Pangestu). In 2016, in line with a recommendation by the Corruption Eradication Commission (KPK), the Ministry of Trade was instructed to reduce the number of import restrictions and no longer to use quantitative restrictions such as quotas (Presidential Instruction No. 10/2016 on the Prevention and Eradication of Corruption).

Jokowi reshuffled his cabinet in August 2015, and again in July 2016. Three years into his presidency, he had already had three trade ministers: Rachmat Gobel, Thomas Lembong and Enggartiasto Lukita. Given the profiles and actions of the three trade ministers, it would appear that the government swung from a protectionist to a market-friendly back to a protectionist policy stance—but the quick turnover of ministers could equally reflect the absence of a clear vision for trade policy. Jokowi also replaced the minister of industry, Saleh Husin, with Airlangga Hartarto, but the minister of agriculture, Amran Sulaiman, was retained despite the two reshuffles (and also survived a third reshuffle in January 2018). This is worthy of note, considering that he is arguably the most populist minister in Jokowi's cabinet. The agriculture minister favours an extreme interpretation of food self-sufficiency that precludes any imports of agricultural products. Given that he remains in cabinet, it would appear that Jokowi supports this view.

How do we explain the rise in economic populism and protectionism under Jokowi? To start with, at the beginning of the Jokowi presidency the rupiah appreciated, making the country's exports more expensive and therefore less competitive. The commodity boom ended around the same time, also reducing Indonesia's competitiveness. Both these factors increased the demand for protection. There has also been a bandwagon effect in which Indonesia has followed the trend set by many other countries to employ a more active industrial policy—perhaps in response to weak global demand. The blame partly goes to the failure of the Doha Round of the WTO, which has damaged confidence in the international economic architecture. Some countries have resorted to beggar-thy-neighbour exchange rate policies while others have continued to erect non-tariff barriers. Even though the protectionist measures themselves have not had much of an impact on trade, the uncertainty they have created about the direction of trade policy certainly has had an impact.

Despite the fact that protectionist measures often have negative consequences, they seem to be spreading almost everywhere, including in Jokowi's Indonesia. The recent rice fracas is a case in point. Indonesia's ambition for self-sufficiency in rice is built on false assumptions: that self-sufficiency means food security (wrong—food security can be obtained without self-sufficiency), that it will benefit the poor (wrong—most Indonesians, including poor farmers and landless peasants, are net consumers of rice), that Indonesia has an abundance of rice and hence is a natural rice exporter (wrong—Indonesia has exported more rice than it has imported in only seven years since 1870, which is as far back as reliable data can go) and that the world market for rice is thin (wrong—the world rice market is much larger and more stable now than it was in the 1970s).

Some populist and protectionist fallacies can be debunked with data and economic reasoning but the politics of this issue are far more complicated. This may be because economic nationalism pays politically (exhibit one: Trump), or because the gains from globalisation are diffused and take a long time to materialise, whereas the costs are concentrated and materialise more quickly. In addition, politicians like to frame economic nationalism in anti-colonial and anti-imperialist terms (see Chapter 3 by Aspinall). Or perhaps economic arguments do not really matter, because politicians view jargon such as 'food sovereignty' and 'food self-sufficiency' as politically potent rhetoric that can ensure their political longevity (see Chapter 5 by Neilson).

STRUCTURE OF THE BOOK

This book consists of five parts. Part 1 highlights Indonesia's experience with globalisation, nationalism and sovereignty.

Chapter 2 by Anthony Reid traces the history of Indonesian trade and commerce from the United East India Company (VOC) times of mercantilism and monopoly, to the rise of free trade under the British during the nineteenth century, to modern-day Indonesia. Given its archipelagic nature, Indonesia is an unlikely place for mercantilist exclusivity, argues Reid. In fact, 'the fundamental reality of the region before 1650 was of multiple port-states competing to attract the world's traders' (p. 17). Yet somehow the idea of state monopoly of trade took deep root in Indonesia. The country was the battleground of competing monopolies for centuries as policy collided dangerously with geography. The lesson from Indonesia's experience, according to Reid, was that state power exercised strategically and pragmatically, in alliance with diverse market forces, could tie together a very plural place without sacrificing economic efficiency.

In the early years of independence, however, the Indonesian government sought state control of all the levers of the economy. Under President Sukarno theories of autarchy and command economy gained popularity, foreign investment and capitalism were associated with the colonial enemy, and capital and expertise fled the country. After Suharto came to power, the technocrats were able to convince the president to institute market-friendly reforms. Suharto also gradually eased the military out of business with Malaysia and Singapore and built cooperative relationships with other countries in the region. But although policy-making has come closer to economic reality, monopolies and rent-seeking remain alluring to a nationalist lobby convinced that indigenous Indonesians suffer a disadvantage in their own country. In a globalised world Indonesia will thus continue its search for a stable equilibrium between state ambition and economic reality.

In Chapter 3, Edward Aspinall argues that nationalist discourse and policy-making are more prominent under President Joko Widodo than under any other post-Suharto government. Aspinall discusses the core features of the new nationalism along its channels of mobilisation: territorial, economic and cultural. He agrees with Reid that the 'new' nationalism is not in fact particularly new. Indonesia's contemporary nationalism is shaped—in fact, trapped—by its historical roots. What is different now, according to Aspinall, is that the contemporary nationalism is strikingly less ideological and less theorised than during either the politically leftist Sukarno era or the politically conservative Suharto era. In the absence of a clear ideology, however, Indonesia still has plenty of 'recyclers of old tropes' and 'promoters of base emotional appeals' (p. 44), among them the notion that foreign powers harbour hostile designs on Indonesia, and a preoccupation with national dignity. Understanding the new nationalism thus requires an understanding of politics in particular, and of the country's economic, social and cultural dynamics in general.

In Chapter 4, Shafiah F. Muhibat discusses the dispute between China and several Southeast Asian countries that have overlapping territorial claims in the South China Sea. She explains that Indonesia has become more cautious in this matter, although it has consistently declared that it is not a party to the dispute. Although China does not claim any of Indonesia's landmass, in 2009 it asserted its 'historic' rights over waters that lie within Indonesia's exclusive economic zone in the province of Natuna, a remote group of islands in the southern part of the South China Sea. In 2016, Chinese fishing vessels operating without permission in Natuna waters clashed three times with Indonesian patrol boats and the Indonesian navy, sparking tension between the two countries. To signify the seriousness with which Indonesia viewed this matter, the Indonesian president visited the area on board a warship (as shown on the cover of this book), and the military held two high-profile exercises in Natuna waters, observed by the president. Muhibat argues that, while the government is taking tougher measures to protect Indonesian interests in Natuna, there is little chance of a dramatic change in its foreign policy on the South China Sea, particularly if it would be likely to jeopardise the relationship with China. Indonesia will continue to maintain its non-claimant position while at the same time emphasising its long-held position that it does not recognise China's claim to 'historic' rights in the South China Sea. It can, however, help to manage the dispute between China and other Southeast Asian countries through the ASEAN framework.

Part 2 of the book provides an assessment of nationalism in Indonesia in practice. The first two chapters discuss sovereignty and nationalism in terms of food protection and mineral protection, respectively. The third chapter reports the results of a recent survey on the perceptions of Indonesians towards globalisation and nationalism.

In Chapter 5, Jeff Neilson examines the ways in which food sovereignty discourses are articulated in Indonesia, exploring their recent emergence and their current deployment by state-based actors. Food sovereignty, or *kedaulatan pangan*, writes Neilson, is a fundamentally endogenous political construct in Indonesia that is only marginally related to its broader global discourses. It should thus be understood primarily as a rhetorical device to strengthen the role and function of the state, and to reinforce existing associations between food security, state control and national-scale food self-sufficiency. It responds primarily to the scalar and emotive notion of feeding the *bangsa*, the abstract Indonesian term for 'the nation'. The conceptual malleability and emotiveness of the term *kedaulatan pangan* allow it to be harnessed by different actors for considerably different ends. It also acts to provide a powerful discursive legitimacy for the state, which is able to extend its material control over the *bangsa* even as the problems of malnutrition, the poor's lack of access to food and geographical inequality remain inadequately addressed.

Chapter 6 by Eve Warburton deals with resource nationalism. The global mining boom between 2003 and 2013 caused a frenzy of mineral extraction across Indonesia's resource-rich regions, particularly Kalimantan, Sulawesi and Sumatra. Indonesia's central and regional governments enjoyed a huge boost in revenues as a result. But many policy-makers, activists and politicians became concerned that Indonesia's finite resources were being shipped overseas too quickly and too cheaply, and that not enough Indonesians were feeling the economic benefits of the minerals boom. In response, in 2009 President Yudhoyono introduced a law requiring mining companies to add domestic value to their mineral ores. This was followed by a ban on the export of minerals in January 2014. The new president elected in 2014, Joko Widodo, initially expressed strong support for the ban, as it fitted with his nationalist economic rhetoric. But then, in January 2017, his administration made the controversial decision to relax the ban, jeopardising three years of downstream investment and development. Warburton argues that this decision was taken primarily to support state-owned mining company PT Aneka Tambang (Antam), whose profits had suffered during the export ban, and not because resource nationalism was on the retreat. In other words, it was all about political calculations. In Warburton's account, resource nationalism should not be viewed as a temporary response to price booms but as part of a re-emergent developmentalist model. This view is consistent with a broader narrative about Indonesia's struggle against foreign economic exploitation (see Chapter 3 by Aspinall).

In Chapter 7, Yose Rizal Damuri and Mari Pangestu dissect the results of a public opinion survey conducted by the Centre for Strategic and International Studies (CSIS) in 2017. Their analysis reveals that anti-globalisation sentiment is strongest with regard to foreign labour and second strongest with regard to foreign imports. However, Indonesians are broadly welcoming of foreign investment and are strongly in favour of foreign visitors. As expected, those who are younger, better educated, working and relatively satisfied with the current economic state of the country are more likely to be positive about globalisation. Those who voted for President Jokowi in the 2014 elections also have a more positive attitude towards globalisation. Damuri and Pangestu find that people with good access to information through the media are actually *less* positive towards economic openness. This has important implications for the communication strategy of the government on the issue of openness, and for the possible angles to be used by politicians in proposing their programs.

Part 3 of the book focuses on the impact of and response to globalisation. In Chapter 8, Arief Anshory Yusuf and Peter Warr examine the relationship between anti-globalisation, poverty and inequality. In the decade and a half after the 1997–98 Asian financial crisis (2000–16), the average growth rate of real GDP per capita in Indonesia was marginally lower than the rate during the two decades preceding the crisis (1976–96) but the rate of poverty reduction slowed significantly. In other words, growth became substantially less effective in reducing poverty. Around the same time, there was a huge increase in measured economic inequality within Indonesia. Yusuf and Warr hypothesise that anti-globalisation (or protectionism in general) caused at least some of the slowdown in poverty reduction and rise in inequality. Their research shows that the increase in protectionism both globally and within Indonesia between 2008 and 2015 had a negative but small effect on the rate of poverty reduction. It also increased inequality, but the effect was smaller still. They conclude that anti-globalisation was harmful for both poverty reduction and inequality, but it was not the major cause of either the slowdown in poverty reduction or the increase in inequality observed in Indonesia.

In Chapter 9, Krisztina Kis-Katos, Janneke Pieters and Robert Sparrow assess the gender-specific effects of trade reform, with a focus on the female labour market implications of trade liberalisation in Indonesia in the 1990s. While the 1990s were a period of stagnation in aggregate female labour force participation, in the post-decentralisation era Indonesia experienced an increase in female participation, especially after 2003. The authors find no evidence that international trade has been conducive to improving women's employment opportunities since the early 2000s, in contrast to their earlier finding that 'trade liberalisation in the 1990s led to larger increases in female (but not male) work participation in those districts that were more strongly exposed to falling tariffs on intermediate products' (p. 176). The authors conclude that whereas female labour force participation has been rising slowly in Indonesia since the turn of the century, the relative role of international trade in improving employment opportunities for women seems to have declined between 2000 and 2010. At the same time, the focus of trade activities shifted towards sectors that were relatively male intensive, such as mining, leading to a reduction in the female labour needs of trade. In addition, female intensity of the labour force increased predominantly in sectors that saw a relative reduction in their exposure to international trade.

Manggi Habir in Chapter 10 looks at the response of Indonesian companies to the shifts in globalisation trends. He focuses on the changes that can be observed during three periods: the formative years of the Sukarno era (1945–65), the development-focused Suharto period (1966–98) and the more open era of *reformasi* (1998 to the present). Habir argues that, even with the country's current protectionist bias, the disruptive impact of globalisation cannot be avoided. Industry players and regulatory authorities have struggled to adapt to heightened competition, to rapid changes in technology and to the changes in how business operates. Globalisation is associated with increased deforestation, pollution and the devastating global financial crisis. Yet it has also increased the efficiency of resource allocation across countries, lifting levels of productivity, growth and development. With advances in technology, this often disruptive and transformative process is accelerating. As a result, there has been a rise in income disparity, leading in turn to a more uncertain and volatile political environment. Businesses generally prefer certainty and thus are usually in favour of maintaining the status quo. In Indonesia, this has translated into two different responses to globalisation: the larger, more established companies are biased towards maintaining the status quo and towards protecting domestic markets; while the new, smaller and less established entrants are seeking to disrupt the status quo and are more tolerant of an open economy.

The three chapters in Part 4 concentrate on the human face of globalisation. In Chapter 11, T. Yudo Wicaksono and Chris Manning discuss the benefits and costs of globalisation for labour in Indonesia. The key channels of globalisation they observe are international trade and investment, with migration playing a supporting role. They argue that, in general, globalisation has been good for labour, although there have been backwash effects for jobs in lagging industries. Moreover, the future for jobs appears less certain than it has for some time as the digital revolution takes hold across the economy. Digital technology will make many unskilled workers redundant and will probably increase inequality. But there are also likely to be benefits for labour, including unskilled labour, from the internet age. To ensure that these benefits are enjoyed by workers, Indonesia will need to be proactive in dealing with the competitive challenges posed by the rapid absorption of this new wave of technology from abroad.

In Chapter 12, Anis Hidayah examines the livelihoods of Indonesian migrant workers in light of globalisation. In particular, she discusses how the Village of Care for Migrant Workers (Desbumi) program is helping to address the problems faced by migrant workers at the village level.

According to Hidayah, most low-skilled migrant workers are women from poor Indonesian villages with little access to decent jobs at home. Unfortunately, these villages have become a major market for job brokers, many of whom use intimidation and other practices that verge on, or constitute, human trafficking. As a result, trafficking often starts at the village level, disguised as a job placement program for migrant workers. Indonesian NGO Migrant CARE established the Desbumi program in 2014 to respond to this situation. Hidayah describes how this initiative is helping to improve the safety of migrants, the returns to migration and the migrant worker system. Among other things, Desbumi provides information on how to have a safe migration, assistance with document preparation, grievance mechanisms and post-migration economic empowerment, supported by compilations of the relevant village rules and regulations and a migrant worker database.

In Chapter 13, Dominggus Elcid Li sharpens the focus of the previous two chapters by examining the link between migrant worker schemes and human trafficking. Although trafficking of migrant workers is widespread in Indonesia, the state's institutions have not yet come up with a coordinated strategy to wipe it out. The free movement of people is part of globalisation, but what the state has failed to anticipate is the threat to vulnerable citizens when human beings are treated as a commodity. In Indonesia human trafficking is considered a crime, but it has yet to be treated as an extraordinary crime. Based on his research in East Nusa Tenggara, Li concludes that Indonesia's state institutions are unable to shield citizens from the risk of human trafficking today. The main problem faced by the vulnerable communities that are the targets of human trafficking is the absence of a clear strategy to prevent labour exploitation in the recruitment areas. Human trafficking networks like to operate in places where vulnerable groups have limited access to resources and no way out of the poverty trap. Rather than relying on civil society organisations to provide an ad hoc solution to the problem, Li argues, the government must develop a comprehensive strategy to deal with the organised crime networks engaged in human trafficking.

Part 5 of the book examines the ways in which Indonesia is navigating the new globalisation. In Chapter 14, Hal Hill and Deasy Pane argue that, after progressively disengaging from the global economy during the first two decades of independence, Indonesia has created a policy regime that has been broadly open since 1966. There were major and successful reform episodes in the late 1960s and the first half of the 1980s, and the economy and polity recovered surprisingly quickly from the deep economic and political crises of 1997–98. But there continues to be widespread ambivalence towards globalisation, and as a result, Indonesia is missing out on some of the opportunities available to more open economies. Hill and

Pane illustrate these issues by examining the link between the policy environment and export performance in Indonesia. In particular, they focus on the three most important footloose manufactured exports for most developing economies: garments, footwear and electronics. They find that when Indonesia embraced globalisation through well-constructed and well-implemented policy reform, as in the 1960s and 1980s, there was a clear policy dividend in terms of stronger export performance, leading to faster employment generation and poverty reduction. When reform regressed, or did not proceed as quickly as in neighbouring countries, Indonesia missed out on these opportunities.

Chapter 15 by Titik Anas and Dionisius Narjoko looks at Indonesia's place and role in the international trade architecture, whether in multilateral bodies such as the WTO, in regional organisations such as APEC, ASEAN and the Regional Comprehensive Economic Partnership (RCEP) or in bilateral trade agreements. Anas and Narjoko argue that it is in Indonesia's interest to have a more open trade and investment regime. Indonesia should engage more in cooperative international arrangements, which have proven instrumental in reducing the barriers to trade and in providing the policy discipline to withstand rent-seeking activities. Beyond Indonesia, the authors call for ASEAN to exercise leadership in the finalisation of the RCEP negotiations. This can be done by using the momentum of the withdrawal of the United States from the TPP, which has increased the potential benefits of regionalisation for RCEP member countries.

CONCLUSION AND WAYS FORWARD

Examining Indonesia's position in the new world requires a broad understanding of the extent to which the state and the people engage with the many dimensions of globalisation, nationalism and sovereignty. First, geographic and historical features matter. In considering the best approach to trade and international affairs, policy-makers should take heed of the fact that Indonesia's archipelagic nature makes the country an unlikely place for mercantilist exclusivity. Globalisation today is more complex than ever. But as history has shown, strategically and pragmatically exercised state power in alliance with multiple market forces can tie together a very plural place without sacrificing economic efficiency.

Second, while the current rise in nationalism is not an entirely new thing, it is manifesting in a less ideological and more pragmatic way than in the past. In this regard, analyses should allow for more nuanced interpretations of its manifestations. For example, political constructs such as food sovereignty and food self-sufficiency may constitute necessary rhetoric by the state in order to strengthen its position with the people. Resource nationalism, on the other hand, may indicate the re-emergence of a developmentalist model.

While it is acknowledged that globalisation can have both positive and negative results, reform should continue to allow the country to make the most of the opportunities to engage with globalisation. At the same time, improving compensation mechanisms and labour market flexibility would help to reduce the risks and costs of globalisation. The labour market issue is especially important because it involves sensitive issues — mistreatment of migrant workers, job losses, a perceived excess of foreign workers — that, if wrongly managed, would further strengthen the public anxiety about globalisation.

Finally, it is important for Indonesia to increase its engagement with the international economic architecture. Even though the multilateral WTO agreement is not working effectively, Indonesia should not risk contributing to the proliferation of costly bilateral agreements. Instead, it should concentrate on upholding the non-discriminatory principles in regional agreements such as the RCEP.

PART 1

Globalisation, nationalism and sovereignty: the Indonesian experience

2 Challenging geography: asserting economic sovereignty in a porous archipelago

Anthony Reid

The world's largest archipelago, lying athwart one of the world's major trade arteries, is an unlikely location for a single mercantilist or protectionist nation-state. The much smaller Caribbean provides the closest comparison to Indonesia in terms of tropical archipelagos that are highly accessible to world trade, but it is divided among 14 sovereignties, heirs to the world's contesting powers. Even other centres of world trade without an archipelagic character, such as the Middle East and the Low Countries of Europe, have been marked by a plurality of commercial city-states or autonomous cities, morphing into a variety of competing modern states.

Throughout recorded history, the strategic location of the Malacca and Sunda Straits, and the alternation of monsoon winds carrying sailing ships between the Indian and Pacific Oceans, made the archipelago and peninsula—Nusantara—a natural centre for mercantile city-states living by trade (Reid 2000). Its spices were the chief prize of the global maritime struggles of the fifteenth to seventeenth centuries, motivating explorers such as Christopher Columbus and Vasco da Gama to discover new sea routes to this part of the world. Despite the modern nationalist imaginings of the ancestral 'empires' of Sriwijaya and Majapahit, the fundamental reality of the region before 1650 was of multiple port-states competing to attract the world's traders. Yet somehow the *idea* of a state monopoly of trade developed very deep roots in this region, despite having to contend with a very different reality.

This idea seems to have taken deepest root in Imperial China. The curious fiction that China needed no external trade meant that for lengthy periods before 1567 the only form of international exchange the Chinese court would accept as legal was that associated with the so-called tribute missions from a few 'barbarian' kingdoms that were able to play this game. Those that did play it successfully — from Sriwijaya in the seventh to eleventh centuries to Pasai (northern Sumatra) and Melaka in the fifteenth — gained a kind of theoretical monopoly over the lucrative trade with China. Indeed, Chinese court records make it appear as though the only legitimate traders were those from the tribute-sending polities. Meanwhile, the coastal peoples of Fujian and Guangdong on the one hand, and of Champa (occupying the central coast of modern-day Vietnam) and Nusantara on the other, were never averse to maritime exchanges that turned a profit, even though successive Chinese dynasties regarded such activity as smuggling and piracy. The conflict between high ideology and the practical livelihoods of maritime peoples has a regional pedigree stretching back over a thousand years.

The other exotic source of the drive for monopoly was Europe. Cut off by the rise of Islam from the natural routes to Asian spices and other luxuries, the Europeans devoted enormous resources to finding viable alternative routes. When the Portuguese and Spanish state enterprises finally succeeded in finding those routes, they were determined to keep their European rivals out of them. Portugal's trade with Asia, and even its intra-Asian trade, was in principle a state monopoly, with private traders permitted to participate only under royal licence. The Portuguese made great efforts to keep their maps and commercial information secret. Of course, the reality was utterly different, with a high degree of competition between Asian and Asia-based merchants, generally without any state control at all. The Portuguese gradually became more Asian in their habits during the century in which they monopolised European maritime dealings with Asia, yet their *ambition* to monopolise trade with the region remained to tantalise later Europeans.

THE VOC MODEL

The heritage of greatest importance for modern Indonesia is of course the Dutch one. The Netherlands was the most advanced capitalist economy in the seventeenth-century world. The United East India Company (VOC), which listed on the Amsterdam stock exchange in 1602, was the world's biggest joint-stock company, and a pioneer in the scale and efficiency of its bookkeeping, the strength of its shipbuilding and navigation, and its accountability to shareholders. Moreover, it employed the great pioneer of international and maritime law, Hugo de Groot (Grotius), to set out an argument in eloquent Latin for the freedom of the seas, in his *Mare Liberum* of 1608. The young prodigy had been well paid by the VOC to develop his ideas during a court battle over a rich Portuguese cargo seized in the waters off Singapore in 1603, when Holland and Portugal were at war.

Since Holland had the strongest fleet both in the North Sea/Baltic waters of Europe and in Southeast Asia, it was able to use Grotius' doctrine of free trade repeatedly to penetrate markets, thwarting English, Scandinavian, Portuguese and Asian attempts to control their own seas. The 'most specific and unimpeachable axiom of the Law of Nations, called a primary rule or first principle', Grotius declared, was that the seas were more like the air than the land, the patrimony of humanity. Hence, 'Every nation is free to travel to every other nation, and to trade with it' (Grotius 1916: 28).

Ironically, the little trading republic that had pioneered the idea of free trade became, through the VOC, the most ruthless and effective exponent of monopoly whenever it saw an opportunity in Asia. The most lucrative opportunity was precisely in the Spice Islands of eastern Indonesia, where all the world's nutmeg and clove trees grew on just a few small islands in the Banda and north Maluku archipelagos, respectively, making total world monopolies possible. For more than a century after the establishment of these monopolies by ruthless force in the 1650s, the VOC sold the spices in Amsterdam at 14 times the prices it had paid in Maluku.

The history of the VOC spice monopolies provides a classic example of the ruinous effects of monopoly on the overall economy. In the long term the VOC monopoly killed innovation and drove European consumers to find other ways of seasoning their meat. The trade-oriented states (Banten, Makassar, Aceh, Banjarmasin and so on) that had flourished because of the intense competition for spices during the 'Age of Commerce' turned away from cash crops and trade to concentrate on self-sufficiency in food (Reid 1993a: 298–303). The Dutch company itself made ever sparser profits from its monopoly of Malukan spices and pepper as the emphasis shifted in the eighteenth century to Chinese ceramics and tea, Japanese silver, Indian textiles and opium. By the 1920s Indonesia had become a net *importer* of cloves.

The consequences were ruinous for Indonesians, who had initially profited hugely from producing spices and trading them for Indian cloth and Chinese manufactures. Bulbeck et al. (1998: 11) have calculated that the total export values of Southeast Asia's four key long-distance exports — cloves, pepper, sugar and coffee, all mostly from Indonesia — peaked in the 1640s and then suffered a prolonged slump, 'the combined value of our four key products not again reaching the levels of 1600–50 until the 1720s'. Indonesia underwent one of the more notable historic cases of de-urbanisation as societies became more self-sufficient and agricultural (Reid 1993a: 302–3). Banten, 'formerly so opulent and prodigal in its daily clothing, now made a very impoverished and desolate' impression, wrote a VOC officer in 1634 (cited in Meilink-Roelofsz 1962: 258).

The VOC had also attempted to restrict the importation of Indian textiles to the ports it controlled, but found that the market collapsed not only because of the higher Dutch prices, but also because of increasing poverty. A Dutch governor-general complained that since

> the Javanese and most eastern people [...] flourished more formerly than now, most of these peoples sought Coromandel and Surat cloths [for everyday use,] not as luxuries, and gave large amounts of money for that. [...] Now most of the surrounding countries are impoverished, and the [Coromandel] Coast and Surat cloths have become limited to the use of the wealthy (Willem van Outhoorn 1693, cited in Reid 1993a: 302).

After the British replaced the Dutch as the dominant maritime power in the early nineteenth century, British liberals claimed self-righteously that all Indonesia's ills were caused by the VOC's 'sordid, vulgar and worthless [...] pursuit [of] a commercial monopoly' (Crawfurd 1856: 127; see also Raffles 1835: 75-6). In reality the end of Southeast Asia's Age of Commerce in the mid-seventeenth century had multiple causes — environmental, military and political, as well as commercial. But there can be no doubt that the virtual elimination of competition among buyers for the spices of the Indies drastically reduced the wealth of Indonesia's trading cities and its spice growers, even as it made Batavia the richest city in Southeast Asia and Amsterdam the richest in Europe in the late seventeenth century.

In the endless battle between free trade and protection, Holland could well have become a champion of free trade, and the Indonesian archipelago the natural forum for unfettered commercial interaction. After all, Holland had a small, open, merchant-run commercial oligarchy that lived by trade, as did many port-states in Nusantara. What changed the archipelago into the 'cradle of monopoly' was the irresistible lure of clove and nutmeg, and the ruthless genius of Jan Pieterszoon Coen — the VOC governor-general (1618-23 and 1627-29) and founder of Batavia — in seizing a short-term military advantage to monopolise these products. Ironically it was Banda, a little Amsterdam in its pluralist, merchant-run oligarchy, that became the site of Coen's most cold-hearted tyranny, and one of the few Asian examples of a slave-based mode of monopoly production under Coen's blueprint (Hanna 1978).

Even after the end of the VOC naval hegemony and the decline of Holland as a major power, the company's legacy lingered in the mind-set that control, at least of the Java Sea, was both a right and a necessity for the Netherlands.

FREE TRADE RETURNS, 1780-1824

The period after about 1780 marked a return to a high degree of openness in the trade of the archipelago—one might even call it a return to 'normalcy' for such a trade-oriented scattering of islands. The VOC's monopolies were weakened in the late eighteenth century by the decline of Dutch naval power—especially after Holland was occupied by Napoleonic forces in 1795—and the VOC was declared bankrupt in 1800. With Holland under pressure from a British blockade of Napoleonic Europe and the seizure of many of its strongholds in Asia, the number of free traders ignoring Dutch pretensions—Chinese, American, European, Asian— expanded greatly. Yankee ships from Boston and Salem used America's new-found independence first to break British monopolies in Asia, then to profit from Britain's blockade of Napoleon's Europe to become the neutral (in Anglo-French terms) and untrammelled suppliers of Indonesian coffee and pepper to Europe. In exchange they tended to offer American rifles, helping to further decentralise authority. There was also a surge of activity among Chinese traders, no longer focused on the European enclaves of Batavia and Manila, but on independent, competitive ports such as Sulu in southwest Philippines, Terengganu in east Malaysia, Sambas in west Kalimantan, Riau in east Sumatra and Aceh in north Sumatra (Blussé 1986: 123; Reid 1993b). At the same time, many new indigenous (and Chinese) enterprises were established, growing pepper, coffee, tobacco, sugar and the astringent tanning agent *gambir*. So neatly did Acehnese and American enterprises mesh that 30 American clippers a year were visiting the Aceh coast in the early nineteenth century, turning Aceh into the supplier of half the world's pepper (Bulbeck et al. 1998: 65-7, 147-51; Reid 1997).

For all its monopolies in India, the English East India Company was dogmatic about the merits of free trade east of its headquarters in Calcutta. Singapore (from 1819) and Hong Kong (from 1841) became the bastions of this doctrine of free trade, in which British-manufactured cloth and Indian opium were used to penetrate the markets of East and Southeast Asia. Chinese, Bugis, Malay, Indian and European traders quickly recognised that Singapore was a convenient base to exchange the produce of the Indonesian archipelago for the goods of the world. Until the advent of regular steamer routes in the mid-nineteenth century, about 35 per cent of Singapore's total trade was with the archipelago, most of it carried by Chinese, Bugis and Malay vessels. Singapore's trade with the islands outside Java exceeded Java's trade with those islands during much of this period (Reid 1996: 284).

The Anglo-Dutch Treaty signed in London in 1824 that brought this period to an end would have profound long-term consequences, far beyond the immediate diplomatic calculations of its authors. Its demarcation of the Straits of Malacca and Singapore as the boundary between the British and Dutch spheres would not only determine the future boundary between Malaysia/Singapore and Indonesia, but also form a gulf between the dynamic free-trading hub linking the region to the world on the northern side, and the more defensive, unwieldy, Batavia-based trading hub on the southern side. In the treaty Britain readily surrendered its moribund attempt at a local pepper monopoly in Bencoolen (Bengkulu) in southwest Sumatra in exchange for Dutch Melaka. The real prize for the British was to oblige the Dutch to accept the existence of the booming free port Thomas Stamford Raffles had established at Singapore. The great legacy of the treaty was that the commercial hinge between the Indian and Pacific Oceans now became concentrated on the northern side of the Straits, in what Britain called its Straits Settlements — Singapore, Melaka and Penang. These port-enclaves lived by trade, permitting anyone to trade or settle there. Instead of duties, their expenses were met by farming out the collection of 'sin taxes' on opium, spirits and gaming — which fell overwhelmingly on their immigrant Asian populations (Trocki 1990).

While Singapore boomed, Batavia's share of trade declined to the point that the city became a branch office of global trade. The problem facing the Dutch was how to use their territorial control, first of Java and eventually of the other islands, to economic advantage in the unequal struggle against free-trading Singapore.

THE TRADE BATTLE WITH SINGAPORE

During the brief British occupation of Java (1811–15), Raffles had declared the island open to foreign trade (1814), and British-manufactured cloth had flooded in, to exchange for Java's coffee and sugar. By 1823, when the Dutch began to move systematically against this trade, over 3 million guilders worth of British cloth was arriving in Java each year, at the expense of both Indian and local hand-made cloth. Discriminatory tariffs evading the intent of the 1824 agreement reduced British cloth imports from 96 per cent to 30 per cent of Java's total textile imports over the next six years. Following the unification of the Netherlands and Belgium in the post-Napoleonic settlement of 1815, textile factories established in the more industrialised Belgian provinces provided a new source of imports. But when Belgium became an independent country in 1830, a shrunken and impoverished Netherlands had to start again, and opted for a fundamental shift to mercantilism in the 1830s.

Since the 1824 Anglo-Dutch Treaty required Holland to restrict levies on British goods to no more than double the levies on Dutch goods, the Netherlands Indies government imposed a tariff of 12.5 per cent on Dutch manufactures for the first time in 1835, allowing a 25 per cent tariff to be imposed on British goods. Under a secret agreement, the state-owned Netherlands Trading Society (NHM) was given the proceeds of the 12.5 per cent duty as a subsidy to boost Dutch manufactures. This was also the time when the notorious *cultuurstelsel* (cultivation system) was inaugurated, giving NHM a monopoly of the exports produced by the forced cultivation of sugar, indigo and coffee in Java. By these monopolistic means, Dutch state control of Java's economy reached its peak in the middle of the nineteenth century (Fasseur 1986; Reid 2009: 48–50; van der Kraan 1998).

Nevertheless, in terms of knitting the archipelago as a whole together, Singapore and Penang continued to play a more crucial role than any Dutch port. In complete contrast to the Dutch dominance of trade at the height of the VOC period, when Batavia maintained its centrality through commercial hegemony, Dutch trade became a minnow in the industrial nineteenth century. Even though it hated to acknowledge it, the Netherlands government knew that its supremacy in the archipelago was dependent on the goodwill of the only global maritime power, Britain, which preferred to bolster the Netherlands rather than risk advances by France, Germany or the United States. Britain insisted that its support for the gradual expansion of Dutch control out to the modern 'national' boundaries envisaged by the 1824 and subsequent treaties was conditional on access for British trade. The constant commercial and diplomatic squabbles between the two nations over the implementation of trade restrictions did not change this fundamental reality. Merchants in the Straits Settlements sought to arouse British outrage against Dutch advances that threatened to disrupt their trade, sometimes dressing this up as sympathy for the independence of Aceh and other states. Dutch journalists and politicians, meanwhile, whipped up patriotic outrage among the Dutch when the concessions to Britain appeared humiliating. This contest was most acute during the first two decades of the Aceh–Dutch war (1873–1911), a festering wound that epitomised the problems of prioritising political claims over economic realities. Straits traders insisted on buying Acehnese pepper and freely selling cloth, opium and even rifles, their self-interest briefly meshing with sympathy for local Aceh patriotism. Fear of alienating the British constantly frustrated Dutch attempts to use their naval power to blockade Aceh ports (Reid 1969: 187–279, 1996: 285–91).

As Dutch control of the archipelago expanded by fits and starts in the nineteenth century, British–Dutch relations became more symbiotic. The shipping company that best tied the archipelago together was Nederlandsch-Indisch Stoomvaart Maatschappij (NISM), a British-owned company that was headquartered in Singapore, despite carrying a Dutch name, flying the Dutch flag and enjoying the subsidy of the Dutch mail contract. Straits-based merchants helped Holland sustain the heavy military burden of attempting to subdue Aceh (while also undermining its efforts). The Penang shipping magnate Chang Chen-hsun (or Thio Taiuw Siat), who was also the first Chinese consul in Penang, held the contract to supply the Dutch navy in Aceh, as well as holding interests in opium and spirit farms throughout northern Sumatra (Godley 1981: 10–12). From mid-century, Singapore and Penang became staple ports for the international steamer companies through which Indonesian travellers and goods had to transit. NISM did not even need to transfer Indonesian passengers and goods in Singapore to the two major Dutch shipping lines, Rotterdamse Lloyd and Scheepvaart Maatschappij Nederland, transferring them instead to the British shipping companies to which it was tied — Alfred Holt and British India. Dutch officials going out to the colony also had to tranship in Singapore or Penang. So did Indonesian pilgrims proceeding to Mecca, if they could not ship clandestinely out of still-independent Aceh (before 1873). British influence became so strong on the Sumatran coast near the Straits Settlements — the booming plantation area around Medan that had opened to tobacco in 1867 — that the Straits dollar was the major currency there, and English-medium mission schools were as influential as the Dutch schools.

This dependence on Singapore and Malaya was as irritating to Dutch nationalists as it would later be to Indonesian ones. The Dutch minister for colonial affairs complained in 1864 that Singapore was the gathering place not only for all the pilgrims from the Indies travelling to Mecca, but also for 'many malcontents, adventurers, etc.' who sought to undermine Dutch control in the archipelago (Fransen van de Putte 1864, cited in Reid 1996: 287). It did not help that Singapore-based Hadhrami Arabs, such as Sayyid Ahmad al-Sagoff and his son Muhammad al-Sagoff, played a large part in taking the pilgrims from Singapore to Jeddah. Penang's role in hardening Acehnese resistance to the Dutch was an even greater irritant, as Christiaan Snouck Hurgronje, the architect of eventual Dutch success in Aceh, noted:

> For the Acehnese Penang is truly the gateway to the world, yes, the world itself. […] Exclusively on the experience of the Acehnese in Penang rests the *general* conviction in Aceh that the rule of the English would be infinitely preferable to ours (Snouck Hurgronje 1893, in Gobée and Adriaanse 1957, I: 115).

Perceived humiliation at British and Acehnese hands did much to galvanise Dutch nationalist resolve to end Holland's debilitating dependence on Britain. In 1883–84 Britain offered to mediate between Aceh and the Netherlands to end the conflict — the alarming implication being that Britain might no longer recognise Dutch sovereignty over Aceh. In 1888, the Dutch government pressured the two big Dutch international shipping companies to form a competitor to the British-owned NISM, the Koninklijke Paketvaart Maatschappij (KPM) (Reid 1969: 218–70). In 1890 KPM took over the mail contract from NISM, and was given many other monopolistic advantages and subsidies. Initially the plan was to bypass Singapore and Penang by turning Dutch ports into alternative hubs of international commerce. As always, however, reality intervened, since the ports of Sabang (in Aceh), Belawan (Medan) and Tanjung Priok (Batavia) could never match the efficiency and price advantages of Singapore and Penang. Instead, KPM was forced to include the British ports in its archipelagic network. Hence, the 'internal' trade between Java and the outer Indonesian islands still amounted to only 5.5 per cent of the 'international' trade of all the islands with the outside world (most of it to the Straits Settlements) in 1914, and to only 17 per cent in 1939. While accommodating the Straits ports, KPM was able to use its government support to gradually squeeze its competitors out of the most strategic domestic arteries (à Campo 1994; Dick 1987, 1996: 40).

KPM became the economic arm of the ruthlessly expansionist administration of J.B. van Heutsz, the governor-general of the Dutch East Indies from 1904 to 1909. Under van Heutsz, indigenous rulers throughout the archipelago were forced to sign a 'Short Declaration' (Korte Verklaring) surrendering all sovereignty to the colonial state, and agreeing to accept its instructions. The feared British objections were not forthcoming. The modern idea of state absolutism had spread to the Asian colonies, and European commercial interests became less interested in maintaining colourful if chaotic autonomies, and more interested in seeing colonial order established in the notoriously unruly Indonesian archipelago. Straits-based British traders had by this time lost interest in the archipelago, having either cut deals with KPM or been squeezed out of the archipelagic trade. The two international Dutch shipping companies began calling regularly at Jeddah in 1883, and in the subsequent decades waged a fierce battle with the Singapore-based al-Sagoffs for the pilgrim trade. By 1900, they and KPM had gained the upper hand (Clarence-Smith 2002; de Goey 2016: 56–8).

The Straits-based Chinese shippers put up stiffer resistance to KPM. They had a lower cost base than the Dutch shipping firm and were able to respond flexibly to new opportunities not serviced by KPM routes. KPM initially tried to run them out of business through price wars and legal sanctions, but it had little success until it adopted the more subtle strategy of encouraging the smaller Chinese steamers into complementary niches. According to à Campo (1994: 21), 'by supporting the cooperative Chinese in many respects, KPM transformed its former adversaries into vassals. In 1911, the maritime pacification was almost complete'. Where there were 33 Straits-based Chinese steamers and 12 KPM steamers serving the archipelago in 1891, by 1913 KPM had 85 steamers — more than double the number of Chinese ones.

From an inherently weak position, the Dutch had managed to create a viable and more-or-less integrated state in the East Indies by 1910. This was achieved despite what in colonial terms had to be an exceptionally open and pluralist approach to foreign investment and trade. In the period 1910–40, Holland's share of Indonesian exports dropped from 29 per cent to below 20 per cent, and its share of Indonesian imports from 33 per cent to 20 per cent (Korthals Altes 1991: 87–90, 100–3). These proportions were much higher than in British, Japanese and especially French colonies. France responded to equally formidable competition from Hong Kong, Singapore and Japan by adopting an extreme protectionist policy, such that over half of Indochinese imports came from France during the period 1897–1939. In the 1930s, France accounted for an even higher share of Indochinese imports — 60 per cent — and for 50 per cent of Indochinese exports (Nørlund 1991: 83).

Singapore remained an important commercial and informational hub for the Indonesian archipelago, especially for Muslims and Chinese, but a stable symbiosis between the city-state and the Indonesian islands had been achieved. The Dutch made periodic attempts to replicate (and in that way undermine) Singapore's success by establishing Dutch-controlled free ports at Tanjung Pinang in Riau in 1829, Pontianak in west Kalimantan in 1833, Makassar in south Sulawesi in 1847 and Manado in north Sulawesi in 1849. Finally, Sabang in Aceh was developed in the 1890s as the challenge *par excellence* to Singapore, perfectly positioned on Indian Ocean routes. Yet these ports attracted limited shipping and made no observable dent in the trade to Singapore and Penang.

The three decades from about 1910 to 1940 when the Netherlands Indies state effectively controlled the area occupied by present-day Indonesia marked a rare point when ruling aspirations matched on-the-ground realities. The authorities in the Straits Settlements and Batavia were relatively cooperative with each other, and smuggling and piracy were at a minimum. Despite the commercial advantages of the free-trading Straits Settlements, Maddison (2001: 215) has calculated that Indonesia's per capita GDP was higher than (the future) Malaysia's in 1913, and not far behind it in 1940. This was the period when the idea of an 'imagined community' of Indonesia took hold. The lesson of this 30-year period appeared to be that state power, exercised strategically and pragmatically in alliance with diverse market forces, could achieve the political objective of tying together a very plural place without sacrificing economic efficiency, whereas headlong confrontation with such forces, especially by an essentially weak government, probably could not.

NATIONALISM AT WAR WITH PRAGMATISM

During the following three decades of heroic chaos, 1940–70, the policies of the new power-holders and the reality of what they could actually control diverged markedly. Theories of autarchy and a command economy became popular; foreign investment and even capitalism itself were tainted by association with colonial and neocolonial ideology; and capital and expertise fled the country. Mackie (1996: 341) has pointed to the stark contrast between the cosy relationship between government and big business in the late colonial era and the 'antagonistic relationship that prevailed almost everywhere between 1945–1966'. The search for alternatives to the pragmatism of the past, he says, led to 'such wildly unrealistic policies and programs that the country's problems were compounded rather than ameliorated'. The post-war period was also the time when Indonesia parted company with rapidly growing Singapore, Malaysia and Thailand in its capacity to cope with poverty, though it would be simplistic to attribute this wholly, or even primarily, to the country's unrealistic economic policies.

During the war, the Japanese occupiers erased some of the boundaries that had been so painfully imposed on the economic realities of the region, but created destructive new ones. They now ruled both sides of the busy Malacca Straits, undoing the work of the 1824 Anglo-Dutch Treaty. Singapore, renamed Syonan, was enlarged with the addition of the Riau archipelago and made the capital for a 25th Army administration of a combined Sumatra and Malaya—'the nuclear zone of the Empire's plans for the Southern Area' (Benda, Irikura and Kishi 1965: 169). This interesting experiment hardly had time to reap any rewards before being reversed in May 1943 as Japanese control of the seas deteriorated. Sumatra and Malaya were put under separate commands, though still sharply separated as economic units from Java. By the following year economic conditions in Japanese-controlled Nusantara had deteriorated sharply. The local Japanese governors (*chōkan*) declared a kind of local autarchy that made trade even between provinces illegal. In theory, the wartime economy was to be tightly controlled to suit the needs of the military. But with the big European players eliminated and the larger vessels that had once plied the archipelago either sunk or fled, the Japanese struggled to control the activities of hundreds of newly built, smaller wooden vessels.

For Indonesians living through the war and the revolutionary period that followed, smuggling—especially between Singapore and the arc of islands around it—became a matter of survival. The smugglers established ways of evading state authority that would develop further strength in the revolutionary period. Towards the end of the war, Karimun Island, strategically located near Singapore, sprang into life as an under-the-radar 'little Syonan' of smuggling between Sumatra and Singapore. The Japanese tolerated this trade because they relied on it themselves for essential foodstuffs such as rice. Twang (1998: 266–91) has documented the new breed of Chinese risk-takers who came to the fore during this period, replacing the established European and Chinese firms accustomed to the calmer pace of Dutch regulation. Most of these newcomers were China-born (*totok*) and had few assets. Many were Hok-chia outsiders like Liem Sioe Liong in Central Java, rather than the long-dominant Hokkien.

South Sumatra continued to be a hotbed of smuggling during the revolutionary period, when the richest operators moved to Singapore for security. During these dangerous times, the republic was beholden to these new men for its economic survival. After getting a start in the risky Sumatra–Malaya trade during the Japanese occupation, they teamed up with equally risk-taking Indonesian officials and warlords during the revolution. A Chinese newspaper in Jakarta, the *Sheng Hua Pao*, reported that, 'Unlike the pre-war Chinese capitalists who are night and day expecting the return of the Dutch government, these newly prosperous merchants are hoping for complete independence for the Indonesians' (cited in van Langenberg 1976: 530).

After the war, Singapore again became the focal point of Indonesian trade with the world. The return of KPM and the 'big five' Dutch trading firms was slow and troubled. The Dutch navy was in no position to intercept the armada of small smuggling boats that made the nightly crossing between Sumatra and Singapore. In both 1947 and 1948, at the height of the conflict between the republicans and the Dutch, Singapore registered over 200,000 tons of rubber imports from Indonesia, more than double the pre-war level. Indonesia provided 22 per cent of Singapore's declared total imports in 1948, though there seems little doubt that a large amount of goods escaped official monitoring altogether. In a compromise designed to establish common criteria on where the boundary lay between legal small-vessel trade and smuggling, in March 1948 the Dutch Indies and British Malayan authorities agreed to a more restrictive system of 'barter trade' between Singapore/Malaya and the Netherlands Indies than had obtained before the war. Indonesian governments have continued the struggle against this barter trade ever since, intermittently trying to suppress it altogether, while Singapore has been content to allow it to flourish (Yong 2003: 153–60).

Unfortunately, the transfer of sovereignty to the fragile new Indonesian government in 1950 was not accompanied by a transfer of the tools needed to integrate the economy. As Dick (1987) has documented, Indonesian officials wanted to take over KPM but did not have the capital to do so legally, while fearing the ramifications of a blatant seizure. Militant trade unions forced the issue by seizing KPM's Jakarta offices in December 1957, triggering prearranged instructions to the captains of KPM vessels to head immediately for foreign ports. The Indonesian government had already established its own shipping company, Pelni, to replace the KPM service, but it proved much less successful than its Dutch-run predecessor in excluding the Singapore-based shipping companies from trade with Indonesia. Even Indonesia's official figures, which overlook the large amount of smuggling, reveal that the proportion of Indonesia's exports going to Singapore rose from 20 per cent in 1938 (probably realistic) to 23 per cent in 1956 and 32 per cent in 1958 (certainly well below the real figure).

The first decades of Indonesian sovereignty witnessed a more exceptional contrast between aspiration and reality even than the nineteenth century. The Indonesian government assumed responsibility for a vast archipelago but had only a rudimentary navy and customs service to control it. At a time when nationalist enthusiasm was at a peak, pragmatic experience of how to handle world markets was at a minimum. The conflict between politics and geography was most starkly on display in the 1950s.

Smuggling became the lifeline of the more prosperous, trade-dependent outer islands of Indonesia. The copra exports of Sulawesi and the rubber, coffee and tobacco exports of Sumatra had flourished in a thousand hands once Dutch blockades were lifted. Controlling and drawing revenue from them became a matter of survival for the young republican government in Jakarta, though it had initially little but moral suasion and the prestige of its perceived victory over the Dutch to bring this trade under its control. It was the local military commands who first took advantage of more stable political conditions and high Korean-War prices for rubber to dominate the trade, by absorbing or neutralising the plethora of local authorities, warlords and revolutionary bands.

Surrendering control of this honeypot to Jakarta was a much bigger step, and could happen only to the extent that the national army gained functional control of its regional constituents. In 1956 this conflict came to a head as the Jakarta press began to report on the vast scale of local military smuggling. Colonel Maludin Simbolon, Toba Batak commander of north Sumatra since 1950, was shown to be in partnership with Medan businessman Chin Hock to smuggle rubber out through the small east Sumatran port of Teluk Nibong (Smail 1968: 135–8). In north Sulawesi six foreign ships were seen unloading consumer goods and loading copra in Manado's new deep-water port of Bitung in broad daylight, seemingly without any central government oversight. Jakarta's attempts to bring the hitherto largely autonomous commanders to heel very quickly led to what we know as the PRRI and Permesta rebellions of 1958, in Sumatra and Sulawesi respectively (Feith 1962: 487–500).

Jakarta extinguished these uprisings with great determination, despite the human and material cost. This victory unified the command structure of the military, which played an ever-larger role in economic affairs thereafter with each nationalisation of 'foreign' business. The government had less success in meeting populist demands to transfer economic assets to indigenous (*pribumi*) hands while retaining entrepreneurial capital and expertise. Soon after the transfer of sovereignty, the government instituted its *benteng* (fortress) policy, intended to build an effective indigenous entrepreneurial class by favouring *pribumi* applicants in the granting of import licences. This was rightly seen as the easiest way for the government to intervene in the market, since it controlled the licences, while the thresholds for capital and expertise in this field were low. The policy succeeded in the sense that, by the mid-1950s, about 70 per cent of import licences were in *pribumi* hands. The most prominent economist of the day, Sumitro Djojohadikusumo, later recalled that he had calculated that even if most beneficiaries 'turned out to be crooks, the remaining three [out of ten] might well develop into real entrepreneurs' (cited in Thee 1996: 317; see also Booth 1998: 312–14). This turned out to be overoptimistic, as an official review in 1955 revealed that only 10 per cent of the people who had been given licences were bona fide importers; the others had mostly either sold their licences to more experienced Chinese-Indonesian businessmen or become silent partners in joint ventures with them.

The same unstable conditions that had allowed risk-taking, China-born newcomers to get ahead in the 1940s proved even more advantageous to a handful of *pribumi* businessmen who had been overtly favoured by both Japanese and republican power-holders. Enough had emerged by the 1950s to form a nationalist lobby against their Chinese-Indonesian business rivals. In March 1956, Minangkabau lawyer, businessman and politician Assaat delivered a speech explicitly denouncing ethnic Chinese businessmen, whether Indonesian citizens or not, as exclusive and monopolistic, and demanding that 'Native Indonesian citizens must receive special protection in all their endeavours in the economic field, from the competition of foreigners in general and the Chinese especially' (cited in Feith and Castles 1970: 346). Although the political establishment was reluctant to endorse his racialised policies openly, the government did respond to popular pressure by introducing various anti-Chinese measures that would prove counterproductive. It restricted government contracts and licences, and forcibly removed Chinese who were deemed to be foreign nationals from rural areas (Presidential Decree No. 10/1959), leading to an exodus to China or Singapore of many actual or potential entrepreneurs (Feith 1962: 481–7).

This anti-Chinese sentiment not only weakened economic activity at a time when Dutch businesses and capital were also departing precipitately, but drove what remained into informal or illegal channels. As the nationalist rhetoric became more extreme during Sukarno's Guided Democracy period, smuggling and evasion of the law became ever more necessary. The depressing legacy of this nationalist mind-set has not been easy to overcome.

The crescendo of the conflict between policy and reality, the 'Confrontation' of Malaysia (Konfrontasi), also proved to be the turning point towards more pragmatic policies. All trade with Malaysia and Singapore was banned in September 1963, with Indonesian 'free ports' declared in Sabang, Belawan and Makassar the following month. This attempt to replace Singapore and Penang with a domestic alternative had as little success as in the Dutch days a century earlier. Food supplies became scarce in the Riau archipelago, which had long been accustomed to using Singapore as its basic market. Smuggling revived, despite the high risks. Established merchants lost their businesses, but once again newcomer Chinese merchants made the necessary connections with some power-holders and bore the risk of being penalised by others. By 1965 things had become desperate in Riau: 'all the government officials had two functions (*dwifungsi*). On weekdays they sat in their offices, but on Saturday they'd catch a boat straight to Singapore or Malaysia and buy stuff to smuggle back' (school principal in Karimun, cited in Ford and Lyons 2012: 96).

The long recovery from this episode of unreality is still not complete. During the period of Konfrontasi and the subsequent military assumption of power amid the massacres of leftists, the guardians of the nation again became the smugglers: 'the generals owned the ships. They flew a yellow flag so if they were caught by customs, the customs officers would know who owned them' (Malay teacher in Karimun, cited in Ford and Lyons 2012: 97). When short of funds in crushing the PRRI in 1958, and again in managing the transition of a bankrupt economy in 1965–66, the central military leadership itself organised some smuggling to Singapore (Sukendro 1970).

Barter trade/smuggling continues to constitute an important but opaque category of unauthorised exports. To take an example, Indonesia has been one of the world's leading tin producers since the 1980s, while Singapore produces none (despite Bukit Timah — 'Tin Hill'), and does not show up in statistics as a significant tin importer. Yet in most years, at least up to the 1990s, tin producers in Bangka seeking to escape the state tin monopoly smuggled enough tin to Singapore to make the latter a bigger tin exporter than Indonesia. In 1993 (the latest year for which such data are accessible), Singapore accounted for 16 per cent of world tin exports, and Indonesia for only 10 per cent (UNCTAD 1995: 24).

Over the 30 years in which he held power, Suharto gradually eased the military out of business with Singapore and Malaysia and built cooperative relationships with these nations. The formation of ASEAN in 1967 and the establishment, in the 1990s, of the ASEAN Free Trade Area and the growth triangles linking Indonesia's borderlands to Singapore, Malaysia, the southern Philippines and southern Thailand were extremely helpful in bringing Indonesian policy-making closer to economic reality. Yet monopolies and rent-seeking naturally remain alluring to a nationalist lobby convinced that indigenous Indonesians are disadvantaged. The gap between politics and geography has again narrowed, but remains daunting.

REFERENCES

à Campo, J.N.F.M. (1994) 'Steam navigation and state formation', in R. Cribb (ed.) *The Late Colonial State in Indonesia: Political and Economic Foundations of the Netherlands Indies, 1880–1942*, KITLV Press, Leiden: 11–30.

Benda, H., J.K. Irikura and K. Kishi (1965) *Japanese Military Administration in Indonesia: Selected Documents*, Yale University Southeast Asian Studies, New Haven CT.

Blussé, L. (1986) *Strange Company: Chinese Settlers, Mestizo Women, and the Dutch in VOC Batavia*, Foris, Dordrecht/Providence.

Booth, A. (1998) *The Indonesian Economy in the Nineteenth and Twentieth Centuries: A History of Missed Opportunities*, Macmillan, Basingstoke.

Bulbeck, D., A. Reid, L.C. Tan and Y. Wu (1998) *Southeast Asian Exports since the 14th Century: Cloves, Pepper, Coffee and Sugar*, Institute of Southeast Asian Studies, Singapore.

Clarence-Smith, W.G. (2002) 'The rise and fall of Hadhrami shipping in the Indian Ocean, c. 1750 – c. 1840', in R. Barnes and D. Parkin (eds) *Ships and the Development of Maritime Technology on the Indian Ocean*, RoutledgeCurzon, London: 227–76.

Crawfurd, J. (1856) *A Descriptive Dictionary of the Indian Islands and Adjacent Countries*, Bradbury & Evans, London.

de Goey, F. (2016) *Consuls and the Institutions of Global Capitalism, 1783–1914*, Routledge, Abingdon.

Dick, H. (1987) *The Indonesian Interisland Shipping Industry: An Analysis of Competition and Regulation*, Institute of Southeast Asian Studies, Singapore.

Dick, H. (1996) 'The emergence of a national economy, 1808–1990s', in T. Lindblad (ed.) *Historical Foundations of a National Economy in Indonesia, 1890s–1990s*, North-Holland for Royal Netherlands Academy of Arts and Sciences, Amsterdam: 21–52.

Fasseur, C. (1986) 'The cultivation system and its impact on the Dutch colonial economy and the indigenous society in nineteenth-century Java', in C.A. Bayly and D.H.A. Kolff (eds) *Two Colonial Empires: Comparative Essays on the History of India and Indonesia in the Nineteenth Century*, Nijhoff, Dordrecht: 137–54.

Feith, H. (1962) *The Decline of Constitutional Democracy in Indonesia*, Cornell University Press, Ithaca NY.

Feith, H., and L. Castles (eds) (1970) *Indonesian Political Thinking, 1945–1965*, Cornell University Press, Ithaca NY.

Ford, M., and L. Lyons (2012) 'Smuggling cultures in the Indonesia–Singapore borderlands', in B. Kalir and M. Sur (eds) *Transnational Flows and Permissive Polities: Ethnographies of Human Mobilities in Asia*, Amsterdam University Press, Amsterdam: 91–108.

Gobée, E., and C. Adriaanse (eds) (1957) *Ambtelijke Adviezen van C. Snouck Hurgronje, 1889–1936* [Advisory Reports to the Government of C. Snouck Hurgronje], Nijhoff, The Hague.

Godley, M.R. (1981) *The Mandarin-Capitalists from Nanyang: Overseas Chinese Enterprise in the Modernization of China, 1893–1911*, Cambridge University Press, Cambridge.

Grotius, H. (1916) *The Freedom of the Seas*, Oxford University Press, New York NY. First published in 1608.

Hanna, W.A. (1978) *Indonesian Banda: Colonialism and Its Aftermath in the Nutmeg Islands*, Institute for the Study of Human Issues, Philadelphia PA.

Korthals Altes, W.L. (1991) *Changing Economy in Indonesia: General Trade Statistics, 1822–1940*, Volume 12A, Nijhoff, The Hague.

Mackie, J.A.C. (1996) 'The 1941–1965 period as an interlude in the making of a national economy: how should we interpret it?', in T. Lindblad (ed.) *Historical Foundations of a National Economy in Indonesia, 1890s–1990s*, North-Holland for Royal Netherlands Academy of Arts and Sciences, Amsterdam: 331–47.

Maddison, A. (2001) *The World Economy: A Millennial Perspective*, OECD Development Studies Series, Paris.

Meilink-Roelofsz, M.A.P. (1962) *Asian Trade and European Influence in the Indonesian Archipelago between 1500 and about 1630*, Nijhoff, The Hague.

Nørlund, I. (1991) 'The French empire, the colonial state in Vietnam and economic policy, 1885–1940', *Australian Economic History Review* 31(1): 72–89.

Raffles, S. (ed.) (1835) *Memoir of the Life and Public Services of Sir Thomas Stamford Raffles*, James Duncan, London.

Reid, A. (1969) *The Contest for North Sumatra: Atjeh, the Netherlands and Britain, 1858–1898*, Oxford University Press and University of Malaya Press, Kuala Lumpur.

Reid, A. (1993a) *Southeast Asia in the Age of Commerce, 1450–1680*, Volume II: Expansion and Crisis, Yale University Press, New Haven CT.

Reid, A. (1993b) 'The unthreatening alternative: Chinese shipping in Southeast Asia, 1567–1842', *Review of Indonesian and Malaysian* Affairs 27(142): 13–32.

Reid, A. (1996) 'Chains of steel; chains of silver: forcing politics on geography, 1865–1965', in T. Lindblad (ed.) *Historical Foundations of a National Economy in Indonesia, 1890s–1990s*, North-Holland for Royal Netherlands Academy of Arts and Sciences, Amsterdam: 281–96.

Reid, A. (1997) 'A new phase of commercial expansion in Southeast Asia', in A. Reid (ed.) *The Last Stand of Asian Autonomies*, Macmillan, Basingstoke: 57–82.

Reid, A. (2000) '*Negeri*: the culture of Malay-speaking city-states of the fifteenth and sixteenth centuries', in M.H. Hansen (ed.) *A Comparative Study of Thirty City-state Cultures*, Royal Danish Academy of Sciences and Letters, Copenhagen: 417–29.

Reid, A. (2009) 'Southeast Asian consumption of British and Indian cotton cloth, 1600–1850', in O. Prakash, G. Riello, T. Roy and K. Sugihara (eds) *How India Clothed the World: The World of South Asian Textiles, 1500–1850*, Brill, The Hague: 31–52.

Smail, J. (1968) 'The military politics of north Sumatra December 1956 – October 1957', *Indonesia* 6(October): 128–87.

Sukendro, Brigadier-General (1970) Interview with Harold Crouch, in Harold Crouch Papers, Australian National University Archives, Canberra.

Thee, K.W. (1996) 'Economic policies in Indonesia during the period 1950–1965, in particular with respect to foreign investment', in T. Lindblad (ed.) *Historical Foundations of a National Economy in Indonesia, 1890s–1990s*, North-Holland for Royal Netherlands Academy of Arts and Sciences, Amsterdam: 315-30.

Trocki, C. (1990) *Opium and Empire: Chinese Society in Colonial Singapore, 1800–1910*, Cornell University Press, Ithaca NY.

Twang, P.Y. (1998) *The Chinese Business Élite in Indonesia and the Transition to Independence, 1940–1950*, Oxford University Press, Kuala Lumpur and New York NY.

UNCTAD (United Nations Conference on Trade and Development) (1995) 'Market situation and outlook for tin, 1994', report by the UNCTAD secretariat, 7 June. unctad.org/en/Docs/pocomd54.en.pdf

van der Kraan, A. (1998) *Contest for the Java Cotton Trade, 1811–40: An Episode in Anglo-Dutch Rivalry*, Centre for Southeast Asian Studies, University of Hull, Hull.

van Langenberg, M. (1976) 'National revolution in North Sumatra: Sumatra Timur and Tapanuli, 1942–1950', PhD thesis, University of Sydney, Sydney.

Yong, M.C. (2003) *The Indonesian Revolution and the Singapore Connection, 1945–1949*, Singapore University Press, Singapore.

3 The new nationalism in Indonesia

*Edward Aspinall**

Over the last decade or so, as Indonesia has recovered from the blows of the 1997-98 Asian financial crisis, resumed economic growth and stabilised as a successful democracy, a mood of assertive nationalism has entered the country's public discourse and domestic politics. Politicians, intellectuals, journalists, leaders of religious and social organisations, and many ordinary citizens frequently state publicly that foreign countries habitually insult, exploit and mistreat Indonesia, and do not accord it the respect it deserves as a great nation. From time to time, there are angry eruptions of public protest and media condemnation in response to alleged insults that other countries — usually neighbours such as Malaysia or Australia — have directed in Indonesia's direction. Candidates for political office increasingly draw upon nationalist themes, and political leaders are increasingly moulding public policy to match the nationalist mood, with a host of measures to protect sectors of the Indonesian economy and restrict activities by foreigners. Though nationalist discourse and policymaking have featured in all post-Suharto governments, they are becoming even more prominent under President Joko Widodo, sworn into office in October 2014.

This chapter sketches core features of this new nationalism, analyses its historical roots and identifies the factors driving its contemporary manifestation. The first section introduces the new nationalism, noting three key arenas of nationalist mobilisation: territorial, economic and

---

* The author thanks Paul Kenny, Evan Laksmana, Citu Rahadian and Eve Warburton for useful comments on an earlier draft, but accepts full responsibility for the content. This chapter is a revised version of a paper that first appeared in *Asia & the Pacific Policy Studies* (Aspinall 2016).

cultural. The second section explains the historical sweep of Indonesian nationalism, in order to identify both the roots of the contemporary phenomenon and its novel characteristics. The next two sections focus on two features that define the contemporary nationalism: first, a sense of suspicion, sometimes bordering on paranoia, about the allegedly hostile intentions harboured by foreign countries; and second, an obsession with insults allegedly directed at Indonesia, and an overwhelming concern to defend Indonesia's 'national dignity'.

The final section of the chapter considers factors driving the new nationalism. Indonesia's post-1998 democratisation, and the absence of strong policy or ideological differences between its major parties, provides a domestic political context strongly conducive to nationalist outbidding. The new nationalism is also moulded by insecurity about Indonesia's place in the world. The emphasis on national dignity, for example, derives largely from the anxieties attending Indonesia's transformation from a relatively poor and underdeveloped nation into a more successful economic player, but one that still lags behind neighbouring countries.

Before proceeding with the argument, let us note three caveats. The first is that the primary focus of this article is Indonesian nationalism as it relates to the country's external relations. Nationalism is always Janus-faced, looking simultaneously outward, to assert a place for the nation within the international community of nation-states, and inward, to identify and define the critical features of national identity to which citizens should owe their loyalty, and (often) to punish those who deviate. These two sides are connected, but this essay focuses on the outward orientation. Accordingly, this chapter does not much discuss Indonesian nationalism's achievements with regard to the creation of an inclusionary national identity in which ethnic and religious minorities are accommodated, nor the difficulties that have attended this process.

Such topics have, of course, been a matter of not merely academic interest in the post-Suharto period. As the country has embarked on the process of reinventing its institutions, so too have various groups tried to stretch, challenge or redraw established concepts of Indonesian nationhood. The communal conflicts that accompanied the transition from Suharto's presidency often involved attempts to remake the rules of national belonging (Bertrand 2004); similarly, both Islamists and pluralists have challenged the 'godly nationalism' (Menchik 2016) forged during the first decades of Indonesian independence, by which Indonesian identity was seen as indissolubly linked to monotheistic religion. In any country, the boundaries of national membership and the core components of national identity are never truly fixed, but are constantly renegotiated and redrawn through processes of political contestation and social change. Indonesia is certainly no exception to this rule, and contestation about what it means to be an Indonesian has been a major feature of contemporary politics. In the interests of focus, however, such issues are largely set aside in this essay.

Second, it should be stressed that nationalism involves notably amorphous ideas and dispositions. Because nationalism is typically linked to structures of feeling and emotion more than to the world of rationality and intellect, its advocates often pay little heed to the logical consistency or implications of their positions. Nationalism is also highly fungible, with nationalists able to combine different aspects of nationalist thinking, and overlay them on other political philosophies and ideas, with almost infinite variation. Accordingly, though the piece discusses contemporary Indonesian nationalism in rather sweeping terms, we should remember that there is in practice considerable variety in how Indonesians articulate, combine and act upon nationalist ideas. Many Indonesians would disagree with the discourses outlined below, or aspects of them. Even so, the nationalist mood described here represents a widely shared and distinctive feature of Indonesia's contemporary political landscape.

Third, and in a related point, it is important to note that, while some of the features of nationalism discussed in this article are unique to Indonesia, increasingly assertive nationalism is part of a broader global trend. A rising tide of nationalism can be observed in countries as diverse as India, China, the United States and Hungary, to name just a few. Numerous factors have been identified to explain this trend, including growing inequality and disillusionment with democratic institutions in established democracies, and the strains generated by authoritarian modernisation in countries such as China. Whatever one makes of such arguments, the breadth of the trend across a wide range of countries with widely differing political institutions and economic trajectories serves to underline the fungible nature of nationalism.

But we should also point out that in the context of widespread nationalism, in many ways Indonesian nationalism does *not* appear to be particularly virulent. The slipperiness of nationalism makes it notoriously difficult to measure, but some guidance can be found in international surveys that show that Indonesians do not appear to be unusually nationalistic. For example, as part of the fifth wave of the World Values Survey (2005–09), residents of 59 countries were asked how proud they were to be Indonesian, Rwandan, Georgian and so on. Among Indonesians, 91.6 per cent said they felt 'quite proud' or 'very proud'—a high figure, but not much higher than the average of 87.9 per cent for all the countries surveyed. But only 45.7 per cent said they felt 'very proud' to be Indonesian, which was significantly lower than the global average of 58.5 per cent (World Values Survey 2005–09).

THE 2014 ELECTION, JOKOWI AND THE NEW NATIONALISM

One sign that assertive nationalism was re-emerging at the centre of Indonesian politics came with the presidential election campaign of 2014. One of the two contestants, Prabowo Subianto, a retired military general who had played a leading role in Suharto's New Order regime (1966–98), built his campaign appeal almost exclusively on a nationalist platform. Although all mainstream politicians in Indonesia, as in other countries, are nationalist to one degree or another, the vehemence of Prabowo's nationalist message, and the passion with which it was delivered, was distinctive. In his stump speeches, Prabowo frequently condemned the foreign actors who were conspiring — in concert with (unnamed) domestic traitors — to drain Indonesia's national wealth, with the consequence that Indonesia had become a 'nation of slaves' (*bangsa kacung*). Foreigners were sneering at Indonesia, he repeatedly said, and it was time for Indonesia to assert itself as a dignified and great nation. In large part, this meant throwing off the shackles of foreign economic exploitation and limiting the role of foreign companies — especially in the natural resources sector — but it also meant asserting Indonesia's greatness in fields ranging from military power to culture. Presumably to underline the seriousness of his nationalist message, Prabowo even styled himself on Indonesia's founding father President Sukarno, wearing a black *peci* cap and an old-fashioned military-cum-safari suit modelled on those worn by Sukarno in his heyday (Aspinall 2015).

Although Prabowo's rival, the ultimately victorious Joko Widodo (Jokowi), had a less strident approach (Mietzner 2015), he also adopted a fundamentally nationalist platform, promoting a three-fold emphasis on political sovereignty, economic autarchy and cultural renaissance. When Prabowo tried to outflank him on nationalist issues in the televised debates, Jokowi responded effectively. For example, when Prabowo implied that Jokowi was weak on national security by asking him what he would do if a foreign country claimed or occupied Indonesian territory (a live issue because of disputes with Malaysia), Jokowi responded that he would first negotiate, but after that: 'If it is clearly our possession then we would have to do anything, if it concerns our sovereignty, yeah, we'll make trouble [*kita buat ramai*]. Don't think I can't be tough. I am tough and bold in making decisions and taking risks!' (Waskita 2014). After Jokowi's inauguration, his government adopted a host of new nationalist measures. These included new import restrictions, such as a ban on the import of rice as part of a proclaimed goal of achieving complete food self-sufficiency, but also other acts such as the much-publicised burning of foreign fishing boats captured in Indonesian waters and the execution of persons, mostly foreigners, convicted of narcotics crimes.

Stepping back from the immediate context of Jokowi's government and surveying the years since the fall of Suharto, we can identify three main arenas in which nationalist mobilisation and policy-making have played out.

Territorial nationalism

A consistent concern of nationalists in the post-Suharto era has been to maintain Indonesia's territorial integrity in the face of alleged external aggression and internal separatism. Indeed, in the minds of most nationalists these threats are inextricably linked, for reasons touched on below. Nationalist discourse on this issue reached fever pitch during and immediately after the Australian-led United Nations intervention in East Timor in 1999. Despite the fact that this intervention occurred on Indonesia's invitation, after an Indonesia-initiated referendum process that was followed by widespread Indonesian military abuses, most mainstream Indonesian politicians blamed the 'loss' of East Timor on the intervention and did not concede that the history of Indonesian military occupation and human rights violations in the province was responsible.

Similar themes still feature in mainstream discourse on other trouble spots. Military leaders, national parliamentarians and other politicians routinely state that political unrest and pro-independence sentiment in Papua are linked to foreign plans to destabilise Indonesia and access Papua's mineral wealth. In October 2014, Jokowi's new home affairs minister justified a policy to split up the provinces of Papua and West Papua by claiming that the policy was necessary to prevent increasing foreign intervention in Papua (Sasmita 2014). It need hardly be stated that this attitude does not help policy-makers to accurately diagnose the roots of political conflict in these provinces, or to design appropriate responses.

Unresolved territorial disputes with neighbours, especially Malaysia, have also caused tension. In 2002, the International Court of Justice ruled in favour of Malaysian claims over the islands of Sipadan and Ligitan, located off the northwest coast of Borneo, causing great angst and contributing to a widespread belief that Indonesia's maritime regions and outlying islands were vulnerable to predation. Several near-clashes between Malaysian and Indonesian navy vessels in the disputed oil-rich Ambalat block, also near Borneo, have prompted outpourings of public hostility towards Malaysia involving, among other things, demonstrations at which protestors threw human excrement at the Malaysian embassy in Jakarta and called for volunteer forces to participate in a new version of the 'Ganyang Malaysia' (Crush Malaysia) campaign of the 1960s. These issues, alongside cultural and other tensions discussed below, have combined to make Malaysia the leading target of nationalist ire in Indonesia in the post-Suharto period (Clark and Pietsch 2014).

Economic nationalism

Nationalist policies designed to protect domestic producers or markets against foreign competition have a long history in Indonesia, but the country was forced to open large segments of the economy to foreign investment and trade under IMF rescue packages after the 1997-98 financial collapse. After Indonesia had paid off its debts and begun to enjoy the fruits of the international commodity boom, a return to economic nationalist policies became visible, starting from around 2009-10 at the beginning of Yudhoyono's second term. The government imposed a raft of new import restrictions, typically with the express purpose of protecting vulnerable industries from foreign competition and, especially, supporting agricultural producers. Minerals became the target of a new 'resource nationalism', with new regulations imposing limits on foreign ownership and banning the export of unprocessed ore (Warburton 2014, 2017). Yudhoyono's government also for a time stopped the import of rice, immediately leading to an increase in the price of the commodity and bumping up the poverty rate (because rice forms a large part of the daily expenditure of poor people). Some of these policies were driven by vested interests and rent-seekers, and others (such as the rice ban) by public pressure, including mobilisations by farmers and other producer groups. Many of these policies were continued, or even expanded, in the Jokowi period.

One striking aspect of this economic nationalist turn has been how politicians have framed it in anti-colonial and anti-imperialist terms. The fevered nature of Prabowo's denunciations of foreign control of Indonesia's natural wealth has already been mentioned, but Jokowi, too, frequently slips into similar language. In early 2015, for example, the president urged young entrepreneurs to compete more actively in the domestic market and so prevent 'foreign businesspeople' from 'occupying' (*menduduki*—a word usually associated with military conquest) the Indonesian market (Siregar 2015).

Cultural nationalism

The cultural arena has become an increasingly important sphere of nationalist mobilisation, prompted in part by the spread of modern communication technologies, especially the internet and social media. This new trend has been most visible in a series of disputes with Indonesia's neighbours, especially Malaysia. Indonesians accuse Malaysians of cultural theft—of laying claim to various Indonesian traditions (dances, songs, culinary products and the like) in their own promotional and marketing activities. Thus, for example, when the Discovery Channel featured footage of the distinctive Balinese Pendet dance in advertisements promoting a series on Malaysia, there was an eruption of condemnation of Malaysia by political leaders, in the media and online, as well as angry demonstrations and calls to 'crush Malaysia'. The tourism and culture minister sent an official letter accusing Malaysia of a violation of ethics; parliamentarians called on the government to withdraw the ambassador. Similar anger has arisen in response to alleged Malaysian appropriation of, among other things, a famous Ambonese song, a Batak dance, the distinctive Reog masked dance from East Java and even a particular variety of spring roll. Though such incidents may seem trivial, together with the territorial disputes and other tensions between the two countries, they have contributed to great popular hostility towards Malaysia.

HISTORICAL ROOTS

In many respects, the 'new' nationalism in Indonesia is not particularly new. As numerous theorists of nationalism have pointed out, nationalism always functions to connect individual citizens to a wider national narrative and birth myth (see Anderson 1983 for a classic statement). In the Indonesian case, the birth myth focuses on the struggle against Dutch colonial exploitation and subjugation. Throughout seven decades of independent statehood, Indonesian nationalism has consistently turned to this early anti-colonial struggle for its myths, symbols and idiom. Contemporary nationalists continue to draw heavily on the terminology and symbols of the anti-colonial struggle. Every Indonesian school child learns about the epochal moments in Indonesia's national awakening, about the various officially designated 'national heroes' who led anti-colonial resistance, and how to sing the 'struggle songs' of that era. They all become intimately familiar—through re-enactments, dioramas, public monuments, movies and other cultural productions—with the iconic image of a long-haired, headbanded and heavily muscled revolutionary youth (*pemuda*) holding aloft a sharpened length of bamboo. Much is made of the 'spirit of struggle' (*semangat perjuangan*) of the early nationalists and how this spirit should guide contemporary Indonesians.

Despite a consistent orientation to the myth of the anti-Dutch struggle, Indonesian nationalism has had distinctive features in different periods, and it has been shaped by changing political imperatives. In the first two decades of Indonesian independence, especially during the period of Guided Democracy under President Sukarno (1957–66), nationalism was generally leftist in orientation and focused on the unfinished anti-colonial mission of the revolution (notably, the nationalisation of foreign enterprises and the 'liberation' of Papua). In the final years of his rule, Sukarno tried to focus Indonesia's revolutionary energies outward, including through a policy of Confrontation (Konfrontasi) with the newly formed Federation of Malaysia, which he described as a neocolonial dagger aimed at the heart of Indonesia. He did so, most analysts agree, to solve a domestic political problem: Sukarno was trying to hold together a political spectrum undergoing rapid polarisation between supporters of the Indonesian Communist Party on the left, and the army, Islamic forces and their allies on the right.

After the army emerged victorious from this conflict, Suharto's New Order regime turned Indonesian nationalism to the purposes of regime maintenance and authoritarian legitimation. The regime's leaders were not interested in highlighting the revolutionary content of Indonesia's nationalist history even as they kept alive its iconography and terminology. Instead, they promoted a version of nationalism that stressed an Indonesian national 'personality' founded on harmony and group interests rather than conflict and individual rights. In stark contrast to the Sukarno government, which had harboured grand ambitions to mobilise the world's New Emerging Forces (NEFOs) against imperialism, Suharto's government was inward looking and conservative in its international relations. However, as the government came under increasing pressure for political reform in its final decade, and as the international environment became less supportive after the collapse of the Soviet Union, the country's leaders began to revive nationalism in order to buttress the regime against internal and external ideological threats. Senior military officers regularly accused persons who sought political reform of deviating from Indonesia's national personality and of being 'national traitors'. Under Suharto, nationalism was above all a tool to keep government in the hands of a highly conservative military–bureaucratic caste.

Indonesia's contemporary nationalism is still shaped by its historical roots. For example, the belief that political unrest on Indonesia's periphery arises from a fusion of separatism and foreign intervention is directly traceable to the years of the revolution, when the Dutch sponsored a federal Republic of the United States of Indonesia as part of their strategy to defeat the nationalists, and to the 1950s when the United States supported regional rebels and contemplated splitting Indonesia into two or more states (Kahin and Kahin 1995). Many other aspects of contemporary Indonesian nationalism — for instance, the militant anti-colonial language in which opposition to foreign investment is often expressed — are also linked to this historical legacy. Indeed, it should be stressed that the three key arenas of nationalist mobilisation discussed above — territorial, economic and cultural — have been major focuses of Indonesian nationalist debate and mobilisation since the early years of independence.

In fact, to say that contemporary Indonesian nationalism is a product of its history is a significant understatement. In many ways, it seems trapped by it, with much current nationalist discourse sounding very anachronistic, as if ripped straight from an earlier era and transplanted unmodified into the present. What, for example, are we to make of the following remark by Indonesian National Army (TNI) commander Moeldoko at a February 2015 meeting with members of Banser, a security group linked to the mass Islamic organisation Nahdlatul Ulama? 'Other countries will be really horrified if they find out that the TNI and Banser are working in synergy', he told the meeting (Detikcom 2015). In the context of Indonesia's contemporary international relations, this statement makes no sense: what country would care in the slightest to learn that the Indonesian military was cooperating with a ramshackle organisation of village youths whose regular security function consisted of little more than providing guards of honour for respected religious scholars in their communities? In the context of mainstream readings of Indonesia's national history, however, Moeldoko's statement is more comprehensible, invoking as it does the myth of a national struggle in which military units fought side by side with popular organisations to drive out the Dutch. The statement also expresses Indonesian military doctrine concerning the mobilisation of popular militias in the event of external aggression, and reflects the TNI's perception of itself as a people's army.

It is easy to find similar examples in almost any contemporary nationalist controversy. On social media, it is common for individuals to jump from a discussion of, say, whether a particular type of spring roll should be considered part of Indonesian or Malaysian cuisine, to invocations of massacres by Dutch troops in Sulawesi in the 1940s, or the 1960s 'Crush Malaysia' campaign. When the Discovery Channel broadcast the images of the Pendet dance, some Indonesians in Jakarta carried sharpened bamboo spears and headbands as they set about trying to 'sweep' the streets and capture Malaysian citizens (Koran Tempo 2009). In short, there often seems to be a mismatch between the tenor of current nationalist rhetoric and the seriousness of the underlying issue.

Setting aside such instances of discursive and symbolic fossilisation, we still need to identify the defining features and underlying political motivations of the new nationalism. As noted above, Sukarno-era nationalism was politically leftist, and shaped by Sukarno's desire to manage domestic political conflict. Suharto-era nationalism was politically conservative and functioned primarily to justify authoritarian rule. Both versions, in their own ways, were highly ideological. Sukarno talked at great length about NEFOs and OLDEFOs (Old Established Forces), borrowed freely from political philosophers of various stripes and coined a plethora of acronyms and slogans to encapsulate his grandiose concepts and ambitions. Suharto presided over equally arcane ideological production, though of a more leaden variety, with regime-approved intellectuals producing a huge volume of turgid tracts on the official Pancasila ideology.

In contrast, contemporary nationalism is strikingly un-ideological and un-theorised. Indonesian nationalism today has few ideologues, but it has many recyclers of old tropes and many promoters of base emotional appeals. But what are those appeals?

FOREIGN THREATS

One distinctive feature of the contemporary nationalism is its preoccupation with the notion that various (usually unnamed) foreign powers harbour nefarious and hostile designs on Indonesia. The most articulate spokesperson of this view in recent times was Prabowo during the 2014 presidential campaign. He frequently claimed that foreigners were sucking Indonesia dry of its natural wealth. However, statements along similar lines are unremarkable in contemporary Indonesia, and are made on virtually a daily basis in national political debate.

Let us take an example involving another senior military officer, army chief of staff General Gatot Nurmantyo. From late 2014, Gatot received much media coverage when he appeared in a series of speaking engagements at campuses. His purpose, he said, was to warn Indonesian youth about the danger of 'proxy war' in Indonesia, which he defined as 'a confrontation between two major powers using proxy actors so as to avoid direct confrontation'. The proxies of choice were usually small states but could also be non-state actors such as non-government organisations, social organisations, community groups and individuals. Proxy war was *already* threatening Indonesia, he insisted, as manifested by the emergence of separatist movements, mass demonstrations and intergroup clashes (Thohari 2014). In one speech, the general said that the growing narcotics problem in Indonesia was another sign of proxy war, because 'This condition happens in order to damage the younger generation of Indonesians […] Through an international conspiracy, the Indonesian younger generation can unknowingly be destroyed, without having to use armed force' (Liputan6 2014). Though Gatot clearly believed proxy war was being waged on Indonesia, he did not identify the culprit or produce evidence to explain or support his assertions. Nevertheless, during his subsequent tenure as armed forces commander (2015–17), the general continued to expound on the theory of proxy war, making it a frequent theme of Indonesian political discourse.

This is a particularly elaborate example, but casual references to Indonesia being the target of foreign conspiracies, economic or political subjugation, moral or political subversion and so on are all part of mainstream debate in Indonesia and rarely raise an eyebrow when uttered even by ministers or members of parliament. The belief that foreign countries represent a territorial, physical or security threat is often intertwined with more general moral panic about cultural and social change. Public figures frequently state that social ills such as sexual promiscuity, drug use, prostitution, sexually transmitted diseases, pornography and the like are attributable to globalisation and foreign (especially Western) cultural influence. Moreover, such concerns cross the political spectrum — it is easy to find remarkably similar statements about foreign threats to Indonesia's sovereignty and culture from Islamist groups on the one hand through to secular–nationalist groups on the other.

Over the last five years or so, various government policies have been reshaped to deal with such foreign dangers. As well as deploying the military to areas that are seen as vulnerable (such as remote islands and parts of the maritime border with Malaysia), the government has tightened regulations governing foreigners within the country. For example, in 2010 the minister of home affairs issued new 'Guidelines for the Monitoring of Foreigners and Foreign Organisations in the Regions' (Minister of Home Affairs Regulation No. 29/2010) mandating increased surveillance of non-citizens. The ministry has also implemented new requirements for Indonesian-language competence for expatriate workers and tightened government control over both government and non-government aid programs.

Of course, at one level, the concern with foreign threats is not surprising: nationalists always define the identity of their nation in opposition to some foreign 'other', whether explicitly or implicitly. There is, however, a notable disproportionality about the current Indonesian discourse. The regional security context in which Indonesia finds itself is benign and no country has expressed hostile intent towards Indonesia. Yet, much contemporary discourse represents Indonesia as being under assault. It is hard to avoid concluding that this discourse in fact points to deep insecurities about Indonesia's identity and place in the world, a point we return to below.

NATIONAL DIGNITY

A second theme of the contemporary nationalism is a preoccupation with Indonesia's 'national dignity', or *martabat bangsa*. This is a key phrase that recurs constantly in political debate. Contemporary political leaders demonstrate a sometimes overwhelming obsession with insults, denigration and devaluing of Indonesia by foreigners, and repeatedly assert that

Indonesia needs to stand up to foreign nations more strongly in defending its own interests. For example, when various foreign governments appealed to Jokowi not to execute their nationals for drug crimes in early 2015, there was a chorus of public commentary from ministers down that the president should resist such pressures in order to preserve Indonesia's 'national dignity'. Indeed, politicians and public commentators represent virtually any instance of problematic relations with other countries in this way: as a test of Indonesia's ability to assert and defend its dignity.

A striking feature of the national dignity discourse is that it is also directed at changing the behaviour of Indonesians themselves in ways that policy-makers believe will improve Indonesia's image in the eyes of both Indonesian citizens and others. Thus, for example, in February 2015 Jokowi announced that he wanted to stop the outflow of household domestic workers from Indonesia, saying that this was a matter of 'dignity and self respect'. He claimed that 'Worldwide, there are only three countries that supply foreign domestic workers, two in Asia and one in Africa' (a patently incorrect statement). 'One of the Asian ones', he said, 'is Indonesia. This is a matter of our dignity. When we have bilateral dealings with Malaysia, we are really ashamed' (Wismabrata 2015). Around the same time, the agriculture minister announced a ban on the import of offal — an important ingredient in many Indonesian dishes — because it was used as dog and cat food in exporting countries. 'I want our republic to be respected by other nations', the minister explained, saying that he was willing to weather a negative response from exporting countries: 'If we are attacked it doesn't matter. I'm willing to do anything for the Republic of Indonesia' (Pratama 2015). Not to be outdone, the trade minister announced a ban on the import of second-hand clothes, which, he said, were often contaminated by fungal spores and bacteria. (He also said they posed a risk of HIV transmission, but later apologised for this statement.) The minister described the ban as a matter of national dignity: 'Let's maintain our dignity and honour as a nation. Why on earth should we be wearing the used bras and underpants of other nations?' (Ritonga and Ernis 2015). Even though such clothes are eagerly bought up by poor consumers in Indonesia, who like both their cheapness and their quality, the minister (one of Indonesia's wealthiest men) did not like the image the trade projected. Indonesians, especially poor ones, were thus called upon to regulate their own behaviour in the service of national dignity.

EXPLAINING THE NEW NATIONALISM

What explains this new nationalist mood? One source is political. It is possible to see political manipulation at play in most if not all of the new expressions of nationalism. TNI officers' trumpeting of Indonesia's vulnerabilities reflects efforts by the military to reassert itself and regain a domestic security role. Similarly, the strongly nationalist tenor of the Jokowi government's first months in office expressed the new president's attempt to demonstrate toughness at a time when his handling of domestic issues — notably an assault by corrupt officers within the national police on the Corruption Eradication Commission (KPK) — showed that he could easily be pushed around by powerful interest groups.

More deeply, the emergence of the new nationalism is a product of the democratisation of Indonesian political life that has occurred since 1998. To be sure, at first sight the new nationalist mood seems out of kilter with the tenor of Indonesia's generally stable democratic politics. Nationalism no longer serves the purpose of overcoming ideological polarisation, as was the case in the 1960s when Sukarno mobilised nationalist sentiment in order to bridge the widening gulf between left and right. On the contrary, contemporary Indonesian politics is marked precisely by the *absence* of divisive ideological cleavages (Mietzner 2008), with all the major parties relying on basically similar clientelist strategies to mobilise electoral support (Aspinall 2014).

But in fact, the very thinness and fungibility of nationalism makes it a useful tool for politicians seeking to build popular support in such a denuded ideological landscape. In conditions such as those in contemporary Indonesia, in which the major parties and aspirants to executive office differ very little in policy and programmatic terms, nationalism is a useful legitimating device by which such actors can try to distinguish themselves from rivals and court public support. In other words, both the shallowness and the vehemence of the new nationalism are reflections of the *absence* of other salient cleavages in Indonesian politics — such as a clear right–left split on economic policy. Indeed, nationalist outbidding is common in newly democratic countries, often leading to the targeting of ethnic minorities (Snyder 2000). Indonesia went through a period of violent ethnic mobilisation of this sort in the immediate post-Suharto years (Aspinall 2008: Bertrand 2004), but since that time domestic politics has stabilised and the search for a threatening 'other' on which to focus public attention has led politicians to emphasise foreign dangers.

We should also seek explanations for the new nationalism in broader economic, social and cultural dynamics. One explanation for the tenor of the new nationalism is simply that it reflects the hyper-reality of the internet age, in which a Malaysian advertisement appropriating an Indonesian cultural artefact, or a misjudged statement by an Australian prime minister, can instantly be disseminated, reproduced, memed, mocked and reinterpreted by millions of people in ways that give rise to sudden eruptions of nationalist feeling, only to dissipate just as rapidly.

More deeply, however, the new nationalist mood arguably points to deep insecurities among both the Indonesian elite and the public about Indonesia's own record of achievement and its place in the world at this particular historical juncture. Many of the calls to uphold national strength and dignity point to an underlying belief that Indonesia is in fact sadly lacking in both qualities. Certainly, Indonesia for the past two decades has been undergoing changes that hold great promise but that have exposed many systemic economic and political failings. Nationalism is a distorted reflection of these failings.

Economically, Indonesia has been transforming itself from a poor, largely agrarian society that was a major recipient of foreign aid to a middle-income country that is far more modern and economically successful. However, it still exhibits many signs of poverty (almost half the population lives on $2 a day), and lags visibly behind many of its neighbours. The new nationalism can thus be read partly as a displaced reaction to the continuing problems of social inequality and poverty. Anger about foreign exploitation of Indonesia's natural resources and the related lament that Indonesia has become a 'nation of slaves' are expressions of disappointment about the country's continuing reliance on commodities rather than modern sectors, and about its inability to generate indigenous firms that can compete effectively against the foreign resource giants. Moreover, growing regional economic integration heightens rather than diminishes awareness of the gap between Indonesia and its neighbours. The large outflows of Indonesian labour to Singapore and Malaysia deserve particular mention. They have become a painful reminder for many Indonesians of their country's relative state of underdevelopment. Malaysian, Singaporean and other employers often mistreat and humiliate these workers, arousing justifiable anger among many Indonesians, but also undercutting claims that their country is a great nation, at least economically.

This dynamic helps to explain another striking feature of the new nationalism: its tendency to target Indonesia's closest neighbours and natural allies, notably Malaysia and Australia (and Singapore to a lesser extent), rather than countries that might be considered to pose a greater long-term military or cultural threat, such as China or the United States. Border issues have certainly played a role in producing this outcome, but another factor is that Indonesia's more intense engagement with these countries creates opportunities for Indonesians to look at the 'other', as it were, through an unflattering mirror. The popular hostility towards Malaysia — a country that shares great cultural commonalities with Indonesia — is particularly revealing in this regard.

The economic disappointments are part of a broader pattern. Indonesia has been experiencing a period of difficult democratic transition for the last decade and a half, prompting painful awareness among Indonesians of their country's weaknesses in law enforcement, corruption, educational achievement and other areas. Many of those who are virulently nationalist when it comes to discussing Indonesia's relations with other countries, also excoriate national performance in such fields, and switch freely from berating Malaysia for cultural theft to, say, bewailing the perfidies of Indonesia's elite or its political system. Similarly, the very elites who trumpet the need for self-reliance are at the same time avid consumers of prestigious international brands and are likely to seek medical treatment in Singapore and deposit their wealth in Singaporean bank accounts. To make matters worse, for the last several decades Indonesia has had a poorly performing diplomatic corps and few notable successes on the international stage. Even the military — the pride and joy of many nationalists — is repeatedly exposed in the domestic media as being a hopelessly ramshackle organisation wracked by poor discipline and corruption and burdened with outdated and inadequate equipment. Most ardent Indonesian nationalists are aware of such failings, so it is hard to avoid seeing a subtext of frustration in the overweening confidence they express in the military.

In other words, hostility and admiration are two sides of the same coin. There is plenty to indicate that most Indonesians respect the very countries that are most frequently the targets of nationalist opprobrium. For example, in an opinion survey conducted by Singapore's Institute of Southeast Asian Studies in 2014, respondents were asked which countries they admired. It turned out that the countries that were most admired by Indonesians were Singapore and Malaysia, with 85.6 per cent and 85.3 per cent of respondents respectively saying they admired these countries. In fact, Indonesians were generally admiring of most countries they were asked about: the *least* admired countries were the United States and Australia, but they were still admired by 79.3 per cent and 79.5 per cent of respondents respectively (Fossati, Hui and Negara 2017: 40). Read this way, the increasing assertiveness of Indonesian nationalism is not in fact a sign of growing self-confidence, but rather its reverse.

REFERENCES

Anderson, B. (1983) *Imagined Communities: Reflections on the Origin and Spread of Nationalism*, Verso, London.

Aspinall, E. (2008) 'Review essay: ethnic and religious violence in Indonesia', *Australian Journal of International Affairs* 62(4): 558–72.

Aspinall, E. (2014) 'Indonesia's 2014 elections: parliament and patronage', *Journal of Democracy* 25(4): 96–110.

Aspinall, E. (2015) 'Oligarchic populism: Prabowo Subianto's challenge to Indonesian democracy', *Indonesia* 99(April): 1–28.

Aspinall, E. (2016) 'The new nationalism in Indonesia', *Asia & the Pacific Policy Studies* 3(1): 72–82.

Bertrand, J. (2004) *Nationalism and Ethnic Conflict in Indonesia*, Cambridge University Press, Cambridge.

Clark, M., and J. Pietsch (2014) *Indonesia–Malaysia Relations: Cultural Heritage, Politics and Labour Migration*, Routledge, New York NY.

Detikcom (2015) 'Panglima TNI: negara lain ngeri kalau TNI–Banser bersinergi' [Army commander: other countries will be horrified if TNI and Banser work in synergy], *Detiknews*, 23 February. http://news.detik.com/read/2015/02/23/125609/2840028/10/panglima-tni-negara-lain-ngeri-kalau-tni-banser-bersinergi?nd772204btr

Fossati, D., Hui Y.-F. and S.D. Negara (2017) 'The Indonesia National Survey Project: economy, society and politics', *Trends in Southeast Asia*, No. 10, 2017, ISEAS – Yusof Ishak Institute, Singapore.

Kahin, A., and G. Kahin (1995) *Subversion as Foreign Policy: The Secret Eisenhower and Dulles Debacle in Indonesia*, New Press, New York NY.

Koran Tempo (2009) 'Razia warga Malaysia dinilai tak beradab' [Sweeps of Malaysians considered uncivilised], *Koran Tempo*, 10 September. https://koran.tempo.co/konten/2009/09/11/176380/Razia-Warga-Malaysia-Dinilai-Tak-Beradab

Liputan6 (2014) 'KSAD: penyalahgunaan narkoba miliki keterkaitan "proxy war"' [Army chief of staff: abuse of illegal narcotics tied to a 'proxy war'], *liputan6.com*, 11 October. http://news.liputan6.com/read/2117518/ksad-penyalahgunaan-narkoba-miliki-keterkaitan-proxy-war

Menchik, J. (2016) *Islam and Democracy in Indonesia: Tolerance without Liberalism*, Cambridge University Press, Cambridge and New York NY.

Mietzner, M. (2008) 'Comparing Indonesia's party systems of the 1950s and the post-Suharto era: from centrifugal to centripetal inter-party competition', *Journal of Southeast Asian Studies* 39(3): 431–54.

Mietzner, M. (2015) *Reinventing Asian Populism: Jokowi's Rise, Democracy, and Political Contestation in Indonesia*, East West Center, Honolulu HI.

Pratama, A.F. (2015) 'Mentan: jeroan itu makanan anjing, impor saya tutup' [Agriculture minister: offal is dog food, I'm shutting down imports], *Kompas*, 27 January. http://bisniskeuangan.kompas.com/read/2015/01/27/100132626/Mentan.Jeroan.Itu.Makanan.Anjing.Impor.Saya.Tutup

Ritonga, E., and D. Ernis (2015) 'Gobel: masak pakai celana dalam bekas bangsa lain' [Gobel: why on earth should we be wearing used underpants from other countries], *Tempo*, 4 February. https://bisnis.tempo.co/read/639971/gobel-masak-pakai-celana-dalam-bekas-bangsa-lain

Sasmita, I. (2014) 'Mendagri prioritaskan pemekaran dua provinsi di Papua' [Home affairs minister prioritises formation of two provinces in Papua], *Republika*, 31 October. http://nasional.republika.co.id/berita/nasional/umum/14/10/31/neanre-mendagri-prioritaskan-pemekaran-dua-provinsi-di-papua

Siregar, D.I. (2015) 'Jokowi puji anak jaman sekarang lebih kreatif baca peluang' [Jokowi praises today's youth for being more creative in seeing opportunities], *Metrotvnews.com*, 12 March. http://ekonomi.metrotvnews.com/read/2015/03/12/370224/jokowi-puji-anak-jaman-sekarang-lebih-kreatif-baca-peluang

Snyder, J. (2000) *From Voting to Violence: Democratization and Nationalist Conflict*, W.W. Norton, New York NY.

Thohari, H. (2014) 'Kasad: pemuda dan mahasiswa harus waspadai proxy war' [Army chief of staff: youth and students need to be vigilant about a proxy war], *Tribun Jogja*, 18 September. http://jogja.tribunnews.com/2014/09/18/kasad-pemuda-dan-mahasiswa-harus-waspadai-proxy-war

Warburton, E. (2014) 'In whose interest? Debating resource nationalism in Indonesia', *Kyoto Review of Southeast Asia* 15. http://kyotoreview.org/yav/in-whose-interest-debating-resource-nationalism-in-indonesia/

Warburton, E. (2017) 'Resource nationalism in post-boom Indonesia: the new normal?', Analysis, Lowy Institute for International Policy, Sydney, 27 April.

Waskita, F. (2014) 'Jokowi: kedaulatan diklaim negara lain, kita akan buat ramai' [Jokowi: If other countries make claims on our sovereignty, we'll make trouble], *Tribunnews.com*, 22 June. http://www.tribunnews.com/pemilu-2014/2014/06/22/jokowi-kedaulatan-diklaim-negara-lain-kita-akan-buat-ramai

Wismabrata, M. (2015) 'Jokowi akan stop pengiriman TKI' [Jokowi will stop the sending of Indonesian migrant workers], *Kompas*, 14 February. http://regional.kompas.com/read/2015/02/14/03274001/Jokowi.akan.Stop.Pengiriman.TKI

World Values Survey (2005–09) 'Wave 5 2005-2008 OFFICIAL AGGREGATE v.20140429', World Values Survey Association, Madrid. http://www.worldvaluessurvey.org/WVSDocumentationWV5.jsp

4 Nationalism, sovereignty and foreign policy: Indonesia and the disputes over the South China Sea

Shafiah F. Muhibat

Since independence in 1945, Indonesia has sought to play a role in regional affairs proportionate to its size and location, while at the same time avoiding involvement in the rivalries among major powers. This has become known as the 'independent and active' foreign policy doctrine of Indonesia. Territorial integrity and national security are two of the most important facets of the country's foreign policy. As early as 1957, as part of its Archipelagic Outlook (Wawasan Nusantara) policy, the Indonesian government issued a declaration stating that all the waters surrounding and between the islands in the territory came within Indonesia's sovereignty. Although the declaration met with almost universal international condemnation at the time, two and a half decades later, in one of the country's best-known diplomatic and legal successes, Indonesia succeeded in having the 'archipelagic principle' incorporated into the 1982 United Nations Convention on the Law of the Sea. This effectively gave legal and political support to Indonesia's territory as consisting of the islands, the intervening seas and the wider economic zone around the edges, thus greatly expanding the jurisdictional boundaries of the country.

With the ascension of President Suharto in the late 1960s, Indonesian foreign policy shifted from the confrontational character of the Sukarno years to an emphasis on close bilateral and multilateral cooperation, especially with other countries in the region. Post-Suharto governments have continued to stress pragmatism and good neighbourly relations, although national sentiment does flare up occasionally, sparked by incidents in which Indonesia's national pride has been 'offended' (mostly by Malaysia and Australia). As Anwar (2014) points out, pragmatism continues to act as a brake in most of these cases, preventing them from escalating into more severe conflicts. In summary, for the past half-century Indonesia has pursued a foreign policy that is geared towards protecting the national interest through cooperation rather than confrontation, through economic development rather than political adventurism, and through independent and active policy-making rather than alliances. The big question is whether such an approach to foreign policy still serves Indonesia well in dealing with the current regional and global dynamics, in particular the multiple territorial disputes in the South China Sea.

In January 2015, at her first annual press statement, Indonesian foreign minister Retno Marsudi said that her main foreign policy priority would be to maintain Indonesia's sovereignty. The minister said she aimed to accomplish this by responding firmly to any intrusions into Indonesian territory and by settling the country's maritime borders. A year later, she again emphasised that 'sovereignty is a home that must be safeguarded' (Marsudi 2016). The message was even more pointed and direct in January 2017, when the minister stated that 'Maritime areas around the Natuna Archipelago will continue to be safeguarded' (Marsudi 2017).

The South China Sea is the focal point of escalating territorial disputes between China and several Southeast Asian states, namely the Philippines, Vietnam, Malaysia and Brunei. Although not officially a claimant state, Indonesia has also been drawn into a dispute with China, owing to incidents involving Chinese fishing vessels operating without permission inside Indonesia's exclusive economic zone. In this chapter I will discuss three major incidents that took place in 2016, and how the Indonesian government reacted to these breaches of territorial integrity and sovereignty. Although the government took a number of tough measures in response to the incursions, I argue that there is little chance of a dramatic change in Indonesian foreign policy in relation to the South China Sea, considering the bigger interests at stake, particularly economic interests, and Indonesia's familiar preference for good neighbourly relations.

THE NINE-DASH LINE AND NATUNA

Throughout the 1980s and 1990s, Indonesia was generally unaffected by the territorial disputes between China and other countries involving the South China Sea. Nevertheless, the government was concerned about the potential threat the disputes posed to regional autonomy from outside hegemony, and to the ASEAN norm of peaceful settlement of disputes. In the late 1980s to mid-1990s, Indonesia organised a series of informal workshops to manage the potential conflicts in the South China Sea. Hasjim Djalal, the convener of the workshops, later wrote that 'Indonesia had no ulterior motive except to promote peace, stability, and cooperation in the South China Sea because this was important for the peace, stability, and development of the region as a whole' (Djalal 2001: 97). Although the first meeting was attended only by ASEAN members, the following workshops attracted Chinese participation as well.

In the 1990s China became more open to participating in the multilateral frameworks initiated by ASEAN. Ultimately, this led to the signing of the 2002 Declaration on the Conduct of Parties in the South China Sea, which — when implemented — would commit ASEAN members and China to the peaceful settlement of disputes, the non-use of force and the exercise of restraint. Importantly, it called for all claimants to refrain from occupying uninhabited islands, reefs and shoals in the South China Sea.

Only a few years after the declaration was signed, however, the various claimants were again at loggerheads. In 2009, China submitted a *note verbale* to the secretary-general of the United Nations in which it produced a map delineating, with a dashed line, China's territorial claims in the South China Sea. China claimed that the map, originally drafted in 1914 and republished by the Kuomintang government in 1947, supported its claim to 'historic' rights in the South China Sea. Problematically for Indonesia, Beijing's territorial claims encroached on the exclusive economic zone that Indonesia derived from its possession of the Natuna Islands, although China did not claim any of the landmass of the islands themselves. Inevitably this would draw Indonesia into a dispute with China over the area within Indonesia's exclusive economic zone off the coast of Natuna that slightly overlapped the area delineated by China's now-famous nine-dash line.

Natuna is a group of 272 islands located 400 miles northeast of Sumatra, between mainland Malaysia and the island of Borneo. The islands are administered by the provincial government of Riau Islands. Natuna first became the subject of a dispute with China in the early 1990s when Beijing published a map claiming rights to a large (and as yet undeveloped) gas field to the north of the islands but within Indonesia's exclusive economic zone. China renounced its claim to the Natuna Islands (but not to the gas field) in 1995, meaning that there are no land features within the island chain that China could use as a basis to claim the surrounding waters under the rules of the United Nations Convention on the Law of the Sea.

In July 2010, in a bold retort to China's *note verbale*, Indonesia contested the validity and legality of China's nine-dash line in its own diplomatic note to the United Nations secretary-general. Indonesia's *note verbale* stated that China's map could not be recognised under international law because it lacked an international legal basis and contravened the United Nations Convention on the Law of the Sea. 'Thus far', the *note verbale* stated, 'there is no clear explanation as to the legal basis, the method of drawing, and the status of those separated dotted-lines' (United Nations 2010: paragraph 2).

Beijing refrained from pursuing the case too vociferously, most likely in order to avoid having to clarify — and possibly regularise — its position in relation to the Convention on the Law of the Sea. This allowed China to maintain a form of 'strategic uncertainty' about its position, while allowing Indonesia 'to uphold its status of neutral mediator' (Hellendorf and Kellner 2014). China has never responded directly to Indonesia's *note verbale*, but it has acknowledged Indonesia's ownership of the Natuna Islands on at least three occasions since 2015. The first was on 12 November 2015, when, in the foreign ministry's first ever public statement on the Natuna Islands, a spokesperson said that 'The Chinese side has no objection to Indonesia's sovereignty over the Natuna Islands' (Yu 2015). The second was on 21 March 2016, when a foreign ministry spokesperson said that the 'Natuna Islands belong to Indonesia, and there is no objection from China on that' (PRC Foreign Ministry 2016a). On 20 June 2016, Beijing reiterated its position that 'China has no territorial sovereignty dispute with Indonesia', while admitting to 'overlapping claims for maritime rights and interests' (PRC Foreign Ministry 2016b).

INCIDENTS IN NATUNA WATERS AND THE ARBITRAL TRIBUNAL RULING

During the first half of 2016, on three separate occasions, fishing vessels from China operating without permission within Indonesia's exclusive economic zone clashed with Indonesian maritime authorities. The first incident took place 4.3 kilometres off the coast of the main Natuna island, Natuna Besar. A patrol boat operated by the Indonesian Ministry of Marine Affairs and Fisheries seized a 300-tonne Chinese fishing boat, the *Kway Fey 10078*, and arrested its eight crew members for fishing illegally within Indonesia's exclusive economic zone. The Indonesians commandeered the *Kway Fey* after transferring its crew to their own vessel. As the *Kway Fey* was being towed back to shore, however, a Chinese coast guard vessel rammed the fishing boat, forcing it to stop, and at almost the same time, a second Chinese coast guard vessel appeared in the vicinity. To avoid an escalation of the dispute, the patrol boat's officers abandoned the *Kway Fey* to the Chinese, who removed it from Indonesian waters.

As one would expect, the media covered this incident relentlessly, questioning in particular whether the altercation had finally pulled Indonesia directly into the ongoing territorial disputes between China and various Southeast Asian nations. Indonesia's foreign minister lodged a strong protest with the Chinese embassy's *chargé d'affaires*, demanding to know why the Chinese coast guard had entered Indonesian territory and violated Indonesia's sovereignty. The minister told reporters that the government had asked for clarification from its Chinese counterparts and emphasised that 'Indonesia remained a non-claimant state in the South China Sea' (Salim 2016a).

The second incident took place in May 2016, when the *Gui Bei Yu 27099* was arrested for fishing illegally in the same waters as the *Kway Fey*. In this case an Indonesian frigate, the *Oswald Siahaan-354*, fired several rounds to stop the *Gui Bei Yu* from escaping, and successfully prevented a Chinese coast guard vessel from rescuing the vessel. The Indonesian navy was able to prevail on this occasion because its vessel was equivalent in size and capacity to the Chinese coast guard vessel.

On board the *Gui Bei Yu*, the Indonesians found a map designating parts of Indonesia's exclusive economic zone as Chinese-government-endorsed fishing grounds. Indeed, in each of the protest notes delivered to Indonesia after the three incidents in 2016, China insisted that its fishermen had the right to fish in Natuna waters on the basis of the 'traditional fishing ground' concept (Juwana 2016).

On this occasion, Indonesia decided not to make a formal protest to the Chinese authorities about the presence of a Chinese coast guard vessel in its waters. The commander of Indonesia's Western Fleet concluded that the Chinese vessel had not committed an offence, despite being in the proximity of the fishing vessel intercepted by the navy (Fadli 2016).

The third incident occurred on 17 June 2016, when an Indonesian naval vessel again opened fire on a Chinese fishing vessel to force it to comply with a directive to cease fishing and allow Indonesian authorities to detain the vessel. Analysts noted that this was the second instance in which an Indonesian navy vessel, rather than a less powerful vessel of the Ministry of Marine Affairs and Fisheries, had been used to protect Natuna waters from foreign fishing violations (Morris 2016).

This incident occurred less than a month before an arbitral tribunal constituted under Annex VII to the United Nations Convention on the Law of the Sea issued its ruling on a case filed by the Philippines against China in 2013 (Permanent Court of Arbitration (PCA) Case No. 2013-19). The Philippines had asked the tribunal in The Hague to consider the 'rights and entitlements' of the parties in disputed areas of the South China Sea that lay within China's nine-dash line. Despite being a signatory to the convention, China refused to participate in the arbitration process.

On 12 July 2016, the tribunal ruled against China's claim to the disputed areas, stating that 'China's claims to historic rights […] with respect to the maritime areas of the South China Sea encompassed by the relevant part of the "nine-dash line" are contrary to the Convention and without lawful effect'; the tribunal also rejected China's claim to an exclusive economic zone or continental shelf in the disputed areas.

A few hours later, Indonesia's foreign ministry issued a statement calling on all parties involved in the dispute to respect the applicable international laws:

> Indonesia once again calls on all parties to exercise self-restraint and to refrain from any actions that could escalate tensions, as well as to protect Southeast Asia region particularly from any military activity that could pose a threat to peace and stability, and to respect international law including [the 1982 Convention on the Law of the Sea] (Indonesian Foreign Ministry 2016).

Although the foreign minister would insist she had done all she could to manage the vexed South China Sea issue, including at the ensuing meeting of ASEAN foreign ministers in Vientiane, critics called Indonesia's response 'soft' and 'underwhelming' (Laksmana 2016a, 2016b; Salim 2016b; Supriyanto 2016).

The South China Sea issue has now entered the domestic political discourse in Indonesia. Because sovereignty is an extremely sensitive issue for Indonesians, as can be seen from other cases as well,[1] there is bound to be more pressure from the public for the government to take a tougher stance towards China.

A SHIFT IN APPROACH TO THE SOUTH CHINA SEA DISPUTES?

The March 2016 incident was not the first confrontation involving Indonesian patrol boats and Chinese coast guard vessels, although it was the first to occur during the administration of President Joko Widodo. Similar incidents had occurred near the Natuna Islands in 2010 and 2013, but Indonesia tried to keep them quiet, apparently concerned about disrupting bilateral relations with China (Leavenworth 2016).

Not all Indonesian officials went along with this policy of avoiding public criticism of China. In March 2014, during an event in the Natuna Islands, a senior military official, Air Commodore Fahru Zaini, stated openly that China claimed Natuna as its territorial waters, adding that 'This dispute will have a large impact on the security of Natuna waters' (Antaranews 2014). In April 2014, General Moeldoko, then the commander-in-chief of the Indonesian armed forces, warned in an opinion piece in the *Wall Street Journal* that Indonesia intended to strengthen its military forces in the Natuna Islands to prevent Beijing from occupying them (Moeldoko 2014).

The foreign ministry was quick to clarify Indonesia's position. Less than a week after the air commodore made his remarks, then foreign minister

---

1 One example would be Indonesia's stern displeasure with Australia's policy of turning back boats carrying refugees (Lindsey 2014).

Marty Natalegawa stressed that there was no territorial dispute between China and Indonesia over Natuna. While conceding that Indonesia had sent a *note verbale* to the United Nations protesting China's nine-dash line, he said that this did not translate into an unresolved territorial dispute, or indeed have anything to do with the Natuna Islands (Prabowo 2014).

Shortly after winning the presidential election in July 2014, Widodo elaborated on his policy plans with regard to the South China Sea in an interview with a major Japanese newspaper. He told the *Asahi Shimbun* that Indonesia was ready to act as an intermediary to calm rising tensions over territorial disputes in the South China Sea, and would help expedite the drafting of a code of conduct between China and the 10 member states of ASEAN (Today 2014). In 2015, before embarking on a state visit to Tokyo, President Widodo told the *Yomiuri Shimbun* that Indonesia rejected China's nine-dash line claim because it had no legal basis in international law (Kapoor and Sieg 2015).

Weatherbee (2016: 3) has described the Widodo government's reaction to the first, March 2016, altercation as 'uncoordinated, with the voices of different officials having different responsibilities being heard'. Thus, the minister for marine affairs and fisheries demanded that China return the *Kway Fey* to Indonesian custody; the coordinating minister for political, legal and security affairs insisted that the crew of the vessel would be prosecuted for poaching in the face of Chinese demands for their repatriation; and the minister of foreign affairs dispatched a protest note to the Chinese foreign ministry demanding that China explain its actions.

As noted earlier, after the third incident in June 2016, a Chinese foreign ministry spokesperson reiterated Beijing's position that China had 'no territorial sovereignty dispute' with Indonesia. She added, however, that the incident had taken place in waters that were 'Chinese fishermen's traditional fishing grounds and where China and Indonesia have overlapping claims for maritime rights and interests' (PRC Foreign Ministry 2016b; Taylor Fravel 2016). This was the first time China had used the term 'overlapping claims' in relation to Natuna, and signalled a stronger stance by China towards its claim to 'historic' rights in the South China Sea.

Would Indonesia, too, take a tougher stance? It would appear that President Widodo did change his approach after the 2016 incidents. A few days after the third clash, he led a high-level delegation to the Natuna Islands in a conspicuous show of force. Standing on the deck of the same warship that had fired on the Chinese fishing trawler the previous week, flanked by his ministers and the chief of the armed forces, the president ordered the defences around the Natuna Islands to be increased.

On 14 July 2017, as part of what it said was its 'regular' updating of maps, the Coordinating Ministry of Maritime Affairs announced that the northernmost part of Indonesia's exclusive economic zone, the site of significant oil and gas activity, would be renamed the North Natuna Sea. On the same day, Indonesia's military signed a memorandum of understanding with the Ministry of Energy and Mineral Resources to provide land and maritime security for resource exploration activities.

The new map reflected the results of Indonesia's completed maritime boundary negotiations with Singapore and the Philippines. However, it was the renaming of the sea to the north of the Natuna Islands that would prove most controversial. At a press conference in Jakarta on 14 July, the deputy minister of the Coordinating Ministry of Maritime Affairs observed that, as a sovereign state, Indonesia had the right to name every area in the country's territory, and would officially register the new name of the sea with the United Nations and the International Hydrographic Organization. The objective of the renaming, he said, was 'to provide certainty and a connection between the continental shelf boundaries and the waters to its north' (Sapiie 2017a).

The government's decision to rename the sea triggered an immediate response from Beijing. A Chinese foreign ministry spokesperson stressed that 'South China Sea' was the standard, internationally recognised name for a clearly defined geographical area that included the renamed area (Sapiie 2017b). At the time, Jakarta seemed to shrug off the response, with high-profile parliamentarians openly offering their backing for the government's position (Nadlir 2017).

On 25 August, the Chinese foreign ministry sent an official note to the Indonesian embassy in Beijing demanding that Indonesia rescind its decision to rename the southwestern part of the South China Sea. The letter said that the China–Indonesia relationship was 'developing in a healthy and stable way' and that the South China Sea dispute was 'progressing well', but that 'Indonesia's unilateral name-changing actions are not conducive to maintaining this excellent situation' (Ismail 2017). Renaming the area would not change the fact that China and Indonesia had overlapping maritime claims in the Natuna area, the letter said.

The Indonesian government has since backtracked on its decision to rename the sea, for reasons that have never been made clear. On 13 September 2017, the coordinating minister for maritime affairs, Luhut Panjaitan, told journalists that the government had not yet decided whether or not to rename the area, and that an official decision would be made only after a lengthy period of consideration (Aziza 2017).

It is clear that the Indonesian government has become more vigilant in addressing China's claims in the South China Sea. The current policy is a stronger version of earlier policies of firm law enforcement when dealing with illegal fishing activities in Indonesian waters. Owing to extensive media coverage, the general public is now well aware of the South China Sea issue, and strongly supportive of the government's position—especially the hard line taken against illegal fishing by the minister for marine affairs and fisheries, Susi Pudjiastuti, since being appointed in 2014.

Nevertheless, in its public rhetoric, the Indonesian government remains cautious. This is consistent with the longstanding nature of Indonesian foreign policy, which, as already mentioned, is geared towards protecting the national interest through cooperation rather than confrontation, and through economic development rather than political adventurism.

Some analysts argue that Indonesia's cautious language is justified given the importance of good bilateral relations with China for Indonesian economic development (Jennings 2016; Utama and Kim 2016). In its Medium Term Development Plan for 2015–19, for example, the National Development Planning Agency (Bappenas) estimated that the Indonesian government would be able to supply only a third of the $450 billion in infrastructure investment required over the five years from 2015 to 2019; the remainder would need to be sourced from foreign investment, particularly from China. Other analysts have described Indonesia's attitude to the rise of China and the South China Sea issue as 'ambivalent', involving the interplay of domestic political factors and personalities. They point out that some of President Widodo's strategic initiatives, such as his ambitious plan to turn Indonesia into a global maritime fulcrum, are at odds with the independent aims of his ministers and the defence establishment (Arif 2016; Dharma Agastia 2016; Laksmana 2016a).

A CODE OF CONDUCT FOR THE SOUTH CHINA SEA

ASEAN was formed in 1967, primarily to focus on economic matters. A push for a formalised, more comprehensive role for the institution in the early 2000s led to its defining achievement, the ASEAN Charter. Signed in 2007 and ratified in 2008, the accord established a formal institutional framework for the association that has been credited, among other things, with contributing to geopolitical stability in the region.

ASEAN solidarity has been put to the test by the South China Sea issue, which continues to dominate the region's geopolitical landscape. At a meeting of ASEAN foreign ministers in Vientiane in July 2016—two weeks after the arbitral tribunal in The Hague had issued its ruling—the ministers could not agree on a joint approach to the verdict to form part of their joint communiqué. According to reports, the Philippines and Vietnam both wanted the communiqué to refer to the ruling and the need to respect international law, but Cambodia opposed the proposed wording, throwing the meeting into disarray (Connor 2016). The final version of the communiqué said merely that the ministers were 'seriously concerned over recent and ongoing developments [in the South China Sea,] which have eroded trust and confidence, increased tensions and may undermine peace, security and stability in the region'. It did, however, recommend 'full and effective implementation' of the ASEAN–China Declaration on the Conduct of Parties in the South China Sea, while urging all parties 'to work expeditiously for the early adoption of an effective Code of Conduct' to regulate behaviour in the South China Sea (ASEAN Joint Communiqué 2016).

Indonesia has long been a proponent of a code of conduct for the South China Sea, but efforts to finalise a legally binding document have dragged on for years without any sign that they will ever be successful. In July 2011, after many years of negotiation, China and ASEAN agreed on an in-principle set of guidelines for cooperation within the disputed areas of the South China Sea. Senior officials from both the ASEAN countries and China applauded the outcome as a significant milestone in accelerating implementation of the Declaration on the Conduct of Parties in the South China Sea, but not much progress was reported afterwards.

At the 9th ASEAN–China Joint Working Group in September 2013, both sides agreed to give renewed impetus to the code-of-conduct negotiations. In the years that followed, however, China rapidly expanded its land reclamation activities in the Spratly and Paracel islands and increased its military presence in the disputed waters. Pessimism about the conclusion of a code of conduct was therefore inevitable.

One month after the meeting of ASEAN foreign ministers in Cambodia, in August 2016, senior officials from ASEAN and China met in Manzhouli, Inner Mongolia, to discuss how to implement the Declaration on the Conduct of Parties in the South China Sea. After the meeting, China said the officials had made several breakthroughs, including approving guidelines for an ASEAN–China hotline for use during maritime emergencies; finalising a joint statement on the application of the Code for Unplanned Encounters at Sea to the South China Sea; and agreeing to finish the draft framework for a code of conduct in the South China Sea by mid-2017 (PRC Foreign Ministry 2016c). A year later, on 6 August 2017, the foreign ministers of ASEAN and China announced in Manila that they had finally endorsed the framework for a code of conduct.

Analysts have been sceptical about these 'breakthroughs' (Nguyen 2017; Poling 2017; Prameswaran 2016). Both the hotline and the application of the Code for Unplanned Encounters at Sea had been agreed upon at least a year earlier. The code of conduct, meanwhile, had been pursued for more than a decade with virtually no progress, and there was no reason to believe this would change any time soon. Without any clarification of Beijing's claims, it would be virtually impossible to agree on the geographic scope of a code of conduct. It also seemed unlikely that China would agree to make any such agreement binding. 'Without overcoming those hurdles', Poling (2017) concludes, 'any framework reached [in 2017] would be a largely hollow gesture'.

Indeed, a perusal of the text released on 6 August 2017 shows that the framework is short on detail and contains many of the same principles and provisions already found in the (as yet unimplemented) Declaration on the Conduct of Parties in the South China Sea. Most importantly, it does not say anything about the code of conduct being 'legally binding', which has been the most contentious part of the negotiations.

Moreover, there are still doubts about China's sincerity in proceeding with the process. As Poling (2017) observes, satellite imagery ahead of the arbitral tribunal's ruling revealed that China was constructing hangar space for 24 fighter jets (a full regiment) and three or four larger planes at each of its three largest artificial islands in the South China Sea, Fiery Cross Reef, Mischief Reef and Subi Reef. The level of mistrust towards China among the Southeast Asian states is relatively high, contributing to the pessimism that lingers around the code-of-conduct talks. Nevertheless, Storey (2017: 6–7) argues that, 'despite its shortcomings, ASEAN and China's endorsement of the framework is a step forward in the two-decade long conflict management process for the South China Sea'. At the same time, however, he warns that the process of reaching agreement on a code of conduct to regulate behaviour in the South China Sea 'is likely to be protracted and frustrating'.

OPTIONS FOR INDONESIA

Unhappiness at the direction ASEAN has taken over the past few years has given rise to a discourse on a post-ASEAN foreign policy for Indonesia (Sukma 2009a, 2009b). For example, Tan (2014: 119) argues that 'Indonesia's longstanding role as "first among equals" in ASEAN has increasingly been frustrated by the obduracy of some member nations of the organisation who resist efforts by Jakarta and others to deepen regional integration and strengthen institutional cohesion', leading to 'allusions to an Indonesian foreign policy no longer necessarily bound by an abiding commitment to ASEAN'.

If Indonesia is to play a greater role in dispute resolution in the South China Sea, it may need to cooperate more closely with countries other than ASEAN, or to take stronger unilateral action. Let us consider some of the possibilities in light of recent events.

First, in terms of unilateral action, Indonesia's proposal to rename the waters around Natuna and its shows of force in the region have demonstrated that Indonesia is willing and able to take a strong stance towards China. In October 2016, for example, the Indonesian air force conducted a major exercise in the area where the incidents with the Chinese fishing vessels had occurred. F-16, Sukhoi and Hercules planes took part in the drill, with President Widodo in attendance. This exercise involved 2,000 personnel. The armed forces conducted an even bigger exercise in May 2017, in the shape of a war simulation involving fighter jets, tanks and warships, as well as parachute landings. President Widodo dubbed the exercise 'a show of [the army's] preparedness in maintaining the Unitary State of the Republic of Indonesia' (Fadli and Ompusunggu 2017). This exercise involved 5,900 defence personnel.

The plan to shore up defences in Natuna includes extending the air base runway at Ranai (the district capital) to better accommodate jet fighters, building port facilities for frigates and (possibly) developing a radar facility (Parlina and Halim 2016). At the same time, President Widodo has made the economic development of Natuna, especially the fishery and energy sectors, a high priority.

Second, Indonesia may consider working more closely with major non-ASEAN states. There have been some interesting developments in this regard. In October 2016, following the fourth 2+2 Dialogue between the Indonesian and Australian foreign and defence ministers, Indonesian defence minister Ryamizard Ryacudu told reporters that he had proposed joint patrols by Indonesia and Australia in the eastern part of the South China Sea to combat illegal fishing and 'bring peace' to the region (Topsfield 2016). Australian foreign minister Julie Bishop confirmed that Australia was considering the proposal, telling local media it was 'consistent with our policies of exercising our right of freedom of navigation' (Guardian 2016). Given the sensitivity of the issue, the comments from both sides attracted considerable (but, as it turned out, overblown) media attention.

Shortly before he embarked on a two-day visit to Australia in February 2017, President Widodo told reporters that he was in favour of joint patrols with Australia, but only if it did not intensify tensions with China (Reuters 2017). However, the matter was not mentioned by either the Indonesian president or the Australian prime minister during their joint press conference in Canberra, and not long afterwards, it became clear that both countries had completely backtracked on the idea. Indeed, on the sidelines of the Indian Ocean Rim Association summit in Jakarta in March 2017, Julie Bishop claimed that President Widodo had never suggested joint patrols in the South China Sea, and was simply talking about 'cooperation in maintaining freedom of overflight and freedom of navigation' in the area (Topsfield 2017). In short, despite the hype surrounding the proposal, it was probably never a real prospect (Muhibat 2017).

Indonesia may also be interested in forming closer ties with the United States. As reported by *IHS Jane's Navy International*, a delegation of five senior Indonesian navy officers visited the United States in September 2016 to seek funding under Washington's foreign-military financing program to upgrade Indonesia's naval bases in the South China Sea (Rahmat 2016). The report said that Indonesia was already in the process of upgrading its naval facilities at Ranai to support a larger deployment of ships in the South China Sea region, and planned to locate its third submarine base on the same island. Funding from the foreign-military financing program would assist not only with upgrading the Natuna facilities, but also with upgrading another naval base at Piabung in Lampung. Situated in the south of Sumatra, the province of Lampung is strategically located on the Sunda Strait—a major sea line of communication through the archipelago.

In addition to pursuing partnerships with Australia and the United States, Indonesia is forging partnerships with multiple powers with security interests in the region, including India, the United Kingdom and the Netherlands. This is being done within the bigger framework of President Widodo's electoral promise to focus on maritime issues.

I believe that for some time to come ASEAN will continue to be the main vehicle for Indonesia to exert its influence in the Southeast Asian region, in spite of the criticisms about its effectiveness (Muhibat 2016a, 2016b). On the South China Sea issue, the Indonesian government is unlikely to abandon its customary rhetorical caution. Using the consensual approach it has favoured in the past, it will continue to push for a united approach by all ASEAN members to resolving the disputes in the South China Sea.

CONCLUDING NOTES

While the Indonesian government may continue to take tough measures against foreign incursions in Indonesian waters, there is little chance of any dramatic change in its South China Sea policy, particularly if it could be perceived as being directed against China. Indonesia will continue to pursue a foreign policy that is geared towards protecting the national interest through cooperation rather than confrontation. The government's backtracking on the renaming of the North Natuna Sea reveals two things: problems of coordination within the government; and the government's susceptibility to external pressure, even on issues where it has strong public support. Strong unilateral action against China is unlikely ever to get off the ground. The same is true of the proposals to create real defensive collaborations with countries such as Australia, which remain a distant prospect.

Rather than a shift in Indonesia's direct response to China, what observers can expect is an increase in Indonesia's efforts to unify ASEAN and make it a more effective framework to manage the South China Sea issue. There is still an opportunity for Indonesia, as the largest country in ASEAN, to play a role in encouraging a resurgence of ASEAN centrality in managing the South China Sea disputes.

REFERENCES

Antaranews (2014) 'China includes part of Natuna waters in its map', *Antaranews*, 13 March. http://www.antaranews.com/en/news/93178/china-includes-part-of-natuna-waters-in-its-map

Anwar, D.F. (2014) 'Indonesia's foreign relations: policy shaped by the ideal of "dynamic equilibrium"', *East Asia Forum*, Australian National University, Canberra, 4 February. http://www.eastasiaforum.org/2014/02/04/indonesias-foreign-relations-policy-shaped-by-the-ideal-of-dynamic-equilibrium/

Arif, M. (2016) 'Behind Indonesia's ambivalence in the South China Sea: the push of domestic politics', *APPS Policy Forum*, Asia & the Pacific Policy Society (APPS), Australian National University, Canberra, 15 August. https://www.policyforum.net/behind-indonesias-ambivalence-south-china-sea/

ASEAN Joint Communiqué (2016) 'Joint Communiqué of the 49th ASEAN Foreign Ministers' Meeting, Vientiane, 24 July 2016'. http://asean.org/storage/2016/07/Joint-Communique-of-the-49th-AMM-ADOPTED.pdf

Aziza, K. (2017) 'Luhut pastikan tak ada pengubahan nama Laut China Selatan menjadi Laut Natuna Utara' [Luhut confirms there is no name change from South China Sea to North Natuna Sea], *Kompas*, 13 September. http://ekonomi.kompas.com/read/2017/09/13/193437026/luhut-pastikan-tak-ada-pengubahan-nama-laut-china-selatan-menjadi-laut

Connor, N. (2016) 'China claims victory as ASEAN countries issue watered down statement on South China Sea', *The Telegraph*, 25 July. http://www.telegraph.co.uk/news/2016/07/25/china-claims-victory-as-asean-countries-issue-watered-down-state/

Dharma Agastia, I.G.B. (2016) 'Indonesia's Global Maritime Fulcrum: an updated Archipelagic Outlook?' *The Diplomat*, 17 December. https://thediplomat.com/2016/12/indonesias-global-maritime-fulcrum-an-updated-archipelagic-outlook/

Djalal, H. (2001) 'Indonesia and the South China Sea initiative', *Ocean Development & International Law* 32: 97–103.

Fadli (2016) 'Indonesia will not file protest against China over another Natuna incident, *Jakarta Post*, 31 May. http://www.thejakartapost.com/news/2016/05/31/indonesia-will-not-file-protest-against-china-over-another-natuna-incident.html

Fadli, and S. Ompusunggu (2017) 'Jokowi observes massive TNI exercise near S. China Sea', *Jakarta Post*, 20 May. http://www.thejakartapost.com/news/2017/05/20/jokowi-observes-massive-tni-exercise-near-s-china-sea.html

Guardian (2016) 'South China Sea: Australia considers joint naval patrols with Indonesia', *The Guardian*, 1 November. https://www.theguardian.com/world/2016/nov/01/south-china-sea-australia-considers-joint-naval-patrols-with-indonesia

Hellendorf, B., and T. Kellner (2014) 'Indonesia: a bigger role in the South China Sea?', *The Diplomat*, 9 July. http://thediplomat.com/2014/07/indonesia-a-bigger-role-in-the-south-china-sea/

Indonesian Foreign Ministry (2016) 'Indonesia calls on all parties to respect international law including UNCLOS 1982', Ministry of Foreign Affairs, Republic of Indonesia, 12 July. https://www.kemlu.go.id/en/berita/Pages/Indonesia-Calls-On-All-Parties-To-Respect-International-Law-Including-UNCLOS-1982.aspx

Ismail, S. (2017) 'China demands Indonesia rescind decision to rename part of South China Sea', *Channel News Asia*, 2 September. http://www.channelnewsasia.com/news/asiapacific/china-demands-indonesia-rescind-decision-to-rename-part-of-south-9179992

Jennings, R. (2016) 'Indonesia balances maritime sovereignty, economic ties to China', *VOA News*, 25 November. http://www.voanews.com/a/indonesia-china-south-china-sea/3611198.html

Juwana, H. (2016) 'Opinion: Indonesia's position in the South China Sea', *Kompas*, 23 June. http://cdn.assets.print.kompas.com/baca/english/2016/06/23/OPINION-Indonesia-s-Position-on-the-South-China-Se?utm_source=bacajuga

Kapoor, K., and L. Sieg (2015) 'Indonesian president says China's main claim in South China Sea has no legal basis', *Reuters*, 23 March. http://www.reuters.com/article/us-indonesia-china-southchinasea-idUSKBN0MJ04320150323

Laksmana, E.A. (2016a) 'The domestic politics of Indonesia's approach to the tribunal ruling and the South China Sea', *Contemporary Southeast Asia* 38(3): 382–8.

Laksmana, E.A. (2016b) 'A statement on the South China Sea ruling', *New Mandala*, 27 July. http://www.newmandala.org/statement-south-china-sea-ruling/

Leavenworth, S. (2016) 'South China Sea: Indonesia summons Chinese ambassador as fishing dispute escalates', *The Guardian*, 21 March. https://www.theguardian.com/world/2016/mar/21/south-china-sea-indonesia-summons-chinese-ambassador-as-fishing-dispute-escalates

Lindsey, T. (2014) 'Why Indonesia is so touchy about borders', *Sydney Morning Herald*, 18 January. http://www.smh.com.au/federal-politics/political-opinion/why-indonesia-is-so-touchy-about-borders-20140117-310gg.html

Marsudi, R.L.P (2016) 'The annual press statement of the Indonesian Minister for Foreign Affairs 2016', Ministry of Foreign Affairs, Jakarta, 7 January. https://www.kemlu.go.id/en/pidato/menlu/Pages/The-Annual-Press-Statement-of-the-Indonesian-Minister-for-Foreign-Affairs-2016.aspx

Marsudi, R.L.P (2017) 'Annual press statement Minister for Foreign Affairs of the Republic of Indonesia Retno L.P Marsudi 2017', Ministry of Foreign Affairs, Jakarta, 10 January. https://www.kemlu.go.id/id/pidato/menlu/Documents/PPTM-2017-EN.pdf

Moeldoko (2014) 'China's dismaying new claims in the South China Sea', *Wall Street Journal*, 24 April. https://www.wsj.com/articles/moeldoko-chinas-dismaying-new-claims-in-the-south-china-sea-1398382003

Morris, L. (2016) 'Indonesia–China tensions in the Natuna Sea: evidence of naval efficacy over coast guards?', *The Diplomat*, 28 June. http://thediplomat.com/2016/06/indonesia-china-tensions-in-the-natuna-sea-evidence-of-naval-efficacy-over-coast-guards/

Muhibat, S.F. (2016a) 'Whither the honest broker? Indonesia and the South China Sea', Maritime Awareness Project, National Bureau of Asian Research and Sasakawa Peace Foundation USA, Seattle WA and Washington DC, 20 May. http://maritimeawarenessproject.org/2016/05/20/whither-the-honest-broker-indonesia-and-the-south-china-sea/

Muhibat, S.F. (2016b) 'National interests and the role of major and middle powers in the South China Sea: the case of Indonesia', National Asian Security Studies Program Issue Brief No. 4.3, UNSW Canberra at the Australian Defence Force Academy, Canberra, December. https://www.unsw.adfa.edu.au/sites/default/files/uploads/nassp-pdf/4.3%2C%20National%20Interests%20%26%20Role%20of%20Major%20and%20Middle%20Powers%20in%20SCS.pdf

Muhibat, S.F. (2017) 'Indonesia–Australia ties: joint patrols in the South China Sea?', RSIS Commentaries CO17050, S. Rajaratnam School of International Studies (RSIS), Nanyang Technological University, Singapore, 22 March. https://www.rsis.edu.sg/rsis-publication/rsis/co17050-indonesia-australia-ties-joint-patrols-in-the-south-china-sea/#.WYKSzYiGO70

Nadlir, M. (2017) 'DPR minta pemerintah abaikan China soal penamaan Laut Natuna Utara' [Parliament calls on government to ignore China's protests about North Natuna Sea], *Kompas*, 17 July. http://ekonomi.kompas.com/read/2017/07/17/173056326/dpr-minta-pemerintah-abaikan-protes-china-soal-penamaan-laut-natuna

Nguyen, H.T. (2017) 'A code of conduct for the South China Sea: effective tool or temporary solution?', Maritime Awareness Project, National Bureau of Asian Research and Sasakawa Peace Foundation USA, Seattle WA and Washington DC, 28 March. http://maritimeawarenessproject.org/2017/03/28/a-code-of-conduct-for-the-south-china-sea-effective-tool-or-temporary-solution/

Parlina, I., and H. Halim (2016) 'Govt to fortify flashpoint island', *Jakarta Post*, 30 June. http://www.thejakartapost.com/news/2016/06/30/govt-to-fortify-flashpoint-island.html

Poling, G. (2017) 'Prepare for a stormy 2017 in the South China Sea', Asia Maritime Transparency Initiative, Center for Strategic and International Studies (CSIS), Washington DC, 12 January. https://amti.csis.org/prepare-stormy-2017-south-china-sea/

Prabowo, P.H. (2014) 'Indonesia pernah sampaikan keberatan atas peta Natuna'[Indonesia has objected to [China's] map of Natuna], *Antaranews*, 19 March. http://www.antaranews.com/berita/424961/indonesia-pernah-sampaikan-keberatan-atas-peta-natuna

Prameswaran, P. (2016) 'Beware the illusion of China–ASEAN South China Sea breakthroughs', *The Diplomat*, 17 August. http://thediplomat.com/2016/08/beware-the-illusion-of-china-asean-south-china-sea-breakthroughs/

PRC Foreign Ministry (2016a) 'Foreign ministry spokesperson Hua Chunying's regular press conference on March 21, 2016', Ministry of Foreign Affairs of the People's Republic of China, Beijing, 21 March. http://www.fmprc.gov.cn/mfa_eng/xwfw_665399/s2510_665401/t1349416.shtml

PRC Foreign Ministry (2016b) 'Foreign ministry spokesperson Hua Chunying's regular press conference on June 20, 2016', Ministry of Foreign Affairs of the People's Republic of China, Beijing, 20 June. http://www.fmprc.gov.cn/mfa_eng/xwfw_665399/s2510_665401/t1373744.shtml

PRC Foreign Ministry (2016c) 'The 13th Senior Officials' Meeting on the Implementation of the DOC held in Manzhouli, Inner Mongolia', Ministry of Foreign Affairs of the People's Republic of China, Beijing, 16 August. http://www.fmprc.gov.cn/mfa_eng/wjbxw/t1389619.shtml

Rahmat, R. (2016) 'Indonesia explores possibility of obtaining US aid to finance base in South China Sea', *IHS Jane's Navy International*, 21 September.

Reuters (2017) 'Indonesia to raise prospect of joint patrols with Australia in South China Sea: report', *Reuters*, 24 February. https://www.reuters.com/article/

us-southchinasea-indonesia-australia/indonesia-to-raise-prospect-of-joint-patrols-with-australia-in-south-china-sea-report-idUSKBN1622Q2

Salim, T. (2016a) 'RI–China sea spat continues', *Jakarta Post*, 22 March. http://www.thejakartapost.com/news/2016/03/22/ri-china-sea-spat-continues.html

Salim, T. (2016b) 'We all have made an effort to move things forward in Vientiane', *Jakarta Post*, 1 August. http://www.thejakartapost.com/news/2016/08/01/we-all-have-made-effort-move-things-forward-vientiane.html

Sapiie, M.A. (2017a) 'New map asserts sovereignty over Natuna', *Jakarta Post*, 15 July. http://www.thejakartapost.com/news/2017/07/15/new-map-asserts-sovereignty-over-natuna.html

Sapiie, M.A. (2017b) 'Indonesia shrugs off China's protest over North Natuna Sea's name', *Jakarta Post*, 18 July. http://www.thejakartapost.com/news/2017/07/18/indonesia-shrugs-off-chinas-protest-over-north-natuna-seas-name.html

Storey, I. (2017) 'Assessing the ASEAN–China framework for the code of conduct for the South China Sea', ISEAS Perspective No. 62, ISEAS – Yusof Ishak Institute, Singapore, 8 August. https://iseas.edu.sg/images/pdf/ISEAS_Perspective_2017_62.pdf

Sukma, R. (2009a) 'Indonesia needs a post-ASEAN foreign policy', *Jakarta Post*, 30 June. http://www.thejakartapost.com/news/2009/06/30/indonesia-needs-a-postasean-foreign-policy.html

Sukma, R. (2009b) 'A post-ASEAN foreign policy for a post-G8 world', *Jakarta Post*, 5 October. http://www.thejakartapost.com/news/2009/10/05/a-postasean-foreign-policy-a-postg8-world.html

Supriyanto, R.A. (2016) 'Indonesia's ASEAN leadership lost at sea', *East Asia Forum*, Australian National University, Canberra, 16 September. http://www.eastasiaforum.org/2016/09/16/indonesias-asean-leadership-lost-at-sea/

Tan, S.S. (2014) 'Indonesia among the powers: should ASEAN still matter to Indonesia?' National Security College Issue Brief No 14, Australian National University, Canberra, May. https://nsc.crawford.anu.edu.au/sites/default/files/publication/nsc_crawford_anu_edu_au/2017-05/indonesia-briefs-final.pdf

Taylor Fravel, M. (2016) 'Traditional fishing grounds and China's historic rights claims in the South China Sea', Maritime Awareness Project, National Bureau of Asian Research and Sasakawa Peace Foundation USA, Seattle WA and Washington DC, 11 July. http://maritimeawarenessproject.org/2016/07/11/traditional-fishing-grounds-and-chinas-claims-in-the-south-china-sea/

Today (2014) 'Indonesia prepared to mediate in South China Sea dispute', *Today*, 13 August. https://www.todayonline.com/world/asia/indonesia-prepared-mediate-south-china-sea-dispute

Topsfield, J. (2016) 'Australia and Indonesia consider joint patrols in South China Sea', *Sydney Morning Herald*, 31 October. http://www.smh.com.au/world/australia-and-indonesia-consider-joint-patrols-in-south-china-sea-20161031-gseta5.html

Topsfield, J. (2017) 'Julie Bishop denies Indonesian president suggested joint patrols in South China Sea', *Sydney Morning Herald*, 6 March. http://www.smh.com.au/world/julie-bishop-denies-indonesian-president-suggested-joint-patrols-in-south-china-sea-20170306-gurxlb.html

United Nations (2010) Unofficial translation of *note verbale* from the Permanent Mission of the Republic of Indonesia, No. 480/POL-703/VII/10, United

Nations, New York, 8 July. http://www.un.org/depts/los/clcs_new/submissions_files/mysvnm33_09/idn_2010re_mys_vnm_e.pdf

Utama, J., and M. Kim (2016) 'More than just economy: maritime implications of China's investment', *Jakarta Post*, 27 June. http://www.thejakartapost.com/academia/2016/06/27/more-than-just-economy-maritime-implications-of-chinas-investment.html

Weatherbee, D.E. (2016) 'Re-assessing Indonesia's role in the South China Sea', ISEAS Perspective No. 18, ISEAS – Yusof Ishak Institute, Singapore, 21 April. https://www.iseas.edu.sg/images/pdf/ISEAS_Perspective_2016_18.pdf

Yu, M. (2015) 'Et tu, Jakarta?' *Washington Times*, 19 November. http://www.washingtontimes.com/news/2015/nov/19/inside-china-china-concedes-natuna-islands-to-indo/

PART 2

Nationalism in practice

5 Feeding the *bangsa*: food sovereignty and the state in Indonesia

*Jeff Neilson**

There has been a shift in Indonesian political rhetoric on food policy over the last decade, away from food security (*ketahanan pangan*) and towards food sovereignty (*kedaulatan pangan*). This shift is not unique to Indonesia; it reflects a broader movement by activist peasant organisations around the world to emphasise sovereignty over security in relation to food. The way in which the concept is being interpreted and applied by political actors in Indonesia, however, is distinctive, in that it draws strongly on a perceived need to protect the nation — the *bangsa* — although not necessarily the individual citizens within it.

This chapter examines the processes by which food discourses have been constructed, recast and deployed in Indonesia. The first section looks at the wider global discourses on food security and the second focuses on the history of food policy in Indonesia. The third section explains the more recent embrace of the concept of food sovereignty by the state and addresses the implications of this rhetorical shift for Indonesian food policy.

This discursive arena responds to the very real challenges that Indonesia faces in terms of ensuring that adequate and nutritious food is accessible to a population that exceeds 250 million. The Food and Agriculture Organization has estimated that, in 2014–16, Indonesia had 20.3

---

* This is a highly modified and updated version of an article previously published in *Geographical Research* (Neilson and Wright 2017).

million undernourished people (FAO et al. 2017: 89).[1] Child malnutrition presents a critical and unresolved challenge for the country, with stunting affecting 37 per cent of Indonesian children aged under five in 2013, compared with only 12 per cent across the entire East Asia and Pacific region (DKP and WFP 2015). Unlike many other indicators of food insecurity, rates of malnutrition have actually worsened in recent years, indicating that current policy is ill equipped to address key nutritional challenges. Patterns of food insecurity in Indonesia have a strong geographical dimension: 52 of the 58 districts identified by Indonesia's Food Security Council (Dewan Ketahanan Pangan) and the World Food Programme in 2015 as 'severely vulnerable to food and nutrition insecurity' were located in the far eastern regions of Papua, Maluku and East Nusa Tenggara (DKP and WFP 2015). This raises serious questions about the scale at which food insecurity should be addressed.

Debates about food security are politically charged in Indonesia, as they are in many countries. While Indonesian food policy presents a broad and inclusive vision of food security, the nation's political rhetoric relies overwhelmingly on a limited, scale-specific and state-centric approach. A state discourse that conflates food self-sufficiency at the national scale with food sovereignty (*kedaulatan pangan*) has dominated the food security conversation in Indonesia in recent years. This chapter presents the contemporary Indonesian food discourse as a complex product of selective engagement with international debates, but that is ultimately informed by the peculiar cultural and political history of the Indonesian nation. The analysis suggests that many of the contesting discourses about food security and food sovereignty in Indonesia can be explained by the prioritisation of the national scale over other possible scales of action, and as an attempt by the state to assert its political legitimacy.

INTERNATIONAL DEBATES ON FOOD SECURITY

During the Cold War, Western nations promoted a package of agricultural advances, generally known as the Green Revolution, as being fundamentally necessary to avert an impending Malthusian food disaster in the Third World (Cullather 2010). Food security was overwhelmingly

---

[1] Undernourishment is defined as the inability, over at least one year, to acquire enough food to meet one's dietary energy requirements. Highlighting some of the challenges in this field, data from the National Socio-Economic Survey (Susenas) indicate that a staggering 52.5 per cent of the Indonesian population failed to meet the international threshold of 2,000 kilocalories per capita per day in 2013 (DKP and WFP 2015).

conceptualised and measured in terms of food availability at the national level, gauged largely by whether a country produced more food (or food staples) than its population consumed. From this perspective, national food self-sufficiency was the central mechanism to ensure food security, and the terms came to be used somewhat synonymously (Pinstrup-Andersen 2009).

Over the past 30 years, however, the international understanding of food security has undergone a significant transformation. The production-centric perspective of food security was challenged most notably by Amartya Sen in his 1981 book, *Poverty and Famines: An Essay on Entitlement and Deprivation*. Through case studies of the Bengal famine of 1943 and the famines in Ethiopia, Bangladesh and the Sahel in the 1970s, Sen showed that famine does not arise primarily from food shortages, but rather from the absence of resources at the household level to access food. As Sen (1981: 1) asserts, 'Starvation is the characteristic of some people not *having* enough food to eat. It is not the characteristic of there *being* not enough food to eat' [emphasis in original].

Sen's work produced a significant change in the way food insecurity was understood, and informed the three main principles of food security — availability of food, access to food and food utilisation — developed by the Food and Agriculture Organization (FAO) of the United Nations. At the World Food Summit in Rome in 1996, the FAO proposed a new definition:

> Food security exists when all people, at all times, have physical and economic access to sufficient, safe and nutritious food that meets their dietary needs and food preferences for an active and healthy life (FAO 1996: paragraph 1).

This access-oriented understanding of food security remains broadly accepted by international organisations today, although the FAO later identified a fourth dimension: the stability of the other three dimensions over time (FAO 2014). Food availability at the national scale clearly does not necessarily equate to access to food by individuals, households or communities.

Some food security discourses, perhaps paradoxically, emphasise the need to act on a global scale. Rapid globalisation has encouraged a discourse in which food security transcends national borders, to become a unifying global issue. This global construction of food security was evident at the 2009 World Food Summit, where delegates were told that global food production would need to increase by 50 per cent by 2030 to meet rising demand, and that it would need to double by 2050 to feed a projected world population of 9 billion (Maye and Kirwan 2013: 1). These two projections have since become a common refrain of the food security discourse. The international focus on such projections has had the effect of reinvigorating a productionist bias, while assuming that there are few impediments to cross-border trade. Such presentations frame food security as essentially a problem of inadequate agricultural production (availability), and ignore or downplay the role of food access, food entitlements and critical distributional issues. They tend to identify nation-states as potential impediments to the free flow of food rather than as strategic managers of food systems (Hopma and Woods 2014).

While the international organisations describe food availability as a global problem, they increasingly present food access in classical liberal terms as a problem affecting the individual, with the solutions to be framed accordingly in terms of individual freedom and empowerment. Cloke (2013: 623) argues that the praxis of food security has been complicated by the international food organisations' 'growing intimacy with the discursive constructions of a global neoliberal imaginary', which disguises the reality of food scarcity in a food-abundant world. The discourses prioritising food sovereignty that have emerged in recent years need to be understood in this context—as a reactionary, critical response to the emphasis on food security solutions based on global productivism and market-based liberalism (Hopma and Woods 2014).

The term 'food sovereignty' is closely associated with the international peasants' organisation La Via Campesina (Jarosz 2014). Its secretariat was based in Indonesia from 2005 until 2013, under the leadership of Henry Saragih, the longstanding chair of the Indonesian Peasants Union (SPI). La Via Campesina is part of a broader movement agitating against globalisation and the influence of transnational corporations; its agenda emphasises redistributive land reform, peasant rights, community assertiveness and trade protectionism (La Via Campesina 2006). At a widely attended food sovereignty colloquium held at Yale University in 2013, food sovereignty was defined as 'the right of peoples to democratically control or determine the shape of their food system, and to produce sufficient and healthy food in culturally appropriate and ecologically sustainable ways in and near their territory' (as reported by Li 2015: 205). From this perspective, food sovereignty offers an alternative to the dominant neoliberal models of agriculture and trade. The movement is understandably reluctant to be overtly prescriptive. As Schiavoni (2009: 685) explains: 'There is no single path or prescription for achieving food sovereignty. It is the task of individual regions, nations, and communities to determine what food sovereignty means to them based on their own unique set of circumstances'. Food sovereignty is more than a mere discursive strategy, however. The movement has generated genuine oppositional practices, such as the international solidarity networking and agro-ecological practices described by Martínez-Torres and Rosset (2014), and it has influenced law-making and policy-making in several countries (McKay, Nehring and Walsh-Dilley 2014), including Indonesia.

Food sovereignty advocates tend to look 'beyond the concept of food security, which says nothing about where the food comes from' (Rosset 2011: 22). Similarly, while international organisations have promoted an emphasis on food access for decades (see, for example, World Bank 1986), and on the ability of an individual to produce or buy food, the food sovereignty movement criticises a reliance on volatile market forces. Food sovereignty is perhaps best understood as an oppositional stance against the dominant corporate food system. The inherent injustices of this system are most forcefully and comprehensively articulated through the notion of a global corporate food regime (McMichael 2009); indeed, McMichael (2016) explicitly links the corporatisation of the global food regime with the rise of the food sovereignty movement.

While the food sovereignty movement consistently appeals to notions of 'community', the position of the state remains intensely problematic (Bernstein 2014). The very same actor that is widely implicated, according to food regime theory, in progressing and abetting the corporate interests of capitalism—that is, the state—is simultaneously, and somewhat paradoxically, expected to implement policies and practices to defend peasant producers. The adoption of the food sovereignty discourse by the Indonesian state highlights some of these contradictions.

FOOD DISCOURSES IN INDONESIA: FEEDING THE *BANGSA*

The Indonesian state's perspective on food policy departs somewhat from the above-mentioned international articulations of both food security and food sovereignty. Strong nationalist sentiment consistently underpins state policy and the broader political rhetoric on food provisioning in Indonesia (Rafani 2014). Accordingly, the state frames the issue of food sovereignty in terms of the necessity to achieve food self-sufficiency at the national scale, reflecting the dominant international food security discourse prior to Amartya Sen's work, but also, more critically, the state's desire to defend the *bangsa*—often translated as 'the nation'.

National-scale self-sufficiency has long been of central ideological importance in Indonesia, with successive post-colonial leaders selecting rice production as a key indicator of prosperity, security and wellbeing. On one level this is somewhat surprising, given that Indonesia has actually been a net rice importer for the last 100 years, with the exception of three brief periods in which exports exceeded imports (Patunru, forthcoming). Sukarno established the foundations of this discourse in 1952 when he asked, in an impassioned speech, 'Why bother talking about political freedom if we don't have the freedom to manage our own rice, and always have to beg for help to buy rice from neighbouring nations?' (Sukarno

1952: 15).[2] Sukarno's key concern was 'food availability for the people' (*soal persediaan makanan rakyat*), expressed as an arithmetical need to increase domestic rice production based on the per capita calorie requirements of the population.

Even today, the 1952 oration continues to be read and embraced as a source of contemporary policy guidance. The speech was the centrepiece of an edited book by Fariyanti et al. (2012); President Joko Widodo quoted from it in his foreword to the 2015 *Food Security and Vulnerability Atlas* (DKP and WFP 2015); and throughout 2017, the president used Sukarno's exact wording to stress that food was a matter of survival for the nation (*soal hidup mati bangsa kita*) (see, for example, Afrianto 2017). In the speech, Sukarno does not explicitly consider access to food by individuals and households. In this respect it is a product of its times, reflecting both the prevailing international food discourse and the revolutionary spirit of the post-colonial period. Nevertheless, the speech continues to have deep cultural resonance.

In his foreword to the *Food Security and Vulnerability Atlas*, Widodo refers to Sukarno's insistence on 'the importance of the fulfilment of food needs for the continuation of the life of the nation [*keberlangsungan kehidupan bangsa*]' (DKP and WFP 2015: i). Sukarno presented the availability and production of food as a matter of life or death for the nation; he talked about the *bangsa* in a highly personified way, as if this abstract notion was capable of feeling hunger, or indeed dying. Anderson (1966: 105) argues that, like *kedaulatan* (sovereignty), *bangsa* is one of a set of highly emotive words that 'stem from the seedtime of the Republic [...] Virtually all the emotive words in Indonesian are centred round the struggle and violence of the physical revolution and almost all have highly political-heroic connotations'. While the literal feeding of an 'imagined community' (to use Anderson's 1991 term) may appear incongruous, the 'feeding the nation' narrative is considered almost sacrosanct in modern Indonesia. The pre-eminence given to the *bangsa* in relation to food security, fortified by emotive appeals to the notion of food sovereignty (*kedaulatan pangan*), has profound implications for current practice. Anderson (1999) reminds us that nationalism is frequently misunderstood as implying that the 'state' and the 'nation' are somehow identical; in Indonesia, this is reinforced by the use of the term *negara dan bangsa* (the state and the nation) throughout

---

2 Sukarno delivered the speech on 27 April 1952, on the occasion of laying the first stone for an agricultural faculty in Bogor. The speech was written down so that (in Sukarno's words) it would become a *risalah* (Arabic for 'message', especially a message from Allah) that would be read and reread by youth right across Indonesia.

Law No. 18/2012 on Food (the 2012 Food Law), as if the two were equivalent and inseparable.

Following the overthrow of Sukarno, President Suharto developed the 'feeding the *bangsa*' discursive logic further by investing heavily in rural infrastructure. Indeed, Suharto considered his (momentary) attainment of national rice self-sufficiency in 1985 as the greatest achievement of his presidency (Abdulgani-Knapp 2007). Rice production has since remained close to national consumption levels, although accurate data on rice production and consumption in Indonesia are notoriously hard to come by. Simatupang and Timmer (2008) argue that, while rice self-sufficiency is technically feasible, it is costly both fiscally and in terms of foregone economic opportunities, and does not guarantee an end to hunger and malnutrition. Importantly, though, Suharto's fleeting achievement in attaining self-sufficiency was accompanied by considerable progress in poverty alleviation, which declined (in terms of absolute poverty) from 60 per cent in 1970 to 15 per cent in 1990 (World Bank data, cited in Salim 2011), simultaneously improving food access for many.

Indonesia's food logistics agency, Bulog, was established in 1967 to implement a rice price stabilisation policy through a floor price for farmers and a ceiling price for consumers. It performed a pivotal role during the Suharto era, and gained considerable bureaucratic power. Although Bulog was transformed from a parastatal government agency into a state-owned enterprise in 2003, its social function in ensuring price stability and administering government rice delivery programs has continued, as has its ability to exploit price differentials between the domestic and world markets. In 2017, the Widodo government not only attempted to resurrect the trading and regulatory role of Bulog, but even appeared willing to act against private rice traders to ensure Bulog's access to supply.[3] The key policy tool used to achieve self-sufficiency has been the tight regulation of imports. The gap between domestic and international rice prices—which has increased sharply in recent years, according to the World Bank (2016: 55)—generates lucrative rents for those companies granted import licences by Bulog, even as the agency itself has had a history of making staggering losses through inefficiencies (Arifin 2008).

While import restrictions appear to have had a negative effect on poverty in the short term, their longer-term effects are less clear. The Indonesian food system proved relatively resilient during the 2007–08 global food crisis, even if trade restrictions raised prices for poor consumers

---

3   The police raided the rice warehouses of PT Tiga Pilar Sejahtera in late July 2017, apparently justified by the logic that the government provides subsidies for fuel, fertiliser and irrigation, and is therefore entitled to preferential access to farmers' agricultural produce (Tempo 2017).

(Warr and Yusuf 2014). Global food price hikes and the instability they prompted in many parts of the world provided political momentum for enhanced protectionism in Indonesia. Timmer (2014) describes the world rice market as 'highly unstable'. In addition to this inherent volatility, the risks of being dependent on foreign food producers were again highlighted in 2011 when Australia imposed a ban on the export of live cattle to Indonesia based on animal welfare concerns. This highlighted, for many Indonesians, the risks of a food supply chain that could be held hostage by a foreign power.

The *reformasi* period has been increasingly protectionist, with all post-1998 administrations continuing to regulate imports and maintain agricultural subsidies in an attempt to protect and promote domestic producers (Soesastro and Basri 2005; Pangestu, Rahardja and Ing 2015; Patunru and Rahardja 2015). Indonesia has also seen a rising tide of economic, cultural and territorial nationalism, coinciding with the start of President Yudhoyono's second term in office in 2009 and reaching fever pitch during the 2014 presidential elections (Aspinall 2016). Yudhoyono created ambitious targets to attain national self-sufficiency in corn, soybean, sugar and beef, and aimed to produce a 10-million-tonne rice surplus by 2014 (none of which were achieved). It was in this political environment, and with the 2007–08 global food crisis still at the forefront of law-makers' minds, that the parliament enacted the 2012 Food Law. The law gives a tangible insight into the state's current thinking on food, constituting a formal articulation of the government's position. It introduces the concept of food sovereignty (*kedaulatan pangan*) into Indonesian legislation (apparently) for the first time, defining it as 'the right of the state and the nation [*negara dan bangsa*] to independently determine a food policy that ensures a right to food for the people, and that ensures rights for the community to determine a food system appropriate to its local resources' (article 1(2)). Thus defined, *kedaulatan pangan* borrows from the international discourse, but also departs from it by foregrounding both the centrality of the state and the importance of the nation.

Under the 2012 Food Law, the state is expected to play a pivotal role in all aspects of food policy, and is given a mandate to regulate the production, trade and sale of food products. The law is also explicit about the aim of achieving national food self-sufficiency. However, it does not specify which food products should be produced domestically, thereby implying a normative goal for all food products. Notably, the law does not provide a specific definition for 'food accessibility', and the expression 'food security, food sovereignty and food self-sufficiency' (*ketahanan pangan, kemandirian pangan dan kedaulatan pangan*) is used throughout the document without making any distinction between the three terms. The law thereby conflates all three into a single objective, to be achieved through a single set of policy prescriptions (McCarthy and Obidzinski

2017). 'Food sovereignty' is deployed rhetorically to strengthen the case for state intervention to achieve national-scale food self-sufficiency. While the emphasis on *kedaulatan pangan* should be interpreted as an attempt by the state to assert control over the food system, it also reflects the perceived need for the state to assert its legitimacy amidst re-emergent nationalism.

Widodo has enthusiastically embraced the rhetoric of *kedaulatan pangan*, as articulated in his pre-election policy statement, known as the Nawacita (Widodo and Kalla 2014). The guiding vision of the document is a sovereign and self-sufficient nation (*bangsa yang berdaulat dan mandiri*), with an economic policy based on the Sukarnoist rhetoric of *berdikari* (*berdiri di atas kaki sendiri*), or 'standing on one's own two feet'. According to Lassa and Shrestha (2014: 1), on his Facebook page Widodo clarified what he saw as the conceptual differences between food security and food sovereignty as follows:

> Food security (*ketahanan pangan*) is different from food sovereignty (*kedaulatan pangan*). Food security is simply the availability of foodstuffs (logistically) in warehouses and in the markets regardless of the origin, whether from import or from locally produced. Food sovereignty means we produce and market our foodstuffs ourselves, while the surplus of agricultural crops is exported.

There continues to be silence on the matter of food access.

The Widodo administration has significantly increased spending on irrigation infrastructure, fertiliser subsidies and other agricultural supports to achieve its ambitious self-sufficiency targets (Damuri and Day 2015; World Bank 2016). Presumably using a national sovereignty logic, the government has even enrolled the services of the military's village-level units to 'supervise' farmers—a potentially worrying development given the military's past role in violently suppressing the Indonesian peasant movement (Lassa and Priamarizki 2015). The new programs appear to have increased both the domestic production of rice (in which the government claimed to be self-sufficient in 2017) and of corn (with significant reductions in imports). The World Bank (2016) argues, however, that the investments have been poorly targeted and have not resulted in a commensurate increase in agricultural GDP. The retail prices of rice continue to be nearly twice as high in Indonesia as in other parts of Southeast Asia, suggesting an implicit tax on Indonesian food consumers.

THE FOOD SOVEREIGNTY DISCOURSE AND POLICY OUTCOMES IN INDONESIA

In a political sense, achieving *berdikari* and national-level self-sufficiency in rice and other food items is clearly appealing to President Widodo, whose re-election in 2019 may even depend on it, especially if he again confronts

Prabowo Subianto and his ultra-nationalist, pro-farmer rhetoric.[4] In the policy arena, his government's emphasis on food sovereignty is evident in a series of state-led policy interventions intended to boost production and reduce dependence on food imports. I will now briefly discuss these interventions and explain how they may inadvertently be contributing to food insecurity among poor households.

The promotion of large-scale food estates

Perhaps the most problematic feature of Indonesia's food security policy is the recourse to large-scale food estates as a means to achieve *kedaulatan pangan* (McCarthy and Obidzinski 2017). An early forerunner of this model was the Suharto-era Mega Rice Program, which aimed to convert 1.4 million hectares of peat-swamp forest in Central Kalimantan into rice paddies (Rieley 2001; Law et al. 2015). The program failed to meet its agricultural targets, but it did manage to disrupt the peat-land hydrology through timber clearing, contributing significantly to the fires that raged across Kalimantan in 1997 and 1998 (Cattau et al. 2016). In 2014, the land previously identified for the Mega Rice Project was estimated to be 38 per cent forest, 50 per cent degraded land and 12 per cent agricultural land; 29 per cent of the region was covered by (mainly undeveloped) oil palm concessions, and poverty rates among the inhabitants (in 2005) were as high as 36 per cent (Law et al. 2015).

Aspects of this food estate model were incorporated into the Master Plan for the Acceleration and Expansion of Indonesia's Economic Development (MP3EI), released by President Yudhoyono in 2011. It proposed a 1.2-million-hectare estate in West Papua: the Merauke Integrated Food and Energy Estate (MIFEE). According to Ito, Rachman and Savitri (2014: 29), the project was expected to 'increase the production of rice by 1.95 million tons, maize by 2.02 million tons, soybeans by 167 thousand tons, cattle by 64 thousand head, sugar by 2.5 million tons and crude palm oil by 937 thousand tons, thereby reducing net food imports by US$514 million'. However, MIFEE has been criticised as a thinly veiled resource grab by domestic and international investors, and for creating serious environmental problems (AGRA 2012). The Widodo government has continued to champion food estate development as part of its food security policy, announcing a new 500,000-hectare food estate in Kalimantan in 2015 (McCarthy and Obidzinski 2017). The almost inevitable consequences of such large-scale land allocations are disenfranchised local populations

---

4 Prabowo was formerly the (contested) chair of the Indonesian Farmers Association (HKTI), a position claimed (in early 2018) by his Gerindra party colleague, Fadli Zon.

and landscapes either denuded of their timber resources or planted with oil palm.

The Indonesian state has repeatedly used food sovereignty discourses to justify the development of food estates, despite such estates being associated with the conversion and replacement of large areas of sago palms (a local food staple in food-insecure Papua) and swidden rice (in Kalimantan). According to the MP3EI, the MIFEE project was necessary to 'anticipate a food crisis', with Merauke projected to become a metaphorical food barn (*lumbung pangan*) for eastern Indonesia. Moreover, MIFEE embodied Sukarno's 1952 aspirations, through its explicit promotion of large-scale, capital-intensive, industrial agriculture. As argued by Jarosz (2014: 169) for other contexts, such 'large-scale land acquisitions ensure national food and energy security for purchasers or lease-holders, while threatening or eroding food security for those who depend upon the land and water resources for their livelihoods and who are barred from them through eviction and resettlement'. Ito, Rachman and Savitri (2014) assert that, in partnership with corporate actors and local elites, the Indonesian state is trying to manipulate discourses of food sovereignty to make the prospect of large-scale corporate investment in food crops and biofuels more politically appealing. In the wake of the food and energy crises of 2007–08, for example, President Yudhoyono adopted the slogan 'Feeding Indonesia, feeding the world', whose overtones of sovereignty proved rhetorically very powerful (Ito, Rachman and Savitri 2014).

The Widodo government has since reaffirmed its support for MIFEE (Indrawan, Caldecott and Ermayanti 2017). The state's conflation of national-scale self-sufficiency with food sovereignty has, in this case, facilitated a corporate land grab to promote mono-crop agriculture to produce palm oil, sugarcane and wood chips. Paradoxically, this has reduced the livelihood options for local communities, whose traditional access to local resources has been curtailed (Hadiprayitno 2017). This is exacerbating the problem of local food insecurity for these communities.

Trade protectionism: who really benefits?

Despite food-related price inflation in Indonesia throughout 2015 and 2016, President Widodo sought to prevent food imports at all costs as a matter of national pride, or as a matter of *kedaulatan*. This uncompromising approach to imports (especially rice and beef imports) contributed to significant inflationary pressures and ultimately led to a rise in poverty (Yusuf and Sumner 2015; World Bank 2016).

Most tellingly, the increases in rice prices occurred in an international context of relatively low prices. The government argued that the restrictions on imports would increase the prices farmers received for their produce, and therefore their profits, encouraging them to increase production. This argument has long been contentious, with earlier work (such as Warr 2005) establishing a relationship between protectionist policies and an increased incidence of poverty, and by extension an increase in food insecurity at the individual level.

While the link between import restrictions and agricultural profits itself remains questionable, such restrictions almost certainly make food more expensive for the majority of the population and reduce the overall competitiveness of the agricultural sector. It is widely argued that such measures undermine rather than improve access to food for poor consumers, including the urban poor as well as the majority of farmers, who are also net buyers of food staples (OECD 2012; Warr and Yusuf 2014; Yusuf and Sumner 2015). From the perspective of poor households, a public policy that prevents rice imports 'at any cost' is difficult to defend. Some researchers argue that the impact of trade restrictions is not always negative. Timmer (2014), for example, believes that transparent import and export restrictions can be effective in stabilising rice prices. He argues that price stability is always preferable to price fluctuation, whether up or down, because it protects consumers from sudden spikes in world markets, as occurred during the 2007–08 food crisis.

Regardless of the effect that import restrictions have on the welfare of the poor in Indonesia, the widening gap between domestic and international food prices certainly generates lucrative rent-seeking opportunities related to the allocation of import licences, for both government officials and their corporate cronies. The high-profile politicians who have been tried for receiving bribes to grant import licences include the former president of the Prosperous Justice Party (PKS), Luthfi Hasan Ishaaq, who was jailed in 2013 for manipulating beef import quotas (Maharani 2013), and the then Regional Representative Council (DPD) leader Irman Gusman, who was found guilty in 2017 of accepting kickbacks for doctoring sugar import licences (Firmanto 2017). While there is some public recognition of the ill effects of such practices, with frequent references in the media — and explicitly in the Nawacita (Widodo and Kalla 2014) — to an 'import mafia', the public does not seem to recognise that this mafia in fact thrives on the existence of import restrictions. Thus, while politicians claim to be standing up to a nebulously defined 'import mafia', traders are engaged in illegal stockpiling to drive up domestic prices (McCarthy and Zen 2013) — opportunities that are only possible due to the country's import restriction regime.

In summary, due to the hegemonic status of *kedaulatan pangan* in food discourses, there is very little public debate about the efficacy of food import restrictions and who really benefits from them. The perils of 'opening the floodgates to imports' (*buka keran impor*) are considered to be self-evident, motivating powerful vested interests linked to the state to actively perpetuate food sovereignty discourses to advance their own interests.

CONCLUSIONS

Discourses of food sovereignty — *kedaulatan pangan* — are malleable, highly political, historically contingent and culturally embedded. With both the causes of and solutions to food insecurity remaining contested, political and economic actors in Indonesia have been able to harness the rhetoric of food security and food sovereignty discourses to suit their own specific political and economic agendas. While aspects of food policy in Indonesia seem to indicate engagement with inclusive and multi-scalar visions of food sovereignty, the overriding political discourse favours a state-centric and production-focused vision of what it means for the nation as a collective — the *bangsa* — to be food secure.

Kedaulatan pangan emerges as a fundamentally endogenous political construct that is only marginally related to the broader global discourses of food sovereignty as espoused by organisations like La Via Campesina and SPI. In Indonesia, the term connotes the state's capacity to shape policy without external interference, to be achieved through national-scale self-sufficiency in selected 'strategic' commodities. The development of Indonesian food policy exemplifies the process by which elements of international discourse are selectively adopted and shaped by particular place-based political contexts to create new, historically contingent discourses. As it is deployed in Indonesia, *kedaulatan pangan* prioritises the national scale above all others, sidelining alternatives such as the neoliberal imaginary of a globalised food security agenda, the individualised concerns about food access and land reform, and the intermediate, community-based notions of food sovereignty. To a large extent, this distinctive version of food sovereignty was made possible by the Sukarnoist rhetoric on food security established more than 60 years ago, when the notion of a hungry *bangsa* appeared both logical and conceivable.

McKay, Nehring and Walsh-Dilley (2014) observed a similarly high degree of co-optation of food sovereignty discourses by the Bolivian state under Evo Morales, but remained somewhat optimistic (at the time they were writing) that, at least in the case of Venezuela, it would be possible to achieve 'the continuous symbiotic interaction between empowered pro-reform state and societal actors [that] is a necessary prerequisite for food sovereignty' (p. 1,195). The co-optation of food sovereignty discourse and practice by the Indonesian state leaves less room for optimism. The reason lies in the rhetorical association of *kedaulatan pangan* with a resurgent nationalism, and the specific historical trajectory of nationalism in Indonesia. Aspinall (2016: 76) states that, 'under Soeharto, nationalism was above all a tool in the hands of a highly conservative military–bureaucratic caste'. My concerns therefore echo those of Anderson (1999), who provided ample evidence that the Indonesian state actually subjugated individuals and communities who were ostensibly part of the *bangsa*.

The conceptual malleability and emotive connotations of the term *kedaulatan pangan* allow it to be harnessed by different actors for considerably different ends. Not only has the distinct framing of food sovereignty in Indonesia been embraced by political actors to further vested interests, but it appears to have contributed directly to policy interventions that are having perverse outcomes for some of Indonesia's most vulnerable individuals and communities. While the dominant framing of *kedaulatan pangan* in Indonesia borrows selectively from international debates, it has also been reconstructed, through Sukarnoist logic, in a mould shaped by historical contingency and cultural specificity, and then perpetuated by the vested interests of a powerful political economy. The concept also functions to provide a powerful discursive legitimacy for the state, which has been able to extend its material control over the *bangsa*, even as problems such as malnutrition, inability of the poor to access to food and geographical inequality remain inadequately addressed.

REFERENCES

Abdulgani-Knapp, R. (2007) *Soeharto: The Life and Legacy of Indonesia's Second President*, Marshall Cavendish, Singapore.

Afrianto, D. (2017) 'Jokowi: pangan adalah hidup mati bangsa!' [Jokowi: food is a matter of life or death for the nation!], *Okezonefinance*, 13 June. http://economy.okezone.com/read/2017/06/13/320/1715066/jokowi-pangan-adalah-hidup-mati-bangsa

AGRA (Aliansi Gerakan Reforma Agraria) (2012) 'Land grabbing for food and biofuel: Merauke Integrated Food and Energy Estate (MIFEE) case study', AGRA and Pesticide Action Network Asia & the Pacific (PAN AP), Penang, April. http://archive.panap.net/sites/default/files/casestudy-mifee-land-grabbing.pdf

Anderson, B.R.O. (1966) 'The languages of Indonesian politics', *Indonesia* 1(April): 89–116.

Anderson, B.R.O. (1991) *Imagined Communities: Reflections on the Origin and Spread of Nationalism*, Verso, London.

Anderson, B.R.O. (1999) 'Indonesian nationalism today and in the future', *New Left Review* I(235): 3–17.

Arifin, B. (2008) 'From remarkable success to troubling present: the case of Bulog in Indonesia', in S. Rashid, A. Gulati and R. Cummings, Jr (eds) *From Parastatals to Private Trade: Lessons from Asian Agriculture*, Johns Hopkins University Press, Baltimore MD: 137–64.

Aspinall, E. (2016) 'The new nationalism in Indonesia', *Asia & the Pacific Policy Studies* 3(1): 72–82.

Bernstein, H. (2014) 'Food sovereignty via the "peasant" way: a sceptical view', *Journal of Peasant Studies* 41(6): 1,031–63.

Cattau, M.E., M.E. Harrison, I. Shinyo, S. Tungau, M. Uriarte and R. DeFries (2016) 'Sources of anthropogenic fire ignitions on the peat-swamp landscape in Kalimantan, Indonesia', *Global Environmental Change* 39: 205–19.

Cloke, J. (2013) 'Empires of waste and the food security meme', *Geography Compass* 7(9): 622–36.

Cullather, N. (2010) *The Hungry World: America's Cold War Battle against Poverty in Asia*, Harvard University Press, Cambridge MA.

Damuri, Y.R., and C. Day (2015) 'Survey of recent developments', *Bulletin of Indonesian Economic Studies* 51(1): 3–27.

DKP and WFP (Dewan Ketahanan Pangan and World Food Programme) (2015) *The Food Security and Vulnerability Atlas of Indonesia 2015*, DKP and WFP, Jakarta.

FAO (Food and Agriculture Organization of the United Nations) (1996) 'World Food Summit plan of action, 13–17 November 1996 Rome Italy', FAO, Rome, 13 November. http://www.fao.org/docrep/003/w3613e/w3613e00.HTM

FAO (Food and Agriculture Organization of the United Nations) (2014) 'The state of food insecurity in the world 2014: strengthening the enabling environment for food security and nutrition', FAO, Rome.

FAO, IFAD, UNICEF, WFP and WHO (Food and Agriculture Organization of the United Nations, International Fund for Agricultural Development, United Nations Children's Fund, World Food Programme and World Health Organization) (2017) 'The state of food security and nutrition in the world 2017: building resilience for peace and food security', FAO, Rome.

Fariyanti, A., A. Rifin, S. Jahroh and B. Krisnamurthi (eds) (2012) 'Pangan rakyat: soal hidup atau mati. 60 tahun kemudian' [Food for the people: a matter of life of death. 60 years on], Agricultural Department, FEM–IPB and Perhepi, Jakarta.

Firmanto, D. (2017) 'Terungkap, begini kronologi suap gula Bulog ke Irman Gusman' [Uncovered, this is the chronology of Bulog's sugar bribes to Irman Gusman], *Tempo,co*, 31 January. https://nasional.tempo.co/read/news/2017/01/04/063832658/terungkap-begini-kronologi-suap-gula-bulog-ke-irman-gusman#y0D0sZ2yRXImQ5j1.99

Hadiprayitno, I.I. (2017) 'Who owns the right to food? Interlegality and competing interests in agricultural modernisation in Papua, Indonesia', *Third World Quarterly* 38(1): 97–116.

Hopma, J., and M. Woods (2014) 'Political geographies of "food security" and "food sovereignty"', *Geography Compass* 8(11): 773–84.

Indrawan, M., J. Caldecott and Ermayanti (2017) 'Mitigating tensions over land conversion in Papua, Indonesia', *Asia & the Pacific Policy Studies* 4: 147–57.

Ito, T., N.F. Rachman and L.A. Savitri (2014) 'Power to make land dispossession acceptable: a policy discourse analysis of the Merauke Integrated Food and Energy Estate (MIFEE), Papua, Indonesia', *Journal of Peasant Studies* 41(1): 29–50.

Jarosz, L. (2014) 'Comparing food security and food sovereignty discourses', *Dialogues in Human Geography* 4(2): 168–81.

La Via Campesina (2006) 'Rice and food sovereignty in Asia Pacific', La Via Campesina, Jakarta, 24 July. https://viacampesina.org/en/wp-content/uploads/sites/2/2006/07/2006_07_13_Rice_and_Food_Sovereignty_in_Asia_Pacific.pdf

Lassa, J.A., and A. Priamarizki (2015) 'Jokowi's food sovereignty narrative: military in the rice land?', RSIS Commentary No. 040, S. Rajaratnam School of

International Studies (RSIS), Singapore, 27 February. https://www.rsis.edu.sg/wp-content/uploads/2015/02/CO15040.pdf

Lassa, J.A., and M. Shrestha (2014) 'Food sovereignty discourse in Southeast Asia: helpful or disruptive?', RSIS Commentary No. 231, S. Rajaratnam School of International Studies (RSIS), Singapore, 20 November. https://www.rsis.edu.sg/wp-content/uploads/2014/11/CO14231.pdf

Law, E.A., E. Meijaard, B.A. Bryan, T. Mallawaarachchi, L.P. Koh and K.A. Wilson (2015) 'Better land-use allocation outperforms land sparing and land sharing approaches to conservation in Central Kalimantan, Indonesia', *Biological Conservation* 186: 276–86.

Li, T. (2015) 'Can there be food sovereignty here?', *Journal of Peasant Studies* 42(1): 205–11.

Maharani, D. (2013) 'Luthfi Hasan Ishaaq divonis 16 tahun penjara' [Luthfi Hasan Ishaaq sentenced to 16 years in jail], *Kompas.com*, 9 December. http://nasional.kompas.com/read/2013/12/09/2106550/Luthfi.Hasan.Ishaaq.Divonis.16.Tahun.Penjara

Martínez-Torres, M.E., and P.M. Rosset (2014) 'Diálogo de saberes in La Vía Campesina: food sovereignty and agroecology', *Journal of Peasant Studies* 41(6): 979–97.

Maye, D., and J. Kirwan (2013) 'Food security: a fractured consensus', *Journal of Rural Studies* 29: 1–6.

McCarthy, J.F., and K. Obidzinski (2017) 'Framing the food poverty question: policy choices and livelihood consequences', *Journal of Rural Studies* 54: 344–54.

McCarthy, J.F., and Z. Zen (2013) 'Food security in Indonesia', *Inside Indonesia* 114(October–December).

McKay, B., R. Nehring and M. Walsh-Dilley (2014) 'The "state" of food sovereignty in Latin America: political projects and alternative pathways in Venezuela, Ecuador and Bolivia', *Journal of Peasant Studies* 41(6): 1,175–200.

McMichael, P. (2009) 'A food regime genealogy', *Journal of Peasant Studies* 36(1): 139–70.

McMichael, P. (2016) 'Commentary: food regime for thought', *Journal of Peasant Studies* 43(3): 648–70.

Neilson, J., and J. Wright (2017) 'The state and the food security discourses of Indonesia: feeding the *bangsa*', *Geographical Research* 55(3): 131–43.

OECD (Organisation for Economic Co-operation and Development) (2012) *OECD Review of Agricultural Policies: Indonesia 2012*, OECD Publishing, Paris.

Pangestu, M., S. Rahardja and L.Y. Ing (2015) 'Fifty years of trade policy in Indonesia: new world trade, old treatments', *Bulletin of Indonesian Economic Studies* 51(2): 239–61.

Patunru, A.A. (forthcoming) 'Is greater openness to trade good? What are the effects on poverty and inequality?', in R. Barichello, R. Schwindt and A. Patunru (eds) *Trade, Poverty and Income Distribution: The Indonesian Experience*, University of British Columbia Press, Vancouver.

Patunru, A.A., and S. Rahardja (2015) 'Trade protectionism in Indonesia: bad times and bad policy', Analysis, Lowy Institute for International Policy, Sydney, 30 July.

Pinstrup-Andersen, P. (2009) 'Food security: definition and measurement', *Food Security* 1(1): 5–7.

Rafani, I. (2014) 'The Law No. 18/2012 governing food security in Indonesia', FFTC Agricultural Policy Platform, Food and Fertilizer Technology Center (FFTC), Taipei, 15 January. http://ap.fftc.agnet.org/ap_db.php?id=182

Rieley, J. (2001) 'Kalimantan's peatland disaster', *Inside Indonesia* 65(January–March).

Rosset, P. (2011) 'Food sovereignty and alternative paradigms to confront land grabbing and the food and climate crises', *Development* 54(1): 21–30.

Salim, E. (2011) 'Foreword', in W. Nitisastro, *The Indonesian Development Experience: A Collection of Writings and Speeches of Widjojo Nitisastro*, ISEAS Publishing, Singapore: xi–xxiii.

Schiavoni, C. (2009) 'The global struggle for food sovereignty: from Nyéléni to New York', *Journal of Peasant Studies* 36(3): 682–9.

Sen, A. (1981) *Poverty and Famines: An Essay on Entitlement and Deprivation*, Clarendon Press, Oxford.

Simatupang, P., and C.P. Timmer (2008) 'Indonesian rice production: policies and realities', *Bulletin of Indonesian Economic Studies* 44(1): 65–80.

Soesastro, H., and M.C. Basri (2005) 'The political economy of trade policy in Indonesia', *ASEAN Economic Bulletin* 22(1): 3–18.

Sukarno, President (1952) 'Soal hidup atau mati' [A matter of life or death], speech delivered by President Sukarno on 27 April 1952, Bogor. http://seafast.ipb.ac.id/article/Pidato-Bung-Karno_Peletakan-Batu-Pertama.pdf

Tempo (2017) 'The rice affair', *Tempo*, 1 August. https://magz.tempo.co/konten/2017/08/01/LU/33430/The-Rice-Affair/50/17

Timmer, C.P. (2014) 'Food security in Asia and the Pacific: the rapidly changing role of rice', *Asia & the Pacific Policy Studies* 1(1): 73–90.

Warr, P. (2005) 'Food policy and poverty in Indonesia: a general equilibrium analysis', *Australian Journal of Agricultural and Resource Economics* 49(4): 429–51.

Warr, P., and A. Yusuf (2014) 'World food prices and poverty in Indonesia', *Australian Journal of Agricultural and Resource Economics* 58(1): 1–21.

Widodo, J., and J. Kalla (2014) 'Nawacita: jalan perubahan untuk Indonesia yang berdaulat, mandiri dan berkepribadian: visi misi, dan program aksi' [National Priority Agenda: a path for change towards a sovereign, self-sufficient and honourable Indonesia: vision, mission and action plan], Jakarta, May.

World Bank (1986) 'Poverty and hunger: issues and options for food security in developing countries', Policy Study No. 9275, World Bank, Washington DC, February.

World Bank (2016) 'Indonesia economic quarterly: pressures easing', World Bank, Washington DC, October.

Yusuf, A.A., and A. Sumner (2015) 'Growth, poverty, and inequality under Jokowi', *Bulletin of Indonesian Economic Studies* 51(3): 323–48.

6 Nationalism, developmentalism and politics in Indonesia's mining sector

Eve Warburton

The global mining boom, occurring roughly between 2003 and 2013, caused a frenzy of mineral extraction across Indonesia's resource-rich regions, such as Kalimantan, Sulawesi and Sumatra. During the boom years, Indonesia's central and regional governments enjoyed a huge boost in revenues as demand from China sent commodity prices soaring. But many policy-makers, activists and politicians became concerned that Indonesia's finite resources were being shipped overseas too quickly and too cheaply, and that not enough Indonesians were feeling the economic benefits of the minerals boom.

In response, President Susilo Bambang Yudhoyono's administration (2004–14) introduced Law No. 4/2009 on Mineral and Coal Mining (the 2009 Mining Law), which stated that mining companies must begin adding value to their mineral ores within five years of the law's enactment. The government's goal was to kick-start a downstream mineral-processing industry by forcing companies to smelt or refine their ores domestically. Then, in January 2014, the government went ahead and banned the export of unprocessed minerals (Minister of Energy and Mineral Resources Regulation No. 1/2014). According to the regulation, value-adding activities in the mining sector would help to 'increase the benefits of minerals for the people and for regional development'. Indonesia could then transition away from extracting and exporting cheap primary commodities, and instead produce and export higher-value mineral products.

The policy was primarily justified in nationalist terms. Without policies like the export ban, so the argument went, Indonesia would just continue selling cheap primary commodities to richer, more industrialised nations, and never move up the global value chain. The policy contributed to Indonesia's reputation as a country marked by 'resource nationalism', a term that describes the various ways in which state and non-state actors attempt to extract more value from, and exert more ownership over, their natural resource endowments. Conventional market-cycle theories suggest that resource nationalism emerges in response to commodity booms, and then fades as commodity prices cool and resource-rich governments come under financial pressure (Wilson 2015).

After taking office in late 2014, President Joko Widodo (Jokowi) expressed strong support for the ban. Indeed, the broader agenda of downstream industrialisation aligned with the new president's nationalist economic sensibilities. By the end of 2016 the policy had begun to produce results, with over $18 billion in downstream investment being channelled into 32 smelting facilities (Singgih 2017). But then, in January 2017, the Jokowi administration made the controversial decision to relax the ban, jeopardising three years of downstream investment and development. What compelled the president's change of heart?

Many observers argued that the policy backflip was simply a response to budget pressures, and that resource nationalism was on the retreat—as market-cycle theories predict. But I suggest that this narrow causal narrative misses the broader policy picture in Indonesia's resource sectors. I argue in this chapter that Jokowi's decision to relax the ban was primarily about supporting state-owned mining company PT Aneka Tambang (Antam), whose profits had suffered during the export ban. The Jokowi administration has made the reform and expansion of state-owned enterprises a key pillar of its economic strategy. In the mining sector specifically, the government set out to boost state-owned mining companies and prepare them to make future acquisitions—in particular the acquisition of shares in Freeport Indonesia. In other words, relaxing the ban did not represent a retreat from the nationalist position, but rather a shift in nationalist priorities. This shift in priorities, I suggest, was largely driven by the president's political calculations.

What does this case reveal about the nature of resource nationalism in Indonesia more broadly? I argue that resource nationalism should not be viewed as a temporary response to price booms, as much of the literature maintains. Instead, we should see nationalist interventions in Indonesia as part of a re-emergent developmentalist model. The developmentalist vision for a locally owned and industrialised resource sector enjoys much support within the policy-making elite, and dovetails with the interests of domestic business. The ideas that underpin resource nationalism also resonate with broader narratives about Indonesia's struggle against foreign economic exploitation (Aspinall 2016; see also Chapter 3 of this book by Aspinall).

But the execution of this vision has been disjointed. Indonesia's mining sector is characterised by regulatory ambiguity, as policies are frequently retracted, revised and sometimes revived. Political conflict and competition distort the regulatory regime in Indonesia's resource sectors and prevent the realisation of a nationalist–developmentalist vision.

The rest of the chapter proceeds as follows. I begin by explaining the genesis of the export ban and its various regulatory iterations. I then examine, in turn, the implementation of the ban, the January 2017 decision to relax the ban and the contending explanations for the government's policy reversal. In the final section, I reflect on what this case reveals about the nature of resource nationalism in Indonesia, and its place within a re-emergent developmentalist model under the Jokowi administration.

THE IDEATIONAL BASIS OF THE MINERAL EXPORT BAN

The global commodities boom had a profound impact on Indonesia's economy and its mineral-rich regions. From 2003 to 2013, Indonesia enjoyed significant profits from increasing global prices for coal and minerals (World Bank 2014). Production increased to unprecedented levels, and quickly. According to a report by the United States Agency for International Development, for example, between 2008 and 2011 bauxite exports rose five-fold, nickel exports eight-fold and copper eleven-fold (USAID 2013: 7). Most of Indonesia's raw commodities were destined for China and India, whose rapid industrial growth spurred global demand and sent prices rising. The boom helped drive impressively high GDP growth rates in Indonesia, which averaged 6 per cent between 2005 and 2011 (Tabor 2015: 4).

At the same time, however, studies showed that the boom was having a minimal impact on poverty reduction, the labour market and inequality (Bhattacharyya and Resosudarmo 2015). There were also many within Indonesia's policy-making and political elite, including at the regional level, who felt that more should be done to distribute the economic benefits of the booming resource sectors.

An argument in favour of 'value adding' gained currency during these boom years. A value-added resource economy was an industrialised resource economy in which mining companies invested in downstream facilities and processed and smelted their mineral ores domestically, prior to export. The idea was to expand the economic footprint of Indonesia's enclave mining industry. This vision was translated into policy through the 2009 Mining Law, which laid the legal foundation for the 2014 export ban. Articles 102–103 of the law mandated that mining companies add value to mineral ores prior to export. Article 170 stipulated that companies operating under Contracts of Work (CoWs) or mining licences (IUPs) had five years from the law's enactment in which to prepare processing facilities. After the January 2014 deadline, only minerals at specified purity levels would be allowed to leave Indonesian shores.

Value adding as a policy concept enjoyed support from across the political spectrum, as well as from the bureaucracy and the economic policy-making elite. In interviews, officials framed the policy in terms reminiscent of 'dependency theory', which argues that, within the global capitalist economic system, poor countries are compelled to sell cheap primary commodities to the advanced industrialised countries, which use them to manufacture higher-value products. The system creates a cycle of underdevelopment in the 'global south' and sustained dependence upon the wealthy countries of the 'global north' (Ferraro 2008). Dependency theorists argued that commodity-exporting countries were invariably subject to ever worsening terms of trade with industrialised states — a phenomenon known as the 'resource curse'. The problem, theorists argued, was particularly acute when foreign companies dominated enclave resource industries in poor countries, because those companies repatriated rather than reinvested their profits (Ross 1999: 301–2).

From the late 1980s, economists increasingly agreed that commodity-exporting countries that depended on mining and cash crop sectors, on average, tended to suffer poorer economic and developmental outcomes. One of the causes, according to Humphreys (2015: 41), was 'a systemic bias in the international trading system against commodity producers. Prices of commodities relative to those of manufacturers […] appeared to show a persistent long-run decline'. Downstream integration, value adding and price stabilisation schemes, some economists argued, could protect commodity exporters from the economic pathologies associated with the resource curse (Humphreys 2015: 42).

This was the logic that underpinned nationalist intervention in the resource sector generally, and the mineral export ban specifically. Senior bureaucrats were anxious about Indonesia's sustained reliance on primary commodities, which exposed the economy to poor terms of trade and made it vulnerable to boom–bust cycles. Indonesia needed more backward and forward linkages, so the argument went, in order to reap maximum reward from its natural endowments (Ministry of Energy and Mineral Resources 2010: 23). Without state intervention, Indonesia would just continue selling cheap raw commodities to rich industrialised nations, without ever moving up the global value chain or beyond its lower-middle-income status.

It is worth nothing that not everyone in government, and certainly not everyone in the industry, supported the decision to force downstream development and to ban mineral exports. Several independent studies made a strong economic case against the ban, and projected losses of tens of billions of dollars in export revenue (USAID 2013). Domestic business associations, liberal economists and senior members of the bureaucracy argued that these sorts of export restrictions would hurt the country's smaller and medium-sized miners, and have a negative net impact on the economy (Hukumonline 2014: Stefanie 2015). However, opposition voices were drowned out by those who argued the nationalist case.[1]

Exponents often framed the intervention in emotional terms, tying the policy to Indonesia's economic identity. At the time, President Yudhoyono and his cabinet described the ban as a means of attaining 'economic sovereignty'. When justifying the ban and other nationalist interventions, politicians often invoked article 33 of the Indonesian constitution, which states that strategic parts of the economy, including natural resources, should be controlled by the state and used to ensure the prosperity of the people. If Indonesia failed to invest now in a program of industrial upgrading, the government argued, it would remain 'a nation of slaves' (Riyandi 2013). Hatta Rajasa, the coordinating minister for economic affairs (2009–14), was a key architect of the government's downstream strategy. He explained this nationalist vision in a media interview: 'We say that all raw materials must no longer be exported, everything must have an industry, we must begin down-streaming, and then our engineers can go to work, innovation will emerge, because we will have a value-added economy' (Riyandi 2013). This was the ideational basis for the mineral export ban.

IMPLEMENTING THE BAN

During the period from the introduction of the 2009 Mining Law until the 2014 deadline, both foreign and domestic companies largely failed to invest in downstream refining or smelting facilities. This meant that Indonesia had virtually no new refining capacity as it approached the deadline.[2] Private sector investment was not forthcoming, partly because of the regulatory confusion and mixed messages coming from the government. Back

---

1 It was rumoured at the time that rent-seeking ambitions were behind the government's determination to execute the ban. One rather extreme rumour was that Hatta Rajasa, a leading proponent of the ban, would receive a generous material reward from US Rusal, a Russian mining company with both bauxite and nickel interests, for ensuring that the government implement a tight ban on these two minerals (Metrotvnews 2015). Ultimately, however, these rumours remain unsubstantiated. Almost certainly there were rent-seeking elites waiting in the wings to benefit from the ban, but beneficiation also had broad-based support from across the political and policy-making spectrum.
2 Instead, companies increased the rate of extraction and export of raw minerals, including copper, nickel and bauxite.

in 2012 the Ministry of Energy and Mineral Resources had introduced two new regulations pertaining to value adding. The first, Ministerial Regulation No. 7/2012 on Improving the Value-added of Minerals through Mineral Processing and Purification Activities, attempted to bring the processing deadline forward, and stated that mineral ore exports would be banned within three months. The Indonesian Nickel Association (ANI) and the Association of Indonesian District Governments (Apkasi) challenged the regulation in the Supreme Court, but even before the Supreme Court ruled on the case, the government reinstated the original January 2014 deadline with Ministerial Regulation No. 11/2012 (Koran Tempo 2014). Clearly the ministry perceived the shaky legal ground upon which it stood.

By the end of 2013 the boom was over, the economy was slowing and the current account deficit was at its worst since 1986 (Economist 2014), so companies and industry analysts questioned whether the government would follow through on a policy that was set to limit revenues in the short term. Most assumed that the government would rethink the intervention and retreat from the nationalist position given the changed economic circumstances.[3] Indeed, in the weeks before the January 2014 deadline, policy-makers clashed over what to do about the impending ban. For example, the minister for energy and mineral resources, Jero Wacik, approached the parliament seeking approval to delay the deadline and give companies more time to build smelters (Reuters 2013). But legislators rejected the ministry's proposal.

The evening before the 12 January deadline, senior cabinet ministers met with the president to discuss a revision, and to try to minimise the economic impact of the ban. During these last-minute negotiations at the president's home, some ministers argued in favour of delaying the ban until 2017 (Sullivan 2014). However, as the finance minister at the time, Chatib Basri, explained in an interview on 9 January 2015, 'the law could not be changed, so we had to work within the new economic constraints'.

The result was a compromise in which the ban was to be applied selectively. On 12 January 2014, the Ministry of Energy and Mineral Resources introduced Ministerial Regulation No. 1/2014 on Improving the Value-added of Minerals through Mineral Processing and Purification Activities, which set out the conditions for Indonesia's mineral export ban. The regulation allowed for the export of 'category 1' minerals (copper, iron, limonite, titanium, lead, zinc and manganese concentrates) but maintained a tight ban on minerals placed in 'category 2' (nickel, bauxite, tin, gold, silver and chromium). The ban on category 2 minerals had the most significant

---

3 Interview, Indonesian Mining Association representatives, 12 May 2014; interview, Indonesian Coal Mining Association representative, 5 May 2015.

impact on nickel and bauxite, because tin, gold, silver and chromium were already being processed at the legally mandated levels. Nickel and bauxite, however, were being exported in record volumes during the boom, mostly in raw form. Both minerals also demonstrated potential in terms of smelting investment. According to the Business Monitor International (2015: 43), 'around 80% of the value for nickel and 94% for aluminum are derived from the refining and smelting stages'. But until now companies had not had any incentive to invest downstream, because the prices for the raw ores were high, and the process of extracting nickel and bauxite was relatively simple and cheap. A tight ban, the government argued, was the only way to compel downstream development and ensure investor confidence in the profitability of these investments.

Meanwhile, the concession for category 1 minerals was a boon for the two American companies that dominated Indonesia's copper industry, Freeport and Newmont, which together accounted for over 97 per cent of copper concentrate exports. These mining giants were given another three years to build smelters before becoming subject, in January 2017, to a higher processing requirement for their copper exports. Licences to continue exporting category 1 minerals were contingent on companies demonstrating their financial commitment to building smelters, or to cooperating with another party that was building smelters. In place of a ban, however, the Ministry of Finance introduced an export tax on category 1 minerals that would start at 20 per cent in 2015 and increase to 60 per cent by 2016 (Minister of Finance Regulation No. 6/2014 on the Determination of Exported Goods Subject to Export Duty and Export Duty Tariff). Newmont and Freeport argued that the tax was so onerous that it overshadowed the dispensation they had just received on their copper ore exports.

The ban shocked the domestic and international mining industries. Nickel and bauxite mining came to a virtual standstill, which the government understood would cut exports by approximately $4 billion in the first year (Economist 2014). But despite the immediate economic pain, the Yudhoyono government remained committed to what it regarded as an essential long-term plan for industrialising Indonesia's resource economy.

The policy did begin to pay off in the years that followed, particularly for nickel.[4] The downstream sector attracted billions of dollars in investment (Hewson 2016), and the volume of refined nickel began to increase (Bloomberg 2016). For example, in 2009 nationwide nickel smelting

---

4 The downstream bauxite sector did not experience the same level of investment or progress, largely because Indonesia's energy infrastructure in the bauxite mining areas of Kalimantan simply could not supply the large amounts of energy required for bauxite smelting.

capacity was 98,000 tons, according to Sukhyar, chair of the Indonesian Smelter and Minerals Processing Association. The association claimed that by 2017 capacity had reached 363,000 tons (Bloomberg 2016). Most of the money came from China, with investors sometimes partnering up with local companies in joint ventures. So, despite widespread scepticism and criticism from industry analysts, Indonesia's ban appeared to be doing its job—expanding Indonesia's downstream capacity and pushing it up the global value chain.

THE END OF THE BAN

When President Joko Widodo took office, the mining boom was over and the new government was tasked with managing a growing trade deficit. Yet he and his cabinet initially came out in strong support of the export ban. Given that the investment was beginning to produce results, the consensus among industry analysts and government officials was that Jokowi would stick to the plan for downstream industrialisation—especially for nickel, where most development had taken place.

Then, in January 2017, the government introduced a new regulation that allowed the export of raw nickel, bauxite and copper to resume under certain conditions (Government Regulation No. 1/2017 on the Fourth Change to Government Regulation No. 23/2010 on the Implementation of Mining Company Activities for Mineral and Coal Mining). Mining companies that wished to export unprocessed ores could now apply to the Ministry of Energy and Mineral Resources for a permit, but such permits would only be granted to companies that had demonstrated progress towards building processing plants (Agustinus 2017). The new regulation also forced companies with export permits to allocate 30 per cent of their nickel ores to domestic smelters, to ensure that miners did not simply avoid value adding altogether.

Many in the media interpreted the government's decision as a response to financial pressures (Asmarini and Munthe 2017; Sanderson and Bland 2017). Opening the door to exports would increase tax revenues and help ease the budget deficit. PricewaterhouseCoopers estimated that the mining sector's contribution to Indonesia's total export revenue fell from 18 per cent in 2013 to 14 per cent in 2014 and 2015 (PwC 2016: 3). The Jokowi administration had missed its revenue targets for 2015 and 2016 and was scrambling to find ways to ease the financial pressure. This explanation also reflects conventional market-cycle theories of resource nationalism: the commodity boom was over, and so a resource-rich country such as Indonesia would face increasing financial pressure, and respond by retreating from the nationalist position.

But there are reasons to be sceptical about this explanation. First, the way in which the new rules were structured meant that, in fact, the impact on the budget would be relatively minor. The Ministry of Energy and Mineral Resources was not expecting a huge increase in exports of mineral ores. The conditions for gaining a permit were highly restrictive, and at the time of writing – 10 months after the ban was introduced – only six companies had received such permits (Gumelar 2017). According to one report, the ministry predicted that under the new rules, Indonesia would export up to 5.2 million tonnes of nickel ore per year, or 'less than 9% of what the country used to export prior to the export ban' (de Frutos 2017).

Second, framing the reversal of the export ban simply as a response to low commodity prices mischaracterises the broader policy trajectory in Indonesia's mining sector, and the alternative nationalist agenda of which this latest policy was a part. I suggest instead that the decision to relax the ban served to support state-owned mining company PT Aneka Tambang (Antam). Before the ban, Antam was Indonesia's largest exporter of raw nickel ore.[5] Indeed, raw nickel and bauxite exports accounted for 30 per cent of the company's revenue in 2013 (Antam 2013). Yet back in 2014, Antam received no special dispensations from the Yudhoyono government. The consensus among policy-makers at the time was that Antam would have to withstand the immediate financial pain in order to eventually become a driver of value-added economic growth.

Antam suffered huge financial losses when the nickel ban was introduced. Unable to export raw ore, and without sufficient smelting capacity, Antam's profits nosedived: it booked Rp 743 billion in losses in 2014 and went into the red for the first time in over a decade (Jakarta Post 2015; Maulia 2017b). In the lead-up to the January 2017 deadline, it was even rumoured that the ban would be relaxed for Antam only, and not for Indonesia's hundreds of smaller domestic nickel exporters. When the relaxation was finally announced, Antam's shares jumped 6 per cent. This suggests that the ban's relaxation was designed to fix Antam's bottom line, rather than to fix broader budget troubles.

We also need to view the export relaxation in the context of the Jokowi administration's broader vision for the mining sector. In general, the Jokowi government has been far more sensitive to the financial needs of state-owned enterprises, and has promoted them as locomotives of economic growth (Warburton 2016). For example, in 2015 Jokowi poured Rp 7 trillion (approximately $5.1 million) into Antam in order to boost the company's output and help it invest in several downstream projects (Detikcom 2015). Under Rini Soemarno, the minister for state-owned

---

5 Brazil's Vale is the largest nickel company in Indonesia, but it already processed its nickel ore domestically prior to export.

enterprises, the government has laid out a grand plan to reform and restructure the state-owned sector, in which state enterprises operating in strategic industries will be consolidated under new state-run holding companies. The mining and the oil and gas sectors were identified as a first priority. In the case of the mining sector, the ministry decided to turn PT Inalum, the 100 per cent state-owned aluminium miner, into the mining-sector holding company (Maulia 2017a). The other three state-owned companies in the sector, Antam (nickel, bauxite and gold), Bukit Asam (coal) and Timah (tin), would sit under Inalum. This process was finalised in November 2017 (Sugianto 2017). The goal of the restructuring program was to streamline state-owned companies, make them more efficient and increase their liquidity. But, as minister for finance Sri Mulyani explained to the parliament and the press, the government would only be consolidating the 'healthy state-owned companies' (Glienmourinsie 2016). A holding company with an expanded and diverse portfolio of assets could leverage more capital, the government—and especially Rini Soemarno—argued strenuously, giving it the capacity to acquire shares in expensive, lucrative, privately run mines.

The government's target all along was PT Freeport Indonesia, the Indonesian subsidiary of Freeport-McMoRan. Freeport had been engaged in difficult negotiations with the government for years over the terms of its operating licence at the Grasberg mine in Papua, the most profitable gold mine in the world. Those negotiations began after the introduction of the 2009 Mining Law, which mandated that existing mining contracts be changed to reflect the terms of the new law — including providing new obligations to add value to minerals, and new divestment obligations. Freeport not only wanted to extend its current contract (which was eligible for extension in 2019), but it also opposed the new, more onerous rules for investors. The negotiations became even more fraught in January 2017. At the same time as the government relaxed the export ban, it also obliged foreign miners to divest 51 per cent of their shares by the tenth year of production. The new rule replaced a Yudhoyono-era regulation from October 2014 that had mandated divestment of a maximum of only 30 per cent of shares for foreign-owned mining companies. And in fact, the Jokowi administration almost came to an arrangement with Freeport on those terms back in 2015 (Budiartie and Warburton 2015).

But two years later, the government's priorities had changed. It now wanted the mining giant to divest a controlling share in the Grasberg mine to a state-owned company. In late August 2017 the government finally reached a deal. It agreed to extend Freeport's operating licence to 2041 when the current contract expired, and Freeport agreed to divest 51 per cent of its shares and build a second smelter, among other concessions. However, at the time of writing the parties were yet to agree on fundamental details regarding the share price and the timing of the divestment.

In sum, the administration's nationalist priorities had changed. Rather than prioritise the goal of industrialisation and protect downstream investors, the Jokowi government chose to relax the ban. The administration's priority was to strengthen its state-owned enterprises, and increase state ownership of the country's most profitable, foreign-operated mine. With the reversal of the ban, Antam's profits would rebound, putting Antam, and therefore the planned holding company, in a better financial position to take over foreign-operated mining projects such as Freeport's Grasberg mine (Oktara 2017). After the deal was inked, the government confirmed to the media that Inalum, as the new sectoral holding company, would purchase Freeport's divested shares (Jakarta Post 2017).

THE POLITICAL IMPERATIVE

What explains the Jokowi administration's decision to change tack, and make Inalum's acquisition of Freeport shares an urgent priority? I suggest that political imperatives underpinned the government's shift in nationalist priorities. When he first came to power, Jokowi had no clear agenda when it came to the Freeport contract; indeed, he appeared content for the then minister for energy and mineral resources, Sudirman Said, to direct the Freeport negotiations and find a solution that satisfied 'both parties', without himself articulating any strong personal preference (Majalah Tempo 2015). But by 2017, Jokowi had come to see the Freeport contract as a political liability. Indeed, the new directive that foreign miners divest a majority stake after 10 years came from the president himself. With two years until the next presidential elections, Jokowi was preparing the ground for his re-election bid, and insulating himself from any attacks upon his nationalist credentials.

To recall, Jokowi won the 2014 presidential elections by narrowly defeating Prabowo Subianto. Back then, it was Prabowo that claimed the nationalist ground. At campaign rallies Prabowo decried the exploitation of Indonesia's land and resources by nameless 'foreign forces', and gave impassioned speeches in which he claimed that Indonesia's riches were disappearing (*bocor*) and that the profits were being taken abroad, leaving little for the country's masses of poor people (Gammon 2014; Aspinall 2015). In opinion polls, Jokowi consistently lost to Prabowo when it came to a particular set of leadership qualities. Prabowo was always regarded as stronger (*tegas*) and more powerful and authoritative (*berwibawa*) than Jokowi (Detikcom 2014), while Jokowi was invariably viewed as cleaner and closer to the people. Prabowo cultivated a strongman image primarily through his firebrand nationalism and his identity as a former New Order general. Clearly unnerved by these public perceptions, since coming to office Jokowi has deliberately worked to fortify his political armour against accusations that he is neither strong enough nor nationalistic enough to defend Indonesia against foreign exploitation and insult. Compelling Freeport to divest a majority of its shares became a central part of Jokowi's nationalist strategy.

Jokowi realised in 2015 that the Freeport contract could easily become fodder for his detractors. In October that year, the press revealed that Sudirman Said, the minister for energy and mineral resources, had given Freeport a written assurance that its contract would be extended beyond 2021 (Majalah Tempo 2015). The decision prompted a backlash, including widespread criticism from the media and from other members of the cabinet (Warburton 2015). For example, the cover of the October edition of *Tempo* magazine, one of Indonesia's most prominent and influential political publications, pictured Jokowi dressed in a golden suit, signing a document atop an American flag (Majalah Tempo 2015). The implication was clear: the president had caved in to the demands of an American company at the expense of his country. Shaken by the backlash, the president withdrew the assurances that Said had provided to Freeport.

From mid-2015 onwards, after six months of poor results in the polls, the president's approach to the resource sectors more generally took a nationalist turn. For example, Jokowi made the controversial decision to transfer operating rights for the strategic Mahakam block to the state-owned oil and gas company, Pertamina, denying the request of the French oil and gas company, Total, for an extension of its contract. Mahakam accounts for over 25 per cent of Indonesia's gas production, and most industry analysts argued that handing operating rights to the state-owned company was a high-risk decision. Then, in 2016, Jokowi assisted PT Medco Energi Internasional, owned by Indonesian businessman and former Indonesian Democratic Party of Struggle (PDIP) politician Arifin Panigoro, to acquire 82 per cent of Newmont's Batu Hijau mine, the second-largest copper mine in the country. To finance the acquisition, Medco borrowed from three state-owned banks, Bank Mandiri, Bank Negara Indonesia (BNI) and Bank Rakyat Indonesia (BRI) — a financial arrangement that, according to insiders and press reports, required the president's 'blessing' (Budiartie, Teresia and Nasrillah 2016; Sundaryani 2016). Jokowi reportedly watched the Newmont acquisition carefully, hoping it might constitute a model for transferring the Freeport mine into Indonesian hands in the near future (Budiartie, Teresia and Nasrillah 2016).

In early 2016, the Jokowi administration also decided to force INPEX and Shell to build their LNG terminal for the Masela natural gas block onshore, rather than offshore as their (previously approved) development plans had stipulated. The logic was that an onshore terminal would produce a larger multiplier effect for Indonesian businesses and the communities living on nearby islands (McBeth 2016; Warburton 2017). Finally, as we have seen, in mid-2017 the Jokowi administration managed to reach an agreement with Freeport that would see the government finally take a controlling share in the largest and most profitable gold mine in the world. The deal was portrayed in local media as a significant political win for Jokowi (Daniel 2017; Media Indonesia 2017).

It is important to note that observers have voiced serious concerns about the economic consequences of the government's assertive nationalist approach. Analysts both within and outside Indonesia have expressed doubt about the capacity of Indonesia's companies, both state and privately owned, to access the necessary capital and technology to operate and sustain production at these strategic mineral and hydrocarbon projects (McBeth 2013; Garnaut 2015; Cahyafitri 2013, 2015).

But there are strong material and political imperatives behind the Jokowi administration's nationalist push (Warburton 2017). Taken together, these decisions constitute a solid foundation upon which Jokowi can build a nationalist image. Indeed, Jokowi can now stand in front of a crowd at campaign rallies, or in front of a press conference, and declare that only *he*, and no other president before him, had been able to bring three of the country's most strategic resource projects—Total's Mahakam block, Newmont's Batu Hijau mine and Freeport's Grasberg mine—into Indonesian hands. And if the government can indeed organise for state-owned Inalum to acquire some or all of Freeport's divested shares, the president's nationalist credentials will shine bright in the 2019 presidential campaign. These 'wins' insulate Jokowi against the kind of aggressive nationalist campaign he encountered in 2014.

In sum, the government's nationalist priorities in the mining sector shifted in response to a political imperative. The president became less interested in protecting downstream investors in the minerals sector, and instead sought to boost the financial position of state-owned companies, and facilitate their acquisition of the country's oldest foreign-operated mine.

CONCLUSION: A NEW DEVELOPMENTALISM FOR INDONESIA'S RESOURCE SECTORS?

So what does all of this tell us about the nature of resource nationalism in Indonesia? First, it is clear that nationalist mobilisation and intervention are not tied in a coherent way to an external price mechanism—an assertion that is made in conventional market-cycle theories of resource nationalism. The mining boom ended in 2013, and yet nationalist interventions persist. The sorts of policies that have materialised in the resource sectors over the past five to ten years (export bans, export restrictions, local content requirements and the prioritisation of state-owned companies) approximate, or share some of the features of, a state-led developmentalist model. I suggest, therefore, that resource nationalism is better conceived as a more permanent fixture in the economy policy-making landscape, and as one element of a (re)emergent developmentalism in Joko Widodo's Indonesia.[6]

What constitutes the 'new developmentalism'? This term has become common parlance in recent scholarship on the resource boom in Latin America. Haslam and Heidrich (2016: 5), for example, explain how resource nationalism in that region is 'a visible manifestation of a broader concern with rebuilding the developmental state, or at the very least, rebuilding the state's capacity to regulate and intervene in the economy'. The Brazilian case is particularly instructive. In their study of new developmentalism in Brazil, Döring, Pereira dos Santos and Pocher (2017) demonstrate how the state's industrial policy in the mining and oil and gas sectors favours the domestic business giants, both state owned and private; but how these companies are, in return, expected to contribute to the state's broader industrial and developmental goals. Nem Singh and Massi (2016: 158) agree, showing how the Brazilian state 'facilitate[s] the participation of private firms, while maintaining state control over the ownership of national enterprises'.

The new developmentalism, thus, proposes a greater role for the state in economic planning and resource-based industrialisation; but it is not *radically* nationalist, because it does not reject a role for the private sector or for markets. Instead, this developmental model is premised on the notion that the state should intervene in markets in order to protect and boost local companies, support state-owned enterprises and develop domestic champions as agents of industrial development. The way in which the Jokowi administration supported Medco's acquisition of Newmont's Batu Hijau mine, its plans to develop state-owned sectoral holding companies and its sustained intervention in pursuit of downstream industrialisation all demonstrate features of a new developmentalism that emerged in other resource-rich countries during the mining boom.

These sorts of economic ideas have long been popular in Indonesian policy-making circles. Scholars of Indonesia labelled the New Order a 'repressive developmentalist' regime (Feith 1981). Back then, economic planning was driven by the notion that the state's principal role was to

---

6 I explored this idea in the context of Indonesia's broader political economy, beyond the resource sectors, in a previous paper (Warburton 2016).

provide the conditions for fast-paced economic development, such that Indonesia could begin to catch up with the industrialised nations of East Asia and the west. The Suharto government justified cooptation of societal groups and repression of political dissent in the name of accelerated economic growth.[7]

While the contemporary Indonesian state no longer uses the tools of oppression, developmentalist ideas continue to resonate among the policy-making class. In fact, the transition to democratic government, and the liberalisation of the Indonesian economy after the Asian financial crisis in 1997–98, has, somewhat ironically, produced a broader constituency for economic nationalism generally, and resource nationalism specifically (Patunru and Rahardja 2015: Warburton 2017). Demands for protection, privilege and state intervention come from an expanded domestic business class that is more autonomous than during the New Order days. Political actors also promote nationalist interventions, because they are aware of the broad-based societal support for a locally owned and industrialised resource economy. Developmentalist economic ideas resonate with the electorate, reflect the ideological preferences of many in the bureaucracy and dovetail with the particularistic interests of the domestic private sector.

None of this is to suggest that Indonesia reflects an ideal-type developmentalist state. Far from it. Indonesia's execution of its nationalist vision is often disjointed and incoherent. Nationalist regulations are constantly being amended, and the resource sectors are characterised by high levels of institutional ambiguity. For example, there have been three different regulatory iterations of the export ban since 2009, and four different versions of the divestment law since 2010. This mutability is a function of how bureaucrats and ministers readily adjust regulations to align with new priorities. Sometimes those priorities reflect changed economic circumstances. But as we have seen, regulatory incoherence is often due to the shifting political priorities of elected officials.

While Indonesia's political and policy elite may share a developmentalist ambition for a locally owned and industrialised resource sector, the institutional ingredients are missing. The rules that underpin this nationalist vision are highly unstable and discretionary. The case of the

---

7   Particular policy networks promoted nationalist interventions in the economy in order to advance the cause of industrialisation and nurture Indonesia's small indigenous private sector (Bresnan 1993). Their influence over economic policy was strongest during times of plenty, when natural resource booms flooded state coffers with rents. During times of economic crisis or downturn, Suharto would have to look to the liberal technocrats to open up the economy, invite investment and minimise any negative economic repercussions (Hill and Thee 2008).

mineral export ban and the revised divestment regulations highlight the challenges of executing a coherent developmentalist strategy in a context in which regulations are designed to meet the changing (and often short-term) agendas of Indonesia's fragmented political and bureaucratic class.

REFERENCES

Agustinus, M. (2017) 'Ekspor mineral mentah kembali dibuka, ini penjelasan ESDM' [Mineral ores opened again for export, this is ESDM's explanation], *Detikfinance*, 21 January 2017. https://finance.detik.com/read/2017/01/21/175544/3402098/1034/ekspor-mineral-mentah-kembali-dibuka-ini-penjelasan-esdm

Antam (PT Aneka Tambang) (2013) 'Annual report 2013: managing reality, overcoming uncertainty', Antam, Jakarta. http://www.indonesia-investments.com/upload/bedrijfsprofiel/217/aneka-tambang-antam-annual-report-2013-antm-company-profile-indonesia-investments.pdf

Artani, Q. (2015) 'Disanggah Hatta, ini jawaban Faisal Basri' [Hatta protests, this is Faisal Basri's response], *Metrotvnews*, 26 May. http://news.metrotvnews.com/read/2015/05/26/129935/disanggah-hatta-ini-jawaban-faisal-basri

Asmarini, W., and B.C. Munthe (2017) 'Indonesia eases export ban on nickel ore, bauxite', *Reuters*, 12 January. https://www.reuters.com/article/us-indonesia-mining-exports/indonesia-eases-export-ban-on-nickel-ore-bauxite-idUSKBN14W1TZ

Aspinall, E. (2015) 'Oligarchic populism: Prabowo Subianto's challenge to Indonesian democracy', *Indonesia* 99(April): 1–28.

Aspinall, E. (2016) 'The new nationalism in Indonesia', *Asia & the Pacific Policy Studies* 3(1): 72–82.

Bhattacharyya, S., and B.P. Resosudarmo (2015) 'Growth, growth accelerations, and the poor: lessons from Indonesia', *World Development* 66: 154–65.

Bloomberg (2016) 'Nickel supply seen rising from Indonesia as smelters fire up', *Bloomberg.com*, 20 September. https://www.bloomberg.com/news/articles/2016-09-20/indonesian-nickel-supply-seen-surging-as-local-smelters-start-up.

Bresnan, J. (1993) *Managing Indonesia: The Modern Political Economy*, Columbia University Press, New York NY.

Budiartie, G., A. Teresia and F. Nasrillah (2016) 'Membidik saham Batu Hijau' [Aiming for Batu Hijau's shares], *Tempo Magazine*, 11 April. https://majalah.tempo.co/konten/2016/04/11/EB/150491/Membidik-Saham-Batu-Hijau/07/45

Budiartie, G., and E. Warburton (2015) 'Indonesia's Freeport saga', *New Mandala*, blog, 22 December. http://www.newmandala.org/indonesias-freeport-saga/

Business Monitor International (2014) 'Industry trend analysis: moderation in sight for nickel ore export ban', BMI Research, 17 February. http://www.emergingmarketsmonitor.com/industry-trend-analysis-moderation-sight-nickel-ore-export-ban-17-feb-2014

Cahyafitri, R. (2013) 'Mining shutdown looms', *Jakarta Post*, 6 December. http://www.thejakartapost.com/news/2013/12/06/mining-shutdown-looms.html

Cahyafitri, R. (2015) 'Pertamina's biggest gamble: the Mahakam block', *Jakarta Post*, 9 February. http://www.thejakartapost.com/news/2015/02/09/pertaminas-biggest-gamble-the-mahakam-block.html

Daniel, W. (2017) 'Jonan: dapat 51% saham Freeport, RI berdaulat!' [Jonan: take 51% of Freeport shares, RI is sovereign!], *Detikfinance*, 2 September. https://finance.detik.com/read/2017/09/02/091001/3625252/1034/jonan-dapat-51-saham-freeport-ri-berdaulat

de Frutos, R. (2017) 'Why Indonesia's easing of the ore export ban is bullish for nickel prices', *Metal Miner*, 17 January. https://agmetalminer.com/2017/01/17/why-indonesias-easing-of-the-ore-export-ban-is-bullish-for-nickel-prices/

Detikcom (2014) 'Kenapa elektabilitas Prabowo semakin tempel Jokowi?' [Why is Prabowo gaining on Jokowi in electability?], *Detiknews*, 15 June. https://news.detik.com/read/2014/06/15/173535/2608598/1562/kenapa-elektabilitas-prabowo-semakin-tempel-jokowi

Detikcom (2015) 'Ini proyek-proyek yang digarap antam bila "disuntik" Jokowi Rp 7 triliun' [These are the projects Antam will take on if Jokowi injects Rp 7 trillion], *Detikfinance*, 29 January. https://finance.detik.com/read/2015/01/29/145521/2817748/4/ini-proyek-proyek-yang-digarap-antam-bila-disuntik-jokowi-rp-7-triliun

Döring, H., R.S. Pereira dos Santos and E. Pocher (2017) 'New developmentalism in Brazil? the need for sectoral analysis', *Review of International Political Economy* 24(2): 332–62.

Economist (2014) 'Smeltdown', *The Economist*, 18 January. https://www.economist.com/news/business/21594260-government-risks-export-slump-boost-metals-processing-industry-smeltdown

Feith, H. (1981) 'Repressive-developmentalist regimes in Asia', *Alternatives: Global, Local, Political* 7(4): 491–506.

Ferraro, V. (2008) 'Dependency theory: an introduction', in G. Secondi (ed.) *The Development Economics Reader*, Routledge, London.

Gammon, L. (2014) 'Prabowo's dog-whistling', *New Mandala*, blog, 12 June. http://www.newmandala.org/prabowos-dog-whistling/

Garnaut, R. (2015) 'Indonesia's resources boom in international perspective: policy dilemmas and options for continued strong growth', *Bulletin of Indonesian Economic Studies* 51(2): 189–212.

Glienmourinsie, D. (2016) 'Sri Mulyani: BUMN sakit jangan dijadikan induk holding' [Sri Mulyani: unhealthy BUMN should not become the main holding company], *SINDOnews.com*, 25 August. https://ekbis.sindonews.com/read/1134040/34/sri-mulyani-bumn-sakit-jangan-dijadikan-induk-holding-1472124574

Gumelar, G. (2017) 'Pemerintah beri enam perusahaan izin ekspor nikel dan bauksit' [Government gives six companies export licences for nickel and bauxite], *CNN Indonesia*, 7 September. https://www.cnnindonesia.com/ekonomi/20170906144210-85-239833/pemerintah-beri-enam-perusahaan-izin-ekspor-nikel-dan-bauksit/

Haslam, P.A., and P. Heidrich (2016) *The Political Economy of Natural Resources and Development: From Neoliberalism to Resource Nationalism*, Routledge, London.

Hewson, J. (2016) 'China's virtue dragon joins Indonesian nickel rush', *Nikkei Asian Review*, 7 December. https://asia.nikkei.com/Business/Companies/China-s-Virtue-Dragon-joins-Indonesian-nickel-rush

Hill, H., and Thee K.W. (2008) 'Moh. Sadli (1922–2008), economist, minister and public intellectual', *Bulletin of Indonesian Economic Studies* 44(1): 151–6.

Hukumonline (2014) 'UU tak menyebut eksplisit larangan pemurnian ore', *Hukumonline*, 16 April. http://www.hukumonline.com/index.php/berita/baca/lt534e8339e6a94/uu-tak-menyebut-eksplisit-larangan-pemurnian-ore

Humphreys (2015) 'New mercantilism: a perspective on how politics is shaping world metal supply', *Resources Policy* 38(3): 341–9.

Jakarta Post (2015) 'Antam plunges into the red as export ban hurts sales', *Jakarta Post*, 10 March. http://www.thejakartapost.com/news/2015/03/10/antam-plunges-red-export-ban-hurts-sales.html

Jakarta Post (2017) 'Govt picks Inalum to buy Freeport's shares', *Jakarta Post*, 20 September. http://www.thejakartapost.com/news/2017/09/20/govt-picks-inalum-to-buy-freeports-shares.html

Koran Tempo (2014) 'Pembatasan kadar pemurnian disepakati' [Purification grades agreed on], *Koran Tempo*, 10 January. http://koran.tempo.co/konten/2014/01/10/332047/Pembatasan-Kadar-Pemurnian-Disepakati

Majalah Tempo (2015) 'Angin surga bagi investor tua' [Heavenly breeze for old investors], *Majalah Tempo*, 19 October. https://majalah.tempo.co/konten/2015/10/19/LU/149246/Angin-Surga-bagi-Investor-Tua/34/44

Maulia, E. (2017a) 'Indonesia pressing ahead with SOE mergers', *Nikkei Asian Review*, 12 January. http://asia.nikkei.com/Business/AC/Jakarta-accelerates-merger-of-state-owned-energy-mining-companies

Maulia, E. (2017b) 'Company in focus: Antam faces test as Indonesia shifts mining policy', *Nikkei Asian Review*, 2 February. http://asia.nikkei.com/Features/Company-in-focus/Antam-faces-test-as-Indonesia-shifts-mining-policy

McBeth, J. (2013) 'Nationalism undermining Indonesia's oil and gas sector', *Straits Times*, 8 January.

McBeth, J. (2016) 'Masela: Indonesia's odd LNG plan', *The Diplomat*, 14 April. http://thediplomat.com/2016/04/masela-indonesias-odd-lng-plan/

Media Indonesia (2017) 'Divestasi 51% berarti Indonesia berdaulat atas Freeport' [51% divestment means Indonesia is sovereign over Freeport], *Media Indonesia*, 5 September. http://mediaindonesia.com/news/read/120874/divestasi-51-berarti-indonesia-berdaulat-atas-freeport/2017-09-05

Ministry of Energy and Mineral Resources (2010) 'Rencana Strategis Kementerian Energi dan Sumber Daya Mineral tahun 2010-2014' [Strategic plan of the Ministry of Energy and Mineral Resources for the years 2010-2014], Ministry of Energy and Mineral Resources, Jakarta. https://www.esdm.go.id/assets/media/content/RENSTRA_KESDM_2010-2014_--_Final_280110.pdf

Nem Singh, J., and E. Massi (2016) 'Resource nationalism and Brazil's post-neoliberal strategy', in P. Haslam and P. Heidrich (eds) *The Political Economy of Natural Resources and Development: From neoliberalism to resource nationalism*, Routledge, Abingdon: 158–86.

Oktara, D. (2017) 'Menteri Luhut: dibahas proses BUMN akuisisi Freeport' [Minister Luhut: we are discussing the process for an SOE to acquire Freeport], *Tempo.co*, 27 February. https://m.tempo.co/read/news/2017/02/27/090850607/menteri-luhut-dibahas-proses-bumn-akuisisi-freeport

Patunru, A.A., and S. Rahardja (2015) 'Trade protectionism in Indonesia: bad times and bad policy', Analysis, Lowy Institute for International Policy, Sydney, 30 July.

PwC (PricewaterhouseCoopers) (2014) 'Mining in Indonesia: investment and taxation guide', sixth edition, PwC, May. https://www.pwc.com/id/en/publications/assets/mining-investment-taxation-guide-2014.pdf

PwC (PricewaterhouseCoopers) (2016) 'Mining in Indonesia: investment and taxation guide', eighth edition, PwC, May. https://www.pwc.com/id/en/energy-utilities-mining/assets/May%202016/PwC%20Indonesia-mining-in-Indonesia-survey-2016.pdf

Reuters (2013) 'UPDATE 1: Indonesia trying to skirt its own ban on mineral exports', *Reuters*, 9 December. https://www.reuters.com/article/indonesia-ore-ban/update-1-indonesia-trying-to-skirt-its-own-ban-on-mineral-exports-idUSL3N0JO2M220131209

Riyandi, S. (2013) 'Peningkatan kualitas SDM buat Indonesia tidak jadi negara kuli' [Increasing the quality of human resources will ensure Indonesia does not become a nation of slaves], *Merdeka.com*, 6 May. https://www.merdeka.com/uang/peningkatan-kualitas-sdm-buat-indonesia-tidak-jadi-negara-kuli.html

Ross, M.L. (1999) 'The political economy of the resource curse', *World Politics* 51(2): 297–322.

Sanderson, H., and B. Bland (2017) 'Indonesia eases ban on mineral exports', *Financial Times*, 13 January. https://www.ft.com/content/a077c154-d942-11e6-944b-e7eb37a6aa8e

Singgih, V. (2017) 'Indonesia hopes to ride nickel revival by 2020', *Jakarta Post*, 16 May. https://www.pressreader.com/indonesia/the-jakarta-post/20170516/282016147253672

Stefanie, C. (2015) 'Ketua MPR tak setuju Faisal Basri soal ekspor minerba' [Head of MPR disagrees with Faisal Basri on export of minerals and coal], *CNN Indonesia*, 25 May. https://www.cnnindonesia.com/ekonomi/20150525224203-85-55627/ketua-mpr-tak-setuju-faisal-basri-soal-ekspor-minerba

Sugianto, D. (2017) 'Holding BUMN tambang terbentuk, saatnya caplok Freeport' [State-owned mining holding company established, it's time to seize Freeport], *Detikfinance*, 30 November. https://finance.detik.com/read/2017/11/30/071719/3749272/6/holding-bumn-tambang-terbentuk-saatnya-caplok-freeport

Sullivan, B. (2014) 'The export ban finally introduced: a grand compromise with much residual uncertainty', *Coal Asia Magazine*, January.

Sundaryani, F.S. (2016) 'Medco inks $2.6 billion deal for Newmont NT', *Jakarta Post*, 1 July. http://www.thejakartapost.com/news/2016/07/01/medco-inks-26-billion-deal-newmont-nt.html

Tabor, S. (2015) 'Constraints to Indonesia's economic growth', ADB Papers on Indonesia, No. 10, Asian Development Bank, Manila, December. https://www.adb.org/sites/default/files/publication/178041/ino-paper-10-2015.pdf

USAID (United States Agency for International Development) (2013) 'Economic effects of Indonesia's mineral-processing requirements for export', USAID, April. http://pdf.usaid.gov/pdf_docs/pbaaa139.pdf

Warburton, E. (2015) 'Political turf wars hurting investment in Indonesia', *East Asia Forum*, blog, 11 December. http://www.eastasiaforum.org/2015/12/11/political-turf-wars-hurting-investment-in-indonesia/

Warburton, E. (2016) 'Indonesian politics in 2016: Jokowi and the new developmentalism', *Bulletin of Indonesian Economic Studies* 52(3): 297–320.

Warburton, E. (2017) 'Resource nationalism in post-boom Indonesia: the new normal?', Analysis, Lowy Institute for International Policy, Sydney, 27 April.

Wilson, J. (2015) 'Understanding resource nationalism: economic dynamics and political institutions', *Contemporary Politics* 21(4): 1–18.

World Bank (2014) 'Development policy review 2014. Indonesia: avoiding the trap', Report No: 86025-ID, Poverty Reduction and Economic Management Department, East Asia and Pacific Region, World Bank, March. http://documents.worldbank.org/curated/en/936481468042895348/Indonesia-Avoiding-the-trap-development-policy-review-2014

7 Who is afraid of economic openness? People's perceptions of globalisation in Indonesia

Yose Rizal Damuri and Mari Pangestu

Protectionism and anti-globalisation are on the rise again. Protectionism has been rising since the global financial crisis in 2009, and populist and nationalist tendencies, especially in the United States, have escalated anti-globalisation to a whole new level. The World Trade Organization reported a significant increase in the number of trade-restrictive measures introduced by G20 countries, from a total of 381 in October 2010 to 1,671 in October 2016 (WT0 2016: 4). This is particularly worrying considering that trade growth has stagnated at the same time.

The vote in the United Kingdom in June 2016 to leave the European Union and the presidential election result in the United States in November 2016 caught everyone by surprise. In the former case, the popular vote to leave an economic bloc that has provided many benefits for the British economy was difficult to understand and seemed to run counter to the national interest. In the latter case, Donald Trump's promise to 'make America great again' by changing trading rules that he considered did not benefit the United States clearly struck a chord with many Americans. Since he came to office in January 2017, the United States has withdrawn from the Trans-Pacific Partnership (TPP), reopened negotiations on the North American Free Trade Agreement (NAFTA) and the Korea–US Free Trade Agreement (KORUS), unilaterally imposed tariffs on a number of products in the name of 'fair trade' and 'national security', and signalled that the United States will not abide by WTO rulings. More than any other country, China has been targeted due to its large trade deficit with the United States and its alleged theft of intellectual property rights. These events are indications of a contagious new populism and nationalism that may affect other parts of the world, especially with the retreat of the United States from being the champion of an open world economic order.

Indonesians had an ambivalent attitude towards economic openness even before the rise of the anti-globalisation movement in advanced countries. The increase in trade restrictions in Indonesia since 2001 has been referred to as 'creeping protectionism' (Basri and Patunru 2012; Patunru and Rahardja 2015). Marks (2017) shows that, due to an increase in trade barriers, both the nominal and effective rates of protection continued to increase between 2008 and 2015, notably for food and agricultural products. The effective rate of protection for agricultural products, for example, jumped from 17 per cent in 2008 to 41 per cent in 2015.

There are several possible explanations for the increase in trade restrictiveness in Indonesia. The most popular one is that interest groups have been able to maximise their rent-seeking activities by influencing the policy-making process. In other words, through a complex bargaining process, small but concentrated and well-organised groups have been able to lobby for greater protection for their sectors, allowing them to generate excessive profits. According to Soesastro and Basri (2004), the main beneficiaries of protectionist measures in Indonesia have been the capital-intensive and highly concentrated sectors, which have the resources to lobby government for protection. Damuri (2017) observes a similar tendency, although the form of protection involves the use of more subtle measures, such as import permits, seasonal import restrictions and technical regulations.

Another explanation for the increase in trade restrictions is that trade policy is the easiest and most visible way for politicians to show constituents that they understand what they want and are prepared to act in accordance with their wishes. While the influence of voters' trade policy perceptions has yet to be studied due to a lack of empirical evidence, they clearly do carry weight with Indonesian politicians.[1] In the agricultural sector, for instance, the government justifies the use of protectionist measures by referring to the need to support the millions of farmers in Indonesia and to achieve national food self-sufficiency. The government has long put trade barriers in place to protect most agricultural and food products, even though the restrictions lead to higher domestic retail prices, but not to increases in the prices received by farmers. In the manufacturing sector, the focus has been on protecting small-scale industries and domestic producers until they are able to compete successfully with businesses

---

1 Patunru and Rahardja (2015: 11–12), for example, discuss the tendency of Joko Widodo, initially as the mayor of Solo, then as the governor of Jakarta and now as the president of Indonesia, to listen carefully to the views of business groups and institute ad hoc (often protectionist) measures to support particular sectors.

from abroad. Public opinion is strongly in favour of such actions, as widely reflected in articles and commentary in the mass media.

In this chapter we try to provide a better understanding of Indonesians' attitudes towards economic openness, as a basis for informing the public and political debate, and for formulating trade policy. Based on a national survey conducted in 2017 by the Centre for Strategic and International Studies (CSIS) in Jakarta, we will examine public perceptions on various aspects of openness and analyse the economic and non-economic factors behind those preferences. We will not examine the *effect* of public perceptions on trade policy, however, because we lack the data to do so.

The chapter proceeds as follows. In the next section we review the literature on public perceptions of economic openness. This is followed by a background section on measures of globalisation and openness in Indonesia. We then provide an explanation of the CSIS survey and summarise the most important results. Next, we attempt to identify the factors that are most significant in influencing public perceptions. In the final section of the chapter, we discuss the implications of the main results.

A BRIEF LITERATURE REVIEW

The notion that trade policy is the outcome of a political process is widely recognised in the international trade policy literature. This framework assumes that the individual preferences of society, expressed through interest groups or voters in general, influence the political processes that shape policies on trade and trade openness. Neoclassical trade theory attributes the variety of individual preferences to the uneven distribution of the gains from trade. According to neoclassical trade theory, free trade is beneficial for the country and the world, but there are gainers and losers from free trade. Backed by proper political processes and institutions, coupled with adequate compensation for the losers, this group of individuals could become a politically potent force to increase trade barriers, despite the harm to the economy.

In this chapter we focus on how individual preferences and opinions towards openness are formed in Indonesia, without looking at the political process. Based on the neoclassical theory of trade, the literature on the formation of individual preferences provides two major explanations for people's trade policy preferences. First, under the Heckscher–Ohlin model of comparative advantage, free trade means that a country will specialise in the sectors that make intensive use of its more abundant factors of production. Since factors of production are assumed to be perfectly mobile across sectors within a country, the Stolper–Samuelson theorem further predicts that free trade benefits the abundant factors of production in the country and hurts the scarce ones. Individuals would then base their perceptions of trade policy on the factors of production they own. In a capital-abundant country, the owners of labour would be the losers and could therefore be expected to have a negative perception of free trade.

A second explanation is derived from the so-called specific-factors or Ricardo–Viner model. In this setting, at least in the short run, factors of production cannot move easily to the sectors that have a comparative advantage. Therefore, the owners of the factors of production would base their preferences on how openness affects their industries. In a simple model in which there are two factors of production, the owners of both capital and labour in the sector that is not competitive will be the losers if they cannot move to the more competitive sector, and would therefore perceive free trade negatively.

A growing number of empirical studies are trying to establish which one of these two explanations best fits the reality. In a cross-country study, Mayda and Rodrik (2005) find that trade preferences at the individual level closely follow the prediction of the Stolper–Samuelson theorem. Scheve and Slaughter (2001) find similar results for the case of the United States, and Passadila and Liao (2004) provide an example that supports this prediction for the case of the Philippines. Other studies, however, find evidence of industry-based preferences. Busch and Reinhardt (2000), for example, find that the trade policy preferences of American manufacturing workers are explained by the comparative advantage of the industry in which they work. In other words, American workers in industries with less comparative advantage or that are less competitive are more likely to have a protectionist stance towards trade policy.

In addition to the assumption of neoclassical trade theory that individuals base their preferences on whether they gain or lose from trade, other factors also appear to determine individual views on openness. Mayda and Rodrik (2005), for example, include status, relative income and political opinions among the determinants of preferences. Mansfield and Mutz (2009) argue that the distribution of the gains from trade to the factors of production does not have a major effect on individual preferences; rather, it is people's perceptions of the benefits of trade for the economy in general that determine their opinions. The authors find that ethnocentrism and foreign policy attitudes also affect people's attitudes towards openness.

GLOBALISATION AND THE DECLINE OF ECONOMIC OPENNESS IN INDONESIA

By the conventional definition of openness, the Indonesian economy is not an outward-looking one. The share of trade in GDP was only 37.4 per cent in 2016, well below the average for Southeast Asia countries (Table

Table 7.1 Selected indicators of openness, 2015–16 (% of GDP)

Indicator of openness	2015		2016	
	Indonesia	ASEAN	Indonesia	ASEAN
Trade	41.90	116.30	37.40	110.80
Current account	−2.03	3.33	−1.80	3.87
Net inflows of FDI	2.30	5.48	0.44	4.28

Source: World Development Indicators.

7.1). From an average of 17 per cent per annum before the global financial crisis, Indonesia's exports contracted by 6 per cent per annum in 2012–16, due to a sharp drop in commodity prices, low external demand and stagnant growth in global trade.[2] Inflows of foreign direct investment (FDI) declined from an already low 2.3 per cent of GDP in 2015 to just 0.4 per cent in 2016—far lower than the average for ASEAN. Indonesia is also experiencing a decline in its share of global trade: the country's exports contributed only 0.7 per cent of world exports in 2016, around 30 per cent less than in the mid-2000s, when the figure was closer to 1 per cent.

These trends are partly a result of a weakening global economy, leading to stagnant growth in international trade and investment and falling demand for commodities, which make up 60 per cent of Indonesia's exports. Despite facing similar circumstances to the rest of ASEAN, Indonesia has fared worse than other Southeast Asian countries because of its more inward-looking policies. While Indonesia's tariff rates have been declining across all products, the government's use of non-tariff measures has increased significantly. According to data from the Ministry of Trade, the share of tariff lines subject to border restriction measures rose from 10 per cent in 2011 to 35 per cent in 2015, before falling back slightly to 32 per cent in 2016. These cross-border restrictions included WTO-consistent measures related to health and technical standards (sanitary and phytosanitary measures and technical barriers to trade), but also more restrictive measures such as import bans and seasonal restrictions on imports.[3]

---

2 In 2017, exports jumped by 16 per cent due to an upturn in commodity prices and an improvement in external demand.
3 Although most of Indonesia's non-tariff measures have been consistent with WTO rules, some, such as the quarantine requirements linked to port of entry for horticultural products, have been challenged under WTO rules by Indonesia's trading partners.

Restrictive measures are also observed in the case of FDI. The restrictions on FDI are defined in the government's negative investment list, which lists sectors and subsectors closed to FDI, or open subject to certain conditions. The negative investment list was introduced in 2007 as part of Law No. 25/2007 on Capital Investment in order to create greater transparency and certainty for investors, and thus a more conducive investment climate. The negative list conformed with best practice in the selection of the sectors that were closed to FDI, with the intention of making the foreign investment regime transparent and thus, over time, more open to the relaxation of restrictions. Anything not on the negative list was open. The list was last updated in 2016. While the revised list eases restrictions in a number of fields, such as online marketplaces and film distribution, it also adds a number of sectors, such as construction services, to the areas reserved for micro, small and medium enterprises. The spirit of the negative list, which was to increase investment policy certainty, has shifted in the opposite direction by helping industries to ensure that restrictions in fact remain.

In fact, the negative list for FDI is just the starting point for foreign investors, who face many other regulations and requirements in various sector-level policies and local regulations. This is most obvious in the case of natural-resource-intensive sectors such as mining, fisheries and forestry, where policy-making reflects the rise of resource nationalism (Warburton 2017). In the mining industry, a ban on exporting certain minerals and a requirement to process raw minerals domestically have been in place for more than five years. These are complemented by divestment obligations and foreign investment restrictions for foreign investors in the oil and gas sector.

PUBLIC OPINION SURVEY ON ECONOMIC OPENNESS

Indonesia's nationalist and inward-looking policies are shaped by various factors, including public perceptions. To explore the nature of public perceptions towards economic openness further, we turn to a public opinion survey conducted in 2017 by the Centre for Strategic and International Studies (CSIS 2017). It is part of a nationwide survey on social–political matters conducted annually by CSIS, normally in the third quarter of the year. The questions cover a broad range of issues, including people's level of satisfaction with government policies and actions, their political affiliations and choices, their aspirations and their social activities. Respondents are selected randomly using a multi-stage random sampling method, to ensure even representation across provinces and the total population. The survey is conducted through face-to-face interviews with the respondents.

Table 7.2 Characteristics of the sample

Characteristic	Share (%)
Median age	31.0
Male	50.1
Median expenditure (Rp thousand/month)	1,593.8
Living in Java	56.9
Education	
University graduate	12.6
Secondary school graduate	44.6
Employed	65.9
Self-employed	24.7

Source: CSIS (2017).

Conducted in the last week of August, the annual survey for 2017 involved 1,600 respondents aged 17 or above. The main characteristics of the sample of respondents are shown in Table 7.2.

In addition to the routine questions on social and political issues, respondents were asked about various aspects of globalisation and economic openness, including their perceptions of imported products, foreign investment and foreign workers, and the general impact of globalisation. The questions on the four main aspects of economic openness – trade, investment, tourism and migration – were as follows.

1. Do you think the importation of products from abroad into Indonesia is beneficial or harmful?
2. Do you think it is beneficial or harmful to have companies from abroad operating in Indonesia?
3. What is your opinion about foreigners visiting Indonesia for tourism or business?
4. What is your opinion about having many foreign workers in Indonesia?

Respondents were asked to assess the impact of each aspect on their own economic situation as well as on the Indonesian economy in general. Four answers were available: very beneficial, beneficial, harmful or very harmful.

The results for the impact of economic openness on the Indonesian economy are presented in Figure 7.1. It shows that respondents' perceptions varied substantially depending on the aspect under consideration. In the case of imports, 48 per cent of respondents viewed the importation of products as beneficial or very beneficial for the Indonesian economy, while 50 per cent viewed it as harmful or very harmful. Respondents

Figure 7.1 Survey results: perceptions of the impact of economic openness on the economy (% of respondents)

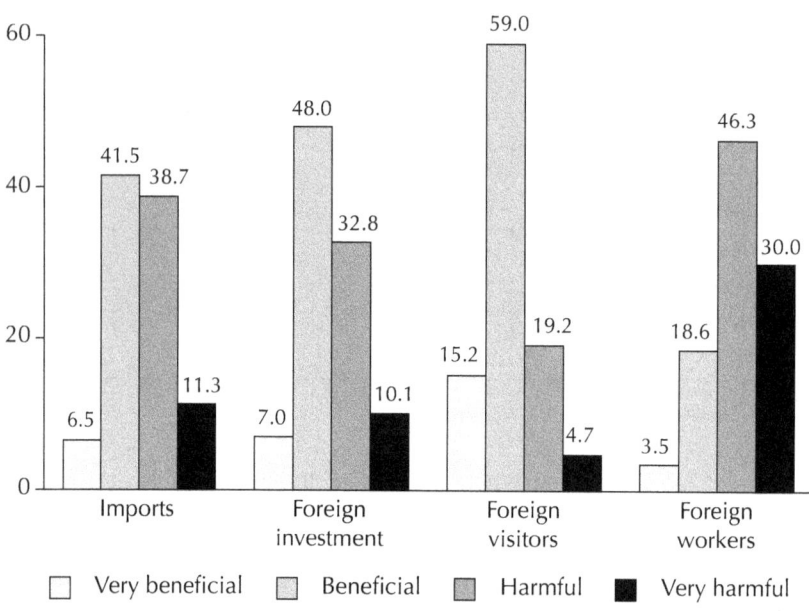

Source: CSIS (2017).

were more positive about foreign investment and foreign visitors, with 55 per cent and 74 per cent respectively viewing these as beneficial or very beneficial. However, the attitude towards foreign workers was very negative, with an overwhelming majority (76 per cent) viewing them as harmful or very harmful.

The results were similar (but slightly more negative) when respondents were asked about the impact on their own situation; for example, around 34 per cent said that foreign workers were very harmful for them personally, whereas only 30 per cent said that they were very harmful for the Indonesian economy. The coefficients of correlation between the two sets of answers — the impact on the respondents themselves and the impact on the Indonesian economy — were quite high: 0.75, 0.82 and 0.84 for imports, foreign investment and foreign workers respectively. This indicates that respondents put roughly equal value on the impact of economic openness, regardless of whether the question was in reference to themselves or to the economy.

In two related questions, respondents were asked about Indonesia's participation in cooperative international economic arrangements, and about globalisation. The questions were as follows.

Figure 7.2 Survey results: perceptions of international economic cooperation and globalisation (% of respondents)

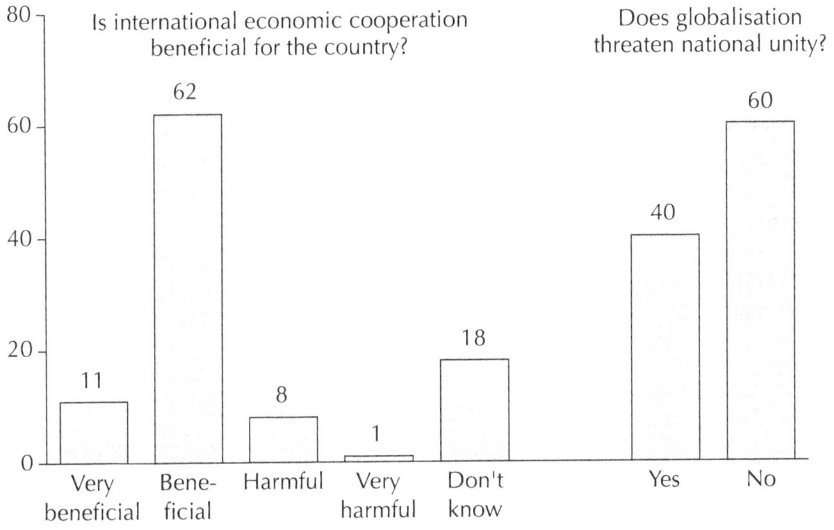

[Bar chart showing two questions:

"Is international economic cooperation beneficial for the country?" — Very beneficial: 11, Beneficial: 62, Harmful: 8, Very harmful: 1, Don't know: 18

"Does globalisation threaten national unity?" — Yes: 40, No: 60]

Source: CSIS (2017).

5   Do you think Indonesia's participation in various cooperative international economic arrangements is beneficial for Indonesia's economic interests?
6   Do you think globalisation poses a threat to the unity of the nation?

The results are shown in Figure 7.2. Respondents were far more positive about international economic cooperation than they had been about imports, foreign investment and foreign workers: 73 per cent thought that it was beneficial or very beneficial and only 9 per cent thought that it was harmful or very harmful. A sizeable 18 per cent of respondents, however, were unable to provide a definitive response to the question. On the second question, most respondents (60 per cent) did not think that globalisation posed a threat to national unity; nevertheless, the percentage that did think it could harm national unity (40 per cent) was relatively high.

DETERMINANTS OF INDIVIDUAL OPINIONS ON OPENNESS

What explains the patterns of responses described above? In this section, we use the data available in the wider CSIS national survey (for example, on the political attitudes and affiliations of the respondents) to draw some conclusions about the determinants of individual attitudes towards openness. We run simple logistic regression models to better understand the individual preferences of respondents. The data and methodology are explained in detail below.

Dependent variables

We examine individual opinions on three aspects of economic openness: imports, foreign investment and foreign workers (questions 1, 2 and 4 in the previous section). The four possible responses to each question are coded as follows: 1 = very harmful; 2 = harmful; 3 = beneficial; and 4 = very beneficial. Therefore, each dependent variable is an ordinal variable, where a higher order represents a more positive attitude towards openness.

Independent variables

To explain variation in individual perceptions of openness, we examine the demographic characteristics and political perceptions of the respondents. Based on the factors identified in the earlier literature review, we group these into three categories of potential determinants: economic factors, demographic factors and political factors.

The economic factors include a variable for education as a proxy for human capital and skills. In our simple model, we differentiate between respondents who have graduated from university and those who have not. The hypothesis is that university graduates will tend to have a more positive attitude towards openness. This is in line with the prediction of the Stolper–Samuelson theorem that the factors used intensively in production will receive greater benefits from economic openness.

The next economic variable is employment. In our study we differentiate between individuals who are employed and those who are not. For those who are employed, we use the information from the survey to identify three types of occupation: student, self-employed and employee.[4] We expect that people with a job will have a more positive attitude towards openness.

The last economic variable is relative income, represented by a dummy variable for individuals who are in the top 33 percentiles of the sample by monthly expenditure. We expect that people in the top group will have a more positive attitude towards openness.

---

4 Each occupation is represented by a dummy variable. In this case, the baseline model defines the case of people who do not work.

Our empirical work also makes use of the demographic characteristics of the sample, namely age, gender, access to information and religion. We hypothesise that older people will be more negative towards economic openness. We measure access to information by formulating an index based on the respondent's frequency of access to four types of media: radio, television, newspapers and online media. Respondents who access at least three of the four media on a daily basis are given a score of 1, while those who do not are given a score of 0. Our hypothesis is that people with better access to information will be more positive towards economic openness. We use another dummy variable to represent the religion of respondents, giving a score of 1 if the individual is a Muslim and 0 otherwise.

The third group of determinants focuses on political affiliations and attitudes. We capture the political dimension by looking at whether the individual voted for the current president, Joko Widodo (Jokowi), during the presidential election in 2014. To capture political attitudes, we use a dummy variable for satisfaction with the current general economic situation. Finally, we use a dummy variable for the level of concern about national unity, which can also be expected to affect an individual's preference for economic openness. The independent variables are summarised in Table 7.3.

Estimation results

We now try to estimate the parameters related to the set of independent variables described above in order to determine which factors are significant in affecting individual preferences towards openness. We estimate three models to examine the determinants of preferences in the three major areas of openness identified above: imports, foreign investment and foreign workers. The results are summarised in Table 7.4.

Here, we discuss only the statistically significant variables from our estimations of the three models. Instead of presenting the estimated coefficients of the models, we choose to show the marginal effect of each variable for the third possible response: '3 = beneficial'. It shows the change in probability that someone with certain characteristics will assert that openness is beneficial for the Indonesian economy. For example, the marginal effect of the variable for a university education on imports, which is 0.074 for the response '3 = beneficial', can be interpreted as indicating that an individual who has graduated from university would be 7.4 per cent more likely to respond that imports are beneficial for the economy. More complete results of the estimations are available in Appendix A7.1.

Among the economic variables, university education is statistically significant in affecting the opinion of the respondents towards economic openness, except in the case of foreign workers. The probability that

Table 7.3 Summary of independent variables and the expected signs

Variable	Explanation	Expected sign
Economic variables		
University graduate	Dummy variable; university graduate = 1	Positive
Student	Dummy variable; student = 1	Positive
Self-employed	Dummy variable; self-employed = 1	Positive
Employee	Dummy variable; employee = 1	Positive
High relative income	Among the top 33 percentiles of the sample by monthly expenditure = 1	Positive
Demographic variables		
Age		Negative
Gender	Dummy variable; male = 1	
Access to information	Index of frequency of access to four types of media: radio, television, newspapers and online media	Positive
Religion	Dummy variable; Muslim = 1	
Political variables		
Political affiliation	Dummy variable; voted for current president = 1	Positive
Political attitudes	Dummy variable; satisfied with current general economic situation = 1	Positive
Unity of the nation	Dummy variable; concerned about unity of the nation = 1	Negative

Source: Authors.

individuals with a university education will view imports and foreign investment as beneficial is 7.4 per cent and 9.5 per cent higher, respectively, than the probability that those without a university education will do so. This is in line with the theoretical prediction that people with more skills and education will have a more positive attitude towards economic openness. The same individuals do not, however, maintain that positive sentiment when it comes to foreign workers. In this respect university graduates are no different to the rest of our sample. Students and the self-employed are more likely to welcome imports than people who are not employed. In addition, students are one of only two groups to welcome foreign workers (the other being Jokowi voters).

Among the demographic factors, age, religion and access to information significantly affect opinions about all aspects of economic openness,

Table 7.4 Marginal effect of statistically significant variables for the response '3 = beneficial'

Statistically significant variable	Dep. variable: imports	Dep. variable: foreign investment	Dep. variable: foreign workers
University graduate	0.074	0.095	Not significant
Student	0.089	Not significant	0.063
Self-employed	0.047	Not significant	Not significant
Age	−0.002	−0.001	Not significant
Religion = Muslim	−0.126	−0.061	−0.073
Good access to information	−0.160	−0.086	Not significant
Political affiliation	0.039	0.056	0.044
Political attitudes	0.044	0.060	Not significant
Unity of the nation	−0.068	−0.087	Not significant

Source: Authors' estimations.

except in the case of foreign workers. Older people are less likely to see the benefits of imports and foreign investment; each one-year increase in age makes an individual 0.2 per cent less likely to view imports and 0.1 per cent less likely to view foreign investment as beneficial. Religion is also a statistically significant determinant of a person's attitude towards all three aspects of openness, with the relationship being negative.

Interestingly, we find that people who have better access to information through the media tend to be less favourable towards openness. Individuals with good daily access to the media are 16 per cent less likely to regard imports, and 8.6 per cent less likely to regard foreign investment, as beneficial for the economy. This suggests that there may be a relationship between the content of the media on economic openness and people's perceptions towards economic openness. This is confirmed by a scan of Indonesian newspapers, which shows that news articles are generally negative on the issues of imports, foreign investment and foreign workers.[5]

---

5 The authors analysed the content of the two biggest newspapers in Indonesia (*Kompas* and *Jakarta Post*) during the six-month period before the presidential election in 2014. We found 327 articles in which we could identify 577 narrations on imports, foreign investment or foreign workers. Of the 577 narrations, 101 claimed that imports would slash Indonesia's industrial competitiveness and flood the domestic market with foreign products, and 58 asserted that economic openness would erode Indonesia's sovereignty in various areas, such as food, energy and policy-making.

Turning to the political factors, our estimation reveals a close relationship between political affiliation and perceptions of economic openness. Individuals who voted for the current president, Joko Widodo, are 3.9 per cent more likely to regard imports, 5.6 per cent more likely to regard foreign investment and 4.4 per cent more likely to regard even foreign workers as beneficial for the economy. People who feel satisfied with the current general economic situation are also more likely to accept the benefits of imports and foreign workers. Finally, as expected, people who feel that globalisation endangers the unity of the nation tend be less likely to view imports and foreign investment as beneficial for the Indonesian economy. The estimation results for the political variables are therefore in line with expectations.

It is interesting to note that most of the factors included in our estimation do not explain respondents' attitudes towards foreign workers. Only three variables are significantly related to the variable for foreign workers: religion (where being a Muslim is negatively related to the acceptance of foreign workers), political affiliation (where voting for Joko Widodo is positively related to the acceptance of foreign workers) and being a student (which is also positively related to the acceptance of foreign workers). Given the strongly negative sentiment towards foreign workers in the CSIS survey, with 76 per cent of respondents—regardless of their economic views or political attitudes—viewing them as harmful or very harmful, it is understandable that we could not find a clear explanatory relationship between this aspect of economic openness and most of the variables.

Some variables do not significantly affect respondents' opinions. Among the economic factors in our model, for example, being an employee does not significantly affect attitudes towards any aspect of economic openness, compared with being unemployed. Having a high relative income also does not affect perceptions of the benefits of the various aspects of economic openness. There is also no evidence that male respondents have different opinions to their female counterparts.

As a simple robustness test, we use ordinary least squares (OLS) to test all the variables explained above, in all three models. The results are quite similar in terms of the significance and direction of the effects, as shown in the tables in Appendix A7.1.

CONCLUSIONS AND IMPLICATIONS

In this chapter, we have attempted to examine the political economy of trade policy and openness in Indonesia. Policies related to economic openness are shaped by the attitudes and preferences of individuals, and by the political process. In this study we have focused on individual attitudes and on the various factors that explain those attitudes. Using a unique dataset compiled from a survey conducted by CSIS (2017), we were able to analyse the patterns of preferences and to identify some factors that may explain people's perceptions of imports, foreign investment, foreign visitors and foreign workers.

We found that the proportion of respondents viewing imports as harmful or very harmful (50 per cent) was about the same as the proportion viewing them as beneficial or very beneficial (48 per cent), and that most respondents had a positive attitude towards foreign investment (55 per cent) and (especially) foreign visitors (74 per cent). However, the sentiment towards foreign workers was strongly negative, with 76 per cent of respondents believing they were harmful or very harmful for the economy.

Interestingly, the majority of respondents (60 per cent) did not think that globalisation threatened national unity, indicating that anti-globalisation sentiment is not particularly strong in Indonesia. Moreover, 73 per cent of respondents viewed international economic cooperation as beneficial or very beneficial. However, the high proportion of respondents who said that they did not know (18 per cent) suggests that the government and other stakeholders need to educate the public on how cooperative international arrangements – such as trade agreements, rules that ensure fair trade, capacity building and technical cooperation – can help to maximise the benefits of open trade and reduce and manage the harmful effects of globalisation.

In analysing the determinants of people's perceptions, we identified three categories of possible explanatory factors: economic, demographic and political. The statistical analysis used ordinary logistic regression to estimate how these characteristics explained perceptions of openness. Basically the estimation showed the probability that a person with certain characteristics would hold the view that openness was beneficial for Indonesia. We found, as expected, that the economic factor of higher education and the demographic factor of younger age were associated with a higher probability of having a positive attitude towards imports and foreign investment. However, there was no evidence to support an association between these characteristics and a more positive attitude towards foreign workers. In fact, it would seem that the attitude towards foreign workers was uniformly negative, irrespective of individual characteristics. One possible explanation is that the public perceives foreign workers as a real and direct threat to jobs, both for themselves and for their communities. Also, shortly before the survey was conducted, the media publicised several high-profile cases of Chinese workers working illegally in Indonesia, including some involving infrastructure projects that had been contracted out to Chinese companies. This is consistent with the interesting result noted earlier, that individuals with good access to information tend to be less favourable towards all aspects of economic openness.

The results for the political variables were generally strong and significant. People who voted for Joko Widodo in the 2014 election had a higher probability of being positive towards imports, foreign investment and even foreign workers. More analysis is needed, but this result would suggest that the use of anti-globalisation rhetoric would probably not persuade Jokowi voters to switch their allegiance. Another expected result was that people who felt satisfied with the current general economic situation were more likely to accept economic openness.

These results imply that the government will need to manage negative perceptions if it hopes to introduce trade policies that promote openness. The most sensitive issue appears to be that of foreign workers. This needs to be dealt with in a balanced way, by providing accurate information, explaining government policy and demonstrating the need for Indonesia to acquire foreign talent that is not available in Indonesia. Without foreign talent, it is difficult to see how Indonesia can encourage innovation and increase productivity and efficiency. The results also point to an anti-globalisation view propagated by the media. More research is needed to understand the causality: does the media have an anti-globalisation perspective because it thinks this will be popular with its audience, or is it the culprit in influencing or reinforcing anti-globalisation sentiment? The government and other stakeholders should develop a communication strategy and narrative that addresses the Indonesian public's perceptions and fears and provides insights into how to manage any perceived or real harm arising from a shift towards openness. Such a narrative is important to balance the growing anti-globalisation sentiment in Indonesia, prevent the country from shifting to the far right or the far left, and protect the country from harmful policies of a protectionist or nationalist nature.

This study is just a starting point to better understand the factors behind the negative attitudes towards openness and the tendency towards protectionism in Indonesia. Further research should be conducted to gain more insights into this issue. First, researchers could link data from other sources that would help to explain the formation of individual preferences to the data from the CSIS survey, and attempt to improve the econometric and statistical exercises. Second, to ascertain whether there is a link between individual preferences and trade policies on openness, researchers could examine how individual preferences are internalised into the political and policy-making processes. Further disaggregation could also be undertaken to see how individual preferences are linked to policies on particular sectors and industries, instead of the general preferences captured by the CSIS survey. Third, as mentioned above, a more in-depth analysis of the influence of the media is needed to determine the direction of causality between media reporting and audience perceptions. This should include an analysis of the new forms of social media, which have become increasingly important in affecting public perceptions, both in other countries and in Indonesia.

REFERENCES

Basri, M.C., and A.A. Patunru (2012) 'How to keep trade policy open: the case of Indonesia', *Bulletin of Indonesian Economic Studies* 48(2): 191–208.

Busch, M.L., and E. Reinhardt (2000) 'Geography, international trade, and political mobilization in US industries', *American Journal of Political Science* 44(4): 703–19.

CSIS (Centre for Strategic and International Studies) (2017) 'Laporan survei nasional 2017' [National survey 2017], CSIS, Jakarta.

Damuri, Y.R. (2017) 'Hidden measures: Indonesia's trade policy in the 21st century', *Indonesian Quarterly* 45(3).

Mansfield, E.D., and D.C. Mutz (2009) 'Support for free trade: self-interest, sociotropic politics, and out-group anxiety', *International Organization* 63(3): 425–57.

Marks, S.P. (2017) 'Non-tariff trade regulations in Indonesia: nominal and effective rates of protection', *Bulletin of Indonesian Economic Studies* 53(3): 333–57.

Mayda, A.M., and D. Rodrik (2005) 'Why are some people (and countries) more protectionist than others?', *European Economic Review* 49(6): 1,393–430.

Passadila, G.O., and C.M. Liao (2004) 'Determinants of individual trade policy preference in the Philippines', PIDS Discussion Paper Series No. 2004-16, Philippine Institute for Development Studies (PIDS), Makati City.

Patunru, A.A., and S. Rahardja (2015) 'Trade protectionism in Indonesia: bad times and bad policy', Analysis, Lowy Institute for International Policy, Sydney, 30 July.

Scheve, K.F., and M.J. Slaughter (2001) 'What determines individual trade policy preferences?', *Journal of International Economics* 54(2): 267–92.

Soesastro, H., and M.C. Basri (2005) 'The political economy of trade policy in Indonesia', CSIS Economics Working Paper Series WPE 092, Centre for Strategic and International Studies (CSIS), Jakarta.

Warburton, E. (2017) 'Resource nationalism in post-boom Indonesia: the new normal?', Analysis, Lowy Institute for International Policy, Sydney, 27 April.

WTO (World Trade Organization) (2016) 'Report on G20 trade measures (mid-May 2016 to mid-October 2016)', WTO, Geneva, 10 November. https://www.wto.org/english/news_e/news16_e/g20_wto_report_november16_e.pdf

APPENDIX A7.1: METHODOLOGY AND RESULTS

Given that our dependent variables are constructed as discreet and ordinal variables, we opted to use ordered logit estimations. Individual opinions of economic openness are assumed to be a function of a vector X, the independent variables that determine the marginal benefits or costs of openness. Unfortunately, these marginal benefits are unobserved. What we can observe is the individual response as a choice between four opinions: 1 = very harmful, 2 = harmful, 3 = beneficial and 4 = very beneficial. Therefore, we can consider the marginal benefits of openness as a latent variable y^* that determines the choice of preferences. Thus,

$$y^* = X\beta + e$$

where β is the coefficient of independent variables X, and e is the error term with a standard logistic distribution with mean zero and variance one.

The value of y^* corresponds to the choice of opinion given certain cut-off points. For example, an individual response of '3 = beneficial' could be interpreted as meaning that the individual's marginal benefits from openness are greater than the category 3 cut-off point ($y^* > \mu_2$), while an individual response of '2 = harmful' would mean that the individual regards the marginal benefits from openness as being less than the category 3 cut-off point ($y^* < \mu_2$).

Another way to interpret the results of the estimations is to calculate the probability that certain characteristics will lead to certain choices. We can therefore calculate the probability that, for example, a person with a university education, or working as an employee, will hold the opinion that imports are beneficial for the Indonesian economy.

Table A7.1 Results of the estimation for dependent variable: opinion of imports (1 = very harmful, 2 = harmful, 3 = beneficial, 4 = very beneficial)

Variable	Ordered logit			OLS
	(1)	(2)	(3)	
University graduate	0.337**	0.362**	0.374**	0.163***
	(0.15)	(0.16)	(0.16)	(0.06)
Student	0.289*	0.361**	0.451**	0.180**
	(0.16)	(0.18)	(0.18)	(0.07)
Self-employed	0.224**	0.241*	0.239*	0.092*
	(0.11)	(0.12)	(0.12)	(0.05)
Employee	−0.099	−0.035	−0.017	−0.017
	(0.14)	(0.15)	(0.15)	(0.06)
Age		−0.007*	−0.010**	−0.004***
		(0.00)	(0.00)	(0.00)
Gender = male		−0.045	−0.044	−0.005
		(0.11)	(0.11)	(0.04)
High relative income		0.022	0.028	0.026
		(0.11)	(0.11)	(0.04)
Religion = Muslim		−0.770***	−0.635***	−0.233***
		(0.16)	(0.16)	(0.06)
Good access to information		−0.842***	−0.808***	−0.314***
		(0.27)	(0.27)	(0.10)
Voted for current president			0.199**	0.088**
			(0.10)	(0.04)
Satisfied with current general economic situation			0.224**	0.104**
			(0.11)	(0.04)
Globalisation threatens unity			−0.341***	−0.131***
			(0.10)	(0.04)
Constant				2.821***
				(0.10)
No. of observations	1,580	1,575	1,575	1,575

Note: Standard errors are in parentheses. * = $p < 0.10$; ** = $p < 0.05$; *** = $p < 0.01$.
Source: Authors' estimations.

Table A7.2 Results of the estimation for dependent variable: opinion of foreign investment (1 = very harmful, 2 = harmful, 3 = beneficial, 4 = very beneficial)

Variable	Ordered logit			OLS
	(1)	(2)	(3)	
	(0.15)	(0.16)	(0.16)	(0.06)
Student	−0.049	−0.004	0.140	0.062
	(0.16)	(0.18)	(0.18)	(0.07)
Self-employed	0.065	0.103	0.097	0.053
	(0.11)	(0.12)	(0.12)	(0.05)
Employee	−0.092	−0.041	−0.015	0.006
	(0.15)	(0.16)	(0.16)	(0.06)
Age		−0.002	−0.007*	−0.003**
		(0.00)	(0.00)	(0.00)
Gender = male		−0.100	−0.102	−0.036
		(0.11)	(0.11)	(0.04)
High relative income		0.109	0.120	0.068
		(0.11)	(0.11)	(0.04)
Religion = Muslim		−0.529***	−0.326**	−0.122*
		(0.16)	(0.16)	(0.06)
Good access to information		−0.510*	−0.461*	−0.195*
		(0.27)	(0.27)	(0.11)
Voted for current president			0.300***	0.117***
			(0.10)	(0.04)
Satisfied with current general economic situation			0.321***	0.140***
			(0.11)	(0.04)
Globalisation threatens unity			−0.467***	−0.175***
			(0.10)	(0.04)
Constant				2.723***
				(0.10)
No. of observations	1,579	1,574	1,574	1,574

Note: Standard errors are in parentheses. * = $p < 0.10$; ** = $p < 0.05$; *** = $p < 0.01$.
Source: Authors' estimations.

Table A7.3 Results of the estimation for dependent variable: opinion of foreign workers (1 = very harmful, 2 = harmful, 3 = beneficial, 4 = very beneficial)

Variable	Ordered logit			OLS
	(1)	(2)	(3)	
	(0.15)	(0.16)	(0.15)	(0.06)
Student	0.330**	0.347**	0.431**	0.169**
	(0.16)	(0.18)	(0.18)	(0.07)
Self-employed	0.057	0.051	0.040	0.002
	(0.11)	(0.12)	(0.12)	(0.05)
Employee	0.050	0.058	0.071	0.015
	(0.14)	(0.15)	(0.15)	(0.06)
Age		−0.002	−0.004	−0.002
		(0.00)	(0.00)	(0.00)
Gender = male		−0.003	−0.000	0.012
		(0.11)	(0.11)	(0.04)
High relative income		0.093	0.103	0.034
		(0.11)	(0.11)	(0.04)
Religion = Muslim		0.603***	−0.499***	−0.196***
		(0.16)	(0.16)	(0.06)
Good access to information		−0.174	−0.199	−0.068
		(0.27)	(0.27)	(0.11)
Voted for current president			0.304***	0.123***
			(0.10)	(0.04)
Satisfied with current general economic situation			0.048	0.040
			(0.11)	(0.05)
Globalisation threatens unity			−0.143	−0.050
			(0.10)	(0.04)
Constant				2.119***
				(0.10)
No. of observations	1,583	1,578	1,578	1,578

Note: Standard errors are in parentheses. * = $p<0.10$; ** = $p<0.05$; *** = $p<0.01$.
Source: Authors' estimations.

PART 3

Impact of and response to globalisation

8 Anti-globalisation, poverty and inequality in Indonesia

*Arief Anshory Yusuf and Peter Warr**

The 1997–98 Asian financial crisis was a turning point for Indonesia, as it was for many other East Asian countries. In addition to the economic consequences, Indonesia experienced dramatic political change, including a transition to electoral democracy and far-reaching government decentralisation. In the post-crisis period, the average growth rate of real GDP per capita has been only marginally lower than during the two decades preceding the crisis, but the rate of poverty reduction has slowed significantly. Something seems to have happened to make growth substantially less effective in reducing poverty. Simultaneously, Indonesia has experienced a huge increase in measured economic inequality. The slowdown in the rate of poverty reduction per unit of growth and the increase in inequality can be viewed as quantitative aspects of the same distributional phenomenon, in which different segments of the population recovered from the crisis at widely divergent rates. What caused this to happen?

The present study marks the initial step in a research program in which the authors aim to explore competing hypotheses that might explain the change in the poverty–inequality nexus since the crisis. The hypothesis examined in this article relates to what we will call 'anti-globalisation': resistance to the increasing reliance on international trade that has been a characteristic of globalisation, with that resistance taking the form of tightened restrictions on international trade. At the same time as inequality has increased in Indonesia, protectionism has also risen, both internationally and within Indonesia. We hypothesise that anti-globalisation has caused at least some of the slowdown in poverty reduction and increase

---

* In fond memory of our colleague, Professor Rina Oktaviani.

Figure 8.1 Poverty incidence, 1970–2016 (% of population)

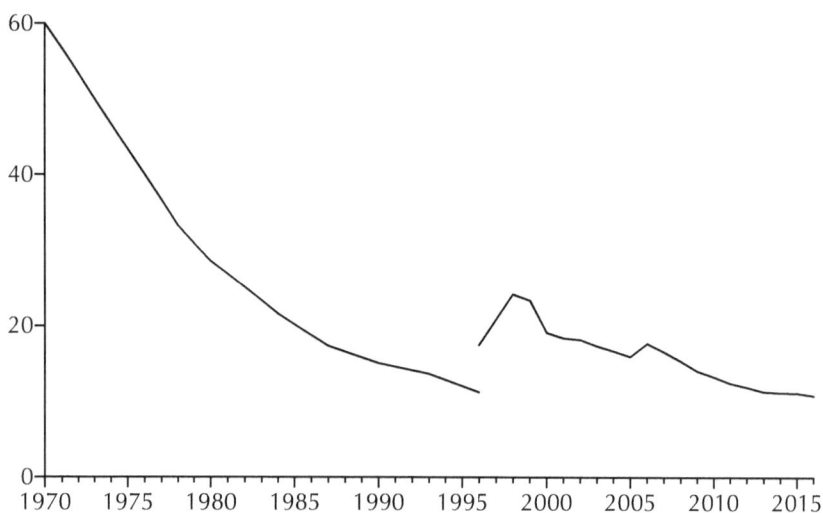

Note: The break in the line marks a change in the way BPS calculates poverty, with the new method leading to higher reported poverty incidence than previously.
Source: BPS.

in inequality. We will examine the extent to which the increase in protectionism in the global economy, and within Indonesia itself, can explain the changes in economic outcomes experienced by different segments of the Indonesian population.

First, we discuss in more depth the slowdown in poverty reduction and increase in inequality experienced in Indonesia since the financial crisis. We then provide more detail on the rise of protectionism, both in the international economy and within Indonesia. Next, we describe the economic model used to analyse the effects of protectionism on poverty and inequality. Finally, we summarise the results.

SLOWDOWN IN POVERTY REDUCTION, RISE IN INEQUALITY

Over the four and a half decades for which data are available, the incidence of absolute poverty has declined dramatically in Indonesia (Figure 8.1). Over the two decades immediately preceding the Asian financial crisis, 1976–96, poverty incidence at the national level declined on average by 1.44 per cent per annum (Table 8.1). This means that each year, on average, 1.44 per cent of the Indonesian population moved from levels of real expenditure per person below the poverty line to levels above

Table 8.1 Change in poverty incidence and inequality, 1976–96, 2000–08 and 2008–16

Year	Poverty incidence (%)	Inequality (Gini)
1976	40.1	0.346
1996	11.3	0.365
Annual change, 1976–96	**−1.4**	**0.001**
2000	19.1	0.303
2008	15.4	0.367
Annual change, 2000–08	**−0.5**	**0.008**
2008	15.4	0.367
2016	10.9	0.397
Annual change, 2008–16	**−0.6**	**0.004**

Source: BPS.

the line, holding the real value of the poverty line constant. This decline occurred in both rural and urban areas and in all parts of the country, though not at the same rate. The damaging effects of the 1997–98 financial crisis included a temporary increase in poverty incidence. The period of economic recovery that began roughly in 2000 brought a resumption of poverty reduction, but at much lower rates than previously. In the post-crisis period (2000–16), national poverty incidence declined on average by 0.53 per cent per annum. Thus, the post-crisis rate was lower than the pre-crisis rate by 1.44 − 0.53 = 0.91 percentage points per year, representing a 63 per cent decline in the rate at which poverty fell each year.

To some extent, a lower rate of poverty reduction after the crisis was to be expected given the fall in economic growth: the average annual rate of real GDP growth per person dropped from 4.44 per cent in the pre-crisis period (1976–96) to 3.93 per cent in the post-crisis period (2000–16). But this 11 per cent reduction in real GDP growth per person was much smaller than the 63 per cent decline in the rate of poverty reduction.

The slowdown in the rate of poverty reduction per unit of economic growth coincided with an increase in economic inequality. Figure 8.2 tracks inequality in Indonesia, as measured by the Gini coefficient, based on expenditure per household member, over the period 1976–2016 (see also Table 8.1). The Gini coefficient can in theory vary between 0 and 1, where higher values indicate greater inequality. Figure 8.2 shows that the Gini coefficient barely changed during the two decades before the Asian

Figure 8.2   Gini coefficient of inequality, 1976–2016

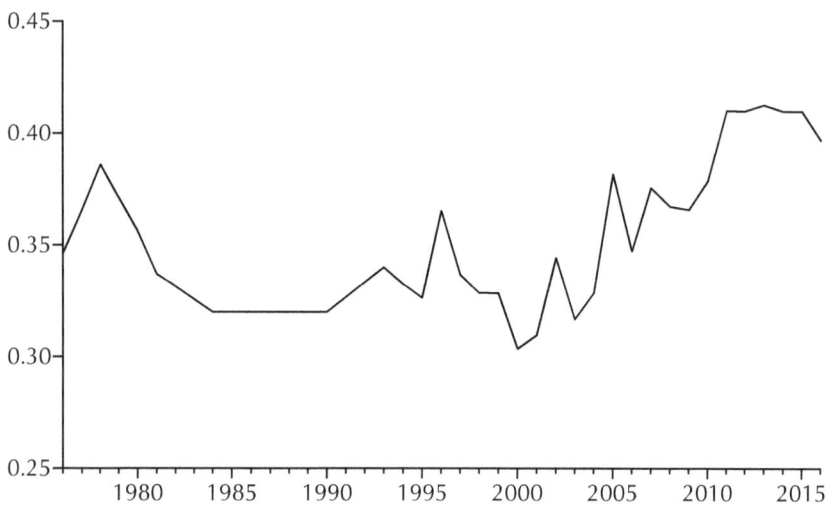

Source: BPS.

financial crisis. It fell during the crisis itself, from 0.365 in 1996 to 0.303 in 2000, because, although the entire population suffered, better-off Indonesians were more seriously affected than poorer Indonesians. The Gini coefficient then increased over the next decade and a half to reach 0.397 in 2016. This post-crisis rise in measured inequality was one of the largest increases ever recorded for any country.[1]

RISING PROTECTIONISM

World trade grew at about double the rate of world GDP over the decade and a half prior to the 2007–08 global financial crisis (Figure 8.3). As a consequence, the ratio of global trade to GDP increased significantly during this period (Figure 8.4). The growth in world trade slowed during the crisis and has still not recovered. World GDP growth was briefly negative but has since rebounded, while not quite regaining its pre-crisis level. Since the crisis, the growth rates of world trade and world GDP have been

---

1   The largest recorded rate of increase in the Gini coefficient is thought to have occurred in the former Soviet Union, immediately following its break-up in 1991. Indonesia's post-crisis rate of increase seems to be the second highest.

Figure 8.3   Growth in world trade and GDP, 1990–2016 (% p.a.)

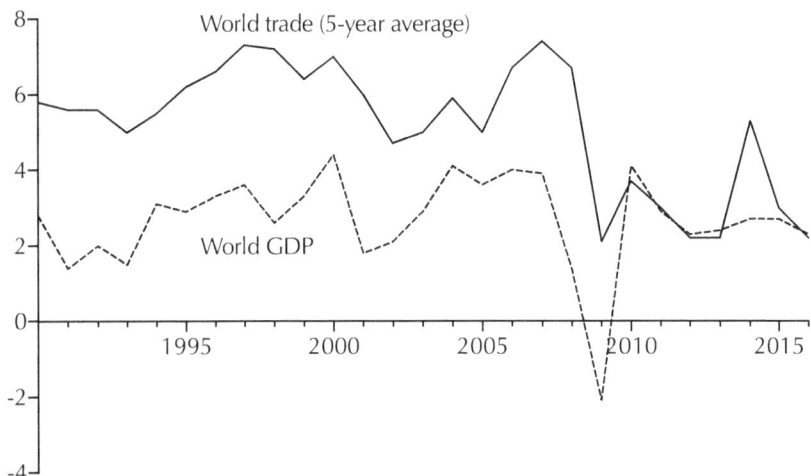

Source: World Bank, *World Development Indicators*, various issues.

Figure 8.4   Trade-to-GDP ratio, Indonesia and the world, 1990–2016 (%)

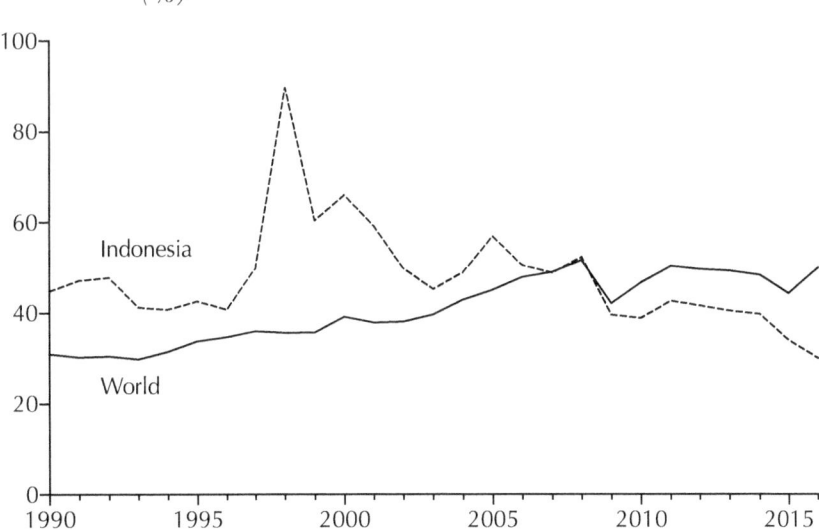

Source: World Bank, *World Development Indicators*, various issues.

Figure 8.5   Trade restrictions in G20 countries since October 2008 (no.)

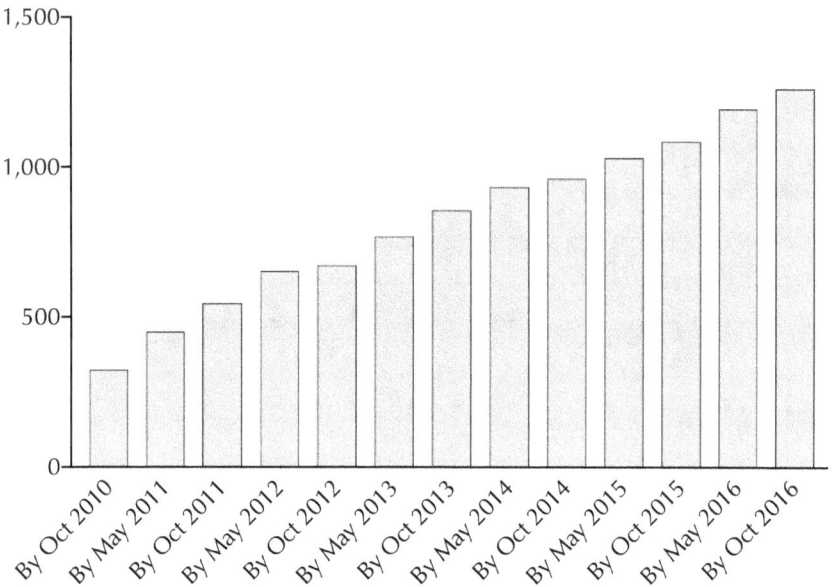

Source: World Trade Organization (2016).

about the same. As a result, the global trade-to-GDP ratio has stagnated in the post-crisis period.

In the case of Indonesia, the trade-to-GDP ratio has fallen steadily since the 1997–98 Asian financial crisis. In 2016 it was only about two-thirds its level prior to the crisis (Figure 8.4).

The 18th Global Trade Alert Report (Evenett and Fritz 2015) draws attention to a retreat from globalisation in many countries. This has taken the form of increased protectionism, especially in response to the global financial crisis (Figure 8.5). The report shows that the commodity categories in which trade declined were the same as the categories in which protection increased. It therefore attributes the slowdown in the growth of global trade relative to global GDP to rising protectionism, particularly in the G20 countries.

Indonesia is one of the G20 countries in which protectionism has increased since the global financial crisis. In an important recent paper, Marks (2017) has estimated the effective rates of protection (ERPs) across 140 tradable-goods sectors in the Indonesian economy in early 2015, using value-added shares as weights. His estimates take into account the effects of most-favoured-nation and preferential-import tariff schedules, anti-dumping and safeguard duties, export levies, duty drawbacks

Table 8.2 Nominal rates of protection by sector, 2008 and 2015 (%)

Sector	2008	2015	Change, 2008–15
Food crops	12.5	27.7	15.2
Estate & other crops	–0.3	2.0	2.3
Livestock & their products	0.9	8.8	7.9
Forestry	–4.0	–4.2	–0.2
Fisheries	0.2	0.3	0.1
Oil & gas extraction	0.6	0.1	–0.5
Other mining	–13.1	–22.1	–9.0
Food, beverages & tobacco	3.0	10.6	7.6
Textiles, apparel & leather	0.7	3.7	3.0
Wood products	–0.1	0.6	0.7
Paper products	0.7	1.4	0.7
Chemicals	1.7	3.2	1.5
Oil refining & LNG	0.2	0.4	0.2
Non-metal products	2.0	4.7	2.7
Metals & metal products	3.3	6.7	3.4
Machinery & transport equipment	4.7	7.7	3.0
Other manufacturing	2.1	4.3	2.2

Source: Marks (2017: Table 4).

and exemptions, domestic subsidies and excise taxes. He finds that both the magnitude and the dispersion of ERPs were higher in early 2015 than in early 2008, and that much of the variability was related to the expanded use of quantitative trade restrictions. In particular, the regulations examined raised a measure of the cost of living by 7.6 per cent in 2015, compared with 2.0 per cent in 2008. Table 8.2, drawn from Marks (2017), indicates that between 2008 and 2015 nominal rates of protection in Indonesia changed most significantly in four product categories, three of them food sectors and the other one a mining sector. In the three food categories, food crops, livestock and their products, and manufactured food (food, beverages and tobacco), nominal rates of protection against imports increased by 15.2 per cent, 7.9 per cent and 7.6 per cent respectively. In the mining category – 'other mining', which includes tin, nickel, bauxite and copper – *dis*-protection, reflecting export taxation, increased by 9 per cent in absolute value.

APPLICATION OF THE INDONESIA-E3 MODEL

Changes in rates of protection in countries other than Indonesia alter the prices for commodities and traded inputs faced by Indonesia in world markets. This in turn affects the domestic prices faced by both producers and consumers within Indonesia, but the transmission of international price changes to domestic price changes is conditioned by Indonesia's trade policies. Changes in Indonesia's own protection policies alter the relationship between domestic prices and international prices. These policies affect the welfare of Indonesian households, by changing both their incomes and the prices they face for consumer goods. In this study, we analyse these complex relationships using INDONESIA-E3, a multi-household, multi-sector computable general equilibrium (CGE) model of the Indonesian economy. The essence of the analysis is a comparison of the welfare of households in the observed circumstance, in which the above anti-globalisation policies are in place, and their welfare under a hypothetical alternative set of policies – the counterfactual – in which those policies are absent.

The distinctive feature of the INDONESIA-E3 model, and one that is very important for this study, is the disaggregation of households by expenditure class. The multi-household feature is applied not only to the expenditure or demand side of the model, but also to the income side. This allows precise estimation of the effect that shocks have on different types of households, facilitating measurement of their impact on inequality and poverty incidence. In the literature on poverty impact analysis using CGE models, this class of model is called an integrated CGE model (Bourguignon, Robilliard and Robinson 2003). In an integrated CGE model, each household is linked to its sources of income (through the market for factors of production) and to its areas of expenditure (through the market for commodities). In the widely used top-down method of integrating data on households into modelling, the CGE model is separate from the poverty module and there is only a one-directional relationship between them. But in an integrated CGE model, such as INDONESIA-E3, there is no separation between the model and the poverty module – both are contained within the one fully integrated model.

INDONESIA-E3 has been used in the past to analyse the effect of fuel pricing reform on the expenditure, income and consumption patterns of Indonesian households (Yusuf and Resosudarmo 2008); the impact of a carbon tax on poverty incidence and other measures of household welfare (Yusuf and Resosudarmo 2015); and the effect of subsidy interventions on land use and carbon emissions (Warr and Yusuf 2011).[2]

---

2 A more detailed exposition of the model can be found in Yusuf (2008).

The INDONESIA-E3 model uses a social accounting matrix (SAM) for its database. The SAM was constructed to allow the integration of highly disaggregated households, sufficient for accurate distributional analysis. It covers up to 175 industries, 175 commodities and 200 household groupings (100 in urban areas and 100 in rural areas, grouped in each case by percentile of real expenditure per capita). The data used to construct the SAM are taken from an Indonesian input–output table, the official SAM published in 2008 by the central statistical agency (BPS) and, most importantly, household-level data from the National Socio-Economic Survey (Susenas) for 2008 conducted by BPS.[3]

Model structure

The CGE model used in this study combines Indonesian data, as summarised above and elaborated below, with a theoretical structure based on the ORANI-G model, an applied general equilibrium model of the Australian economy.[4] This theoretical structure is conventional for static general equilibrium models in that it contains equations describing:

- industry demand for intermediate inputs and primary factors;
- producers' supplies of commodities;
- demand for inputs to capital formation;
- household demand;
- export demand;
- government demand;
- the relationship of basic values of goods and services to production costs and purchaser prices;
- market-clearing conditions for commodities and primary factors; and
- numerous macroeconomic variables and price indices (Horridge 2000: 2).

The demand and supply equations for private sector agents (producers and consumers) are based on the usual assumptions that producers are motivated by the desire to minimise costs and consumers by the desire to maximise utility. These agents are assumed to be price takers, with producers operating in competitive markets with zero-profit conditions.[5]

We modified the standard ORANI-G model in several ways. In particular, we constructed a SAM representing the Indonesian economy in the year 2008 to serve as the core database for our CGE model. The official

---

3   The statistical method used to construct the SAM is explained in more detail in Yusuf (2006).
4   See Horridge (2000) for an in-depth discussion of the ORANI-G model.
5   The equations used in our model are described in detail in Yusuf (2008).

Indonesian SAM published by BPS does not distinguish households by level of income or expenditure, so does not allow an accurate assessment of the effect of policy changes or external shocks on the welfare of different types of households. The SAM used in our study contains comprehensive data on 200 household groupings, 100 in urban areas and 100 in rural areas, grouped in each case by percentile of real expenditure per capita. Constructing a SAM specifically designed to have a distributional emphasis required not only large-scale household survey data but also the reconciliation of various data sources.

In addition to providing detailed, disaggregated data on households, the Indonesian SAM for 2008 acknowledges the typical characteristics of labour markets in developing countries such as Indonesia by distinguishing four types of skills (agricultural, non-agricultural unskilled, clerical and services, and professional), each divided into urban and rural workers, and also into formal and informal (unpaid) workers, making a total of 16 categories of labour. In the model, we aggregate these 16 categories of labour into five labour categories: agricultural labour, unskilled formal-sector labour, unskilled informal-sector labour, skilled formal-sector labour and skilled informal-sector labour.[6]

In our study, the headcount measure of poverty incidence and the Gini coefficient of inequality are calculated using the methods set out in Appendix A8.1. These calculations are based on the distributions of real expenditure per capita ex ante (before the policy change) and ex post (after the policy change). The simulation results are estimates of the percentage changes in the endogenous variables of interest that result from the exogenous policy changes being studied. In this study, these policy changes are increases in rates of protection, first at the global level and second within Indonesia itself, occurring between 2008 and 2015.

For all the simulations, we assume full employment for all types of labour. Real wages for each category of labour are the equilibrating variables. Capital and land are assumed to be sector-specific. Another assumption in the macroeconomic closure is that government spending and real investment demand for each good are fixed exogenously.

We use the model to simulate two scenarios: one in which there is a world globalisation reversal, and one in which there is an Indonesian globalisation reversal. In the first case, we use the World Bank's estimated levels of global protection to simulate the effect on Indonesian households of a 20 per cent increase in all rates of protection in all countries except Indonesia. In the second case, we simulate the effect on Indonesian households of the observed increase in Indonesia's own trade protection between 2008 and 2015, based on Marks (2017), as discussed above.

---

6 For detailed information on how the SAM was constructed, see Yusuf (2006).

In the second of these cases — increased protection within Indonesia — we focus on two contrasting sectors in which significant changes in protection occurred between 2008 and 2015: food (consisting of food crops, livestock and manufactured food), in which Indonesia is a net importer; and minerals, in which Indonesia is a net exporter. The simulations are divided into three parts, covering, in turn, food, minerals, and food and minerals combined. Marks' (2017) estimates of changes in nominal rates of protection distinguish between those that are attributable to changes in tariffs and those that are attributable to changes in quantitative trade restrictions. This distinction is important for modelling the distributional effects of the changes in protection because the revenue from tariffs accrues to the government, while the rents accruing from quantitative restrictions are collected privately. In our simulations, the rents from quantitative restrictions within Indonesia are assumed to accrue to the richest 5 per cent of Indonesian households in urban areas.

RESULTS

Impact of a world globalisation reversal

Protection arising outside Indonesia is represented by the tariff-equivalent of protection facing Indonesia's exports in the world market. We use a 20 per cent increase in this tariff-equivalent to simulate the effect on Indonesian households of an increase in global protection.

The simulated effect that an increase in protection in all countries except Indonesia has on the welfare of the Indonesian population is summarised in Figure 8.6. The left-hand side of the chart shows how an increase in global protectionism affects the real expenditure on all commodities of households living in urban areas, while the right-hand side shows how it affects the real expenditure of households living in rural areas. In each case, the households are divided into 100 per capita expenditure centiles, arranged from the poorest 1 per cent to the richest 1 per cent.

As Figure 8.6 shows, almost all population groups within Indonesia experience a decline in real expenditure, meaning that they all lose from a globalisation reversal. The households living in rural areas experience larger declines in real expenditure, on average, than urban households. In rural areas, the adverse effects of a globalisation reversal are felt most strongly by households in the thirtieth to fiftieth percentiles of expenditure per capita.

Clearly global protectionism has diverse effects on different Indonesian households, through its divergent effects on household incomes and household expenditures. The effects on household incomes are related to changes in the returns to the factors of production that individual

Figure 8.6 Impact of global protectionism on real expenditure per capita (% change)

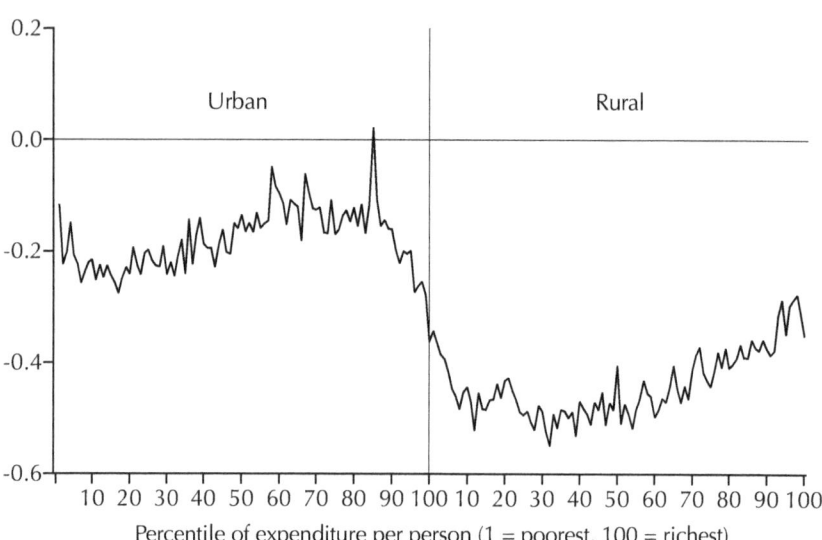

Source: Authors' calculations from INDONESIA-E3 model.

households own; and the effects on household expenditures are related to changes in the prices of the consumer goods that individual households purchase.

In terms of the income effect, Figure 8.7 shows that, with the exception of skilled labour, the real returns to all factors of production (unskilled labour, capital and land) are reduced by a globalisation reversal (where 'real' means nominal factor returns deflated by the Indonesian consumer price index, as estimated by the model). Agricultural workers are the worst affected, followed by landowners. These results are consistent with the finding that rural households experience stronger negative impacts than urban households.

The tendency for the negative impact of global protectionism to be largest for rural/agricultural households reflects the fact that increased global protection lowers the international prices for agricultural commodities relative to manufactured commodities. The effects on the production of different sectors of the Indonesian economy also reflect this fact. As Table 8.3 shows, global protectionism negatively affects the output of many traditional Indonesian export commodities that have a strong rural basis, including sugar cane, tobacco, cloves, tea, coconut and maize. Global protectionism mainly benefits service sectors with a strong urban basis, such as transportation, and hotels and restaurants.

Figure 8.7 Impact of global protectionism on real return to factors of production (% change)

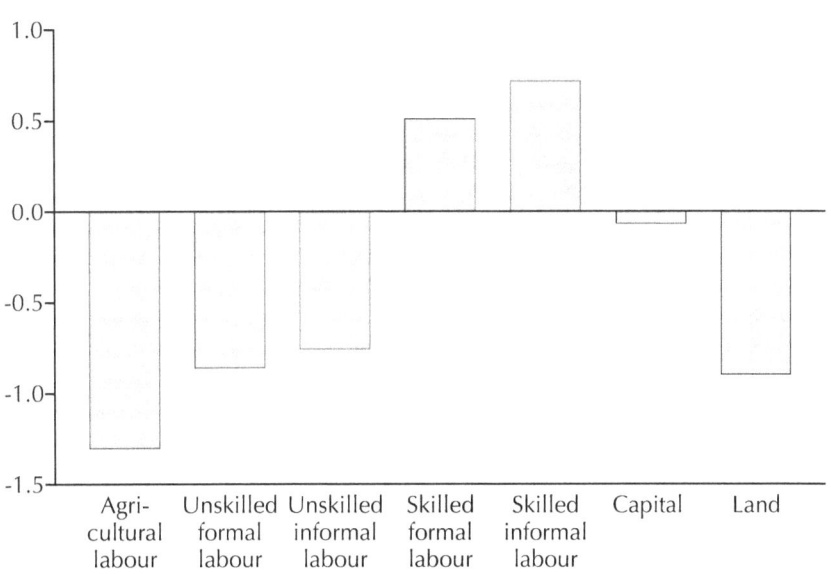

Note: In this figure, 'real' means nominal factor returns deflated by the Indonesian consumer price index, as estimated by the model.
Source: Authors' calculations from INDONESIA-E3 model.

Given its effect on the real expenditure of households, as shown in Figure 8.6, one would expect global protectionism to increase poverty incidence, especially in rural areas. Our calculations indicate that this is indeed the case, but that the effect is small: in rural areas poverty incidence increases by 0.18 percentage points, in urban areas by 0.06 percentage points and nationwide by 0.12 percentage points. The estimated impact on inequality within Indonesia, as reflected in the Gini coefficient, is negligible.

To summarise, these estimates indicate the possible effects of increased global protectionism between 2008 and 2015. Starting with 2008 levels of global protection, for example, a 20 per cent increase in all rates of global protection by 2015 would raise Indonesia's nationwide level of poverty incidence in 2015 by 0.12 percentage points, compared with the level it would *otherwise* have been if global protection had not increased.

Impact of Indonesia's globalisation reversal

We now consider how Indonesia's protection of the food sector (in which Indonesia is a net importer) and dis-protection of the mineral sector (in

Table 8.3 Impact of global protectionism on output by sector (% change)

Sector	%	Sector	%	Sector	%
Water transport	2.32	Root crops	0.17	Rail transport	−0.05
Transport services	1.37	Rice milling	0.15	Other services	−0.06
Other manufacturing	1.10	Paddy	0.15	Finance	−0.10
Hotels & restaurants	0.65	Slaughtering	0.13	Electricity, gas & water	−0.14
Soybeans & other beans	0.60	Rubber plantations	0.12	Basic non-ferrous metals	−0.14
Other estate crops	0.58	Poultry	0.09	Livestock	−0.16
Coffee	0.52	Banking	0.09	Maize	−0.20
Basic ferrous metals	0.50	Other forest products	0.09	Coconut	−0.21
Chemicals	0.47	Coal, metal & other mining	0.07	Beverages	−0.47
Air transport	0.47	Wood	0.07	Tea	−0.58
Machinery	0.44	Metals	0.06	Cloves	−0.78
Transport equipment	0.41	Cement	0.06	Flours	−0.86
Fabricated metal products	0.34	Other agricultural products	0.05	Tobacco	−0.87
Fertilisers & pesticides	0.30	Fuels	0.04	Cigarettes	−1.12
Paper products	0.30	Other mining	0.04	Sugar cane	−1.13
Non-metallic mineral products	0.29	Oil	0.01	Sugar	−1.17
Fuel subsidies	0.29	General government services	0.01	Other food products	−1.22
Wood products	0.27	Natural gas & geothermal	0.01	Textiles, clothing & footwear	−1.45
Rubber & plastics	0.26	Construction	0.00	Oil palm	−1.49
Communications	0.23	Other services	−0.02	Fibre crops	−1.61
Vegetables & fruits	0.23	Social & community services	−0.04	Yarn spinning	−1.61
Other food crops	0.21	Trade	−0.04	Oils & fats	−1.84
Road transport	0.20	Fisheries	−0.05	Food processing	−3.99

Source: Authors' calculations from INDONESIA-E3 model.

which Indonesia is a net exporter) affects the welfare of individual Indonesian households. The answer is complex. It depends on changes in the returns to factors of production, individual households' patterns of ownership of these factors of production, changes in the prices of the consumer goods purchased by households, and individual households' patterns of consumption of these consumer goods. The overall impact of these differing effects at the household level can be decomposed into:

Total Effect (*real expenditure effect*) = *Income Effect* − *Price Effect*

Income Effect measures, for each household, how a shock affects the income derived from a household's ownership of factors of production (labour, capital and land). *Price Effect* measures the impact on the household's cost of living. The latter is household-specific because, even though everyone faces identical changes in the prices of individual commodities, each household purchases a different bundle of commodities. For example, if the prices of food items increase proportionately more than the prices of non-food items, the cost of living (*Price Effect*) of poor households will increase proportionately more than that of rich households, because the share of food in the total consumption of poor households is generally higher than that of rich households. *Total Effect* (in percentage change) is simply *Income Effect* minus *Price Effect*.[7]

This decomposition is implemented in Figure 8.8 for the case of Indonesia's protectionism in the food sector. The income effect is positive for both the rural and urban populations and is proportionately larger, on average, for the rural population. Since the rural population is on average poorer than the urban population, the income effect reduces inequality *between* the rural and urban populations. In addition, the income effect is proportionately larger for the poorer population groups within rural areas. This is also the case within urban areas, with one important exception. Because the richest 5 per cent of urban households receive all the rents from quantitative trade restrictions, their incomes increase, on average, by around 1 per cent, whereas the remaining urban households receive an average increase of less than 0.4 per cent. For this reason, while inequality falls within rural areas, the overall effect on inequality within urban areas is difficult to infer from the diagram alone.

The first column of Table 8.4 helps to clarify these results. It shows that the effect of Indonesia's protection of the food sector is to raise the nominal return to agricultural labour relative to the returns to all non-agricultural forms of labour and the returns to capital and land. Agricultural labour

---

7 This analytical framework is developed more fully in Warr and Yusuf (2014).

Figure 8.8 Impact of Indonesia's protectionism in the food sector on real expenditure per capita (% change)

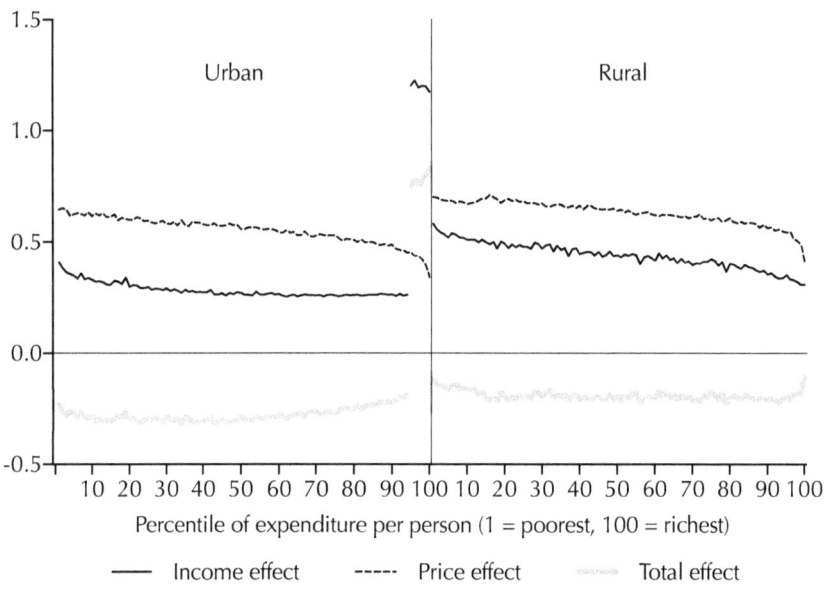

Source: Authors' calculations from INDONESIA-E3 model.

Table 8.4 Impact of Indonesia's protectionism on nominal return to factors of production (% change)

	Food	Minerals	Food + minerals
Agricultural labour	0.885	−0.161	0.722
Unskilled formal labour	0.121	0.188	0.305
Unskilled informal labour	0.229	0.179	0.352
Skilled formal labour	0.273	−0.066	0.205
Skilled informal labour	0.196	−0.066	0.128
Capital	0.179	−0.309	−0.131
Land	0.538	−0.533	−0.005
Memo item:			
Consumer price index	0.551	−0.053	0.496

Source: Authors' calculations from INDONESIA-E3 model.

Table 8.5 Impact of Indonesia's protectionism on poverty incidence (percentage points)

Sector	Urban	Rural	All
Before policy change	11.650	18.930	15.412
Food	11.729	18.992	15.482
Change	**0.079**	**0.062**	**0.070**
Minerals	11.643	18.942	15.415
Change	**−0.007**	**0.012**	**0.003**
Food + minerals	11.722	19.004	15.485
Change	**0.072**	**0.074**	**0.073**

Source: Authors' calculations from INDONESIA-E3 model.

is of course the principal income source for the poorest segments of the rural population.

Turning to the price effect, it is apparent from Figure 8.8 that the effect of Indonesia's protection of the food sector on consumer prices is greater than its effect on income, in both rural and urban areas. The price effect is also regressive, meaning that the increase in the cost of living is felt more strongly by poorer households. The total effect, that is, the overall change in household real expenditure, is negative for all except the richest 5 per cent of urban households, the recipients of the rents from quantitative import restrictions. The fact that the top 5 per cent of urban households experience a positive total effect tends to increase overall inequality.

It is important to note that the fact that our simulation results indicate that all rural *centile groups* lose from increased protection of the food sector does not mean that all rural *households* lose. Within the richer, land-owning centile groups in particular, there will be both households that gain and households that lose. What the results mean is that within each rural centile group the losers outweigh the gainers. The same is true for the urban centile groups, except the richest 5 per cent.

As one would expect from the fall in real expenditure for almost all population groups, an increase in protection in the food sector increases poverty incidence. Table 8.5 indicates that poverty incidence rises by 0.079 per cent in urban areas and 0.062 per cent in rural areas. The nationwide increase in poverty incidence is 0.070 per cent. Thus, protection of the food sector increases poverty, but the size of the effect is small.

Table 8.6 shows that an increase in protection in the food sector leads to a rise in inequality, but the effect is very small. The estimated Gini

Table 8.6 Impact of Indonesia's protectionism on inequality

Sector	Gini coefficient			Top 10%/ bottom 10% (decile dispersion)		Top 10%/ bottom 40% (Palma ratio)	
	Urban	Rural	All	Urban	Rural	Urban	Rural
Before policy change	0.369	0.277	0.371	7.620	3.893	1.276	0.803
Food	0.370	0.277	0.372	7.681	3.892	1.288	0.803
Change	**0.001**	**0.000**	**0.001**	**0.062**	**−0.001**	**0.012**	**0.000**
Minerals	0.368	0.277	0.371	7.602	3.889	1.275	0.802
Change	**0.000**	**0.000**	**0.000**	**−0.018**	**−0.004**	**−0.002**	**−0.001**
Food + minerals	0.370	0.277	0.371	7.663	3.888	1.285	0.802
Change	**0.001**	**0.000**	**0.001**	**0.044**	**−0.005**	**0.009**	**−0.001**

Source: Authors' calculations from INDONESIA-E3 model.

coefficient for rural areas does not change, while the coefficient for urban areas increases by only 0.001 points. Using an alternative measure of inequality, the Palma ratio (Palma 2014), we find that the ratio of the expenditure share of the richest 10 per cent to the share of the poorest 40 per cent of urban households increases from 1.276 to 1.288, or by 0.012 points.

In the case of dis-protection of the mineral sector, the effect of Indonesia's own globalisation reversal on the returns to factors of production is felt most strongly by land and capital owners (Table 8.4). This is because limiting the exports of extractive sectors hurts the factors of production used most intensively in these sectors. As Figure 8.9 shows, the effect on income is strongly progressive (downward sloping), especially for the sections of the urban population whose incomes depend most intensively on capital and land. The effect on prices is relatively neutral across centile groups, shown by the rather flat price effect curves. The overall impact on real expenditure is progressive, particularly in urban areas. As shown in Table 8.5, Indonesia's protectionism in the extractive mineral industries through export limitation tends to reduce poverty in urban areas, increase it in rural areas and increase it nationwide. However, the effect is again very small. The impact on inequality as measured by the Gini index is neutral (Table 8.6).

Figure 8.10 shows the combined effect of protection in the food and mineral sectors on real household expenditure per capita. The effects are

Figure 8.9 Impact of Indonesia's protectionism in the mineral sector on real expenditure per capita (% change)

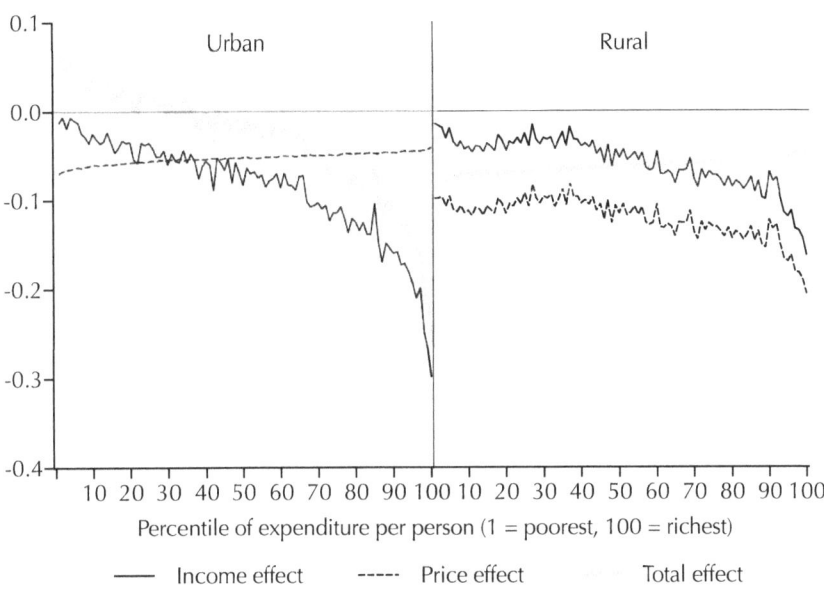

Source: Authors' calculations from INDONESIA-E3 model.

dominated by protection of the food sector, discussed above. First, the income effect tends to be progressive (downward sloping) in both urban and rural areas, but the rural population experiences a greater proportional increase in income than the urban population. Within the rural population, the positive income effect is larger for the poorer parts of the population. In urban areas, the richest 5 per cent of households receive the greatest benefit from the economic rent derived from quantitative trade restrictions.

Second, the price effect is regressive (downward sloping) in both urban and rural areas, because the increase in commodity prices is biased against the basket of commodities consumed more intensively by poorer households, and this effect is larger in rural than in urban areas.

Third, as the price effect is larger than the income effect for all except the richest 5 per cent of urban households, all population groups, except the latter, lose from Indonesia's own globalisation reversal. As a result, poverty incidence increases by 0.072 percentage points in urban areas, 0.074 percentage points in rural areas and 0.073 percentage points nationwide (Table 8.5). In other words, Indonesia's protectionism (represented by the increase in the nominal rate of protection occurring between 2008

Figure 8.10 Impact of Indonesia's protectionism in the food and mineral sectors on real expenditure per capita (% change)

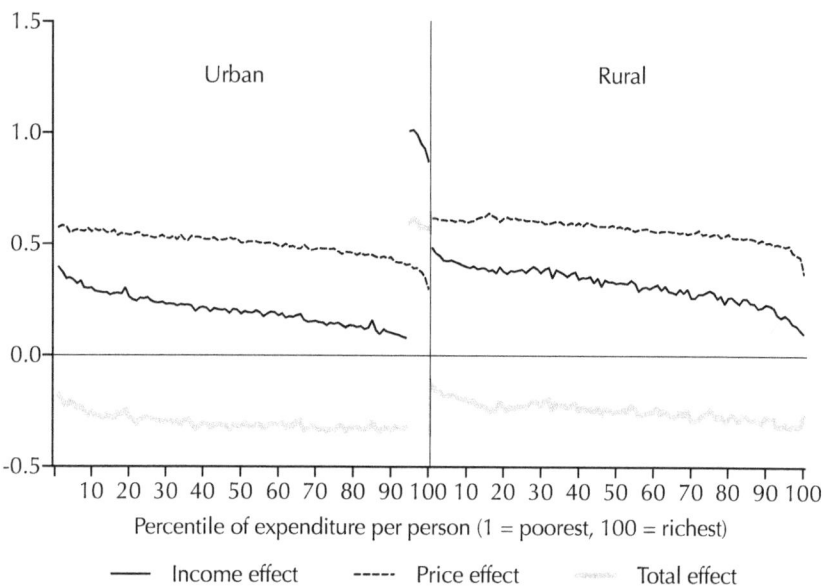

Source: Authors' calculations from INDONESIA-E3 model.

and 2015) results in an increase in poverty, but the impact is small. The estimated effect on inequality, meanwhile, is negligible (Table 8.6).

CONCLUSIONS

Since the 1997–98 Asian financial crisis, the rate of poverty reduction in Indonesia has slowed. From a reduction of 1.44 per cent of the total population per annum between 1976 and 1996, the rate slowed to 0.53 per cent per annum between 2000 and 2016. Thus, the post-crisis rate of poverty reduction was only 37 per cent of the pre-crisis rate, whereas the post-crisis rate of GDP growth per person was 89 per cent of the pre-crisis rate. Following the crisis, economic inequality increased dramatically. The Gini index of inequality increased from 0.303 in 2000 to 0.397 in 2016, one of the largest increases ever recorded for any country. Protectionism also increased, both globally and within Indonesia.

The objective of this chapter has been to estimate the extent to which protectionism, both at the global level and within Indonesia, explains the observed slowdown in poverty reduction and rise in inequality. We did this using the INDONESIA-E3 model, a general equilibrium model of the Indonesian economy that enables detailed calculation of the poverty and inequality effects of policy changes and external shocks. Using this modelling approach, we were able to compare the welfare of households under the existing policies, which included the observed increases in protection, with their welfare under a hypothetical alternative set of policies—the counterfactual—in which these increases in protection did not occur.

The difference between the annual rates of poverty reduction before and after the 1997–98 Asian financial crisis is 1.44 – 0.53 = 0.91 percentage points per year. We find that increased protectionism at the global level between 2008 and 2015 may have reduced the annual rate of poverty reduction in Indonesia during that period by just under 0.02 percentage points (0.12 percentage points over the entire seven-year interval), and that increased protectionism within Indonesia during the same period may have reduced the annual rate of poverty reduction by an estimated 0.01 percentage points (0.07 percentage points over the seven-year interval). We therefore conclude that protectionism increased poverty incidence, but that the effect was small, and not nearly enough to explain the slowdown in the rate of poverty reduction. We also find that the increase in protectionism from 2008 to 2015 increased inequality, but the effect was smaller still.

We conclude that anti-globalisation has been harmful for both poverty reduction and inequality, but that it was not the major cause of either the slowdown in poverty reduction or the rise in inequality that Indonesia has experienced since the Asian financial crisis in 1997–98.

REFERENCES

Bourguignon, F., A.-S. Robilliard and S. Robinson (2003) 'Representative versus real households in the macro-economic modelling of inequality', Document de Travail DT/2003-10, Développement et Insertion International, Paris, September.

Evenett, S., and J. Fritz (2015) 'The tide turns? Trade, protectionism, and slowing global growth', 18th Global Trade Alert Report, Centre for Economic Policy Research (CEPR), London.

Horridge, M. (2000) 'ORANI-G: a general equilibrium model of the Australian economy', Preliminary Working Paper No. OP-93, Centre of Policy Studies and Impact Project, Monash University, Clayton, October.

Marks, S.V. (2017) 'Non-tariff trade regulations in Indonesia: nominal and effective rates of protection', *Bulletin of Indonesian Economic Studies* 53(3): 333–57.

Palma, J.G. (2014) 'Has the income share of the middle and upper-middle been stable around the "50/50 rule", or has it converged towards that level? The "Palma ratio" revisited', *Development and Change* 45(6): 1,416–48.

Warr, P., and A.A. Yusuf (2011) 'Reducing Indonesia's deforestation-based greenhouse gas emissions', *Australian Journal of Agricultural and Resource Economics* 55(3): 297–321.

Warr, P., and A.A. Yusuf (2014) 'Fertilizer subsidies and food self-sufficiency in Indonesia', *Agricultural Economics* 45(5): 571–88.

World Trade Organization (2016) 'WTO report on G20 trade measures (mid-October 2015 to mid-May 2016)', WTO Secretariat, 21 June. https://www.wto.org/english/news_e/news16_e/g20_wto_report_june16_e.pdf

Yusuf, A.A. (2006) 'Constructing Indonesian social accounting matrix for distributional analysis in the CGE modelling framework', Working Paper in Economics and Development Studies No. 200604, Department of Economics, Padjadjaran University, Bandung, November. http://ceds.feb.unpad.ac.id/wopeds/200604.pdf

Yusuf, A.A. (2008) 'INDONESIA-E3: an Indonesian applied general equilibrium model for analyzing the economy, equity, and the environment', Working Paper in Economics and Development Studies No. 200804, Department of Economics, Padjadjaran University, Bandung, September. http://ceds.feb.unpad.ac.id/wopeds/200804.pdf

Yusuf, A.A., and B.P. Resosudarmo (2008) 'Mitigating distributional impact of fuel pricing reform: the Indonesian experience', *ASEAN Economic Bulletin* 25(1): 32–47.

Yusuf, A.A., and B.P. Resosudarmo (2015) 'On the distributional impact of a carbon tax in developing countries: the case of Indonesia', *Environmental Economics and Policy Studies* 17: 1–26.

APPENDIX A8.1: MEASUREMENT OF POVERTY INCIDENCE AND INEQUALITY

Headcount measure of poverty incidence

Let y_c represent real expenditure per capita of a household in the c-th centile, where $c = 1, \ldots, n$. Let the poverty line be y_p, which lies between two levels of real expenditure per capita within c, that is, between the largest real expenditure per capita that is still lower than the poverty line, or $max\{y_c \mid y_c < y_p\}$, and the smallest real expenditure per capita that is above the poverty line, or $min\{y_c \mid y_c > y_p\}$. Thus, poverty incidence is calculated using

$$P(y_c, y_p) = max\{c \mid y_c < y_p\} + \nabla c \qquad (8.1)$$

where

$$\nabla c = \frac{y_p - max\{y_c \mid y_c < y_p\}}{min\{y_c \mid y_c > y_p\} - max\{y_c \mid y_c < y_p\}} \cdot$$
$$\left(min\{c \mid y_c > y_p\} - max\{c \mid y_c < y_p\}\right)$$

The first term in equation 8.1 is simply the highest centile, where real expenditure per capita is lower than the poverty line, that is, the number of households with real expenditure per capita less than or equal to $max\{y_c \mid y_c < y_p\}$. The second term is the linear approximation of the number of households with real expenditure per capita above $max\{y_c \mid y_c < y_p\}$ but still lower than the poverty line.

The change in poverty incidence after a policy shock (simulation) is calculated as

$$\Delta P = P(y'_c, y_p) - P(y_c, y_p)$$

where

$$y'_c = \left(1 + \frac{\hat{y}_c}{100}\right) \cdot y_c$$

and $\hat{y}_c$ is the percentage change in real per capita expenditure of a household of the centile c produced from the simulation of the CGE model.

Gini coefficient of inequality

The Gini coefficient is calculated from the following formula:

$$G(y_c) = \frac{1}{n}\left(n+1-2\frac{\sum_{c=1}^{n}(n+1-c)y_c}{\sum_{c=1}^{n}y_c}\right)$$

9 Gender, labour markets and trade liberalisation in Indonesia

Krisztina Kis-Katos, Janneke Pieters and Robert Sparrow*

A growing body of literature has assessed the distributional effects of globalisation, focusing mainly on inequality by skill level or socio-economic characteristics. Much less is known about the differential effects for men and women, although theory suggests several channels through which trade may affect the employment of men versus women. Globally, gender gaps in labour market outcomes remain large, notwithstanding the fact that differences between men and women in labour force participation and earnings are declining in many countries. Indonesia is one of the countries with relatively low female labour force participation, and a persistently large gender gap in participation. To understand whether and how trade policy and trade performance have played a role in this gender gap, this chapter focuses on the gender-specific effects of trade liberalisation in the 1990s and the relationships between trade and female employment in the period 2000–10.

In the next section, we first consider trade theory, and the mechanisms through which trade reform can induce gendered labour market effects. These channels include labour market discrimination, skill-biased technological change, sectoral segregation and the sectoral structure of employment. We then discuss the international empirical evidence for gendered trade effects. In the second section, we discuss the effects of Indonesia's trade reforms in the 1990s. The evidence suggests that import tariff reductions improved the competitiveness of Indonesian firms by reducing

---

* We thank Oliver Braun for excellent research assistance.

the costs of intermediate inputs. This, in turn, induced job creation and increased female—but not male—work participation. In the third section, we describe the more recent trends in female labour force participation, and in the fourth we relate those trends to Indonesia's trade performance in the period 2000–10. While the 1990s were a period of stagnation in aggregate female labour force participation, in the post-decentralisation period Indonesia experienced an increase in female participation, mainly in the service and trade sectors. But at the same time, the role of international trade in improving employment opportunities for women seems to have declined between 2000 and 2010.

HOW TRADE REFORMS CAN HAVE GENDERED LABOUR MARKET EFFECTS

Gender inequality in the labour market, including not only wage inequality but also differences in labour force participation rates, can be driven by various factors, such as discrimination, skill differences and social norms. By altering one or more of these factors, trade reforms can have an impact on gender inequality. In this section, we will focus on a number of factors that have been emphasised in recent research. We first give a brief overview of how trade liberalisation affects gender inequality according to theory, and then summarise the available empirical evidence.

One potential driving force of gender inequality is discrimination, which can be defined as the situation where women are paid less than equally qualified men for the same work. If firms discriminate against women, preferring to hire men even when qualified women are available, women's wages will be lower on average than those of men. As a consequence, employing more women would reduce firms' costs (Becker 1957). Trade reforms are expected to reduce discrimination by increasing competition among firms, so that discriminating firms are driven out of the market or induced to discriminate less. Hence, by increasing competition, trade reforms can reduce gender inequality in wages and in employment.

Gender differences in pay and employment are also related to the sectoral structure of the economy, because industries differ in the extent to which they hire women, owing to social norms or technological differences (Goldin 1994; Do, Levchenko and Raddatz 2016). These differences are reflected in widespread sectoral segregation by gender; as a share of their workforces, for example, the textiles industry hires more female workers than the mining industry (Borrowman and Klasen 2015). Trade reforms will affect gender inequality in the labour market to the extent that they induce structural change—a reallocation of output and production factors across industries. If the expanding industries are relatively female intensive, then trade reforms will create more employment opportunities for women, but if the expanding industries are relatively male intensive, then men will benefit more.

Trade reforms can also affect the relative demand for women *within* industries by, for example, stimulating technological change. This may occur because increased competition (or improved access to export markets) induces firms to invest in new technology, or because imported capital goods become cheaper with declining import tariffs. Modern machinery and equipment can carry out certain tasks that would once have been carried out by workers. If these tasks require physical strength, and were traditionally carried out by men, then investing in new technology would reduce men's comparative advantage and increase the relative demand for female workers (Galor and Weil 1996; Juhn, Ujhelyi and Villegas-Sanchez 2014).

Several studies have considered the effects of trade on gender discrimination in the labour market, in order to test the predictions of Becker (1957). Black and Brainerd (2004) studied imports in US manufacturing industries in 1977–94 and found that the gender wage gap declined in industries that were initially concentrated and that then experienced an increase in import penetration. Following a similar approach—comparing the effects of trade on concentrated and less concentrated industries— other studies have shown that trade liberalisation reduced gender discrimination through increased competition in the manufacturing sector in Mexico (Artecona and Cunningham 2002; Hazarika and Otero 2002) and in Colombia (Ederington, Minier and Troske 2009). Yet the evidence presented in these studies would also be consistent with other channels through which increased competition could affect gender inequality, such as technology upgrading.

Recent empirical evidence on the role of technology upgrading considers the impact of the North American Free Trade Agreement on manufacturing firms in Mexico. Juhn, Ujhelyi and Villegas-Sanchez (2014) show that in industries with the greatest increase in access to the US market, more firms started to export and firms were more likely to invest in new technology. In addition, the female share of workers in blue-collar occupations increased in these industries, in line with the prediction that new technology reduces the physical strength required for workers to perform tasks.

As noted above, the sectoral structure of the economy also matters, because of differences in the female share of workers across sectors. Do, Levchenko and Raddatz (2016) analyse the link between fertility and the sectoral structure of countries' exports, using export data for 61 manufacturing industries in 145 countries over the period 1980–2007. They find evidence to support the idea that in countries with a comparative advantage in relatively female-intensive goods (such as textiles), there is greater demand for female labour so that women are able to earn higher wages. This is reflected in lower fertility, because women bear most of the burden of child rearing and higher wages for women mean the opportunity cost of raising children increases. The authors also show that in countries with low levels of income and female educational attainment, female labour force participation is significantly higher if the countries' exports are concentrated in more female-intensive industries.

Do, Levchenko and Raddatz (2016) do not assess the impact of trade reforms on fertility or female participation, but rather analyse export composition driven by differences in technology and resource endowment. Another study that illustrates the importance of sectoral structure is the analysis of Brazil's trade liberalisation by Gaddis and Pieters (2017). They find that while import tariff reductions led to lower overall employment growth, male employment was affected much more than female employment because the impacts were concentrated in the male-dominated tradable sector.

Based on their analysis of a panel of 72 countries over the period 1992–2010, Borrowman and Klasen (2015) find little effect of trade openness on gender segregation in the labour market. This would suggest that trade is not related to within-industry shifts in the gender composition of employment, on average. Yet summary measures of labour market segregation may fail to capture some of the dynamics in male and female labour force participation, and because the authors' analysis is based on comparisons across countries and over time, it cannot be ruled out that trade reforms led to significant changes in segregation within particular countries and time periods. Juhn, Ujhelyi and Villegas-Sanchez (2014) is one such example; as discussed above, the authors show that in Mexico the North American Free Trade Agreement led to an increase in the number of female workers in previously male-dominated production work.

THE EFFECTS OF INDONESIA'S TRADE REFORMS IN THE 1990s

Indonesia's strong import tariff reductions in the 1990s reduced not only the costs of goods in output markets that competed with Indonesian products, but also the costs of intermediate inputs imported by Indonesian firms. These two effects of tariff reductions can have countervailing effects on labour market outcomes: the first increasing the competition from foreign products faced by Indonesian firms, the second strengthening the competitiveness of Indonesian firms by reducing production costs.

The empirical evidence for Indonesia suggests that the effects of the reductions in import tariffs on intermediate inputs outweighed the effects of the tariff reductions on output. For example, using Indonesian firm data, Amiti and Konings (2007) show that the cuts to tariffs on intermediate goods increased firms' sales and profits. In terms of the distributional effects on labour market outcomes, Amiti and Cameron (2012) find that low-skilled wage workers benefited more than high-skilled workers, as tariff liberalisation reduced the industrial skill premium.

This is consistent with Kis-Katos and Sparrow (2015), who find that both work participation among the low-skilled and the wages of medium-skilled workers increased as prices on intermediate products fell due to import tariff reductions. These effects at the lower end of the income distribution resulted in a net reduction in poverty. In addition, Kis-Katos and Sparrow (2011) show that tariff liberalisation in the 1990s reduced the incidence of child labour, presumably through these positive income effects.

Kis-Katos, Pieters and Sparrow (2017) find evidence of gendered effects from the tariff reductions in the 1990s by relating changes in labour market outcomes in Indonesian districts to changes in the import tariffs on inputs used by sectors in the districts. The reduction in input tariffs, and the resultant improvement in the competitiveness of Indonesian firms, increased labour market participation specifically among women and reduced their involvement in domestic duties. In contrast, the authors find much weaker effects for male work participation. At the same time, labour market outcomes for both men and women were not much affected by increased foreign competition in local markets due to output tariff reductions.

A combination of channels seems to be at play. First, it appears that female-intensive sectors have benefited the most from reductions in input tariffs and have expanded more relative to sectors that were initially more male intensive. Second, sectoral gender segregation has declined with tariff cuts, especially among low-skilled workers. This may be explained by firms' responses to liberalisation in terms of increased investments in imported capital goods and new technologies, which may have diminished the comparative advantage of men in physically demanding work.

The labour market changes brought about by trade reform have also generated wider effects on the life decisions of young adults. For both sexes, trade liberalisation has raised the age of first marriage. The main explanation would be that the returns to marriage decline as women's labour market opportunities improve and they engage less in domestic duties.

FEMALE LABOUR FORCE PARTICIPATION SINCE 1999

The 1990s were a period of stagnation in aggregate female labour force participation, which hovered around or just below 50 per cent (Kis-Katos,

Table 9.1 Labour force participation rate among people aged 16–64 by gender, 1999–2011 (%)

	1999	2003	2007	2011
Female	50.9	48.4	55.3	56.4
Male	87.2	88.2	88.5	88.2

Source: Authors' calculation using Susenas household surveys, 1999, 2003, 2007, 2011.

Pieters and Sparrow 2017).[1] But in the post-decentralisation period the country experienced a notable increase in female participation, especially after 2003. In this section, we describe the recent trends in female participation, including participation by age group and sector, and we discuss the extent of sectoral segregation by gender.

Table 9.1 shows that labour force participation among women aged 16–64 fell from 51 per cent in 1999 to 48 per cent in 2003, before increasing to 56 per cent in 2011. For men in the same age group, on the other hand, we see a very stable labour force participation rate, of around 88 per cent.

Figure 9.1 disaggregates female labour force participation in 1999–2011 by age group. It shows that the increase in participation towards the end of the decade was driven mainly by women older than 30, while the participation of younger cohorts either stagnated (among those aged 20–29) or decreased considerably (among those aged 16–19, especially after 2007). The same trend can be observed for young men (not shown here). These trends may reflect improvements in educational attainment as well as rising senior secondary school and tertiary enrolment rates.

Figure 9.2 breaks down the total female labour force participation rates (as in Table 9.1) by sector. The main sector of employment for both men and women remains agriculture. The female participation rate in this sector fluctuated around 24 per cent, with agriculture accounting for about 45 per cent of all women active in the labour market. The next two most popular sectors for women were trade and other service industries, which were the main drivers of the increase in female participation after 2003. The participation rate in trade increased by 4.0 percentage points (from 9.9 per cent to 13.9 per cent between 2003 and 2011), and in services by 4.6 percentage points (from 5.8 per cent to 10.4 per cent). Participation in manufacturing remained stable at around 5 per cent throughout the period.

---

1   Labour force participation is defined here as wage employment, self-employment or seeking work.

Figure 9.1 Female labour force participation by age group, 1999–2011

Source: Authors' calculation using Susenas household surveys, 1999, 2003, 2007, 2011.

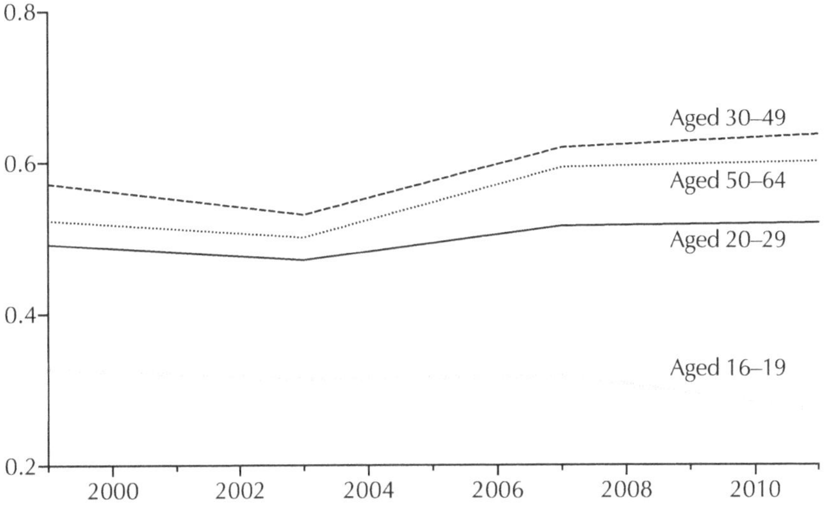

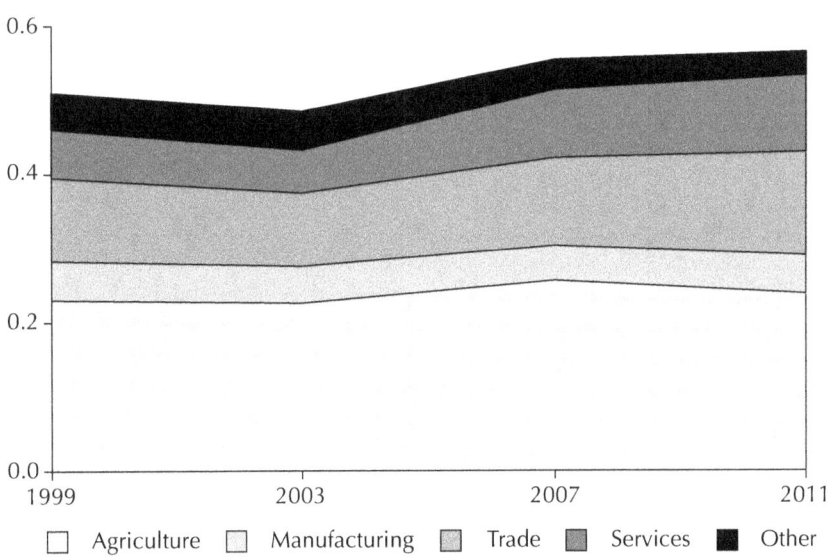

Figure 9.2 Female labour force participation by sector, 1999–2011

Source: Authors' calculation using Susenas household surveys, 1999, 2003, 2007, 2011.

For men, we see similar patterns for the agricultural, manufacturing and service sectors (not presented here), although the increases in the participation rates for services are slightly less pronounced. The main difference, besides higher overall labour force participation, is that the construction, transportation, communication and mining sectors employ substantially more men, with construction in particular showing a surge after 2003.

Segregation by gender is an important aspect of the labour market, as the impact of trade reform will be gender-specific if trade induces structural change while gender segregation across sectors is persistent.

Borrowman and Klasen (2015) find that gendered sectoral segregation is slightly less severe in Indonesia than in low- and middle-income countries for which suitable data are available. For example, they calculate a sectoral index of dissimilarity (*ID*),

$$ID = \frac{1}{2} \sum_s \left| \frac{M_s}{M} - \frac{F_s}{F} \right|,$$

which compares sector *s* shares of male and female labour, and can be interpreted as the percentage of men or women that would have to be reallocated across sectors in order to eliminate all gender segregation from the labour market. For Indonesia, they find a dissimilarity index of 0.18, which is substantially lower than the global cross-country average of 0.26. Their calculation is of similar order of magnitude to what we find using data from the National Socio-Economic Surveys (Susenas) for 1999, 2003, 2007 and 2011. There is no clear trend in the index from 1999 to 2011, suggesting that on average sectoral gender segregation is fairly constant. However, we do see some changes at the provincial level.

We see some clear trends when we look at the concentration index (*CI*),

$$CI_s = \frac{F_s / F}{M_s / M},$$

which simply takes the ratio of the female and male labour shares per sector *s*. The concentration index identifies the sectors in which female labour is over-represented relative to male labour. Agriculture, the largest sector for both male and female labour, remains balanced with an index of around 1. Services and trade, two sectors with relatively high initial female employment shares, have become more female oriented, especially since 2003. By 2011, women outnumbered men in the trade sector in absolute terms, and had almost caught up in the service sector. The opposite has occurred in the traditionally male-dominated sectors of mining, utilities and construction, where the male shares have continued to increase.

FEMALE LABOUR AND INTERNATIONAL TRADE

The previous section described the overall trends in female workforce participation since 1999 and the distribution of female workers across sectors. Given that input tariffs have been relatively low and stable since 2002, it is not possible to analyse the effects of tariff reforms on labour market outcomes in the 2000s. Instead, we assess whether the international trade environment in Indonesia during the more recent period, 2000–10,[2] has been conducive for harnessing the potentially positive effects of trade on female labour market outcomes.

We are interested to see, first, whether the sectoral composition of trade has seen changes in the direction of more (or less) female-intensive activities. For example, have the more female-intensive sectors become more important for Indonesia's exports? Second, we ask whether the exposure to trade is correlated with the female share of workers across sectors. Are the sectors most engaged in importing or exporting those with relatively high female intensities? And is there a link between the changes in trade exposure during the 2000s and the changes in female intensity?

To analyse the exposure of female labour to international trade, we calculate measures capturing exports, imports of intermediate inputs, and imports of final goods using the World Input–Output Database (Timmer et al. 2015). We combine these data with labour force measures from the National Labour Force Surveys (Sakernas) for the years 2000, 2001 and 2010.[3] This gives us 33 distinct sectors, for which we calculate the female share of workers as well as three trade exposure measures. The sectors covered include agriculture, mining, a number of manufacturing industries and various service sectors (see Table A9.1 in the appendix for a complete list).

To calculate the female share of workers (*female intensity*), we divide the number of female workers by the total number of male and female workers in each of the 33 sectors. The numbers of workers are estimated by using individual survey weights to yield nationally representative results. The first trade exposure measure is the *export–output ratio*, which is calculated by dividing the value of exports by the value of total output in each sector; it shows the extent to which the sector engages in exporting. The second measure, the *import–input ratio*, measures the extent to which each sector relies on international markets to source its inputs. It is calculated by

---

2 Our timeframe is constrained by the availability of detailed sectoral data on occupation from the Sakernas labour force surveys.
3 To increase the sample size, data for the year 2000 combine the observations from the 2000 and 2001 Sakernas surveys. The sample size is 121,721 in 2000–01 and 540,800 in 2010.

Table 9.2 Summary statistics at the sectoral level, 2000 and 2010

Variable	Mean	Weighted mean	Standard deviation	Minimum	Maximum
2000					
Female intensity	0.288	0.372	0.166	0.016	0.576
Export–output ratio	0.265	0.082	0.322	0.000	1.020
Import–input ratio	0.250	0.202	0.108	0.100	0.666
Import penetration	0.237	0.076	0.291	0.003	1.044
2010					
Female intensity	0.304	0.368	0.179	0.019	0.636
Export–output ratio	0.188	0.066	0.213	0.000	0.707
Import–input ratio	0.173	0.143	0.089	0.071	0.502
Import penetration	0.180	0.059	0.215	0.000	0.816

Note: The number of observations (sectors) in each year is 33. Export shares can surpass 1 by depleting inventories.

Source: Authors' calculation using data from the World Input–Output Database, 2000, 2010; and Sakernas labour force surveys, 2000, 2001, 2010.

dividing the value of imported intermediate products by the total value of intermediate inputs used by each sector. Finally, *import penetration* measures the extent to which a sector is exposed to international competition. It is calculated by dividing the total value of final goods imported by the value of total domestic demand per sector (sectoral output plus imports minus exports).

Table 9.2 presents descriptive statistics for these variables for the years 2000 and 2010. As well as presenting unweighted means, standard deviations, minimums and maximums, it shows mean values weighted by the size of total sectoral employment in each year.

The weighted average of female intensity in 2000 was 0.372, indicating that, on average, female workers represented 37.2 per cent of the workforce. Across sectors, this share ranged from 1.6 per cent to almost 60 per cent. Appendix Table A9.1 shows that in 2000 inland transportation, water transportation and construction had the lowest female intensities (less than 4 per cent of their workforces were female), while food, textiles, hotels and restaurants, and health had the highest intensities (more than 50 per cent of their workforces were female).[4]

---

4 Note that one very female-intensive sector, private household services, is excluded from the analysis because of the lack of reliable input and output

Overall, the trade exposure of the Indonesian economy declined substantially (Table 9.2). Between 2000 and 2010, the (unweighted) average export–output ratio declined from 26.5 per cent to 18.8 per cent. When weighted by sectoral employment, these figures decrease considerably, because the sectors with the largest employment have the lowest export shares. The weighted average export–output ratio fell from 8.2 per cent to 6.6 per cent. The share of imported intermediate goods in total inputs declined on average from 25.0 per cent to 17.3 per cent or, weighted by sectoral employment, from 20.2 per cent to 14.3 per cent. In a similar vein, import penetration fell from 23.7 per cent to 18.0 per cent on average, or from 7.6 per cent to 5.9 per cent when weighted by sectoral employment. Thus, the Indonesian economy experienced a considerable decrease in the importance of exports and imported intermediate inputs as well as a decline in overall competition from imported goods.

Among the 33 sectors considered in this analysis, the largest in terms of employment are agriculture (with 45 per cent of total employment in 2000 and 39 per cent in 2010) and retail trade (17 per cent in 2000 and 16 per cent in 2010). Both sectors are still relatively closed, with export shares and import penetration well below 5 per cent in 2010. At the same time, their trade exposure in terms of imported intermediate goods was somewhat higher: in 2010 agriculture imported 13 per cent and retail trade 10 per cent of its inputs (figures based on authors' own calculations).

Sectoral composition of trade and female labour

In our analysis of Indonesia's trade liberalisation in the 1990s, we found that female labour force participation increased in part because more female-intensive sectors benefited more from reductions in tariffs on inputs, so that they expanded more (in terms of employment) than the sectors that were initially more male intensive. In this subsection, we ask whether changes in a sector's *observed* trade activity (rather than changes in sector-level trade *policies*) are related to the sector's initial female intensity. We do this by measuring changes in the so-called female labour needs of trade (Do, Levchenko and Raddatz 2016), which captures the extent to which the composition of trade is skewed towards more female-intensive sectors. It combines a sector's female intensity in some base year—the year 2000, in our case—with the sector's share in total trade at different points in time.

Using the data sources described above, we calculate the share of each sector in Indonesia's total exports and total imports of final goods for

---

data. This precludes a direct comparison of the sector-specific results of this section and the aggregate results of the previous section.

Table 9.3 Female labour intensity of international trade, 2000 and 2010

	2000	2010	Change
Female intensity of employment	0.372	0.368	−0.004
Female intensity of exports	0.325	0.295	−0.030
Female intensity of final goods imports	0.282	0.276	−0.006

Note: The number of observations (sectors) in each year is 33.
Source: Authors' calculation using data from the World Input–Output Database, 2000, 2010; and Sakernas labour force surveys, 2000, 2001, 2010.

the years 2000 and 2010. These shares are then multiplied by the female intensity of the relevant sector in 2000, and the products aggregated to calculate the female labour needs of trade (*FLNT*):

$$FLNT_t = \sum_{s=1}^{S} Female\ intensity_{s,t=2000} \frac{trade_{s,t}}{total\ trade_t},$$

where *t* refers to the year (2000 or 2010), *s* refers to the sector, and the last term in the equation is each sector's share in trade, where trade is either exports or imports of final goods. Each *FLNT* measure will be identical to the female intensity of the total workforce, as shown in Table 9.2, if the employment shares of all sectors are equal to their trade shares. But if relatively female-intensive sectors have a relatively high share in total exports, the female labour needs of exports will be higher than the female share of the workforce.

The change over time in the female labour needs of trade reflects the extent to which Indonesia's trade composition has shifted towards more (or less) female-intensive industries. In their study covering 145 countries, Do, Levchenko and Raddatz (2016) found that an increase in the female labour needs of exports was associated with lower fertility, due in theory to the higher earning opportunities for women and the increased opportunity cost of raising children. The female labour needs of final goods imports, on the other hand, would be negatively related to employment opportunities for women, since import penetration is associated with lower employment growth (see, for example, Edwards and Jenkins 2015; Acemoglu et al. 2016).

Table 9.3 presents the two *FLNT* measures for 2000 and 2010, with the female intensity of the total workforce repeated in the first row. It shows that while the female intensity of employment was roughly constant over time, the female labour needs of exports declined by three percentage points. Hence, in 2010 the relatively female-intensive sectors accounted for a smaller share of total exports than in 2000. The female labour needs of imports remained roughly constant over time, declining by only 0.6 percentage points.

The decline in the female labour needs of exports is mainly due to the increase in the share of the male-dominated mining sector in total exports, from 14 per cent in 2000 to 24 per cent in 2010; the female intensity of this sector was only 18 per cent in 2000. And while the food and beverages sector, a relatively female-intensive sector, became more important in total exports, this was offset by a declining importance of textile exports – also a female-intensive sector. The share of each sector in Indonesia's total exports in 2000 and 2010 can be found in Table A9.1 in the appendix, along with the female intensity of each sector in 2000.

The decline in the female labour needs of exports in Indonesia, combined with roughly constant female labour needs of imports, indicates that changes in the sectoral composition of trade between 2000 and 2010 did not improve the employment opportunities for women (relative to men).

Exposure to trade and female intensity

We now analyse the 33 sectors' exposure to trade, and assess the link between female intensity and trade exposure. That is, while the previous subsection focused on the sectoral composition of trade, this subsection focuses on within-sector trade openness.

Figures 9.3–9.5 show the relationship between the sectors' female intensity and their trade openness, as measured by the export–output ratio, the import–input ratio and import penetration (as defined above). Each sector is weighted by its employment size, depicted in the figures by the size of each circle.

There is no clear link between female intensity and trade exposure in terms of exports: there seems to be no correlation between a sector's export–output ratio and its female intensity in 2000 or in 2010 (first two graphs in Figure 9.3). In 2000, the four most export-oriented sectors were machinery, other manufacturing (not elsewhere specified), the fuel industry and electrical and optical equipment, with sectoral export–output ratios close to 1 (first graph). By 2010 their export–output ratios had declined considerably, although the machinery and fuel industries still remained among the most export-intensive sectors, together with manufacturing industries such as metals, leather products, and rubber and plastics (second graph). These sectors have somewhat lower than average female intensities, but the overall correlation between export–output ratio and female intensity is not very strong. The decline in export shares is also not correlated with the initial female intensity in 2000 (third graph in Figure 9.3), although we do see that, over the decade, women appear to

Figure 9.3 Female share of workers and export share, 2000–10

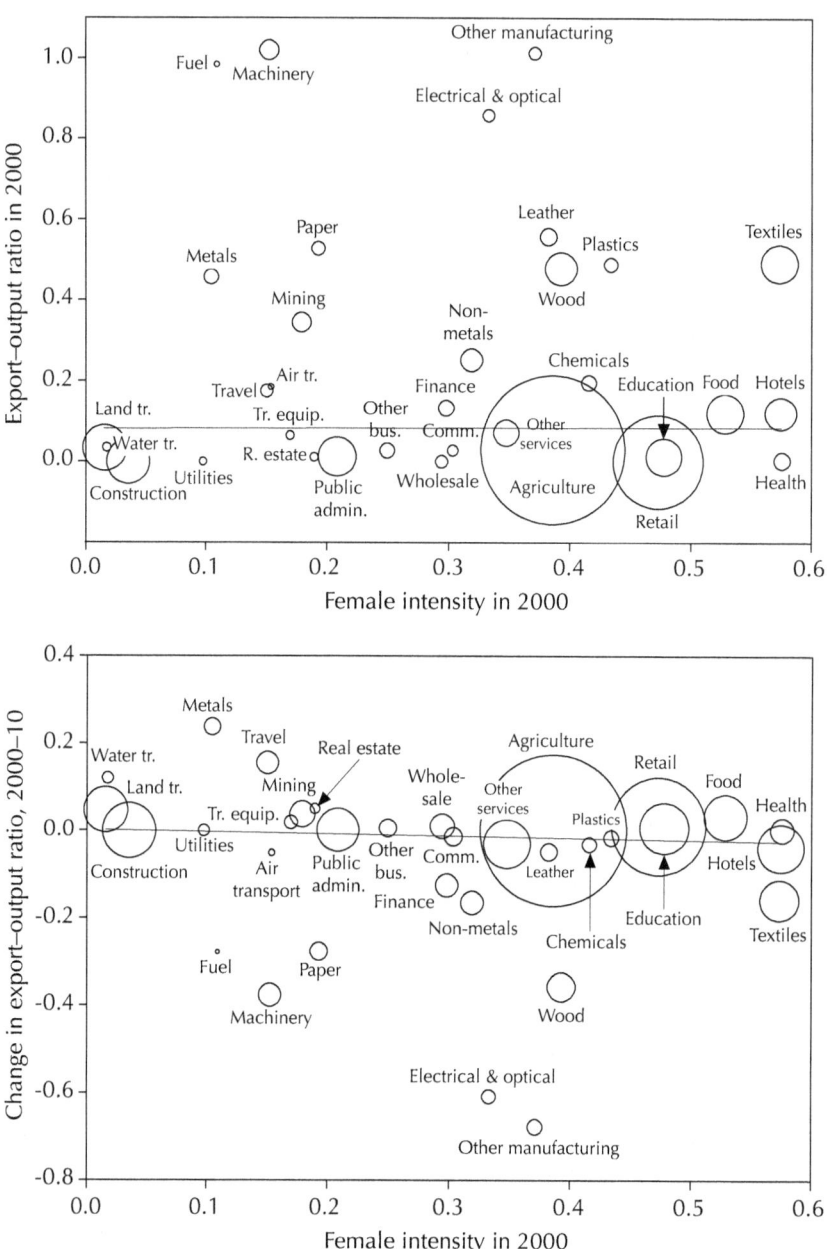

Note: Size of circles denotes overall employment within each sector; linear fit is weighted by sectoral employment.

Figure 9.3 (cont.)   Female share of workers and export share

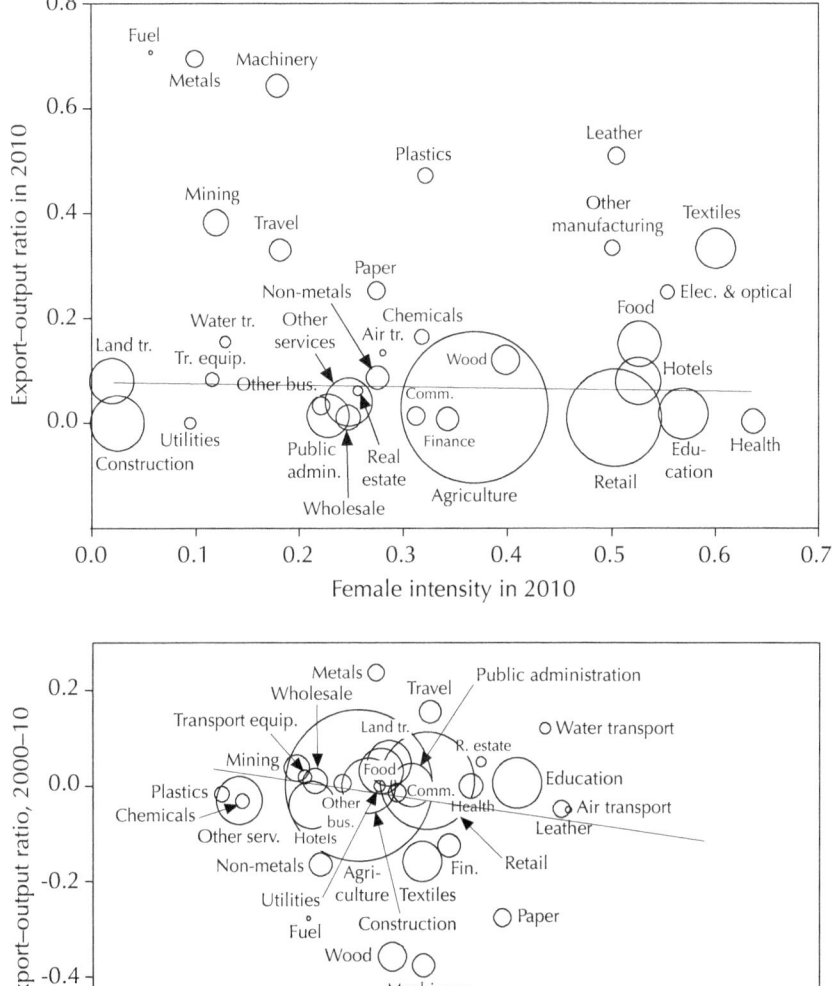

Source: Authors' calculation using data from the World Input–Output Database, 2000, 2010; and Sakernas labour force surveys, 2000, 2001, 2010.

Figure 9.4 Female share of workers and imported input share, 2000–10

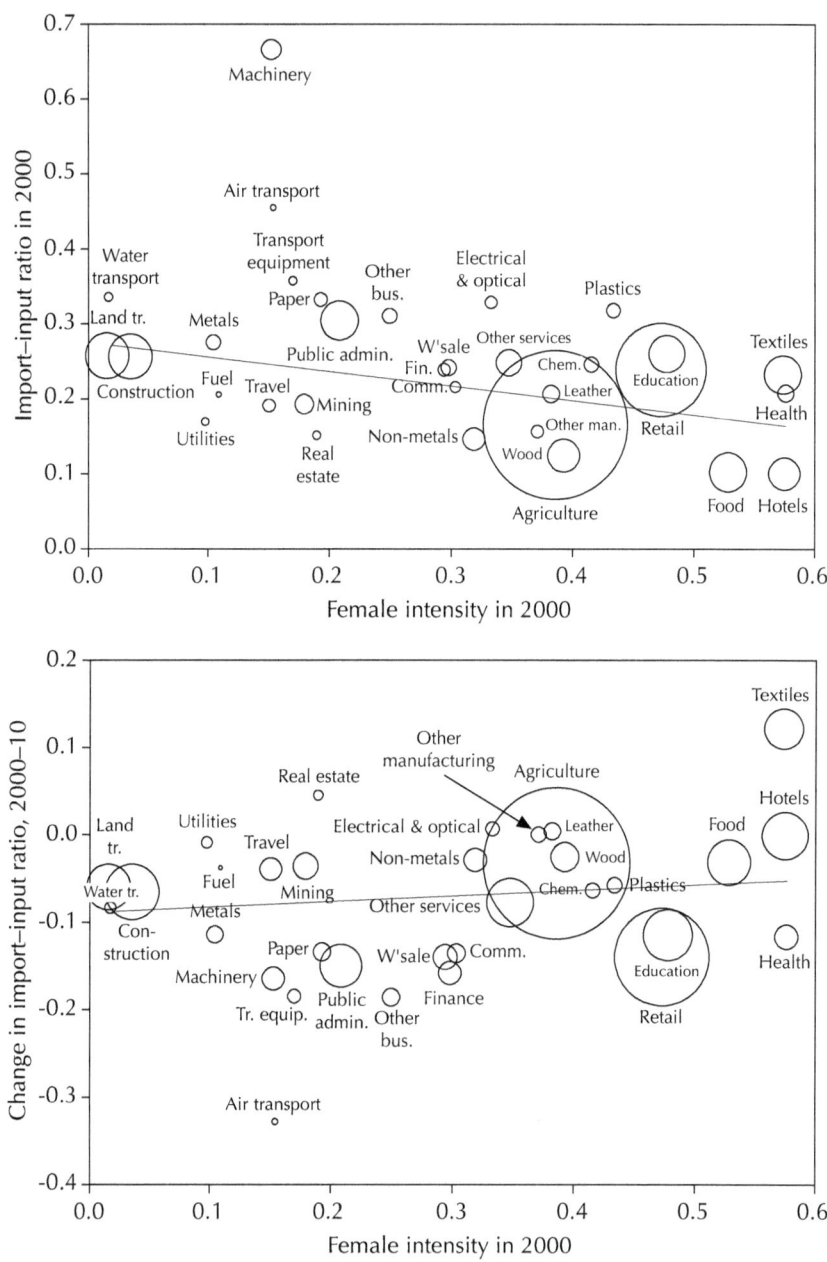

Note: Size of circles denotes overall employment within each sector; linear fit is weighted by sectoral employment.

Figure 9.4 (cont.) Female share of workers and imported input share

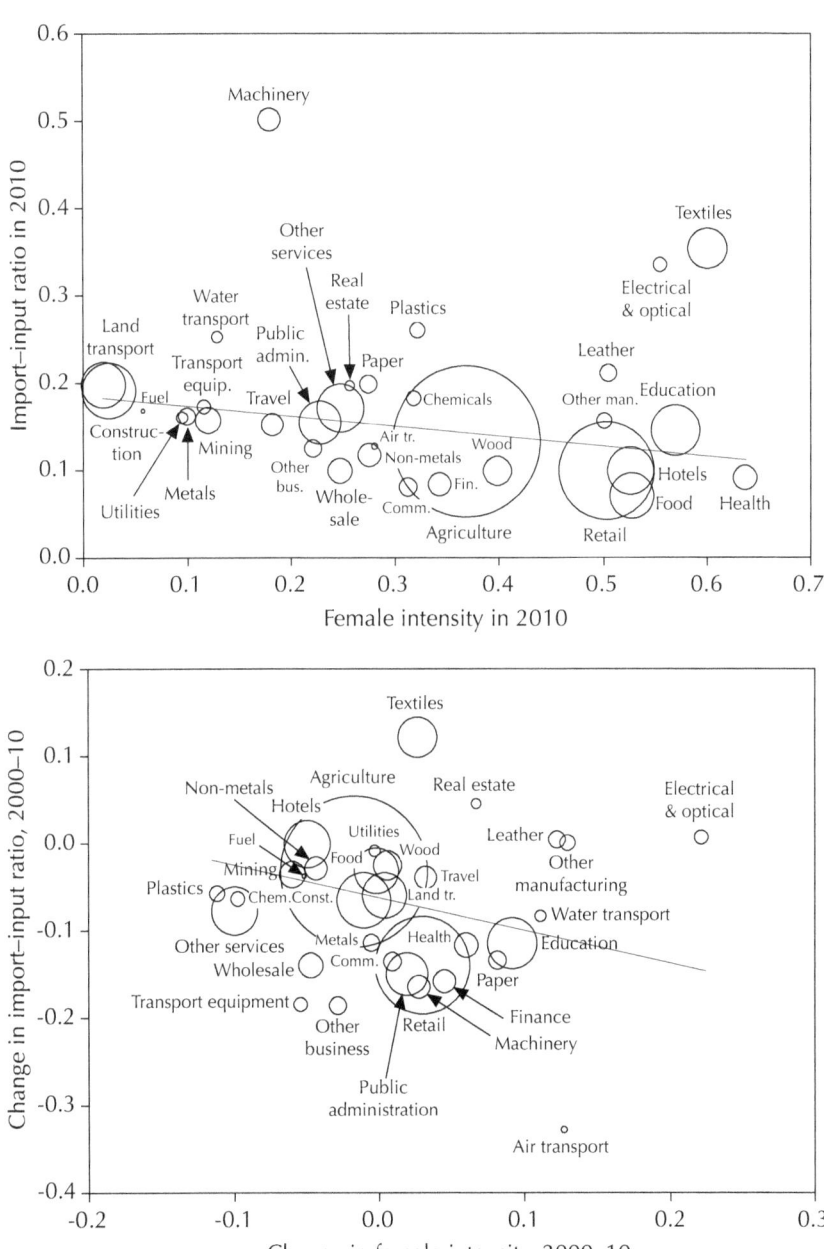

Source: Authors' calculation using data from the World Input–Output Database, 2000, 2010; and Sakernas labour force surveys, 2000, 2001, 2010.

174 *Indonesia in the New World: Globalisation, Nationalism and Sovereignty*

Figure 9.5 Female share of workers and import penetration, 2000–10

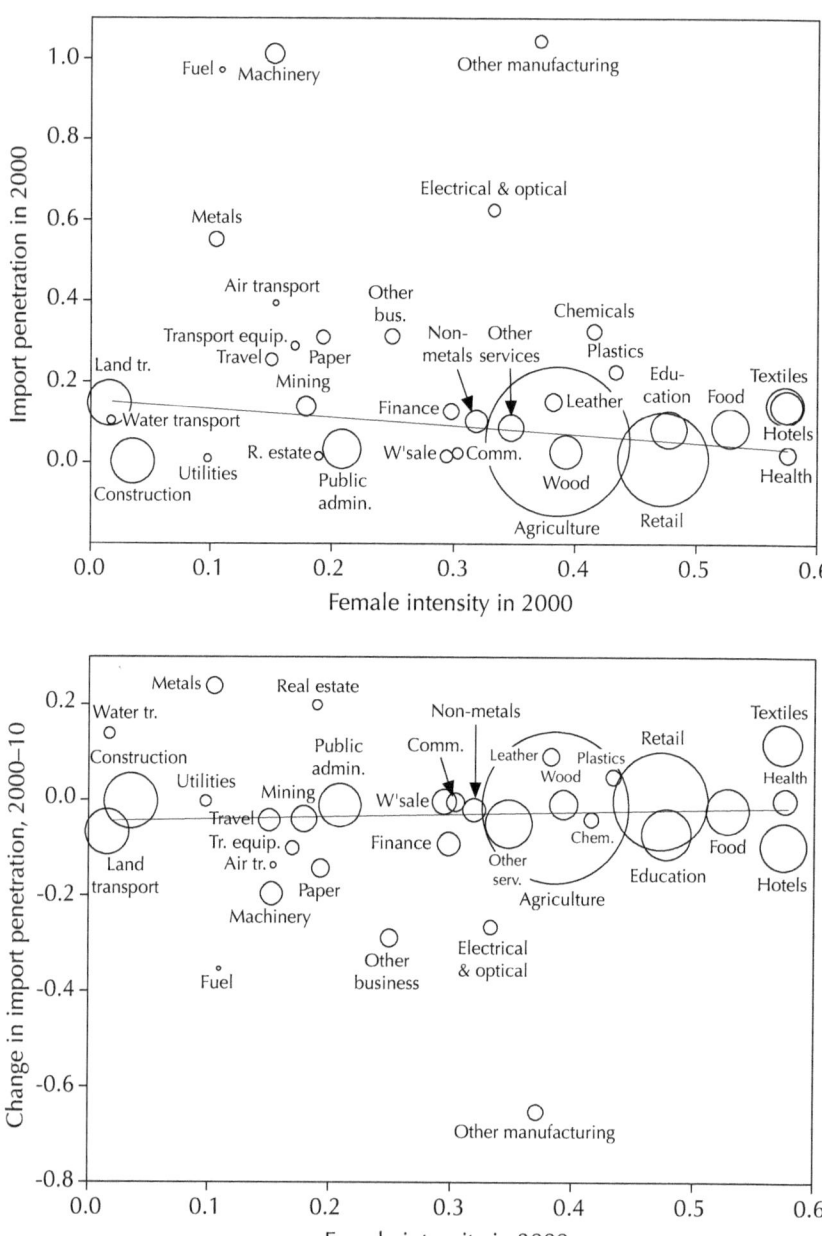

Note: Size of circles denotes overall employment within each sector; linear fit is weighted by sectoral employment.

Figure 9.5 (cont.) Female share of workers and import penetration

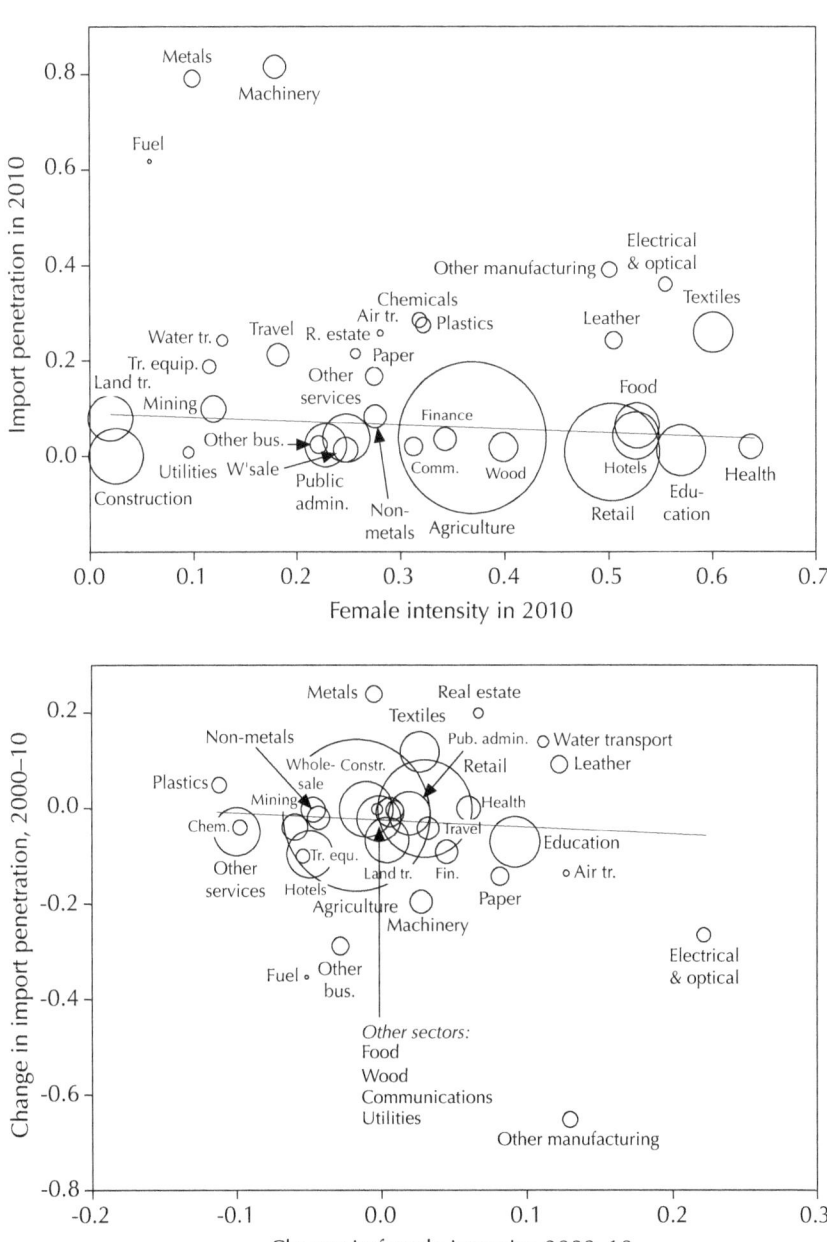

Source: Authors' calculation using data from the World Input–Output Database, 2000, 2010; and Sakernas labour force surveys, 2000, 2001, 2010.

have joined sectors where export activities had declined relative to output (fourth graph). This, of course, does not reflect a causal relationship.

Figure 9.4 correlates female intensity with exposure to trade as measured by each sector's reliance on imported inputs. In both 2000 and 2010, the machinery industry imported the largest share of inputs (first two graphs). In 2000 it was followed by air transport, and in 2010 by the textiles industry and electrical and optical equipment. Similar to exports, the reliance on imported intermediate goods decreased considerably over the period 2000–10. At the same time, we see a stronger correlation between female intensity and imported input share: industries with the largest import shares were less female intensive in both 2000 and 2010. In terms of changes, however, we see that the imported share of intermediate inputs decreased at a slightly slower rate for industries with initially high female intensities (third graph). Nevertheless, these were also the industries with a relative decline in female intensity, so that we find a negative correlation in the fourth graph in Figure 9.4.

Finally, if we consider exposure to international competition through imports of final goods (Figure 9.5), we find that sectors with higher import penetration were slightly less female intensive, in both 2000 and 2010 (first two graphs), and that female intensity fell a bit more in industries with increasing import penetration (fourth graph). All of these correlations are rather weak, however.

Considering the fourth graphs in each of the figures (Figures 9.3, 9.4 and 9.5), it is clear that female intensity increased most in the sectors that experienced reduced trade activity, although the correlation is not always strong.

CONCLUSIONS

The trends in international trade during the post-decentralisation era in Indonesia do not seem to have been favourable for inducing female employment through the channels observed in the decade before the Asian financial crisis, in the 1990s. For example, Kis-Katos, Pieters and Sparrow (2017) show that trade liberalisation in the 1990s led to larger increases in female (but not male) work participation in those districts that were more strongly exposed to falling tariffs on intermediate products. These results link an expansion of imported intermediate use to larger overall female employment. At the same time, intensifying product market competition through imports does not seem to have played a major role.

Whereas female labour force participation rose slowly in Indonesia after 2000, the relative role of international trade in improving employment opportunities for women seems to have declined between 2000 and

2010, although we see large variation across sectors. In general, the Indonesian economy saw a relative decline in trade intensity, in terms of both imports and exports. At the same time, the focus of trade activities shifted towards sectors that were relatively male intensive, such as mining, leading to a reduction in the female labour needs of trade. In addition, female intensity of the labour force increased predominantly in sectors that saw a relative reduction in international trade.

This raises some relevant questions for further research. First, what has been the role of trade policy in Indonesia's dwindling trade performance? In particular, with tariffs low and bound by international agreements, what has been the impact of non-tariff barriers on trade, and how have these affected female employment opportunities? Second, to what extent is sectoral segregation by gender persistent and what drives this sectoral segregation? Answers to these questions would help us better understand how trade and trade policies can strengthen women's labour force participation and reduce gender gaps in labour market outcomes.

REFERENCES

Acemoglu, D., D. Autor, D. Dorn, G.H. Hanson and B. Price (2016) 'Import competition and the great US employment sag of the 2000s', *Journal of Labor Economics* 34(1): 141–98.

Amiti, M., and L. Cameron (2012) 'Trade liberalization and the wage skill premium: evidence from Indonesia', *Journal of International Economics* 87(2): 277–87.

Amiti, M., and J. Konings (2007) 'Trade liberalization, intermediate inputs and productivity: evidence from Indonesia', *American Economic Review* 97(5): 1,611–38.

Artecona, R., and W. Cunningham (2002) 'Effects of trade liberalization on the gender wage gap in Mexico', Working Paper No. 34144, World Bank, Washington DC.

Becker, G.S. (1957) *The Economics of Discrimination*, University of Chicago Press, Chicago IL.

Black, S.E., and E. Brainerd (2004) 'Importing equality? The impact of globalization on gender discrimination', *Industrial and Labor Relations Review* 57(4): 540–59.

Borrowman, M., and S. Klasen (2015) 'Drivers of gendered occupational and sectoral segregation in developing countries', Discussion Paper No. 222, Courant Research Centre: Poverty, Equity and Growth, University of Göttingen, Göttingen.

Do, Q.T., A.A. Levchenko and C. Raddatz (2016) 'Comparative advantage, international trade, and fertility', *Journal of Development Economics* 119: 48–66.

Ederington, J., J. Minier and K.R. Troske (2009) 'Where the girls are: trade and labor market segregation in Colombia', IZA Discussion Paper No. 4131, Institute of Labor Economics, Bonn.

Edwards, L., and R. Jenkins (2015) 'The impact of Chinese import penetration on the South African manufacturing sector', *Journal of Development Studies* 51(4): 447–63.

Gaddis, I., and J. Pieters (2017) 'The gendered labor market impacts of trade liberalization: evidence from Brazil', *Journal of Human Resources* 52(2): 457–90.

Galor, O., and D.N. Weil (1996) 'The gender gap, fertility, and growth', *American Economic Review* 86(3): 374–87.
Goldin, C. (1994) 'The U-shaped female labor force function in economic development and economic history', NBER Working Papers No. 4707, National Bureau of Economic Research, Cambridge MA.
Hazarika, G., and R. Otero (2002) 'Foreign trade and the gender earnings differential in urban Mexico', UNU WIDER Discussion Paper No. 2002/125, World Institute for Development Economics Research (WIDER), United Nations University.
Juhn, C., G. Ujhelyi and C. Villegas-Sanchez (2014) 'Men, women, and machines: how trade impacts gender inequality', *Journal of Development Economics* 106: 179–93.
Kis-Katos, K., J. Pieters and R. Sparrow (2017) 'Globalization and social change: gender-specific effects of trade liberalization in Indonesia', IZA Discussion Paper No. 10552, Institute of Labor Economics, Bonn.
Kis-Katos, K., and R. Sparrow (2011) 'Child labor and trade liberalization in Indonesia', *Journal of Human Resources* 46(4): 722–49.
Kis-Katos, K., and R. Sparrow (2015) 'Poverty, labor markets and trade liberalization in Indonesia', *Journal of Development Economics* 117: 94–106.
Timmer, M.P., E. Dietzenbacher, B. Los, R. Stehrer and G.J. de Vries (2015) 'An illustrated user guide to the World Input–Output Database: the case of global automotive production', *Review of International Economics* 23: 575–605.

Table A9.1 Female intensity and export shares across sectors, 2000 and 2010 (%)

Sector	Female intensity 2000	Share of total exports 2000	Share of total exports 2010
Inland transportation	1.6	0.3	1.7
Water transportation	1.7	0.2	0.7
Construction	3.5	0.0	0.0
Electricity, gas & water supply	9.8	0.0	0.0
Basic metals & fabricated metals	10.5	3.3	3.9
Coke, refined petroleum & nuclear fuel	10.9	10.7	9.7
Supporting transport activities; travel agencies	15.0	0.6	0.9
Machinery, not elsewhere specified	15.2	3.3	3.6
Air transportation	15.3	0.9	0.5
Transport equipment	16.9	1.1	2.5
Mining & quarrying	17.9	14.1	24.2
Real estate activities	18.9	0.1	1.2
Pulp, paper, printing & publishing	19.3	4.9	2.9
Public administration & defence; compulsory social security	20.8	0.2	0.3
Renting of machines & equipment; other business activities	24.9	0.2	0.3
Wholesale & commission trade, except of motor vehicles	29.4	0.0	0.5
Financial intermediation	29.8	1.9	0.1
Post & telecommunications	30.3	0.1	0.3
Other non-metallic mineral products	31.9	1.3	0.6
Electrical & optical equipment	33.3	11.7	6.8
Other community, social & personal services	34.7	1.3	1.5
Manufacturing, not elsewhere specified; recycling	37.1	3.7	2.1
Leather, leather products & footwear	38.2	2.3	1.4
Agriculture, hunting, forestry & fishing	38.6	1.7	2.5
Wood & products of wood & cork	39.3	5.1	1.4
Chemicals & chemical products	41.6	4.7	4.5
Rubber & plastics	43.4	3.7	4.4
Retail trade & repair	47.3	0.0	0.3
Education	47.8	0.1	0.3
Food, beverages & tobacco	52.9	0.0	0.0
Textiles & textile products	57.4	7.0	12.9
Hotels & restaurants	57.5	12.8	6.4
Health & social work	57.6	2.8	1.7

Source: Authors' calculation using data from the World Input–Output Database, 2000, 2010; and Sakernas labour force surveys, 2000, 2001, 2010.

10 The good, the bad and the promise of globalisation: a private sector perspective

Manggi Habir

This is an observer's attempt to shed some light on the impact of globalisation on Indonesian companies, and on their responses to shifts in trends. I will start by describing the trends in globalisation during the formative years of the Sukarno era (1945-66), then in the development-focused Suharto period (1966-98) and finally during the current period of *reformasi* (1998-). The Indonesian economy was closed to the world during the Sukarno era but gradually and often reluctantly opened up during the subsequent two periods. Indonesia's globalisation journey has not been a smooth one, with more than its share of fits and starts. The overall direction, however, has been an unavoidable opening trend.

In the first section of this chapter I will discuss the impact of globalisation on the corporate landscape, especially the financial sector. During the Sukarno era, the relatively open shutters of the colonial economy began to close with the nationalisation of large Dutch companies. The economy gradually began to reopen during Suharto's New Order era, with the impact varying depending on the sector, the state of development and preparedness to compete of individual companies, and the nature of the government's regulatory oversight. In both the Suharto and *reformasi* periods, the most common response of sectors and companies to globalisation was to call for protection, and then to prolong that protection for as long as possible in order to capture domestic market share. This was easier than innovating and improving efficiency to better compete globally.

Even with the country's protectionist bias, however, the disruptive impact of globalisation could not be avoided. Industry players and regulatory authorities struggled to adapt to heightened competition and to the rapid changes in technology and business models. Globalisation helped bring about deforestation, pollution and the devastating 1997–98 Asian financial crisis. Local companies have had to cope with rising working, environmental and product quality standards, whether they liked it or not. Government regulatory oversight has become tighter and more complex, raising the cost of corporate compliance. On the other hand, the Indonesian consumer has benefited from having more options and better-quality products.

In the second section of the chapter, I will highlight the cases of two Indonesian companies that are embracing globalisation to compete head-on with global players: Indofood and Go-Jek. Indofood established its first overseas venture in the early 1990s, while recent start-up Go-Jek is using new ideas and mobile technology to compete with regional and global players.

The new trend of digital globalisation is once again changing the corporate landscape, but this time it is allowing smaller firms to access the global market. The effects are being felt across a wide spectrum of firms, from the developed nations' multinationals to the developing countries' small and medium-sized enterprises. This chapter concludes with a few thoughts on what the Indonesian government can do to help local businesses prepare for the changes ahead.

GLOBALISATION SHIFTS IN MODERN INDONESIA

The Sukarno era (1945–66) and the shutting down of globalisation

After declaring Indonesia's independence on 17 August 1945, President Sukarno inherited a colonial political and economic system. The large corporations and banks were largely Dutch or foreign owned, while the smaller firms had a mix of foreign and local ownership. Independence from Holland did not come easily, with the Dutch sending troops back into Indonesia in 1947–48 in an attempt to regain the Netherlands East Indies. They captured most of Sumatra as well as West Java and East Java, while the Indonesian government moved its capital to Yogyakarta in Central Java. It was only in 1949 that the Dutch finally recognised Indonesia's independence at the Dutch–Indonesian Round Table Conference in The Hague, Netherlands.

The period in which the Indonesian government gradually took control of Dutch colonial institutions and set about altering colonial rules and regulations was a highly disruptive and uncertain one for businesses. Moreover, a considerable number of educated and skilled people opted to leave Indonesia and migrate abroad, mostly to Holland, adding to the confusion and uncertainty, not to mention the loss of talent.

Throughout the 1950s President Sukarno was preoccupied simply with keeping the country together. He focused his political efforts on creating a national identity that could unite a fractious country made up of many different ethnic communities with distinct languages and customs, and comprising a largely Muslim west, a mostly Christian east, and Hindu and Buddhist minorities in the centre. The new government was kept busy putting down secessionist and Islamic rebel movements: the Republic of South Maluku movement in Ambon, the PRRI rebellion in West Sumatra, the Permesta rebellion in South Sulawesi and the Darul Islam Islamic-state movement in West Java.

On the economic front, the government focused inward, promoting self-sufficiency and the ability to 'stand on one's own two feet' (*berdiri di atas kaki sendiri*, or *berdikari*). President Sukarno's well-known remark that Western donors could 'go to hell' with their foreign aid reflected this policy of self-reliance as the country's economic policy direction followed that of China and India. From a more globally connected structure during the colonial period, under Sukarno Indonesia shut itself off from the world in order to focus on reasserting its identity and building its capabilities.

One of the most radical actions the Indonesian government took to assert its control over economic and business activity was to nationalise a number of large Dutch-owned corporations; indeed, many of Indonesia's current state-owned enterprises (SOEs) can still trace their origins back to colonial times. But with insufficient working capital, limited spare parts, a lack of proper maintenance and the departure of many senior and mid-level managers, these companies faced considerable difficulty maintaining their operations.

The corporate landscape was dominated by these nationalised companies and a few new state-owned companies. Private firms largely played a supporting role, producing supplies for the SOEs on the production side or distributing and selling their products on the marketing side. The country's industrial and trade policies were designed to support an import substitution regime. Nevertheless, the seeds of a small and diffuse private sector were planted during this time. A few private sector entrepreneurs had formed close connections with the independence movement, which continued after the new government was formed. They included the indigenous Indonesian (*pribumi*) businessmen Soedarpo Sastrosatomo and Idham, who established Samudera Indonesia (shipping), Bank Niaga (banking) and Asuransi Bintang (insurance). The Sukarno government's 'fortress' (*benteng*) policy was designed to promote such *pribumi* businesses by giving them preferential access to import licences. Despite the intent of the policy, however, the indigenous enterprises often linked up with Indonesian-Chinese businesses, many of which would later flourish during the Suharto period. These companies included Gunung Sewu (agribusiness), Dharmala (coffee) and Sinar Mas (cooking oil).

The 1940s and early 1950s also saw the rise of state-owned banks, with the government establishing Bank Negara Indonesia 1946 (BNI 1946, later shortened to BNI), Bank Rakyat Indonesia, Bank Industri Negara (later Bank Pembangunan Indonesia, or Bapindo), Bank Tani Nelayan (which later merged with Bank Rakyat Indonesia) and Bank Tabungan Pos (which later became Bank Tabungan Negara). Initially these new state banks operated alongside the existing colonial-era banks, which were dominated by three large Dutch-owned banks and a number of regional banks. The major Dutch banks were Nederlandsch-Indische Handelsbank (or Nationale Handelsbank), Nederlandsche Handel-Maatschappij and Escompto Bank; the regional banks were Chartered Bank, Hongkong and Shanghai Banking Corporation (HSBC), Bank of China, Yokohama Specie Bank, Mitsui Bank and Oversea-Chinese Banking Corporation (OCBC Bank) (Lindblad 2009: 85–7).

A decade later, in 1959–60, the Dutch banks were nationalised. Nationale Handelsbank was renamed Bank Umum Negara (which would later become Bank Bumi Daya); Nederlandsche Handel-Maatschappij became Bank Ekspor Impor Indonesia; Escompto Bank became Bank Dagang Negara; and De Javasche Bank became Bank Indonesia, the central bank. Following the completion of these nationalisations, the other foreign banks were closed and the state-owned banks were consolidated into a single large bank, Bank Tunggal – the 'Sole Bank'. This left practically no foreign banks operating in Indonesia by 1965 (Bank Indonesia 1959–66: 7). Thus, by the end of the Sukarno era, the banking sector faced an uncertain and often volatile political environment, a closed economy and an industry going through nationalisation, consolidation and closure.

The transformation from a colonial to a national economy was a disruptive process. Business activity was often restricted and the flow of goods began to dry up. Towards the end of the Sukarno era the economy deteriorated further, leading to rationing and, eventually, hyperinflation. A failed coup followed in 1965, after President Sukarno fell ill. The coup was crushed by General Suharto, who became the country's second president.

The Suharto era (1966–98) and the cautious reopening to globalisation

After taking power, President Suharto stabilised the disruptive political environment by repressing political activity. He allowed only three political parties to hold seats in the country's parliament: the newly formed ruling party, Golongan Karya (Golkar), and two 'opposition' parties, the Indonesian Democracy Party (PDI), formed by five secular–nationalist political parties, and the United Development Party (PPP), formed by four Islamic political parties. The military-controlled Golkar party would dominate political activity throughout the Suharto period. In addition to military representation in parliament, military officers were appointed to key government positions in various ministries, as governors in provinces and key cities, and as ambassadors to important countries. Military influence was further secured by placing the National Police under the military and having its leaders report to the commander in chief of the Armed Forces (ABRI).

With politics under control, the country's new leadership turned to developing and growing the economy. Once economic stability had been restored, the country cautiously opened to outside trade and investment flows. The corporate landscape slowly changed as the private sector was given more room to operate alongside the large and dominant SOEs. It was during this period that some of the country's largest business groups were formed, growing to challenge even the SOEs' dominance in certain sectors. But government control over the economy was still pervasive, and for the private sector it was *who* you knew rather than *what* you knew that counted most. The businesses that flourished were those that could secure licences from the government and take advantage of globalised trade and investment flows to establish joint ventures with foreign partners and gain access to international funding. They included major business groups such as Salim in food, cement and banking; Djarum, HM Sampoerna and Gudang Garam in clove cigarettes; Astra in autos, heavy equipment and palm oil; Sinar Mas in palm oil, paper and property; Raja Garuda Mas and APRIL in plywood and palm oil; Barito Pacific in plywood and later petrochemicals; Lippo in finance and property; Medco in oil; and the Bakrie Group in oil pipes, oil trading and mining. Some of these enterprises dated back to the colonial and Sukarno eras, and all grew rapidly during the Suharto era.

The business environment continued to be protected under an import substitution industrialisation strategy. In manufacturing industries such as autos, private investors were encouraged to invest in the downstream end of the production chain (such as body and assembly) and from there slowly work their way up the value chain to more capital-intensive upstream activities. For those investing in natural resource industries such as plantations and mining, on the other hand, local private investors were encouraged to start at the upstream end and work their way downstream. But these plans were difficult to realise given the heavy capital investment requirements, the lack of supporting infrastructure and the inability of firms to generate appropriate economies of scale (Thee 2012: Ch. 9).

At the beginning of the New Order period, the government adopted a relatively relaxed policy towards foreign investment. This ended with the Malari affair in 1974, when Indonesian students protested violently against Japanese investment in Indonesia during the visit of Japanese prime minister Kakuei Tanaka. After this, policy on foreign direct investment became more restrictive.

This continued until the mid-1980s, when the government again relaxed its foreign investment requirements. The rules differed depending on the sector. In manufacturing, foreign firms were required to set up joint ventures with local partners and were often limited to production activities, with selling and distribution to be carried out by local distributors. In the oil sector, foreign oil companies were permitted to operate as contractors to the state oil company, Pertamina, under production-sharing contracts. In the mining sector, foreign miners were allowed to operate mining concessions for a specified period of time, after which they had to divest enough shares to bring their ownership below a specified level. Despite these restrictions, Indonesia's large domestic market, variety and supply of natural resources, and relatively young labour force were sufficient to attract foreign investment during the Suharto era.

In the case of the banking sector, the large state-owned banks that had been merged into a single consolidated bank in 1965 re-emerged in 1968 when Bank Tunggal was broken up (Bank Indonesia 1959–66: 9). Thus, Bank Indonesia once again became the central bank, while BNI 1946, Bank Bumi Daya (the former Bank Umum Negara), Bank Dagang Negara, Bank Rakyat Indonesia, Bank Ekspor Impor Indonesia, Bank Tabungan Negara (the former Bank Tabungan Pos) and Bapindo again became separate state-owned banks. Some of the larger privately owned Indonesian banks holding foreign exchange licences during the New Order period were Bank Central Asia, Bank Umum Nasional, Bank Niaga, Bank Danamon, Bank Bali, Panin Bank and Bank Duta.

In the 1970s, foreign banks were again permitted to operate in Indonesia. Initially they were allowed to set up wholly owned foreign branches, first in Jakarta and then in six major commercial cities. The foreign banks that established branches in Jakarta in the 1970s were Citibank, Chase Manhattan Bank, Bank of America and American Express from the United States; Bank of Tokyo from Japan; European Asian Bank and ABN AMRO Bank from Europe; Standard Chartered Bank and HSBC from Hong Kong; and Bangkok Bank, the sole ASEAN bank. These foreign banks provided banking services to their own countries' multinational companies and expatriates and to local high-net-worth individuals; they later extended their services to local corporations as well.

In the late 1980s, in the second phase of bank liberalisation, the government issued new banking licences for local banks, and allowed foreign banks to establish a presence in Indonesia by forming joint ventures with local partners. The regional and other banks that entered Indonesia at this time were DBS Bank and United Overseas Bank (UOB) from Singapore; Malayan Banking Berhad (Maybank) from Malaysia; ANZ and Commonwealth Bank from Australia; Korea Exchange Bank and Woori Bank from Korea; Chinatrust Bank from Taiwan; Mizuho Bank and Sumitomo Mitsui

Banking Corporation from Japan; and Rabobank and BNP Paribas from Europe.

A number of local business groups took advantage of the government's issuance of new banking licences to set up their own banks, leading to the establishment, among others, of Bank Internasional Indonesia (Sinar Mas Group), Lippo Bank (Lippo Group), Bank Summa (Soeryadjaya family), Bank Nusa Nasional (Bakrie Group), Modern Bank (Modern Group) and Bank Bumiputera (Asuransi Bumiputera Group). As a result, the number of local commercial banks more than doubled from 66 in 1988 to 165 in 1995, while the number of foreign bank branches and foreign joint-venture banks almost quadrupled from 11 to 41 (Kartasasmita and Stern 2016: 30).

The presence of foreign banks had benefits for Indonesia. Citibank was the first foreign bank to establish a separate consumer banking unit, as distinct from its traditional corporate banking unit, to cater specifically for individual customers. It was also the first to launch consumer products such as credit cards, debit cards, mortgages and car loans, and to install ATMs. Investment in information technology and automation allowed the banks to cut the operating costs of processing individual financial transactions, on both loans and deposits. This made consumer banking services more economical for the banks, and more affordable for individual customers.

Electronic banking services followed, allowing business owners to access their accounts and make transactions without leaving their offices. The foreign banks were also the first to introduce syndicated loans to diversify their loan exposures, and foreign exchange hedging transactions to protect against swings in exchange rate movements.

Citibank and the other foreign banks provided training and experience that led to the development of a cadre of local professionals in the banking sector. Some of these people would eventually become leaders of domestic private banks; Robby Djohan, for example, moved from Citibank to become the head of Bank Niaga.

Innovation was not limited to the foreign banks. The largest private bank, Bank Central Asia, was one of the first to issue a local credit card and it was the first to invest in information technology by linking all its branches, and later its ATMs, through a satellite service, thus allowing real-time transactions. It was also one of the first banks to guarantee same-day fund transfers within Indonesia for its customers, making it the preferred bank for many people. As a result, Bank Central Asia had the lowest cost of funds of all the banks and became one of the most profitable in the country.

With the increase in the number of foreign banks and publicly listed local banks, the banking regulators needed to ensure that bank regulations, standards and disclosure requirements followed global standards as closely as possible. As liberalisation of the banking sector proceeded, Bank Indonesia began tightening bank prudential regulations: it set capital levels in line with Bank for International Settlements standards; prescribed loan-to-deposit ratios to ensure that banks did not rely on interbank funds to maintain liquidity; enacted minimum loan-loss provisions to cover non-performing loans; set foreign currency exposure in the form of net open positions at 20 per cent of bank capital; and set the legal limit for lending to affiliated parties at 10 per cent of bank capital.

The biggest beneficiaries of globalisation and the keen competition among banks were, of course, bank customers. They were able to choose from a wider array of better-designed products, while benefiting from improved services and more competitive pricing. With the dissemination of financial information over television and the internet, bank customers became more knowledgeable, critical and demanding. But it was also bank customers who bore the brunt of the collapse of the banking system during the Asian financial crisis.

The downside of poorly managed globalisation and weak regulatory enforcement turned out to be destructive—and also instructive—for Indonesia. Relaxed environmental and employment standards as well as weak monitoring and enforcement led to environmental damage and poor working conditions in mining and manufacturing. The country's forests and wildlife were damaged irreparably by logging firms and later integrated plywood firms. Palm oil plantation companies cleared forests by burning them, causing smoke and haze to spread across Sumatra and Kalimantan, as well as neighbouring Malaysia and Singapore. Finally, towards the end of the Suharto era, Indonesia was engulfed by a painful and devastating financial crisis that brought about the collapse of the New Order government.

Regulations are effective only if they are enforced strictly and consistently. Unfortunately, this was not the case during the heady days of bank growth in the 1980s and 1990s. The tighter bank prudential regulations that followed the phased opening of the banking industry to new entrants were often not rigorously enforced. This meant that many banks made insufficient provision for bad loans and had limited capital, making them vulnerable to shocks.

Before the crisis, Indonesia also had too many banks, spread too widely across the country, for Bank Indonesia's bank supervision unit to be able to monitor them effectively. With group-affiliated banks avoiding the regulatory lending limits for group-affiliated loans, carrying a high proportion of foreign currency loans that were not sufficiently hedged and having provision levels that were not sufficient to cover problem loans, it only needed a slight market downturn for the banking sector to experience considerable distress.

This was precisely what happened in August 1997. When the Thai baht fell sharply against the US dollar, global market players began to worry about the rupiah. Short-term portfolio funds started to flow out of Indonesia in the last quarter of 1997, causing the rupiah to drop sharply from around Rp 2,500 per dollar in late 1997 to about Rp 10,000 per dollar in early 1998. With their foreign currency loans in rupiah terms ballooning four times, a large portion (about 30 per cent) of their total loans denominated in foreign currency and capital ratios of about 10 per cent, the Indonesian banks started to feel the stress.

To make matters worse, Bank Indonesia's tightening of liquidity to shore up the rupiah led to high interest rates, hurting both businesses and individuals. The deteriorating situation forced the Indonesian government to sign a Letter of Intent (LOI) with the IMF in October 1997, under which a number of distressed, small to medium-sized banks would be closed. This damaged public trust in the banking sector, causing a massive flight of deposits to government- and foreign-owned banks. The government moved quickly to issue a blanket guarantee for all bank deposits to stem the flow and inject liquidity support. Not long after this, most of the large banks (including many government banks) collapsed, as their shareholders were unable to inject the additional capital required to keep them afloat. A number of private banks were either closed or merged, and those that remained were recapitalised by the government. A handful of state-owned banks were also merged and recapitalised (Pangestu and Habir 2002).

The strict requirements of the IMF LOI worsened the economic situation, at least in the beginning, by requiring austerity measures that accentuated the sharp downturn in the economy. Under the LOI, the Indonesian government had to remove most of the major restrictions on trade and investment. The crisis quickly spread from the economic to the political arena, causing a drop in confidence in President Suharto's ability to govern. As he lost his grip on the economy, his 30-year hold on politics also weakened. Students demonstrated in the streets calling for a change in government. When President Suharto could not form a new cabinet, with several ministers refusing to sign up, he resigned and his vice-president, B.J. Habibie, took over as president until a general election could be held.

The *reformasi* era (1998–) and further exposure to globalisation

President Suharto's resignation in 1998 ushered in a more open and democratic political climate. The ban on establishing unauthorised political parties was removed, leading to the formation of several new religious and secular parties. Since then, the country has familiarised itself with the democratic process, successfully holding numerous local, provincial and national elections. Direct elections for local leaders and the president (from 2004) and the decentralisation of central government powers to the regions (in 2001) nurtured a new generation of leaders, including the current president, Joko Widodo, who had been a popularly elected mayor of Solo before becoming governor of Jakarta and then president. The military lost its dominant role in politics and retreated from parliament as well as from its network of government and business positions. The role of the National Police was elevated: it now reports to the Ministry of Home Affairs.

At the same time, however, the ethnic and religious differences that had been repressed during the Suharto era resurfaced. In the early phase of the *reformasi* era, serious clashes erupted between different ethnic and religious groups. Greater regional autonomy for the provinces and increased opportunities for political party representation for some of these groups have helped temper these divisions, but they still tend to surface during election campaigns.

At the height of the Asian financial crisis in 1998, the Indonesian economy had contracted by 13 per cent. But thanks to a world economy that was still growing, Indonesia's economic growth rate rebounded to 2 per cent in 1999 and further to 5 per cent in 2000. Since then, growth has hovered around 5–6 per cent, with a temporary dip below 5 per cent in 2009 as a result of the 2007–08 global financial crisis. Successive *reformasi* governments liberalised several sectors (telecommunications, television broadcasting, airlines, power generation, toll roads) that had previously been restricted to government enterprises and a few well-connected private companies, and privatised some state-owned companies. The trade regime was also relaxed, with tariffs dropping to an average of 5 per cent. Nevertheless, the economic policy bias towards protection remained.

Lately, with the United Kingdom proposing to leave the European Union and US president Donald Trump threatening to impose high tariffs on Chinese imports and to leave NAFTA, there appears to have been a retreat from globalisation. According to the McKinsey Global Institute (2016: 2–3, 4), global flows of goods, services and finance as a share of world GDP declined from a peak of 57 per cent in 2007 to just 39 per cent in 2014, while cross-border flows of data, comprising information, searches, communications, transactions, video and intra-company traffic, grew 45 times between 2005 and 2014. Digital platforms like eBay, Facebook, Alibaba, Amazon and PayPal accounted for a large share of these flows, helping also to boost traditional cross-border flows of goods and services.

Advances in digital technology are lowering the cost of information and transactions, allowing individuals and small firms to participate in the global digital economy alongside larger, more established, multinational companies. The rapid development of mobile technology, the spread of affordable mobiles and smartphones and the downward trend in internet broadband costs have made the internet and global connectivity more accessible for all countries, and for all income levels.

This has fuelled the growth of e-commerce, not only in traditional goods and services, but also in informational products that are easily downloadable, such as movies, music, software programs, mobile apps, computer games and e-publications. The growth of e-commerce is changing the way people consume and is slowly disrupting the business models of traditional retailers and financial institutions, including banks.

The Asian financial crisis severely affected Indonesia's large business groups, with many losing their banking licences and having to sell some of their holdings to cover their debts. In the more open and competitive business environment of the *reformasi* era, the conglomerates had to streamline their portfolios of companies and focus more on areas where they had an edge over their competitors. In other words, these businesses were forced to focus on *what* they knew, rather than *who* they knew as in the past.

The corporate and banking landscape changed accordingly, with some well-known local names becoming foreign owned, while retaining their local brand images. Astra, for example, is now majority owned by Jardines from the United Kingdom and Hong Kong, and most of its auto assembly, component and heavy equipment companies are now joint ventures with major Japanese companies.

In the wake of the crisis, the largest of the private conglomerates, the Salim Group, had to sell its controlling stake in major cement producer Indocement to German-based HeidelbergCement, and its holding in Bank Central Asia to the clove cigarette group Djarum. The Salim Group is now focusing more on its diversified and integrated food business, Indofood. In telecommunications, Singapore's sovereign wealth fund, Temasek Holdings, took a substantial minority stake in Telkomsel; Telekom Malaysia took a controlling stake in XL; and Temasek acquired a minority stake in Indosat, which it later sold to Ooredoo from Qatar.

Lured by the boom in commodity prices driven by China's double-digit growth during the first decade of the century, several private groups began to invest in natural resources. This helped spur growth in Indonesia's outer islands, but also caused worrying levels of environmental damage, deforestation and pollution. It also meant that less money flowed into manufacturing, making Indonesia's exports more vulnerable to swings in commodity prices. With the fall in commodity prices and slowdown in China's economic growth since around 2013, however, there has been renewed, if rather late, interest in manufacturing, especially from regional investors.

President Widodo's push to build much-needed infrastructure using budgetary funds and SOEs has raised two concerns. The first is the exclusion of private sector contractors and, with the government having to issue bonds to fund the gap in government tax revenue, a crowding out of market funds for the private sector and a potential contingent liability for the government. The second, larger, concern is the lack of a level playing field between state and privately owned companies.

In the banking sector, the changes since 1998 have seen more local banks become foreign owned. A handful of larger, locally owned commercial banks that had been acquired and recapitalised by the government after the 1997–98 crisis were eventually sold to foreign banks and regional sovereign wealth funds. Singapore's Temasek bought Bank Danamon (a product of bank mergers) as well as Bank Internasional Indonesia in 2003, and sold its stake in the latter bank to Malaysia's Maybank in 2008. Malaysia's CIMB acquired Bank Niaga in 2002, rebranding it as Bank CIMB Niaga in May 2008. Khazanah Nasional, the investment arm of the Malaysian government, acquired a majority stake in Lippo Bank in 2005 and, as the ultimate shareholder in CIMB, merged Lippo Bank with Bank CIMB Niaga in November 2008. Standard Chartered Bank from the United Kingdom bought Bank Permata (also a product of bank mergers) in 2004.

Foreign banks also acquired some of the banks that had managed to survive the crisis relatively unscathed, including Bank Buana and Bank NISP. In 2004, UOB from Singapore bought a controlling stake in Bank Buana and changed its name to Bank UOB Indonesia, and in the same year Singapore's OCBC Bank acquired a controlling stake in Bank NISP, which became Bank OCBC NISP. After Bank Indonesia limited foreign bank ownership to 40 per cent in 2012 (Bank Indonesia Regulation No. 14/8/PBI/2012 on the Ownership of Shares in Commercial Banks), Japan's Sumitomo Mitsui Banking Corporation bought a stake in Bank Tabungan Pensiunan Nasional, a mid-sized bank focusing on pensioners and micro banking.

Bank consolidation since the crisis has not been limited to the private sector. Four state banks, Bank Bumi Daya, Bank Dagang Negara, Bank Ekspor Impor Indonesia and Bapindo, were merged in 1999 to become Bank Mandiri, the country's largest bank. Nevertheless, reform of the banking sector to improve the efficiency of state banks remains incomplete. A few years ago the government considered merging Bank Mandiri and BNI, as both had a similar focus and customer base, and there was the potential to create efficiencies by merging their back-office operations and streamlining their branches and vast ATM networks. But BNI, the smaller bank, was concerned it would lose its identity, and used its considerable influence to fight off the proposed merger. Bank Rakyat Indonesia and Bank Tabungan Negara are regarded as important policy banks given their respective focuses on agriculture and mortgage financing, and so have been maintained as separate state banks. The number of commercial banks (including foreign, private, national government and provincial government banks) has shrunk by about half since the crisis, from 222 in 1997 to 118 in 2016 (Bank Indonesia 1997; OJK 2016). But the number needs to fall further still before it becomes manageable for the Financial Services Authority (OJK).

The crisis taught the banks to better manage the mix of their loan portfolios, which had been heavily skewed towards large corporations, with concentrated and lumpy exposures. Banks now followed Citibank's consumer bank model, with the result that their loan portfolios became more balanced, diverse and granular. In addition to the large conglomerates, the banks began to target other commercial segments, including small and medium-sized enterprises.

Some banks, including Bank Danamon and Bank Tabungan Pensiunan Nasional, set their sights on providing even smaller, micro loans to small-scale entrepreneurs and traders in traditional markets. Economic growth and the rise of the middle class helped this trend. The share of the population spending $2–20 a day (thus defining them as middle class) grew from 31 per cent in 1999 to 42.8 per cent in 2009 (ADB 2010: 11). In urban areas the increase was even more noticeable: the proportion of the urban population defined as middle class rose from 44.0 per cent in 1999 to 61.9 per cent 10 years later.

With lending rates determined by the country's four largest banks, Bank Mandiri, Bank Rakyat Indonesia, Bank Central Asia and Bank Negara Indonesia, a bank's profitability depends on its ability to lower its cost of funds. This explains the intense competition among banks to attract deposit funds from the market. The total number of bank branches grew from 7,377 before the crisis in 1997 to 32,847 by the end of 2016, giving the banks more capacity to tap into deposits and fund their loans in local rupiah. As a consequence, the proportion of loans denominated in foreign currency fell from 32 per cent to 17 per cent during this period. The proportion of non-performing loans, which stood at 8–12 per cent in 1997, had fallen to 2 per cent by 2016 (Bank Indonesia 1997; OJK 2016).

An improved ability to mobilise deposits and a more cautious lending strategy reduced the banks' average loan-to-deposit ratio from a peak of 110 per cent in 1997 to 87.6 per cent in 2016, while a more conservative capital retention policy boosted the average capital level from 9.2 per cent to 21.0 per cent (Bank Indonesia 1997; OJK 2016). These changes put the banking sector in a far better position to withstand market volatility, as would become apparent during the global financial crisis of 2007–08.

On the regulatory side, there has been a heightened emphasis on governance and enforcement. In 2011, the newly formed Financial Services Authority (OJK) took over the role of bank supervision from Bank Indonesia. With many of the larger banks owning subsidiary insurance, finance and security companies, it made sense to place all financial institutions under one supervisory agency, rather than the old model of Bank Indonesia monitoring the banks and the Ministry of Finance overseeing the non-bank financial institutions. There was also more focus on getting the banks to improve their own governance, especially with respect to disclosure and board independence, to ensure better checks and balances (Habir 2016).

With the rise of e-commerce and e-payments, banks have been struggling to catch up with the more nimble financial technology (fintech) companies, which were far quicker to develop e-payment digital platforms. Not only have the banks been slower to adopt digital technology, but they have also been struggling to integrate the new digital services into their older core systems. Somehow the banks will need to find a way of working with the fintechs, because the digital channel will be critical for distributing banking services. Bank Indonesia has allowed branchless banking through payment agents, including e-commerce platforms, since 2015. To improve the governance and monitoring of the system, in 2016 it issued a regulation requiring both the banks and the e-commerce platforms to obtain a licence to provide e-money facilities. A year later, Bank Indonesia launched its long-awaited National Payments Gateway to process domestic electronic transactions and balance the dominance of the global Mastercard and Visa franchises.

Nearly everyone in Indonesia has at least one mobile phone. This translates into huge potential for anyone trying to take advantage of the digital channel. The government is strongly supporting mobile phone adoption through the provision of infrastructure because it sees this as a way of achieving its financial inclusion policy of providing financial services to all segments of society. At the same time, increasing the number of physical bank branches remains a priority for Indonesia, because of the country's low levels of banking penetration and high bank-branch profitability rates.

INDONESIAN COMPANIES THAT ARE EMBRACING GLOBALISATION

Most Indonesian companies prefer to focus on the domestic market rather than venture overseas. This is understandable given the vast size and relatively high profit margins of the domestic market. Still, some companies are braving global waters, directly or indirectly.

One example is the Salim Group's integrated noodle-producing manufacturer, Indofood. It has a dominant 70 per cent share of the instant noodle market domestically and a 15 per cent market share globally, with manufacturing and marketing arms across the Middle East, Africa and, more recently, Latin America (Suzuki and Tavsan 2016). Indofood set up its first foreign factory in 1994, licensing its brand, formula and technology to a local affiliate in Saudi Arabia. Its familiar, cheap and easy-to-cook products sold quickly to pilgrims from Indonesia travelling to the Middle East for the *haj* and the *umroh*, and became popular among foreign workers in Saudi Arabia. Indofood now has three factories in the country. In 1996, Indofood established a factory in Nigeria under a joint venture; by 2010, the factory was producing 1 billion packets of instant noodles per year. In 2007, Indofood set up a factory in Malaysia through its Malaysian subsidiary. Two years later it built a factory in Egypt and in 2014 it moved into Turkey.

As part of a diversification strategy, Indofood entered into a joint venture with Asahi, the Japanese food and beverage company, to sell non-alcoholic beverages in 2012. In 2013, it took a 50 per cent stake in Brazilian sugar and ethanol producer Companhia Mineira de Açúcar e Álcool Participações and acquired a minority stake in Chinese integrated vegetable producer China Minzhong Food Corporation. Noodle sales still dominate, however, accounting for 65 per cent of Indofood's total sales and 97 per cent of its operating profit in 2014. Foreign sales accounted for a relatively small 9 per cent of total sales in 2014 but the company planned to boost this to 15–20 per cent.

Another company that is taking advantage of globalisation is Go-Jek, the locally owned app-based taxi (transport) and delivery (logistics) company. Go-Jek began offering motorcycle taxi services in 2010 with 10 employees, 20 motorcycle drivers and a call centre. After it launched its mobile phone app in 2015, sales started to take off. Go-Jek now offers at least 12 different types of delivery services through its app, as well as an electronic payments system, Go-Pay (Ford and Honan 2017). In the face of stiff competition from regional transport services provider Grab and global tech company Uber, it managed to raise $550 million from international investors in 2016, and another $1.2 billion in 2017, to fund its expansion (Baziad 2016; Russell 2017). In short, globalisation has been a key factor in driving the development of the mobile application that powers Go-Jek's business and in helping the company to attract sufficient investment from world capital markets to fund its growth.

CONCLUSION

Globalisation increases the efficiency of a country's resource allocation, leading in turn to higher productivity and higher rates of economic growth. With advances in technology, this often disruptive and transformative process is accelerating. The ability of society to adapt to these changes, however, has been slower. At present, people with higher levels of skills and education are benefiting from globalisation; an increasingly tiny segment of the population is growing ever wealthier; and the majority with low levels of income per capita are being left behind. As income inequality has risen, the political environment has become more uncertain and volatile. This trend is being seen across the globe.

In general, businesses prefer certainty. In Indonesia, this has translated into two different responses to globalisation. Among the large, established companies (whether privately or state owned), there is a bias towards maintaining the status quo and protecting domestic market share. Among the new, smaller and less established entrants, however, many want to disrupt the status quo, and are more tolerant of a more open economy.

As we have seen, a strong regulatory framework and effective institutions are required to optimise the benefits of globalisation and minimise its darker side. That is why appropriate standards, clear and consistent rules and regulations, and a level playing field – overseen by a knowledgeable, experienced and decisive government that can ensure enforcement – are critical for business to thrive in an increasingly global market.

In all phases of Indonesian engagement with the world – during the relatively open colonial period, when a minority of society with links to the colonial administration enjoyed the benefits of globalisation, during the inwardly focused and tumultuous Sukarno era, during the cautiously open and development-focused Suharto era and currently during the more politically and economically open *reformasi* era – the power and influence of politics on economic policy to control the flows of globalisation is apparent for all to see. That is why the public's perception of globalisation in a more open political system has considerable influence on how far the doors to globalisation can be opened. If global flows are not managed well, income disparity will increase and the doors to globalisation may close, at least until the miserable consequences push them open once more. Globalisation, it appears, has its own checks and balances.

So how will businesses respond to and manage the next, more technology-driven wave of globalisation, and what is the role of government policy in creating a more conducive ecosystem to help businesses prepare for these changes? In varying ways, businesses are already starting to adopt new digital platforms to better market and sell their products and services, although they have been slower to adopt digital technologies that could reduce their operational and transaction-processing costs. The government can play a role in helping businesses make the transition to new technology by, in particular, providing training in the skills required to help workers shift to technology-based jobs. Over the longer term, the government should add more science and technology content to the school curriculum at all levels.

Given the highly competitive environment in which it operates, the financial industry is perhaps ahead of other sectors in this area. The next phase will be for financial institutions to go beyond simply adopting new technologies and start adding innovative new features specific to the local market and consumer that can enhance their products and services.

The test for the Indonesian government will be to create a more conducive environment in which companies can thrive, while allowing those that are not able to adapt to close at the least cost. The test for local Indonesian businesses will be to use technological platforms and tools to transform themselves, so that they can become more market-relevant. Without these two elements in place, a major replay of the boom, bust and consolidation cycle experienced by the banks during the Asian financial crisis could occur – but among other sectors, and due to globally driven technology disruption rather than to erratic financial flows.

REFERENCES

ADB (Asian Development Bank) (2010) 'The rise of Asia's middle class', in *Key Indicators for Asia and the Pacific 2010*, 41st edition, ADB, Manila, August: 1–52. https://www.adb.org/sites/default/files/publication/27726/key-indicators-2010.pdf

Bank Indonesia (1959–66) 'History of Bank Indonesia: banking. Period from 1959-1966', Special Unit for Bank Indonesia Museum, Bank Indonesia. http://www.bi.go.id/en/tentang-bi/museum/sejarah-bi/bi/Documents/38fb5d2efc3041289c01c555b1bd38a1MicrosoftWordHistoryofBankingPeriod19591966.pdf [in English]; http://www.bi.go.id/id/tentang-bi/museum/sejarah-bi/bi/Documents/880ace647f1d4f0993af369f6a0cd81aSejarahPerbankanPeriode19591966.pdf [in Indonesian]

Bank Indonesia (1997) 'Indonesian financial statistics', Bank Indonesia, Jakarta.

Baziad, M. (2016) 'Go-Jek's US$550mil funding a game-changer for Indonesia', *Digital News Asia*, 18 August. https://www.digitalnewsasia.com/startups/go-jek-us550mil-funding-game-changer-indonesia

Ford, M., and V. Honan (2017) 'The Go-Jek effect', in E. Jurriëns and R. Tapsell (eds) *Digital Indonesia: Connectivity and Divergence*, ISEAS – Yusof Ishak Institute: 275–88.

Habir, M. (2016) 'Indonesia's bank governance trend post-1998 crisis', in P. Verhezen, I. Williamson, M. Crosby and N. Soebagjo (eds) *Doing Business in ASEAN Markets*, Palgrave Macmillan: 45–63.

Kartasasmita, G., and J.J. Stern (2016) *Reinventing Indonesia*, World Scientific, London.

Lindblad, J.T. (2009) *Bridges to New Business, The Economic Decolonization of Indonesia*, NUS Press, Singapore.

McKinsey Global Institute (2016) 'Digital globalization, the new era of global flows', McKinsey & Company, March. https://www.mckinsey.com/business-functions/digital-mckinsey/our-insights/digital-globalization-the-new-era-of-global-flows

OJK (Otoritas Jasa Keuangan) (2016) 'Statistik perbankan Indonesia 2016' [Indonesian banking statistics 2016], Volume 15(01), December. http://www.ojk.go.id/id/kanal/perbankan/data-dan-statistik/statistik-perbankan-indonesia/Documents/Pages/Statistik-Perbankan-Indonesia---Desember-2016/SPI%20Desember%202016.pdf

Pangestu, M., and M. Habir (2002) 'The boom, bust and restructuring of Indonesian banks', IMF Working Paper No. WP/02/66, International Monetary Fund, 1 April. https://www.imf.org/en/Publications/WP/Issues/2016/12/30/The-Boom-Bust-and-Restructuring-of-Indonesian-Banks-15704

Russell, J. (2017) 'Indonesia's Uber rival Go-Jek raises $1.2 billion led by Tencent at a $3 billion valuation', *TechCrunch*, 3 May. https://techcrunch.com/2017/05/03/go-jek-tencent-1-2-billion/

Suzuki, W., and S. Tavsan (2016) 'Company in focus: Indofood finds recipe for growth with halal noodles', *Nikkei Asia Review*, 23 June.

Thee, K.W. (2012) *Indonesia's Economy since Independence*, Institute of Southeast Asian Studies, Singapore.

PART 4

The human face of globalisation

11 Globalisation and labour: the Indonesian experience

T. Yudo Wicaksono and Chris Manning

In the current digital era of rapid technological change, globalisation of labour markets deals with a much broader range of issues than simply the effects of international trade and investment on jobs. Historically a major concern of governments, international trade and investment played a major role in job creation across the globe until the global financial crisis of 2007–08. Since then, the links between computerisation and industrial development — or between cyber and physical systems — have intensified, leading to revolutionary changes in modes of service delivery (Baldwin 2016). These developments have changed the nature of the debate on the labour market consequences of globalisation in Indonesia.

The shift in focus away from the labour market effects of trade in goods is partly a result of the slowdown in world trade since the global financial crisis. This is likely to be exacerbated by the Trump administration's threat to turn its back on the multilateral and regional trading system that has evolved over the past half-century. In addition to the effects of trade, many countries are concerned about the impact of foreign investment on employment, the benefits and costs of international migration and, more generally, the effect of globalisation on inequality (IMF 2007; Helpman 2016). Analysts are increasingly debating the *indirect* effects of foreign trade and capital movements for the labour market, as well as the *direct* effects through migration to and from developing countries.

Indonesia became more wary of trade, capital and labour interactions with the world economy after the Asian financial crisis of 1997–98. Restrictions that slowed the growth in trade and investment accelerated during the second term of the Yudhoyono administration (2009–14), as the boom in resource industries peaked and then came to an end (Hill 2015). At the same time, online shopping and other internet-based services spread rapidly in Indonesia, as in the rest of the world. In the Indonesian case, local start-ups such as app-based transport provider Go-Jek have expanded quickly, usually by gaining an initial foothold in Jakarta before moving quickly to other major cities. In the process they have created new job opportunities, while also threatening old ones (Ford and Honan 2017; Pangestu and Dewi 2017).

This chapter discusses the benefits and costs of globalisation for the labour market in Indonesia. In what respects have the country's interactions with the rest of the world hurt or helped Indonesian workers, either directly or indirectly? The key channels for globalisation are international trade and investment, with migration playing a supporting role. But we also pay attention to developments in the digital economy and their implications for work, employment and skills. The timeframe is the first decade and a half of the twenty-first century, especially the past half-decade or so. The discussion is set in the context of Indonesia's long exposure to international trade and investment, fashioned by geography and history.

In general, we conclude that globalisation has been good for labour, although there have been backwash effects for jobs in lagging industries. We argue that the future for jobs appears less certain than it has for some time as the internet revolution takes hold across the economy. Digital technology will make many unskilled workers redundant, and will probably increase inequality. A simple econometric exercise is performed to demonstrate this point. But digitalisation is also likely to have benefits for labour, including unskilled labour. To ensure that workers enjoy these benefits, Indonesia will need to be proactive in dealing with the challenges posed by the rapid absorption of this new wave of technology from abroad, and the associated increase in competition.

STRUCTURAL CHANGE AND THE SHIFT TOWARDS SERVICES: JOBS AND WAGES

The history of Indonesian workers' long engagement with the world economy has been chequered. Early Muslim traders and later the Dutch East India Company opened up opportunities for the Indonesian islands to sell their primary products to the rest of the world, drawing farmers and later labourers and indentured workers into the world economy (Reid 1990; Booth 1998; Houben, Lindblad and others 1999). In newly independent Indonesia, President Sukarno sent foreign investors home, sparking a cycle of plummeting exports and increasing economic and political instability. During the ensuing New Order period, President Suharto completely reversed the relationship with foreign investors, adopting much more market-friendly policies that were favourable for employment, repressive controls over trade unions notwithstanding.

In response to the Asian financial crisis, Indonesia again took a step back with regard to foreign capital and openness to imports. Immediately after the crisis and the fall of the Suharto regime, employment slowed significantly, investment plunged and economic growth declined. The jobs market struggled for a number of years before the resources boom—led by exports of coal, palm oil and some mineral products—brought about an improvement in economic growth and a better jobs outlook, in both the public and private sectors. When the boom ended in 2011–12, Indonesia faced a different set of macroeconomic challenges associated with a contraction in the foreign sector and an overvalued exchange rate (Garnaut 2015; Basri 2017).

Interestingly, however, the service sector continued to provide new jobs for job-seekers, even after the resources boom ended. Some of this dynamism could be attributed to the digital revolution, which had accelerated with the popularisation of mobile phones, the growth of online businesses, the spread of computerised 3-D design and the beginnings of the 'internet of things and services'. Jobs continued to grow in the modern sector even though labour markets had become more insulated from direct changes in the global economy than at any time during the past half-century.

What, then, has been the impact of structural change in the economy, and especially global interactions, on employment and wages in Indonesia? In the following two subsections we focus on the period after the Asian financial crisis, and especially the past half-decade, during which the economy has moved on from the earlier boom in natural resources.

Employment

The effect of broad economic change on employment over the past 30 years is shown in Figure 11.1. The central message from the figure is the shift in the structure of employment away from agriculture and towards services. However, the trends for each sector have differed during different subperiods, allowing us to gain some insights into how global developments have affected the labour market.

Manufacturing

As is well known, manufacturing exports and jobs surged in the last decade of the Suharto era, during Indonesia's all-too-short manufacturing export boom (Figure 11.2). Indonesia emulated the earlier export-oriented industrialisation strategy of several other East Asian countries—adopting a competitive exchange rate and encouraging exports and foreign capital inflows—and was rewarded with rising exports of labour-intensive commodities, chiefly textiles, clothing and footwear. Jobs in large and

Figure 11.1   Share of jobs by major sector, and unemployment rate, 1989–2016 (%)

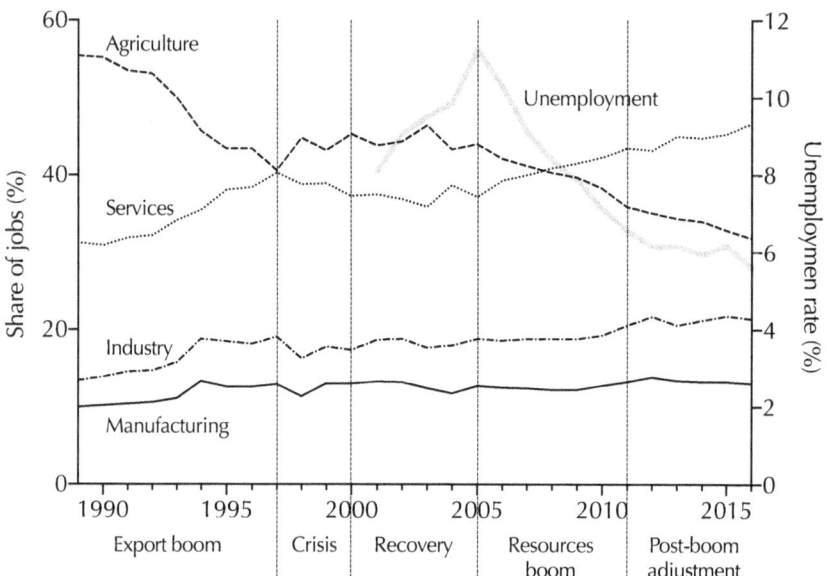

Note: The definition of unemployment was changed in 2001, so the chart shows only post-2001 unemployment data.

Source: BPS, National Labour Force Survey (Sakernas), August round, various years; data for 1995 are interpolated.

medium textiles, clothing and footwear firms almost doubled in just six to seven years, driven by exports emanating from both foreign and domestic investments (Thee 1991). While working conditions in the new factories were very basic, and labour freedoms neglected, many young women gained jobs in these industries that paid higher wages than they could possibly have hoped to earn in their home villages (Manning 1998).

All this was to change with the Asian financial crisis. For most of the 2000s—during the period of economic recovery, during the resources boom and then during the adjustment period after the boom—the output of export-oriented industries stagnated and the number of jobs in industry hardly changed.[1] Manufacturing experienced a sharp fall in employment growth after the crisis and never really recovered. As a consequence, the sector accounted for only 12 per cent of the increase in total employment

---

1   Industry is defined according to international practice as comprising tradable mining and manufacturing industries, as well as non-tradable utilities and construction.

Figure 11.2 Number of jobs in large and medium manufacturing firms by main industry group, 1989–2013

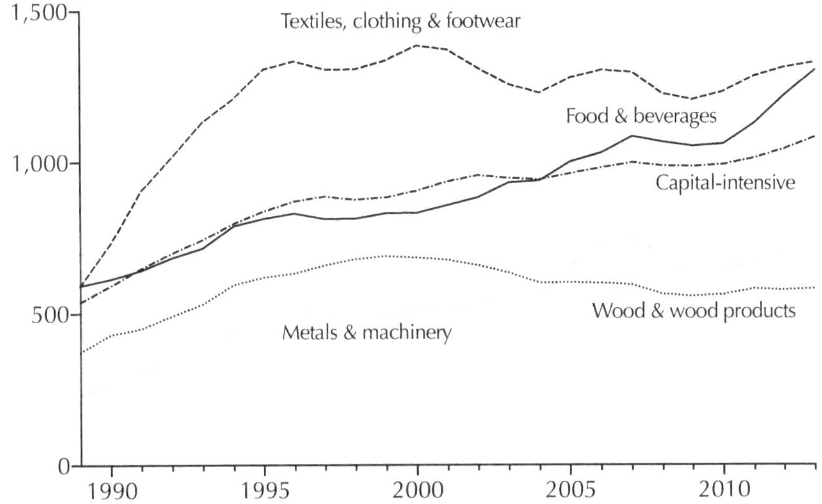

[Figure: Line graph showing number of jobs (0 to 1,500) from 1990 to 2010 for five industry groups: Textiles, clothing & footwear; Food & beverages; Capital-intensive; Wood & wood products; Metals & machinery]

Capital-intensive = paper and printing, chemicals, and non-metallic minerals and metals; metals & machinery = fabricated metals, machinery and equipment.
Source: BPS, Survey of Large and Medium Manufacturing Establishments, various years.

in the 2000s, compared with around 30 per cent in the years leading up to the crisis in 1998.

Indonesia was clearly no longer as attractive as it had been to international investors and buyers in the 1980s and 1990s (Hill 2015). China and to a lesser extent Vietnam began to dominate the inflows of investment and exports of labour-intensive manufactured products that had created so many jobs in Indonesia during the late New Order period. Post-Suharto Indonesian governments failed to invest enough in infrastructure and no longer offered the same incentives to foreign investors. An uncertain regulatory climate also contributed to the contraction in investment in the early 2000s. This included a raft of new labour regulations that threatened to make production less flexible and to raise wage costs (Manning and Roesad 2007). To make matters worse, the exchange rate became overvalued during the boom in resources, eroding the returns to investors.

Primary industries

Although the 2000s marked a partial retreat from globalisation in terms of exports of manufactured products, Indonesia continued to engage intensively with the world economy through its exports of commodities and mineral resources. Production of perennial crops such as palm oil and rubber took off in the outer islands, and by 2010 accounted for approximately one-quarter of all jobs in agriculture, and close to 10 per cent in the economy as a whole. Despite the growth in agricultural jobs in the outer islands, however, total employment in this sector stagnated from the mid-2000s (Edwards 2016). The employment generated by the boom in agricultural exports in the outer islands was not sufficient to counterbalance the steady decline in employment in the food crop sector in other islands, mainly Java.

The experience of the mining industry has been rather different. Although an important part of Indonesia's interaction with the global economy, mainly through the revenue created for the national government and regional governments, mining has never created much direct employment. The number of workers employed by the industry peaked at just over 1.6 million, or 1.4 per cent of the total workforce, at the height of the resources boom in 2012. While many of these workers were employed in high-wage jobs, many others worked for low wages in informal small enterprises, using rudimentary technology to mine on the fringes of the established mining concessions, particularly in the case of coal.[2]

Services

Service industries flourished in the post-crisis period as Indonesia began to retreat from its heavy exposure to the vagaries of the world economy. The mid-2000s through to around 2011-12 were comparatively good years for the Indonesian economy, as reflected in a sharp decline in the unemployment rate from 11.2 per cent in 2005 to 6.1 per cent in 2012, and then to 5.6 per cent in 2016 (Figure 11.1). Within services, the rate of expansion in jobs in two subsectors, finance and business, and public, social and personal services, far exceeded that in the other two major subsectors, trade, hotels and restaurants, and transport and communications (Figure 11.3).

Figure 11.3 shows the changing shares of jobs within services over the past three decades. While the shares of mainly informal sector jobs in trade, hotels and restaurants and in transport and communications fell, the share of finance and business rose from just 2 per cent in 1989-97 to around 12 per cent in 2011-16.[3] The proportion of jobs in 'other' services — public, social and personal services — consisting mainly of formal sector

---

2 Garnaut (2015: Box 1) provides a graphic description of the activities of these informal (and illegal, by official reckoning) mining operations in Indonesia during the resources boom period.

3 Informal jobs are defined according to the BPS definition, as all self-employed and family work, but not including self-employed professionals.

Figure 11.3   Share of service sector employment by major subsector, 1989–2016 (%)

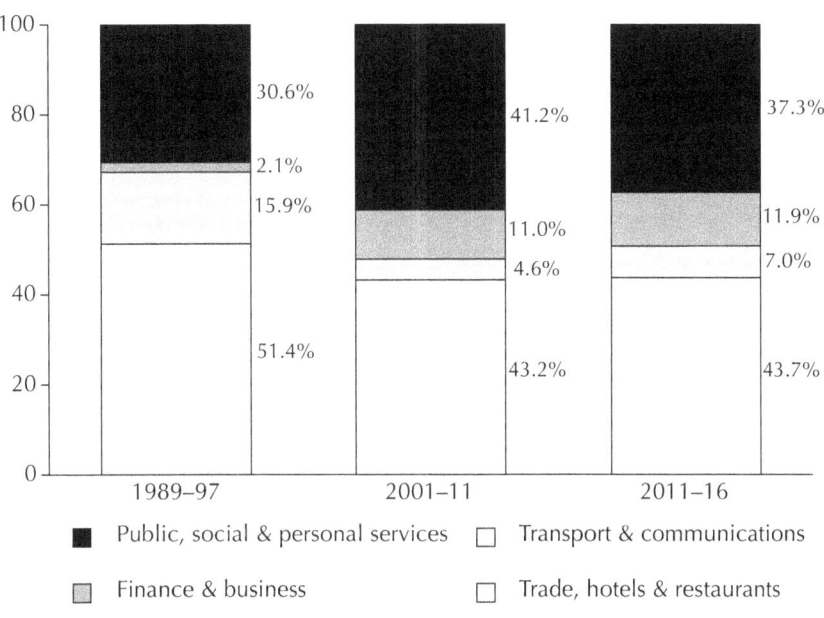

Source: BPS, National Labour Force Survey (Sakernas), August round, various years.

jobs, also rose, to around 40 per cent of all service sector employment. In other words, service sector expansion was associated with strong growth in *formal sector*, wage jobs, in contrast to the earlier experience when new jobs in this sector were associated with expansion of the *informal sector*.

A more detailed breakdown of service sector employment reveals a number of other characteristics related to global trade and investment during 2011–15 (Table 11.1).[4] First, more internationally oriented activities — such as business and tourism-related industries — feature prominently among the mainly formal sector activities that have grown strongly, while employment in food and beverage stalls is the only informal sector activity in this category. Employees in the rapidly growing formal sectors tend to be better educated (with a senior secondary education or higher), female and relatively young.[5] As discussed in the next subsection, they also tend

---

4   The year 2011 is chosen as the starting point because BPS revised its definitions of service sector categories in that year.
5   For example, 45 per cent of all employees in the finance and business sector had a university degree in 2016, compared with less than 10 per cent for the service sector as a whole.

Table 11.1 Service sector jobs in selected industries, 2011–15

Industry	Employment in 2015		Growth in jobs, 2011–15 (%)	Share of formal sector jobs (%)
	(million)	(% of service sector)		
Rapid growth				
Mainly formal sector				
Finance & business	1.45	2.8	35.3	97
Health services	1.40	2.7	25.8	90
Hotels & accommodation	0.58	1.1	30.3	91
Real estate	0.29	0.6	62.0	72
Insurance, pensions	0.15	0.3	49.4	100
Travel agents & tour guides	0.10	0.2	25.1	75
Mainly informal sector				
Food & beverages	4.66	9.0	45.0	23
Slow growth				
Mainly formal sector				
Govt admin. & security	4.03	7.8	2.4	100
Domestic workers	2.49	4.8	5.6	69
Telecommunications	0.33	0.6	–4.7	75
Sea transport	0.19	0.4	–4.2	80
Mainly informal sector				
Retail trade	18.14	35.2	6.3	23

Note: Formal sector employment is defined here as employment in workplaces in which at least 60 per cent of workers are wage workers, rather than self-employed workers, family workers or employers. The balance is classified as informal for the purposes of this table.

Source: BPS, National Labour Force Survey (Sakernas), August round, 2011 and 2015.

to earn higher wages, exacerbating the gap in wages between the formal and informal sectors.

Second, jobs grew less quickly in the mainly formal government sector, and in the mainly informal retail trade sector. In the public sector, limited government budgets meant that fewer new jobs were created.[6] In retail

---

6   The exception was health services, which grew rapidly after the establishment of a new national social security agency (BPJS). There was also a moderate expansion of employment in the very large education sector, which provided more than 4 million jobs, mostly for people with a senior secondary or tertiary education.

trade, which accounted for one-third of all service sector jobs in 2015, the expansion of supermarket chains and retail giants such as Indomart and Carrefour, and the spread of online shopping, probably put a brake on job creation.

Wages

Job creation (and destruction) is just one aspect of labour market adjustment associated with globalisation. Another is the impact of changes in domestic and international demand (especially investment) on wages — for example, the wages paid by foreign firms and firms in export-oriented industries. Critics have coined the term 'race to the bottom' to describe the low wages paid by foreign investors in export-oriented industries (see, for example, Economist 2013; ILO 2013). Alternatively, it is argued that the internationally oriented firms and industries provide opportunities for disadvantaged members of the workforce, especially women, to get better jobs (Moran 2006; Brambilla, Chauvin and Porto 2017).

The literature for Indonesia mirrors these debates. On the one hand, critics of foreign investment in export-oriented and labour-intensive industries, especially garments and footwear, point to abuses of labour rights and standards in Indonesia (Tjandra 2016). On the other hand, economists taking a more quantitative approach highlight the wage bonus derived from foreign investment (and often associated with exports), which is partly explained by the higher productivity of foreign-owned firms (Lipsey and Sjöholm 2004; Takii and Ramstetter 2005; Ramstetter and Sjöholm 2006; Lipsey, Sjöholm and Sun 2010).

Data from BPS's 2014 Survey of Large and Medium Manufacturing Establishments confirm that foreign firms pay higher wages than domestic firms, especially in the case of non-production workers. However, they do not suggest a significant wage premium associated with exporting. Figure 11.4 compares wages in foreign firms and exporting firms. The analysis is restricted to large firms (those with 100 employees or more), bearing in mind that foreign firms and exporting firms tend to be larger than domestic firms and non-exporting companies. In the case of production workers, the figure shows that the wages paid by foreign firms are about 15–20 per cent higher than those paid by exporting firms, except in the more labour-intensive industries (textiles, clothing and footwear, and wood and wood-based products). The foreign firm premium for non-production workers, a rough proxy for more skilled labour, is a much higher 40–60 per cent. The data imply that large foreign firms employ more highly skilled labour than domestic firms, partly because they use more advanced technology, but also because they employ more highly paid workers from overseas.

Figure 11.4 Ratio of wages by firm ownership and trade orientation, 2014 (locally owned and non-exporting firms = 100)

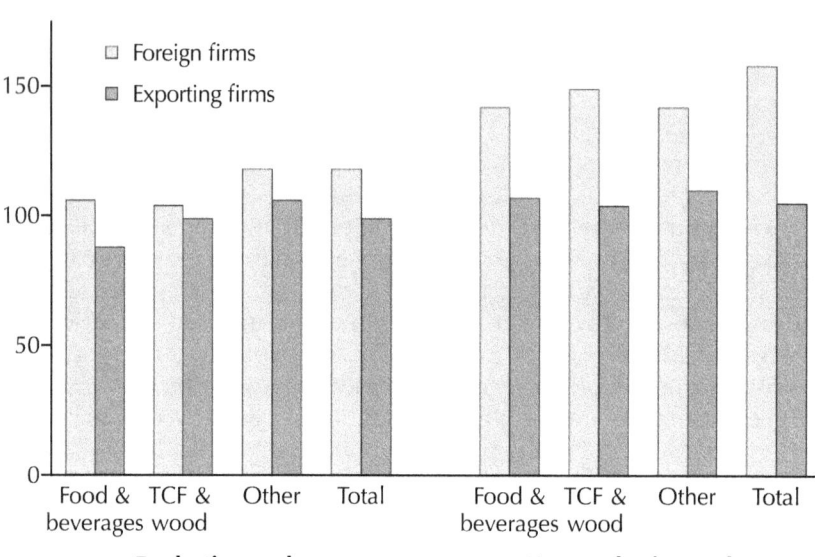

TCF = textiles, clothing and footwear.

Note: The chart shows the ratio of wages in foreign-owned and exporting firms to wages in locally owned and non-exporting firms. Exporters are defined as firms that export 10 per cent or more of their valued added.

Source: BPS, Survey of Large and Medium Manufacturing Firms, 2014.

Exporting firms appear to pay no such wage premium. In fact, the wages exporters in Indonesia's large food-processing industry pay production workers seem to be lower than those paid by non-exporters. The data imply that, unlike foreign companies, exporters derive some of their competitive edge in international markets from the payment of low wages.

Using data from the 2005 and 2014 Surveys of Large and Medium Manufacturing Establishments, we also examined wage growth among production workers in relation to the ownership and trade orientation of manufacturing establishments (Figure 11.5). In general, wage growth seems to have been quite slow among production workers during the period 2005–14 (only 1–2 per cent per annum in the food and beverages, textiles, clothing and footwear, and wood-based industries), reflecting the rather depressed state of manufacturing, as discussed above. Somewhat surprisingly given the greater tendency for foreign manufacturing firms to comply with minimum wage legislation, we find that wages have risen faster in domestic firms than in foreign firms (by 1.5 per cent per annum,

Figure 11.5 Wage growth among production workers in selected industries by ownership and trade orientation, 2005–14 (% p.a.)

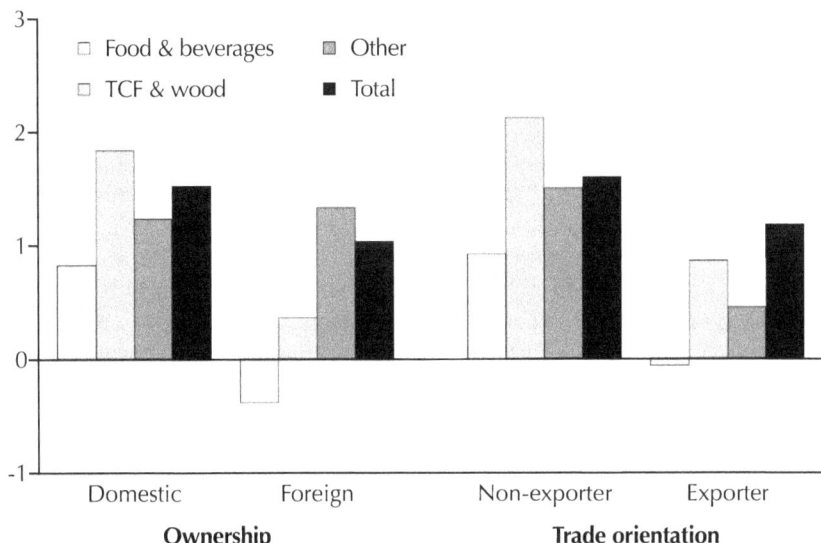

TCF = textiles, clothing and footwear.
Source: BPS, Survey of Large and Medium Manufacturing Firms, 2005 and 2014.

compared with 1.0 per cent), and in non-exporters than in exporters (by 1.6 per cent per annum, compared with 1.2 per cent). One interpretation might be that foreign firms and exporting firms operate in more competitive markets (such as garments and footwear), where wage growth is more tightly controlled.

To sum up, at face value the data confirm that foreign firms pay higher wages, after controlling—somewhat crudely—for industry structure and firm size. However, the wage premium is much smaller and hardly significant among exporting firms. The data lend some support to the claims of globalisation supporters that labour standards are higher in foreign firms. But they also suggest that the magnitude of these benefits has not been increasing over time.

THE DIGITAL REVOLUTION AND EMPLOYMENT

The Indonesian experience described above suggests that globalisation has been good for employment and wages—compellingly so during earlier periods in terms of conventional indicators, and much less so during the decade and a half after the Asian financial crisis. Trade and investment liberalisation in the 1980s and early 1990s led to many workers from villages moving into more productive and better-paid manufacturing jobs (Manning 1998). A different pattern of global growth focused on resource-based industries had no such effect in the 2000s.

The traditional patterns of labour market change associated with global trade and investment remain important for jobs and wages. But new patterns associated with digital and internet-based technology have begun to impinge on both employment levels and incomes in what have traditionally been termed 'tradable' and 'non-tradable' jobs. The distinction between the two types of jobs has become much more blurred. We now turn to some of the processes at work.

Over the last four decades, innovation in information and communication technology (ICT), including digital technology, has grown rapidly. Advances in manufacturing processes, combined with the automation of production following the introduction of computers to manufacturing in the 1970s and 1980s, reduced the costs of production significantly. After the release of the Apple II in 1977 and the IBM PC in 1981, personal computers became more affordable for consumers and their use spread rapidly. This was followed by other waves of innovation, such as the internet, mobile phones and smartphones, and fixed and then mobile broadband (Muro et al. 2017).

Globalisation has also played an important role in driving innovation in digital technology. Significant reductions in trade barriers across countries allowed producers, including ICT manufacturers, to arrange production processes across multiple geographical locations, pushing the production costs of ICT-related products lower. As a result, the adoption of digital technology spread quickly across the world. According to the World Bank (2016: 2), more households in developing countries now own mobile phones than have access to electricity or improved sanitation, and almost 70 per cent of the poorest 20 per cent of the population in developing countries owns a mobile phone.

The digital revolution has increased the flow of information, ideas and innovation around the world. The use of digital technologies—computers, mobile phones and related technologies—has reduced the costs of coordination and information processing and given rise to new ways of organising production. Alibaba's use of a business-to-business e-commerce site to connect smaller Chinese enterprises with the global marketplace, for example, has significantly reduced coordination costs, and boosted the efficiency of the Chinese economy (World Bank 2016). In Indonesia, Go-Jek—an online platform initially providing motorcycle taxi services—has become the exemplar for other Indonesian start-up companies. As these examples show, the use of digital technology can boost employment and earnings in the ICT sector and in sectors that use ICT in their business operations.

The widespread adoption of digital technologies has also transformed features of the traditional workplace. To some extent, it has changed the relative demand for skilled and unskilled workers. Autor, Katz and Krueger (1998) found, for instance, that following the introduction of computers into US manufacturing in the 1980s, the demand for skilled workers rose and wages increased rapidly at the same time, leading to secular increase in the returns to skills. The authors attributed this outcome to skill-biased technological change, that is, to changes in technology that tended to favour skilled workers.

One of the chief concerns about the labour market impact of the digital revolution is that it will accelerate job destruction. While digital technology does have disruptive effects on labour markets, it is also opening up new economic opportunities in many developing countries, both through efficiency gains and through the increased demand for more highly skilled workers. One striking example is the flourishing of call centres in the Philippines and India in recent years.

Digital technologies improve productivity

One mechanism by which digital technology affects employment and wages is through its capacity to increase productivity. Computers and mobile phones can be used to store, retrieve, organise, transmit and transform any type of information that can be digitised. Digital communication technologies are reducing the costs of coordination, communications and information processing. This is transforming economic organisations built in an age of high communication costs.

This transformation is affecting workplaces and employment. An extensive set of empirical studies on developed countries finds that workers who use computers at work earn a wage premium (Krueger 1993; DiNardo and Pischke 1997; Oosterbeek 1997; Autor, Katz and Krueger 1998; Arabsheibani, Emami and Marin 2004). This is the case in Indonesia as well: using data from the Indonesia Family Life Survey (IFLS), Wicaksono (2017) finds that Indonesian workers who use computers in the workplace are more likely to earn higher wages. Consistent with studies for other countries, he concludes that productivity improvements from using computing technology are reflected in higher wages.

Computers, mobile phones and the internet allow individuals to work on different schedules, or from different locations. There are also distributional effects. Women, who generally face more barriers to labour market entry than men, can benefit greatly from technology that provides more flexibility in working schedules. A World Bank report notes, for example, that women's participation in Europe's fast-growing telework industry, and in other occupations with flexible time schedules, has been particularly rapid (World Bank 2016: 114). In Indonesia, Wicaksono (2017) finds that women receive a higher wage premium than men from using computers in the workplace—possibly because their earnings are lower to start with. But the data also imply that computers could help to reduce the gender wage gap in Indonesia.

Do digital technologies always destroy jobs?

The adoption of information and communication technology is accelerating across the world, even among less intensive users such as the retail sector. As we have seen, e-commerce and online-based retail trade have grown significantly. Online transport provider Go-Jek, for example, has expanded from motorcycle taxi services into a range of other services, such as food and goods delivery and even house cleaning.

In the absence of detailed data on the penetration of digital technologies in Indonesia, we use data from the 2009 and 2015 World Bank Enterprise Surveys to assess the intensity of digital technology use across economic sectors. These surveys provide information on whether firms use email to communicate with clients and whether firms have websites (starting in 2015 in the case of service sector industries). Figure 11.6 shows that all firms in the information technology industry use the internet intensively, followed by motor vehicle services and the transportation sector.

Manufacturing has been among the fastest adopters of the internet: the share of non-labour-intensive manufacturing firms using the internet in their day-to-day business operations rose from 27.0 per cent in 2009 to more than half in 2015. We also observe rapid adoption among firms in the trade sector. Surprisingly, even traditional labour-intensive industries such as textiles, clothing and footwear have been quite quick to adopt the internet, with the share of the latter rising from 30.5 per cent in 2009 to 44.4 per cent in 2015. This does not necessarily imply a threat to jobs; greater internet use may actually mean more jobs associated with higher levels of productivity.

The rapid adoption of digital technology has implications not only for factory automation but also for the automation of logistics and processing, digitisation (data entry, publishing and printing) and clerical support. Large-scale automation could speed up job destruction and thus have significant consequences for employment. In most developed countries, factory automation has already destroyed many medium-skilled jobs, leading to the stagnation of median wages (Economist 2016). Frey and Osborne (2017) find that the jobs of around 47 per cent of workers in 702 occupations in the United States are at risk from automation.

Figure 11.6   Share of firms using email and websites in their daily operations by sector, 2009 and 2015 (%)

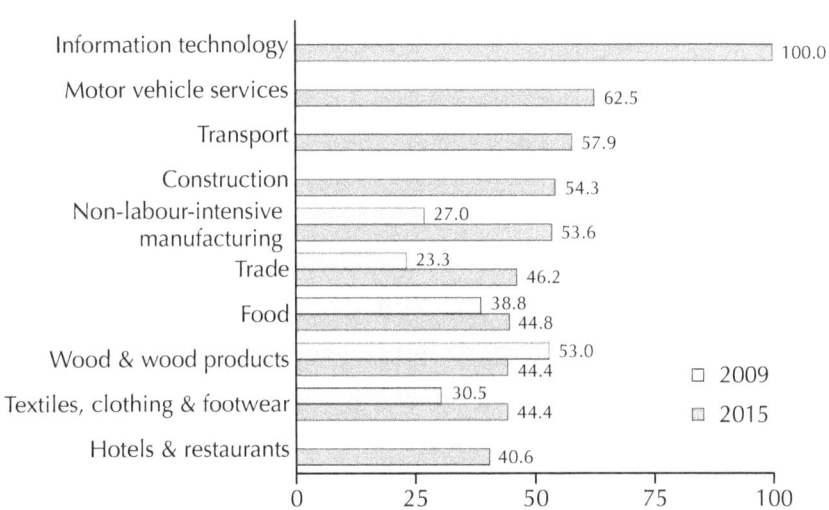

Note: Service sector industries were not asked about their email and website use in 2009.
Source: Authors' calculation, based on World Bank Enterprise Survey, 2009 and 2015.

In Indonesia, the automation of manufacturing processes has been proceeding quickly, even in labour-intensive industries such as textiles and footwear. Part of this may be driven by stringent labour regulations that make employing workers more expensive. Nevertheless, digital technologies are taking job automation to a new level, not only by automating production processes within firms, but also by connecting firms and consumers instantly and directly. That is, digital technologies are improving production efficiency through the optimal use of inputs, while also allowing firms to cater more effectively to consumer demand. The transport sector is a good example of how digital technology is transforming the organisation of firms. App-based transport providers such as Uber and Go-Jek are able to improve their efficiency through better monitoring of idle inputs, which can be put to use as required, instantaneously.

Figure 11.7 depicts the uptake of automation and new technologies in the three years preceding the survey year, 2015. It shows that 36.8 per cent of firms in the transport sector have introduced new technologies, and that 26.3 per cent have either partially or fully automated their manual processes. The rate of new technology adoption in the hotels and restaurants sector is also high. A concerning finding is that the rate of automation in the labour-intensive textiles, clothing and footwear industry (14.0 per cent) is slightly higher than the rate in non-labour-intensive manufacturing

Figure 11.7 Share of firms undertaking automation or adopting new technology in the previous three years, by sector, 2015 (%)

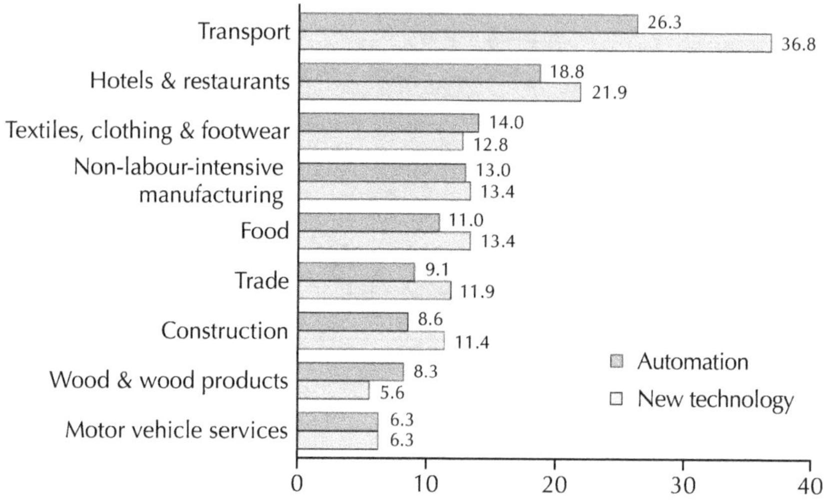

Sector	Automation	New technology
Transport	26.3	36.8
Hotels & restaurants	18.8	21.9
Textiles, clothing & footwear	14.0	12.8
Non-labour-intensive manufacturing	13.0	13.4
Food	11.0	13.4
Trade	9.1	11.9
Construction	8.6	11.4
Wood & wood products	8.3	5.6
Motor vehicle services	6.3	6.3

Source: Authors' calculation, based on World Bank Enterprise Survey, 2015.

(13.0 per cent). While there is no evidence that automation has contributed to significant job losses in labour-intensive industries — slow growth of exports is more likely to be the dominant factor — there is a need to monitor such developments closely. These figures suggest that the introduction of automation and new technologies extends well beyond the capital-intensive industries.

Complementarities between labour and new technology

While it is clear that the use of automation and new technology is spreading, we still do not know how this affects employment. New technologies typically have the capacity to disrupt employment, at least in the short run. However, some technologies may complement labour by increasing demand for workers with particular skills. When first introduced, for example, computers improved the productivity of workers who knew how to use them, and thus increased demand for these workers relative to those who used typewriters.

The impact of technological change on employment remains an open empirical question. Here we adopt a simple model to attempt to estimate the effect of new technology on employment. We borrow liberally from the model of demand for labour, where labour demand is a function of technology, output, unit labour costs and other factors. In this model, we are interested in automation, new technology and the internet.[7] The econometric model is as follows:

$$Emp_{it} = \alpha_i + \beta_1 Auto_{it} + \beta_2 NewTech_{it} + \beta_3 Internet_{it} + X_{it}\gamma + \varepsilon_{it}$$

The dependent variable is employment (in natural logs). We identify four categories of workers: permanent workers, temporary full-time workers, production workers and non-production workers. *Auto*, *NewTech* and *Internet* represent dummy variables for, respectively, automation, new technology and internet use in daily business. We control for other firm characteristics, such as real value added, labour cost per worker, firm ownership (foreign versus domestic), firm export status (exporter versus non-exporter) and a firm's year of establishment.

To estimate the model and address the problem of unobserved heterogeneity, we exploit the panel structure of our dataset, which contains information on the same firms in different years (2009 and 2015).[8] Our data come from the World Bank Enterprise Surveys, which cover small to large Indonesian manufacturing firms. The World Bank surveyed around 1,320 firms in 2009 and 1,444 in 2015—enough to draw meaningful statistical inferences (World Bank 2015). Because our econometric model uses panel data, we were interested only in firms that were observed in both years.

For brevity, in Table 11.2 we present only the coefficients for the three variables of interest. Each column represents a different dependent variable, meaning a different regression. We use a fixed-effects model for all of the estimations. Standard errors are clustered at the two-digit industry level.

We begin with the effect of technological change on permanent workers (column 1 of Table 11.2). The results suggest that automation is associated

---

7   The data on automation and new technology are taken from the section on innovation in the World Bank Enterprise Surveys. Firms were asked whether they had introduced any significant improvements in processes, marketing methods or organisational practices during the previous three years, and, if so, whether the innovation had involved automation of a manual process or the introduction of a new method or technology. Because the self-reported information on automation and new technology is highly subjective, it potentially overestimates the level of innovation at the firm level (Cirera and Muzi 2016).

8   We were concerned that unobserved heterogeneity, α_i, could bias the coefficients for the variables of interest, β_1, β_2 and β_3. It seemed likely that more productive workers would work in more productive firms; but also that more productive firms would be more likely to adopt technologically advanced production systems that allowed them to employ fewer workers. Failure to capture the unobserved heterogeneity would lead to bias in the coefficients. To address this, we used a fixed-effects panel model in which heterogeneity was assumed to be time-invariant. This allowed us to control for unobserved heterogeneity and estimate it as additional parameters.

Table 11.2 Impact of technological change on employment

Variable	Employment by type of contract		Employment of permanent workers by type of work	
	Permanent	Temporary	Production	Non-production
Automation	–0.324***	–0.834***	–0.339**	–0.167
	(0.106)	(0.245)	(0.129)	(0.203)
New technology	0.383***	–0.547**	0.490***	–0.0323
	(0.0999)	(0.265)	(0.149)	(0.159)
Internet	0.0564	–0.335**	0.00777	0.166
	(0.0634)	(0.123)	(0.0912)	(0.130)
No. of observations	860	860	702	702
No. of firms	430	430	351	351
FE model	Yes	Yes	Yes	Yes

*** = significant at 1 per cent; ** = significant at 5 per cent; * = significant at 10 per cent.

Note: The sample consists of firms observed in both periods (2009 and 2015). Columns 1 and 2 include all firms observed in both periods, with no missing variables. Columns 3 and 4 exclude services firms. The dependent variable is the natural log of employment. Standard errors are in parentheses. Standard errors are robust to heteroscedasticity and are clustered at the two-digit industry level. Some variables are not shown, namely real value added, labour cost per workers, a dummy variable for firm ownership (foreign versus domestic), a dummy variable for export status, and year of establishment of a firm.

Source: World Bank Enterprise Survey, 2009 and 2015.

with a reduction in demand for permanent workers. However, new technology is positively associated with the employment of permanent workers, indicating that the introduction of new technologies in the production process complements labour. The role of the internet appears to be rather limited in its impact on the demand for permanent workers.

The adverse effects of technological change are felt chiefly by temporary workers, whom we assume to be mainly unskilled—although that assumption needs to be tested. Automation, the introduction of new technology and internet use are all associated with a reduction in the demand for temporary workers.

If we categorise permanent employees according to whether they work in production- or non-production-related areas,[9] we find that automation

---

[9] We excluded the sectors where there is no distinction between production and non-production workers: hotels and restaurants, information and communication technology, and transport. This reduced the sample size to 702 firms.

is negatively associated with the employment of production workers, but that the introduction of new technology is positively associated with the demand for production workers. This suggests that not all new technologies can substitute for workers—even unskilled ones such as production workers. In the case of non-production workers such as managers, company directors and so on, we find little evidence that automation or the introduction of new technology has had an impact on employment.

Overall, we find some evidence that automation is associated with reduced demand for labour. Low-skilled workers and workers without contracts (that is, temporary workers) are clearly the ones who are disadvantaged most by automation and other kinds of technological change. We also find, however, that the new technologies installed by firms in Indonesia can complement labour—in particular, that the introduction of new technology has had a positive effect on demand for permanent and production workers.

Two qualifications are in order. First, these are partial equilibrium effects. The broader and longer-term effects of technological change depend on adjustments in prices and quantities across firms and industries. While there is cause for concern about the spread of the digital economy, these effects—in particular, the potential role of new technology in driving down costs and prices—also need to be investigated in a general equilibrium context. Second, Indonesia still has a relatively elastic supply of unskilled labour. Unlike in developed countries, in Indonesia the degree of automation driven by labour costs is limited, even in capital-intensive industries such as autos.[10] Despite stringent labour regulations, the labour market remains flexible. The large supply of low-wage workers acts as a brake on the adoption of new technologies that rely on capital, energy and infrastructure, which are all scarce in Indonesia, and are more likely to be subject to periodic bottlenecks.

Online transport: a story of opportunity

Indonesia's transport sector has undergone substantial change, particularly as a result of the phenomenal rise of Go-Jek. Go-Jek was established in 2010 and began operating a phone-based motorcycle taxi service in 2011. In 2015, the company launched an app that allowed consumers to request motorcycle taxis using their mobile phones. In that respect, Go-Jek followed in the footsteps of Uber, the US-based ride-sharing company. Go-Jek

---

10 To take one example, while the assembly stage of car manufacturing is now carried out almost entirely by robots in most developing countries, this is still not the case in Indonesia, where vehicle assembly continues to account for a significant share of manufacturing employment in the auto industry.

has now expanded into a variety of other services that can be delivered to people's homes and workplaces, including logistics (Go-Send, Go-Box), food delivery (Go-Food), medicine delivery (Go-Med) and cleaning and beauty services (Go-Clean, Go-Glam). Go-Jek's extensive range of services is especially valuable for Indonesians living in large cities, where transport is clogged and the subjective costs of moving goods can be substantial. The company clearly competes with the traditional taxi industry, with the largely unregulated *ojek* motorcycle drivers and with established providers in numerous other sectors. In 2016, Go-Jek became Indonesia's first 'unicorn', raising $550 million in new capital.

Like most app-based transport providers, Go-Jek does not own any vehicles. Instead, it provides a platform to match passengers with self-employed motorcycle owner-drivers. As a tech start-up, it employs many highly skilled software engineers and programmers. It also provides work opportunities for a substantial number of low-skilled drivers — around 250,000 nationwide, according to Go-Jek (2017). In other words, tech start-ups like Go-Jek can contribute to demand for both skilled and unskilled labour.

The Go-Jek platform allows self-employed motorcycle drivers to serve potential customers quickly and effectively — that is, it improves transport efficiency by increasing the capacity utilisation of motorcycle taxi drivers. Go-Jek has also increased the efficiency of logistics through its delivery services, and by giving small-scale enterprises such as food vendors access to larger markets. Thus, the multiplier effects generated by companies like Go-Jek can be extensive and substantial.

Our discussions with Go-Jek staff indicate that the company's expansion is constrained by a lack of talented and highly skilled individuals. The company is having trouble finding suitable computer engineering graduates — due either to a lack of supply or to the low quality of these graduates. In this regard, relaxing the restrictive labour regulations on the employment of foreign workers, including foreign software engineers, could benefit some domestic start-up companies. Unlike Go-Jek, which operates only within Indonesia, Grab — one of Go-Jek's fiercest competitors — operates in several ASEAN countries. This puts it in a better position to hire diverse talent from across the region. Moreover, Grab's headquarters are in Singapore, which is more welcoming to foreign talent than Indonesia.

CONCLUDING REMARKS

This chapter has reviewed some of the labour market implications of globalisation in Indonesia, with a focus on the *reformasi* era. While we found that foreign trade and investment have had positive effects for employment and wages in Indonesia, we also noted some of the pitfalls, especially associated with the onset of the digital economy, particularly in more urban contexts. In manufacturing, employment and wages received a boost from foreign capital inflows during the short period of rapid export-oriented growth before the Asian financial crisis, but both have stagnated in the *reformasi* era as Indonesia's manufacturing exports have slowed. Among larger establishments, foreign firms pay higher wages than domestic firms but the reverse is true of export-oriented industries. In contrast to manufacturing, domestic-oriented services have grown strongly since the Asian financial crisis. Many of the new jobs are in business and finance activities that provide mainly formal sector jobs, many of which are held by females.

The adoption of digital technology is spreading quickly, especially among younger cohorts. Digital technologies improve labour productivity, as is evident in the wage premium that workers, especially female workers, earn from using computers in the workplace. We should perhaps be more concerned about the distributional effects, rather than the employment consequences, of new technology. In particular, casual and less skilled workers appear to be at a greater disadvantage when it comes to job automation in manufacturing. One concern is that the new jobs tend to be skill intensive and may thus contribute to higher rates of inequality in Indonesia.

However, there is also complementarity between the technologies installed in Indonesian establishments and the number and types of jobs in those industries. In the transport industry, for example, Go-Jek has been able to generate a large increase in economic activity by linking suppliers and consumers of transport services. That is, despite the concerns about the disruptive effects on employment, new technologies can create employment. Indirect evidence comes from the powerful role that informal jobs still play in the labour market, especially in small businesses.

Migration is one dimension of global labour markets that has not been covered in this survey, mainly due to space constraints. Bank Indonesia data suggest that Indonesia has benefited from out-migration (*tenaga kerja Indonesia*, or TKI) in terms of remittances, which have risen to a not-insignificant $8–9 billion in recent years. Most of Indonesia's registered and unregistered contract workers go to the Middle East and nearby East Asian countries, especially Malaysia. At home, however, the focus has been more on the social costs of migration, especially the abuse of female domestic workers (see Chapter 12 of this book by Hidayah and Chapter 13 by Li). In response to widespread reports of abuse, the Widodo government decided to maintain the previous government's policy of reducing official sponsorship of out-migration of unskilled workers. At the heart of the issue is the failure of host countries both to issue and to enforce satisfactory labour protection regulations (Palmer 2016). In addition, the Indonesian government's tougher stance may signal that it does not expect this form of migration to be a large foreign exchange earner in the near future. So far, however, the clampdown does not appear to have had much effect on remittances.

Turning to the in-migration of workers — the foreign worker presence in Indonesia (*tenaga kerja asing*, or TKA) — the employment of unregistered (illegal) Chinese workers in energy and infrastructure projects has been a politically sensitive issue for several years. The number of unregistered Chinese workers is thought to be around double the number of officially approved Chinese workers, which the Ministry of Manpower estimated to be around 20,000 in 2016/17. Nonetheless, the number of Chinese migrants working in Indonesia is very small relative to the size of the workforce, even if the estimated number of illegal workers is taken into account.

A more important issue for the development and deployment of digital technology is the tight restrictions the government continues to impose on inflows of skilled and professional labour from abroad. ASEAN mutual recognition agreements that aim to free up the movement of professionals within the region are a sound initiative. But partly because of regulations imposed by professional associations on the employment of talent from abroad, they have had relatively little impact on the numbers of professionals working in Indonesia in recent years, despite strong demand in several industries.

Out-migration of unskilled workers can be expected to decline as the government's tougher stance towards the sponsorship of overseas migrant workers takes effect. Meanwhile, restrictions on inward migration of skilled professionals are hampering the development of some Indonesian companies, especially tech start-ups. The government could consider easing these restrictions so that Indonesian companies can make optimal use of digital technology and compete more effectively with foreign companies both within Indonesia and abroad.

REFERENCES

Autor, D.H., L.F. Katz and A.B. Krueger (1998) 'Computing inequality: have computers changed the labor market?', *Quarterly Journal of Economics* 113(4): 1,169–213.

Arabsheibani, G.R., J. Emami and A. Marin (2004) 'The impact of computer use on earnings in the UK', *Scottish Journal of Political Economy* 51(1): 82–94.

Baldwin, R. (2016) *The Great Convergence: Information Technology and the New Globalization*, Belknap Press, Cambridge MA.

Basri, M.C. (2017) 'India and Indonesia: lessons learned from the 2013 taper tantrum', *Bulletin of Indonesian Economic Studies* 53(2): 137–60.
Booth, A. (1998) *The Indonesian Economy in the Nineteenth and Twentieth Centuries: A History of Missed Opportunities*, Macmillan, Basingstoke.
Brambilla, I., N. Chauvin and G. Porto (2017) 'Examining the export wage premium in developing countries', *Review of International Economics* 25(3): 447–75.
Cirera, X., and S. Muzi (2016) 'Measuring firm-level innovation using short questionnaires: evidence from an experiment (English)', Policy Research Working Paper No. WPS7696, World Bank, Washington DC.
DiNardo, J.E., and J.-S. Pischke (1997) 'The returns to computer use revisited: have pencils changed the wage structure too?', *Quarterly Journal of Economics* 112(1): 291–303.
Economist (2013) 'Racing to the bottom: labour standards', *The Economist*, 27 November.
Economist (2016) 'Automation and anxiety', *The Economist*, 25 June.
Edwards, R. (2016) 'Local impacts of resource booms: quantitative case studies from Indonesia', seminar paper, Arndt-Corden Department of Economics, Australian National University, Canberra, 3 February.
Ford, M., and V. Honan (2017) 'The Go-Jek effect', in E. Jurriëns and R. Tapsell (eds) *Digital Indonesia: Connectivity and Divergence*, ISEAS – Yusof Ishak Institute, Singapore: 275–89.
Frey, C.B., and M.A. Osborne (2017) 'The future of employment: how susceptible are jobs to computerisation?', *Technological Forecasting and Social Change* 114: 254–80.
Garnaut, R. (2015) 'Indonesia's resources boom in international perspective: policy dilemmas and options for continued strong growth', *Bulletin of Indonesian Economic Studies* 51(2): 189–212.
Go-Jek (2017) 'Go-Jek's impact for Indonesia', blog, 30 August. https://blog.gojekengineering.com/gojeks-impact-for-indonesia-1d506d2146b1
Helpman, E. (2016) 'Globalization and wage inequality', NBER Working Paper No. 22944, National Bureau of Economic Research, Cambridge MA, December.
Hill, H. (2015) 'The Indonesian economy during the Yudhoyono decade', in E. Aspinall, M. Mietzner and D. Tomsa (eds) *The Yudhoyono Presidency: Indonesia's Decade of Stability and Stagnation*, Institute of Southeast Asian Studies, Singapore: 281–302.
Houben, V.J.H., J.T. Lindblad and others (1999) *Coolie Labour in Colonial Indonesia*, Harrassowitz Verlag, Wiesbaden.
ILO (International Labour Organization) (2013) 'Global wage report 2012/13: wages and equitable growth', ILO, Geneva.
IMF (International Monetary Fund) (2007) 'World economic outlook, October 2007: globalization and inequality', IMF, Washington DC, 11 April.
Krueger, A.B. (1993) 'How computers have changed the wage structure: evidence from microdata, 1984–1989', *Quarterly Journal of Economics* 108(1): 33–60.
Lipsey, R., and F. Sjöholm (2004) 'Foreign direct investment, education and wages in Indonesian manufacturing', *Journal of Development Economics* 73: 415–22.
Lipsey, R., F. Sjöholm and J. Sun (2010) 'Foreign ownership and employment growth in Indonesian manufacturing', IFN Working Paper No. 831, Research Institute of Industrial Economics, Stockholm.
Manning, C. (1998) *Indonesian Labour in Transition: An East Asian Success Story?* Trade and Development Series, Cambridge University Press, Cambridge.

Manning, C., and K. Roesad (2007) 'The Manpower Law of 2003 and its implementing regulations: genesis, key articles and potential impact', *Bulletin of Indonesian Economic Studies* 43(1): 39–86.

Moran, T. (2006) *Harnessing Foreign Direct Investment for Development: Policies for Developed and Developing Countries*, Brookings Institute Press, Baltimore MD.

Muro, M., S. Liu, J. Whiton and S. Kulkarni (2017) 'Digitalization and the American workforce', Metropolitan Policy Program, Brookings Institution, Washington DC, November.

Oosterbeek, H. (1997) 'Returns from computer use: a simple test on the productivity interpretation', *Economic Letters* 55(2): 273–7.

Palmer, W. (2016) *Indonesia's Overseas Labour Migration Programme, 1969–2010*, Brill, Leiden.

Pangestu, M., and G. Dewi (2017) 'Indonesia and the digital economy: creative destruction, opportunities and challenges', in E. Jurriëns and R. Tapsell (eds) *Digital Indonesia: Connectivity and Divergence*, ISEAS – Yusof Ishak Institute, Singapore: 227–56.

Ramstetter, E., and F. Sjöholm (2006) *Multinational Corporations in Indonesia and Thailand: Wages, Productivity, and Exports*, Palgrave Macmillan, Basingstoke.

Reid, A. (1990) *Southeast Asia in the Age of Commerce, 1450–1680. Volume I: The Lands below the Winds*, Yale University Press, New Haven CT.

Takii, S., and E. Ramstetter (2005) 'Multinational presence and labour productivity differentials in Indonesian manufacturing, 1975–2001', *Bulletin of Indonesian Economic Studies* 41(2): 221–42.

Thee, K.W. (1991) 'The surge of Asian NIC investment into Indonesia', *Bulletin of Indonesian Economic Studies* 27(3): 55–88.

Tjandra, S. (2016) 'The *reformasi*: neo-liberalism, democracy, and labour law reform (1998–2006)', Leiden University Repository, Leiden. https://openaccess.leidenuniv.nl/bitstream/handle/1887/37576/03.pdf?sequence=9

Wicaksono, T.Y. (2017) 'Do computers really improve productivity? Evidence from a developing country', SurveyMETER, Yogyakarta.

World Bank (2015) 'Indonesia: Enterprise Survey 2015', World Bank. http://microdata.worldbank.org/index.php/catalog/2665/study-description

World Bank (2016) 'World development report 2016: digital dividends', World Bank, Washington DC.

12 Restoring the rights of Indonesian migrant workers through the Village of Care (Desbumi) program

Anis Hidayah

In 2016 more than 7 million Indonesians were working as overseas migrant workers. Most were low-skilled women from poor villages with little access to decent jobs at home. Under an exploitative, centralistic, high-cost and gender-blind migration scheme, the recruiters who act as middlemen for corporate interests view Indonesian villages simply as marketplaces where they can make large profits from exploiting uneducated, unskilled villagers. Not infrequently, they use intimidation and other practices to force villagers to work overseas. Although Law No. 39/2004 on the Placement and Protection of Indonesian Migrant Workers should protect the interests of those workers, in practice it has served as a vehicle for human rights violations. As a result, human trafficking activities often start at the village level, disguised as an official placement program for migrant workers under Law No. 39/2004.

To address this situation, in 2014 Migrant CARE, an Indonesian non-government organisation, established a village-based program for migrant workers: Village of Care for Migrant Workers (Desbumi). At present, more than 50 villages in East Nusa Tenggara, West Nusa Tenggara, Central Java, East Java and West Java are involved in this program. In each area, Desbumi provides information, assistance with documentation, a migrant worker database, grievance mechanisms, a compilation of relevant village rules and regulations, and post-migration economic empowerment, to ensure that migrant workers from the most at-risk villages have a safe and worthwhile migration experience. All these activities and services are listed on village government websites. The intention is to place the village at the forefront of efforts to protect migrant workers. This is important not only because the village is where the problems start, but also because villages have gained political power and increased funding under Law No. 6/2014 on Villages, which took effect in December 2014.

BACKGROUND

The 1945 Constitution of the Republic of Indonesia states that every citizen has the right to work and to live a decent life, as stipulated in article 27(2): 'Each citizen shall be entitled to an occupation and an existence proper for a human being'. This has not been fully accomplished, however. According to data from the central statistics agency, BPS, 7 million working-age Indonesians were unemployed in 2016, and 28 million people were living below the poverty line.

As globalisation has taken hold, agricultural land has gradually been transformed into industrial land. This has resulted in many farmers being forced off their land and losing their jobs, contributing to the high unemployment rates in Indonesia. The Green Revolution that began in the 1980s has had both positive and negative effects for farmers. On the one hand, agricultural productivity, especially rice productivity, has increased. On the other hand, the gap between rich and poor farmers has widened, and the need for agricultural labour has fallen because of increased use of machinery and technology. In both instances, women have suffered proportionally more than men. Poverty and the loss of livelihoods, especially in rural areas, have forced women to seek employment abroad.

Indonesia's first formal overseas migrant-worker scheme began in 1969. In the following year the government enacted Minister of Manpower Regulation No. 4/1970, which facilitated private sector involvement in migration recruitment and placement through the government's International Labour Placement Program (AKAN) (IOM 2010: 9). When AKAN was dissolved in 1994, responsibility for overseas migrant placements was given to the Directorate General of Labour Force Placement and Expansion of Employment Opportunities (Binapenta), which is now under the Ministry of Manpower and Transmigration.

Since the 1980s, Indonesia has been a major supplier of migrant workers to other countries; the number of Indonesian migrant workers increased significantly from around 96,000 in 1984 to 292,000 in 1989. With labour recruitment businesses springing up to exploit the upsurge in demand, many workers have been forced or deceived into working overseas. Women employed as household domestic helpers have been particularly vulnerable to exploitation.

Poverty is a major factor motivating poor women to leave their homes in search of work, but it is not the only one; others include societal factors ranging from child marriage and domestic violence to government policies that discriminate against women. Based on an analysis of data from the National Socio-Economic Survey (Susenas), BPS and Unicef Indonesia concluded that Indonesia had one of the highest absolute numbers of child marriage in 2015, ranking seventh globally (Unicef Indonesia 2017). According to data collected by the National Commission on Violence Against Women (Komnas Perempuan), 259,150 women in Indonesia were subjected to violence, mostly domestic violence and rape, in 2016 (Komnas Perempuan 2017). In a report to the UN committee overseeing the implementation of the Convention on the Elimination of All Forms of Discrimination against Women, Komnas Perempuan (2016) identified 421 national and regional regulations that discriminated against women in 2016. For these and other reasons, Indonesia—like many other countries—has been experiencing a 'feminisation of migration', in which the proportion of female migrant workers has consistently exceeded that of male migrant workers (Castles and Miller 1998).

Indonesian migrant workers, especially women, face difficult and increasingly complex challenges abroad. These can potentially include human trafficking, organ trafficking, rape, torture, fraud, state-administered punishments that range from deportation to the death penalty, and violations of their basic rights as workers, such as unpaid salaries, excessive working hours, no days off and no right to organise. All this amounts to what may be called 'modern slavery', generally referring to 'situations of exploitation that a person cannot refuse or leave because of threats, violence, coercion, deception, and/or abuse of power' (ILO 2017: 16).[1] Nevertheless, many Indonesians still want to work overseas, motivated by the desire to earn a better livelihood. In 2016, remittances from migrant workers amounted to Rp 119 trillion, or around $9 billion (BNP2TKI 2017). Overseas migrant workers can also expect to benefit from non-monetary rewards, such as increased skills and knowledge and expanded social networks.

To sum up, despite the genuine rewards from migration, migrant workers are generally uninformed about the risks, and may opt to work overseas simply because their domestic and societal conditions leave them with little other choice. The exploitation of migrant workers, especially women, starts in the villages, because brokers view villagers as a big pool

---

1   More specifically, Anti-Slavery International calls someone a slave 'if they are:
    - forced to work—through coercion, or mental or physical threat;
    - owned or controlled by an "employer", through mental or physical abuse or the threat of abuse;
    - dehumanised, treated as a commodity or bought and sold as "property";
    - physically constrained or have restrictions placed on their freedom of movement' (https://www.antislavery.org/slavery-today/modern-slavery/).

Table 12.1 Number of new Indonesian migrant workers, 2011–16

Year	Number	Share by gender (%)	
		Women	Men
2011	586,802	64	36
2012	494,609	57	43
2013	512,168	54	46
2014	429,872	57	43
2015	275,736	60	40
2016	234,451	62	38

Source: BNP2TKI (2017).

of workers they can dip into to make a profit. Although the government says that it is committed to improving the migration process, so far it has failed to provide a legal umbrella to adequately protect migrant workers.

Migrant CARE established the Desbumi program specifically to focus on the village as the basic unit for the protection of migrant workers. Law No. 6/2014 on Villages provides the legal basis, and the funding, for villages to provide services that can improve the welfare of their citizens. This means that the villages that are experiencing strong demand for overseas workers now have the capacity to establish labour migration services.

Against this background, I now explore two questions. First, has the Indonesian government done enough to protect migrant workers, and how do its protection policies and mechanisms work? And second, how does Desbumi, as an instrument developed in the village, contribute to ensuring the rights of Indonesian migrant workers?

THE ROLE OF THE STATE IN LABOUR MIGRATION

According to the World Bank (2017: 11), around 4.9 million documented workers from Indonesia were working abroad in 2016, and over 9 million if one includes both documented and undocumented workers. Official data from the National Agency for the Placement and Protection of Indonesian Migrant Workers (BNP2TKI) show that the number of female migrants consistently exceeded the number of male migrants in the period 2011–16 (Table 12.1). More than half of all migrant workers are employed as domestic workers (maids), while the remainder work in plantations, construction, factories, hotels or cleaning services. Poor working conditions and human rights abuses are rife among migrant workers, but domestic workers are generally considered to be the most vulnerable to exploitation.

In 2011, the International Labour Office adopted Convention No. 189 on decent work for domestic workers, known as the Domestic Workers Convention.[2] It recognised, for the first time, the legal rights of what is essentially an informal segment of the labour force. The Sustainable Development Goals adopted by the United Nations General Assembly in 2015 also address the issue of migrant workers. The aim of the eighth goal is to 'promote sustained, inclusive and sustainable economic growth, full and productive employment and decent work for all' by 2030. The targets include measures 'to eradicate forced labour, end modern slavery and [end] human trafficking' and to 'protect labour rights and promote safe and secure working environments for all workers, including migrant workers, in particular women migrants, and those in precarious employment'.[3]

Indonesia, however, has not ratified the Domestic Workers Convention,[4] and it is not on track to achieve the eighth Sustainable Development Goal. In fact, the Global Slavery Index lists Indonesia among the 10 countries with the largest estimated absolute numbers of people in 'modern slavery' in 2016: 736,100, or 0.3 per cent of the population (Minderoo Foundation 2016: 8, 28).[5] BNP2TKI itself recorded more than 200,000 cases of human rights violations suffered by Indonesian migrant workers during the period 2011–16 (Table 12.2). These are reported cases, so the true numbers may well be higher.

Many factors contribute to the vulnerability of migrant workers— including the migration policies of the Indonesian government, which have often had unintended consequences. Table 12.3 summarises the main migration policies in Indonesia since independence, some of which have exposed migrant workers to human rights violations or modern slavery. In 2015, for example, President Joko Widodo imposed a ban on sending migrant workers to the Middle East, following the execution of two Indonesian domestic workers found guilty of murder in Saudi Arabia. This moratorium violates the right of citizens to seek a better livelihood by working overseas, without addressing the root causes of the problem.

---

2 See http://www.ilo.org/wcmsp5/groups/public/@ed_protect/@protrav/@travail/documents/publication/wcms_168266.pdf.
3 See https://www.un.org/development/desa/disabilities/envision2030-goal8.html.
4 So far, the Philippines is the only ASEAN country to have ratified the convention.
5 The other nine countries are India, China, Pakistan, Bangladesh, Uzbekistan, North Korea, Russia, Nigeria and the Democratic Republic of the Congo.

Table 12.2 Number of cases of human rights violations experienced by Indonesian migrant workers, 2011–16

Year	Number
2011	72,194
2012	47,620
2013	44,087
2014	30,661
2015	19,029
2016	15,157

Source: BNP2TKI (2017).

Migrant CARE's monitoring of departures from Jakarta's international airport suggests that aspiring workers are finding ways around the moratorium, and that many women are still travelling to the Middle East for work. Because the moratorium cannot protect these workers while they are abroad (but can only try to prevent them from going in the first place), they face exactly the same risks as their predecessors.

VILLAGES: WHERE THE PROBLEMS START

A study by Migrant CARE in 2014 found that Indonesian migrant workers recruited from villages obtained most of their information about job opportunities from brokers (62.7 per cent), friends (22.6 per cent) and relatives and neighbours (19.1 per cent), and only a tiny amount (2.5 per cent) from government labour offices (Migrant CARE 2014). This suggests that neither the central government nor local government is an effective provider of information on job opportunities abroad, despite such information being one of the keys to a safe migration.

An earlier study by Migrant CARE showed that some local governments had in fact established programs to protect migrant workers, but those programs were not adequately supported or funded by local parliaments (Migrant CARE 2013). In the district of Central Lombok in West Nusa Tenggara, for example, the budget for the local Commission for the Protection of Indonesian Migrant Workers was only about Rp 50 million ($3,500) per year, which came out of the budget of the Social Affairs and Labour Office. With such a limited budget, this body was unable to provide any services for migrant workers. The provincial government of West Nusa Tenggara has also established a one-stop shop to assist

Table 12.3 Major migration policies in Indonesia

Period	Relevant legislation	Description	Consequences
Sukarno (1945–66)	State Gazette No. 8/1887 on the Deployment of Labour	Regulates the deployment of Indonesians to work overseas	Many workers are sent overseas as forced labour
Suharto (1967–98)	Minister of Manpower Regulation No. 4/1970; and many other ministerial regulations related to the placement of labour	Regulates the setting for and activities of businesses involved in labour migration; regulates the monitoring of private agencies	Migrant workers lack protection, are often treated as a commodity and are vulnerable to human rights violations
B.J. Habibie (1998–99)	Minister of Manpower Decree No. 204/1999 on the Placement and Protection of Indonesian Migrant Workers	Requires returning migrant workers to be processed at a special airport terminal	Exposes returning migrants to extortion
Abdurrahman Wahid (1999–2001)	Minister of Women's Empowerment Decree No. 35/2000	Establishes information service for female workers at airports	For the first time, integrates a gender equality perspective into migration policy
Megawati Sukarnoputri (2001–04)	Law No. 39/2004 on the Placement and Protection of Indonesian Migrant Workers	Regulates the placement and protection of migrant workers	Allows labour agencies to claim legal legitimacy for schemes that exploit migrant workers, especially women
Susilo Bambang Yudhoyono (2004–14)	Law No. 6/2012 on the Ratification of the International Convention on the Protection of the Rights of All Migrant Workers and Members of Their Families	Ratifies the convention but does not harmonise domestic policies with the convention	No significant improvement on the existing rules and regulations
Joko Widodo (2014–)	Minister of Manpower Decree No. 260/2015 Banning the Placement of Indonesian Overseas Workers to Individual Employers in the Middle East	Bans Indonesians from seeking employment in Middle Eastern countries	Violates the citizen's right to work
	Law No. 18/2017 on the Protection of Indonesian Migrant Workers	Brings Law No. 39/2004 into line with the International Convention on the Protection of the Rights of All Migrant Workers and Members of Their Families	Indonesian government has a two-year transition period to implement this law

Source: Author's compilation.

with immigration requirements, pre-departure documents and insurance for migrant workers. However, rather than having its own building and infrastructure, it operates out of an old agricultural high-school building where it is not possible to install data servers.

The districts of East Flores and Lembata (both in East Nusa Tenggara) are the source of many overseas migrant workers. As yet, however, neither of them have enacted regulations to protect migrant workers. Moreover, in each district, the budget allocated to providing information ('socialisation') for migrant workers is very limited: about Rp 16 million ($1,120) per year, or enough to reach about 50 people. The labour and transmigration office in Lembata recorded only 10 migrant workers in 2012, while the office in East Flores recorded 12 migrant workers. These data are at odds with the amount of remittances recorded by each office, which amounts to around Rp 5 billion ($0.35 million) per month.

Further down the government hierarchy, at the village level, there appears to be no government initiative, or clear procedure, specifically designed to protect migrant workers. Instead, the steps in the migration process are handled on an ad hoc basis without any standardised procedure. This causes numerous problems. For example:

- Data on the numbers of migrant workers are not available, either in village archives or in village monographs. Instead, the information on migrant workers mainly comes from brokers.
- Many village government officials also act as migrant worker sponsors and as migration brokers.
- Village regulations relating to migrant workers and their families are unclear and difficult to interpret.
- The difficulties faced by migrant workers are not placed on the list of matters to be discussed at development planning meetings (*musrenbang*).
- The boundaries between brokers, sponsors and field recruiters in the migrant recruitment process are not well defined.

These problems open the door to human trafficking. The three elements of trafficking that form a common chain of abuse of the (formal) migration process — recruitment, displacement and exploitation — commonly start in the villages. As the most basic area of recruitment, the villages may even indirectly encourage trafficking by allowing brokers to offer alluring incentives, such as cultural ambassadorships, scholarships and internships.

Villages as the first place of recruitment of migrant workers need to play a more active role in protecting their citizens. To provide the legal basis for protecting villagers who become migrant workers, village governments need to enact regulations that permit them to establish administrative institutions and services for prospective migrants. They also need to make sure that adequate funding is available to support returning migrants, as part of a strategy to ensure the long-term economic welfare of the community.

The move to reform and empower villages is in step with the provisions of the International Convention on the Protection of the Rights of All Migrant Workers and Members of Their Families.[6] Adopted in 1990, this United Nations convention is the only international instrument that regulates the comprehensive protection of the human rights of migrant workers. The Indonesian government ratified the convention on 12 April 2012 through Law No. 6/2012. This means that the government is obliged to harmonise its policies in accordance with the convention. The reforms Indonesia has been instituting at the village level are also in line with the eighth Sustainable Development Goal, to provide decent work for all citizens, and with the third goal of President Joko Widodo's policy agenda (known as the Nawacita), to promote the 'development of peripheral areas' (UNDP 2015: 8).

The decentralisation of central government powers to the regions, including villages, has the potential to increase the capacity of village governments to protect the human rights of migrant workers. But for this to happen, villages will need to stop focusing solely on the management of natural resources and assert their right to manage local human resources.

Under Indonesia's national migration scheme, local governments, both district and village, have a strategic role to play in in the provision of services for migrant workers. Given that most migrant workers come from the villages, the management of migrant worker placements should be decentralised to the local level. This would avoid the accumulation of large numbers of migrant workers in Jakarta, and support the development of local resources such as hospitals, labour offices, airports, training centres and so on.

Many of the flaws in the formal migration system can be traced back to Law No. 39/2004 on the Placement and Protection of Indonesian Migrant Workers. Recruiters have taken advantage of this law to perpetrate massive human rights violations, both within Indonesia in the pre-migration phase, and in the countries of destination during the post-migration phase. Villages have become the focal point for trafficking practices masquerading as legitimate placements of migrant workers. Commendably, the Widodo administration revised Law 39/2004 in 2017, enacting Law No. 18/2017 on the Protection of Indonesian Migrant Workers. When it is implemented, this law should help to provide greater protection for Indonesian migrant workers.

---

6   See http://www.ohchr.org/EN/ProfessionalInterest/Pages/CMW.aspx.

TACKLING THE ROOT OF THE PROBLEM WITH DESBUMI

Restoring the human rights of migrant workers in villages is part of what it means to respect the right of every person to have decent work. In many cases, Indonesian villagers have no other option but to seek work overseas. Recognising this reality, the goal of the Desbumi program is to ensure that migrant workers have a safe, trouble-free experience and make the best use of their new skills and savings when they come home.

Desbumi stands for Desa Peduli Buruh Migran, which literally means a village that cares about its migrant workers; Desbumi can therefore be translated as 'Village of Care for Migrant Workers'. To care for migrant workers from Indonesian villages, Desbumi offers an integrated package of services to facilitate the migration process while ensuring that the human rights of workers are protected. The program covers people from the time they depart until after they return home. It also encourages local governments to take an active role in establishing policies to assist migrant workers. In the end, the Desbumi program should have the practical result of making migrant workers more prosperous.

Since 2014, 53 villages in East Nusa Tenggara, West Nusa Tenggara, Central Java, West Java and East Java have built, or have started to build, integrated migration service centres. These centres provide information on how to have a safe migration and assistance with documentation. In addition, they are expected to maintain a migrant worker database, establish a standardised complaint-handling mechanism and facilitate post-migration economic empowerment under village regulations. All Desbumi services can be accessed through the village government's website, making them easily accessible to all.[7] The overarching idea behind Desbumi is to make villages the vanguard for protecting migrant workers and to serve as a model for other initiatives to prevent human rights abuses. As an instrument to protect migrant workers, Desbumi would ideally be available in all the main villages of origin of migrant workers.

Desbumi needs to be supported by district-level services to help intending migrants obtain passports, undergo health check-ups and receive pre-departure training, including training in human rights and gender justice. The decentralisation of migration services should help to cut through the complicated administrative procedures of the central government, reduce fees and prevent document forgery and other exploitative practices. A decentralised, government-run scheme would, at the very least, be proof of the presence of the state in protecting its citizens, as mandated by the constitution. It would mean that the fate of migrant workers would no longer be surrendered to predatory agents.

---

7 For an example, see http://www.dulitukan.web.id.

As a relatively new initiative, Desbumi faces both challenges and opportunities. The main challenges can be summarised as follows.

- Villages do not have systematic data on citizens who are working overseas.
- Villages do not provide information to their citizens on how to have a safe migration experience.
- Village government officials often also act as migration brokers, creating opportunities for corruption.
- Village government officials generally have a low capacity to carry out their duties.
- Document forgery and falsification are widespread.
- Private agencies play a dominant role in recruitment, amidst a lack of clear rules.
- Citizens are not aware of their rights, including their rights as migrant workers.
- Funding for the Desbumi program may not be sustainable.

Despite the difficulties, it is important for programs targeting potential migrants to focus on the villages, because village governments are closer to their citizens than any of the higher levels of government. Moreover, direct funding for villages has increased greatly under Law No. 6/2014 on Villages, creating an opportunity for village governments to fund programs such as Desbumi. In a context in which private agencies dominate the recruitment process, village governments can at least ensure that rules and regulations are enacted and enforced. Over time, this can be expected to change the paradigm to one in which villages are expected to provide public services for migrant workers, and private agencies and brokers have fewer opportunities to abuse migrant workers' rights.

The Desbumi program has three pillars: data collection and dissemination; institution building; and empowerment of migrant workers and their families. The practical components of each are shown in Table 12.4. Desbumi is expected to improve village services for migrant workers by ensuring the validity of central and regional government databases; placing stricter controls on the placement of migrant workers; allowing the families of migrant workers and the public to monitor the migration process; encouraging transparency in the placement system; reducing the extent of document forgery; weakening the power of brokers; and cutting the costs of migration (especially the cost of the placement fee).

By September 2017, Desbumi had reached 53 villages in five provinces, with programs operating in 38 villages and in progress in the other 15 (Table 12.5). Most of the 38 villages had allocated funding of around Rp 10 million ($750) to the program, but the amount varied from Rp 4 million to Rp 60 million across villages, and was still under discussion

Table 12.4 The three pillars of the Desbumi program

Pillar	Program	Description
Data collection and dissemination	Collection of data on migrant workers	Desbumi regularly collects data on the numbers and locations of overseas migrant workers, returning migrant workers and the families of migrant workers, including children
	Provision of data and information	Data as well as information on how to have a safe migration are publicly available on village websites
	Management of an online information centre on village websites	Desbumi manages the database and the migration-related information on each village's website
Institution building	Integration of Desbumi into villages' medium-term development plans	Desbumi becomes part of each village's development plan, to make the protection of migrant workers a priority for village administrations and to ensure that a budget for migrant worker services is allocated accordingly
	Establishment of Integrated Information Service Centre (PPIT)	All Desbumi services are available through the Integrated Information Service Centre (PPIT) located in each village
	Establishment of a standardised complaint-handling procedure	
Empowerment of migrant workers and their families	Establishment of community organisations for migrant workers	In every Desbumi village, migrant workers are asked to form an organisation consisting of former migrant workers and members of their families. These organisations have legal status in the form of a decree from the village head. This allows them to participate in development planning meetings (*musrenbang*) and in decision-making on matters affecting migrant workers in the village. The organisations also conduct empowerment and capacity-building programs for migrant workers. Currently, there are 41 groups of female migrant workers with a total of 1,967 active members.

Table 12.4 (continued)

Pillar	Program	Description
	Financial literacy education for returning migrant workers and their families	Financial literacy training is provided to increase the capacity of former migrant workers and their families to make optimal use of remittances
	Development of self-confidence	Development of self-confidence is important to allow former female migrant workers, in particular, to speak directly to policy-makers about their problems and experiences
	Case-handling assistance	Desbumi provides case-handling services for citizens who are experiencing difficulties while working abroad; in such cases, Desbumi coordinates with the local Office of Manpower, the local BNP2TKI office (BP3TKI) and NGOs, as well as Indonesian government representatives abroad
	Gender mainstreaming	Village government officials are given training in gender issues so that they are able to understand the problems faced by female migrant workers, who form the majority of migrant workers
	Economic development	Desbumi provides programs to strengthen the capacity of former migrant workers to identify market opportunities (by, for example, following trends in social media, reading newspapers/magazines or observing successful businesses), and to develop their businesses (covering product packaging, quality control, networking and marketing, and so on)

Source: Author's compilation.

in some villages. This amount of money is by no means large, but it is enough to make a start. All the established programs offer information on secure migration, conduct activities to raise awareness among the community and collect data both on intending migrant workers and on those who have returned home. So far, female migrant workers have formed 41 groups with a total of 1,967 members to advocate on behalf of their communities. Despite limited funding, Desbumi has managed to make real progress, as summarised in Table 12.6.

Table 12.5 Location and funding of Desbumi projects in five provinces

Province	District	Subdistrict	Village	Annual budget (Rp million)	Year of village regulation
West Nusa Tenggara	Central Lombok	Praya Barat Daya	Ndarek	10	2015
		Praya	Gerunung	10	2015
		Jonggat	Nyerot	10	2015
			Gemel	10	2017
		Pringgarata	Pringgarata	10	2017
East Nusa Tenggara	Lembata	Iliape	Tagawiti	60	2016
			Dulitukan	10	2016
			Beutaran	10	2016
		Iliape Timur	Lamawolo	10	2016
			Lamatokan	10	2016
			Bao Lali Duli	10	2016
East Java	Jember	Ledokombo	Sumbersalak	10	2015
		Tempurejo	Wonoasri	10	2016
		Wuluhan	Dukuhdempok	50	2016
		Ambulu	Sabrang	10	2016
			Ambulu	–	–
	Banyuwangi	Pesanggaran	Pesanggaran	7	2017
			Sumberagung	40	–
			Sumbermulyo	40	2017
		Tegaldlimo	Tegaldlimo	4	2016
			Wringinpitu	25	2015
			Kedungasri	–	2016
			Kedunggebang	60	2017
Central Java	Cilacap	Kedungreja	Bojongsari	15	2015
	Kebumen	Puring	Krandegan	5	2015
		Klirong	Tanggulangin	43	2015
			Jogosimo	–	2017
			Tambakprogaten	–	–
			Pandanlor	10	2017
	Wonosobo	Leksono	Lipursari	8	2017
		Sukoharjo	Mergosari	5	2017
			Rogojati	6	2017
		Watumalang	Kuripan	10	2017
			Gondang	7	2017
		Kretek	Ngadikusuman	7	2017
			Sindupaten	7	2017
West Java	Indramayu	Juntinyuat	Juntinyuat	4	2017
	Karawang	Karawang Timur	Tegal Sawah	40	2017

Note: Rp 10 million = around $750; – = budget undecided or regulation not yet passed.
Source: Author's compilation.

Table 12.6 Summary of progress of Desbumi projects in villages

Typical situation in village before establishment of Desbumi	Expected change after establishment of Desbumi	Progress
Official letters for prospective migrant workers are granted only upon request (passive bureaucracy)	Village bureaucracy responds proactively to the needs of migrant workers and their families	Reports and demographic information are available for prospective overseas migrant workers
Data on the numbers of migrant workers are not available, either in village archives or in village monographs	Village provides dynamic data on migrant workers and members of their families	Database on overseas migrant workers and those who have returned are available on each village's website
Problems experienced by migrant workers are considered private, not public	Problems experienced by migrant workers are considered public, not private	Problems experienced by migrant workers are included on the agenda of the village-level development planning meeting (*musrenbang*)
Many village officials also act as migrant worker sponsors and as migration brokers	Village regulations, mechanisms and sanctions are established to prevent officials from acting as sponsors or brokers	Village regulations prohibit village officials from becoming migration brokers
There are no village regulations as the basis for protecting and establishing services for migrant workers and their families	Village regulations are enacted to protect and provide services for migrant workers and their families	Desbumi is acknowledged in village regulations
Village is not involved as an institution in dealing with the problems faced by migrant workers	Village institutes problem-solving mechanisms and minimum service standards for migrant workers and their families	Desbumi provides standard operating procedures and minimum service standards
Problems experienced by migrant workers are not integrated into development planning meetings (*musrenbang*)	Village-level development planning meeting (*musrenbang*) involves the community of migrant workers, and a budget is established for activities to protect migrant workers	Village-level development planning meeting (*musrenbang*) invites migrant worker community to participate

(continued)

Table 12.6 (continued)

Typical situation in village before establishment of Desbumi	Expected change after establishment of Desbumi	Progress
Migrant workers and their families are not organised	Migrant workers and their families are assisted to form groups so that they can exchange information both within each group and with groups in other villages	41 groups of female migrant workers with a total of 1,967 members have been established; these groups are actively involved in advocacy and empowerment programs within their local communities
Boundary between brokers, sponsors and field recruiters is not well defined, leading to rampant recruitment activity in the villages	Village restricts activities of brokers in the villages	Village regulations prohibit brokers from operating in the village
Very little official information on migrant workers is available; most information comes from brokers	Information on the procedures for a safe migration is well socialised in the village	Villagers are easily able to obtain information on the procedures for a safe migration either from leaflets or through the village website
There are no economic empowerment programs to assist migrant workers and the members of their families	Productive enterprises are established to make optimal use of remittances	The 41 groups of female migrant workers are examining how remittances can be used to establish productive enterprises

Source: Author's compilation.

The rollout of the Desbumi program in the villages that are the main targets of the recruiters, combined with the implementation of the amended law on the protection of migrant workers (Law No. 18/2017), should help to improve the treatment of migrant workers, especially women. But the participation of other stakeholders is also required. Bureaucracies managing the migration process in the areas of origin need to make sure that prospective migrants have access to information on how to have a safe migration. Communities need to monitor the migration process to make sure it is conducted transparently and in accordance with human rights. And village governments need to enact clear regulations and provide targeted services to reduce the scope for brokers and private agencies to exploit the system.

CONCLUSION

The development agenda of President Joko Widodo, as described in the Nawacita and in the National Medium-Term Development Plan for 2015–19, emphasises the protection of migrant workers. It commits the government to ensuring the safety and fair treatment of migrant workers before, during and after migration, as set out in the International Convention on the Protection of the Rights of All Migrant Workers and Members of Their Families, which Indonesia ratified in 2012.

The Desbumi projects established in five provinces since 2015 can be used as a model for other participatory migrant-protection initiatives. The program is also a valuable source of data: by involving all relevant parties in the village, especially migrant workers and their families, Desbumi is able to collect and maintain data on citizens who are legally working abroad. Village administrations are now officially involved in the protection of migrant workers, as stipulated in article 42 of the amended law on the protection of Indonesian migrant workers, Law No. 18/2017. This will require them to make adjustments to various aspects of village governance, including regulations and budgeting. Even with village government support, Desbumi is not sufficient to protect migrant workers; it must be reinforced by district government services to help prospective migrants obtain passports, undergo health checks and receive pre-departure training. The decentralisation of migration services to the districts and villages should help to reduce the amount of costly and centralised bureaucracy associated with migration. Law No. 18/2017 mandates the provision of one-stop services for migrant workers at the provincial, district and village levels. This is where the role of Desbumi becomes very relevant, as most of the problems faced by migrants workers start, and can be fixed, in the villages.

REFERENCES

BNP2TKI (Badan Nasional Penempatan dan Perlindungan Tenaga Kerja Indonesia) (2017) 'Data penempatan dan perlindungan tenaga kerja Indonesia tahun 2016' [Data on the placement and protection of Indonesian migrant workers for the year 2016], BNP2TKI, Jakarta. http://www.bnp2tki.go.id/uploads/data/data_08-02-2017_111324_Data-P2TKI_tahun_2016.pdf

Castles, M., and M. Miller (1998) *The Age of Migration: International Population Movements in the Modern World*, Guilford Press, New York NY.

ILO (International Labour Office) (2017) 'Global estimates of modern slavery: forced labour and forced marriage', ILO, Geneva.

IOM (International Organization for Migration) (2010) 'Labour migration from Indonesia: an overview of Indonesian migration to selected destinations in Asia and the Middle East', IOM, Jakarta.

Komnas Perempuan (Komisi Nasional Anti Kekerasan Terhadap Perempuan) (2016) 'National Human Rights Institution independent report', report submitted to the CEDAW Committee, Komnas Perempuan, Jakarta, 30 December. http://tbinternet.ohchr.org/Treaties/CEDAW/Shared%20Documents/IDN/INT_CEDAW_IFN_IDN_26445_E.pdf

Komnas Perempuan (Komisi Nasional Anti Kekerasan Terhadap Perempuan) (2017) 'Labirin kekerasan terhadap perempuan: dari *gang rape* hingga *femicide, alarm* bagi negara untuk bertindak tepat' [Labyrinth of violence against women: from gang rape to femicide, a wake-up call for the country to act properly], press release and factsheet, Jakarta, 7 March. https://www.komnasperempuan.go.id/read-news-siaran-pers-komnas-perempuan-catatan-tahunan-catahu-2017-lembar-fakta-catahu-2017

Migrant CARE (2013) 'Laporan hasil asesmen untuk pembentukan Desbumi' [Report on the results of an assessment of the establishment of Desbumi], Migrant CARE, Jakarta.

Migrant CARE (2014) 'Laporan hasil pendataan buruh migran di desa' [Report on the results of data collection on migrant workers in villages], Migrant CARE, Jakarta.

Minderoo Foundation (2016) 'The Global Slavery Index 2016'. https://www.globalslaveryindex.org

UNDP (United Nations Development Programme) (2015) 'Converging development agendas: "Nawa Cita", "RPJM", and SDGs', UNDP Indonesia Country Office, Jakarta, November. http://www.id.undp.org/content/indonesia/en/home/library/sustainable-development-goals/converging-development-agendas-nawa-cita-rpjmn-and-sdgs.html

Unicef Indonesia (2017) 'Child marriage in Indonesia: progress on pause', research brief, Unicef Indonesia, Jakarta. https://www.girlsnotbrides.org/wp-content/uploads/2016/11/UNICEF-Indonesia-Child-Marriage-Research-Brief-1.pdf

World Bank (2017) 'Indonesia's global workers: juggling opportunities and risks', World Bank Office, Jakarta, November. http://pubdocs.worldbank.org/en/357131511778676366/Indonesias-Global-Workers-Juggling-Opportunities-Risks.pdf

13 Globalisation, the role of the state and the rule of law: human trafficking in eastern Indonesia

Dominggus Elcid Li

HUMAN TRAFFICKING AND GLOBALISATION

Human trafficking is a global phenomenon. Like flows of financial resources and traded goods and commodities, flows of people in the form of international migration are rising, thanks in part to better transportation and communications technology. Labour migration from rural or remote areas to the cities or to major centres of production is part of this phenomenon. For poor, rural workers, labour migration can offer a path out of poverty. But for those who are deceived into working in other countries, it may represent the worst form of labour exploitation and hence is one of the dark sides of globalisation (Jones et al. 2007: 108).

Globalisation can provide a road back to slavery if the movement of labour is not regulated, and if those regulations are not enforced. One form of exploitation of migrant labour is human trafficking. In Indonesia, human trafficking needs to be addressed not only through regional mechanisms such as ASEAN, but also though strategies to reduce social exclusion—because the most commonly targeted victims are the poor and those living on the margins of society.

Law enforcement agencies have not been able to keep up with the criminal networks that have arisen to take advantage of the opportunities for human trafficking offered by globalisation. Castells (2010: 172) says that 'global crime, the networking of powerful criminal organizations, and their associates, in shared activities throughout the planet, is a new phenomenon that profoundly affects international and national economies, politics, security, and, ultimately, societies at large'. The global criminal networks base their management and production functions in low-risk places where they can control the formal institutions of state (Castells 2010: 173). Surprisingly, this is the picture in certain parts of Indonesia today.

This chapter analyses the impact of human trafficking based on findings from East Nusa Tenggara, one of the poorest provinces in Indonesia. I argue that severe disparities between regions in Indonesia and lack of access to justice in peripheral areas have allowed human trafficking to take hold. Access is understood as 'the match between societal commitment and institutional capacity to deliver rights and services and people's capacity to benefit from those rights and services' (De Jong and Rizvi 2008: 4). Lack of access to justice for the victims of human trafficking in East Nusa Tenggara is reflected in the low rates of prosecution of perpetrators.

This chapter uses the definition of human trafficking given in article 3(a) of the United Nations Protocol to Prevent, Suppress and Punish Trafficking in Persons Especially Women and Children, namely:

> 'Trafficking in persons' shall mean the recruitment, transport, transfer, harbouring or receipt of persons, by means of the threat or use of force or other forms of coercion, of abduction, of fraud, of deception, of the abuse of power or of a position of vulnerability or of the giving or receiving of payments or benefits to achieve the consent of a person having control over another person, for the purpose of exploitation. Exploitation shall include, at a minimum, the exploitation of the prostitution of others or other forms of sexual exploitation, forced labor or services, slavery or practices similar to slavery, servitude or the removal of organs.

It is important to distinguish here between human trafficking and people smuggling. The term 'people smuggling' implies that the subject is a willing party to a transaction in which the person is smuggled across judicial borders. The term 'human trafficking', on the other hand, is used when the subject is unequivocally a victim of exploitation. This chapter presents only the cases of people who can be considered victims of human trafficking.

The chapter is based on my experience as an anti-trafficking activist in the eastern part of Indonesia and on my work as a researcher at the Institute of Resource Governance and Social Change (IRGSC) in Kupang, the capital of East Nusa Tenggara. IRGSC is part of the non-government organisation, Alliance Against Human Trafficking (Ampera). As an activist and researcher, I have interviewed numerous officials from various ministries in Kupang (East Nusa Tenggara), Sukabumi (West Java), Batam (Riau Islands) and Jakarta, and analysed media reports on all the human trafficking cases in East Nusa Tenggara as covered by three local newspapers (*Timor Express*, *Pos Kupang* and *Victory News*) in the three years from 2014 to 2016.

The main finding of this research was that agents in state institutions are often involved in human trafficking. The pull factor of strong demand for labour has created opportunities for corruption in village administrations (Antara 2016), civil registration and police offices (Alawi 2014b, 2015), immigration offices (Alawi 2014a) and airports (Seo 2016b). Local newspapers, online media and some national television networks regularly publicise such cases. For instance, the testimony of Rudy Soik, a police whistleblower who exposed corruption within the East Nusa Tenggara police force in 2014, can be accessed online (Najwa 2014a), and reports on a bird's nest entrepreneur who enslaved female workers from East Nusa Tenggara in Medan are available on YouTube (Maia 2016; Najwa 2014b).

According to a global report on human trafficking produced by the US government, Indonesia ranks among the 'tier 2' countries 'whose governments do not fully meet the TVPA's [Trafficking Victims Protection Act's] minimum standards, but are making significant efforts to bring themselves into compliance with those standards' (US Department of State 2017: 45). In 2015, those efforts included rescuing hundreds of fishermen from Myanmar, Laos, Thailand and Cambodia from slavery-like conditions in the remote hamlet of Benjina in Maluku province, where they had been forced to work as crew on fishing vessels (Dillon 2015; Patty 2015). An internal report by the Ministry of Social Affairs indicates that Indonesia returned 19,485 foreign victims of human trafficking to their own countries in 2016.

Although several state institutions share responsibility for dealing with human trafficking issues, including the Ministry of Social Affairs, the Ministry of Women's Empowerment and Child Protection, the National Police, the National Agency for the Placement and Protection of Indonesian Migrant Workers (BNP2TKI) and the Ministry of Justice and Human Rights, Indonesia still does not have an overarching, integrated policy on human trafficking. Even within institutions, the data on human trafficking are very scattered, reflecting the low priority of this issue.

I argue below that, despite the reforms of the post-Suharto period, the gap in access to justice, and hence the extent of social exclusion, has actually widened in the *reformasi* era. In contrast to Suharto's corporatist state, when state institutions controlled the market, the post-corporatist, *reformasi* state has been keen to offer more flexibility to investors. In a labour market context, this means that the state has encouraged private recruitment agencies and investors to take a bigger role in employing labour, in an effort to promote growth and reduce unemployment. This has allowed various actors in society to take advantage of less protected workers, resulting in an industrial relations system that is 'more predatory than liberal' (Juliawan 2010: 25). When government agencies themselves collude with corrupt agencies and industrialists, it is not surprising to find that they do not investigate cases of human trafficking.

In this chapter, I use the term 'migrant labour' to refer to both Indonesians working overseas and those migrating from one province to another within Indonesia, that is, internal migrant workers. The related hypotheses in this regard are that unequal development between regions causes labour migration from poorer areas to more prosperous areas within Indonesia; and that discrimination against (or even exploitation of) migrant workers is tolerated in the destination areas because these people are, by definition, 'newcomers' (*pendatang*).

An important point to note is that human trafficking has both local and global dimensions: although an industry implicated in the use of trafficked labour may operate within Indonesia, the trading network itself is global, and there is a global market for the 'commodity' — the workers. Examples include the multinational Malaysian oil palm companies active in Kalimantan, the small-scale bird's nest enterprises in North Sumatra with global links to Hong Kong, and the Thai-owned fishing companies operating in Indonesia. All have been implicated in the trafficking of workers not only within Indonesia, but also between countries.

While globalisation has opened up new avenues of production, the Indonesian government has been unable to prevent the exploitation of workers within the country's borders, especially those working as maids, plantation workers and fishers. It is important to notice this particular form of trafficking and slavery, since both the Indonesian government and civil society organisations tend to focus solely on overseas migrant workers, while neglecting the human trafficking that occurs inside Indonesia. If the government does not take a strong stance towards human trafficking that takes place within Indonesia, it can hardly expect other countries' governments to protect Indonesian migrant workers abroad. Another overlooked aspect is the changing landscape of migrant workers' mobility, especially the increased flows of workers from the eastern part of Indonesia, both to other provinces and to other countries. The government needs to gain a better understanding of these changes before formulating any policy intervention.

Indonesian government policy focuses on attracting investors but has been short on protecting labour. In particular, it has not been sensitive to the possibility that human trafficking and forced labour may occur in Indonesia. Market liberalisation has arguably made labour more prone to exploitation, not only by legally registered companies and migration brokers, but also by criminal networks of human traffickers (Juliawan 2010; Lindquist, Xiang and Yeoh 2012). Although Xiang and Lindquist (2014) claim that state intervention in the labour market in China has made the problem worse, I argue that it still has an important role to play in the Indonesian case, where government intervention is far less excessive than in China. In the Indonesian context, the consequences of less control over recruitment agencies would be catastrophic.

In this chapter I highlight the role of labour recruitment agencies, brokers and multinational and national companies in targeting poor workers from East Nusa Tenggara and other parts of eastern Indonesia. Two well-researched examples are the recruitment of men to work as daily workers (*buruh harian*) in oil palm plantations in Indonesia or Malaysia (Lindquist 2017; Palupi et al. 2015) and the recruitment of women from Lombok (West Nusa Tenggara) to work as domestic servants in Malaysia or Saudi Arabia (Lindquist 2010). In both cases, these workers face low wages, poor working conditions and lack of access to justice (Lindquist 2010; Rambu 2017).

In the 1980s, when the Suharto government first began to send migrant workers to the Middle East, mostly to work as maids, its focus was on reducing unemployment and increasing remittances, not on the risks potentially facing these overseas migrant workers (Amjad 1989). The current government is aware of the need to negotiate protections for Indonesian citizens working in foreign countries, and the foreign affairs minister in particular has responded quickly to allegations of abuse of overseas Indonesian workers. In 2015, for example, the government imposed a ban on sending domestic workers to the Middle East, in response to reports of inhumane treatment of Indonesians working there. This moratorium remains in place, despite heated debate about its effectiveness, including criticism by BNP2TKI (Amrullah 2017). I believe, however, that the moratorium is the only way to ensure that governments in the Middle East invest in better systems to protect Indonesian women from being treated like slaves (for a different view, see Patunru and Uddarojat 2015). The Chinese government does not allow labour migration to Singapore, Hong Kong, Taiwan or Macau, based on the argument that the dissimilar treatment of workers in countries with similar cultural identities can trigger conflict (Xiang and Lindquist 2014). This can also be argued for the Indonesian case, in that the Middle Eastern countries and Indonesia have a shared Muslim identity.

At the regional level, while the Indonesian government has been involved in forums to protect migrant workers through the ASEAN Ministerial Meeting on Transnational Crime, there is as yet no firm agreement among ASEAN countries on how to protect foreign workers. This lack of coordination among ASEAN governments causes its own problems. For instance, in January 2018 the Malaysian government launched an online recruitment system that would allow Malaysian employers to hire foreign domestic servants directly, without going through an employment agency (Asia Times 2018); within a few days, however, the Indonesian government objected to the system, citing potential conflicts with Indonesian labour regulations (Fauzi 2018).

The problem of the value chain in labour migration — in particular, the role of the labour recruitment agency — has been examined by researchers in several countries. According to Xiang (2012), government intervention in labour recruitment in China has increased the power of the agency. The Malaysian and Indonesian governments have adopted contrasting policies towards recruitment agencies: the Malaysian government has chosen to employ a liberal policy of cutting migration controls, resulting in a reduction in the role of the agency; while the Indonesian government has opted for an interventionist approach that has strengthened the role of the agency. The differing approaches of the two countries show the lack of regional institutional capacity to solve the problems affecting regional migration among ASEAN countries, and especially the labour value chain from the recruitment place to the destination area.

At home, Indonesia is struggling to fight human trafficking not only of its own citizens, but also of citizens from other ASEAN countries, such as Cambodia, Myanmar, Thailand and Laos (Dillon 2015). The problems include lack of judicial capacity to deal with human trafficking cases, poor coordination among state institutions and corruption. The small number of prosecutions of human traffickers — only 46 in 2016, resulting in at least 30 convictions (US Department of State 2017: 209) — is one indicator of incapacity and possible corruption in Indonesia's judicial institutions. The lack of data on human trafficking victims is another sign of incapacity; according to a member of the Criminal Investigation Agency (Bareskrim) of the National Police, whose responsibilities include human trafficking cases, the database on human trafficking is no longer maintained due to a lack of budgetary resources (personal interview with Bareskrim investigator).

Like many other post-authoritarian states, Indonesia is struggling to manage the consequences of market liberalisation, including criminal involvement in labour migration. While Indonesians now live under a less repressive regime, the current political system also provides space for transactional democracy, in which the commodification of voters is common (Aspinall and Sukmajati 2015; Widyatmoko 2013). The market plays a very big role in Indonesian politics and public life, resulting in a struggle to separate the interests of the private sector from those of the state apparatus in national and provincial labour offices.

To prevent human trafficking, state officials are required to check the identity of applicants for migrant worker schemes. The problem with this approach is that the counterfeiting of documents is commonplace and government agencies themselves may be complicit in issuing false documents. Moreover, the Indonesian government's plan to issue a single 'smart' identity card (the e-KTP) to replace all other forms of identification has been halted, following a serious corruption scandal involving members of the national parliament (DPR).

The human trafficking networks aim not only to take advantage of vulnerable populations, but also to control the state institutions that are supposed to be in charge of protecting citizens. They do not hesitate to bribe state officials to achieve their goals. In 2014, for example, Rudy Soik, a whistleblower in the East Nusa Tenggara provincial police office, revealed that senior police officers were facilitating the trafficking of minors to Malaysia (Soik 2014). In 2017, a judge in East Nusa Tenggara released a trafficker who was well known for her ability to bribe officials, and she remains a fugitive (Padeng 2017a, 2017b). Moreover, the police tend to have a circumscribed view of what constitutes a human trafficking victim. According to Farrell and Pfeffer (2014), police in the United States focus mainly on cases that involve the trafficking of minors for sex. This is also the case in Indonesia, in part because human trafficking cases are easier to prosecute when the victim is a minor.

HUMAN TRAFFICKING WITHIN INDONESIA

Since adopting the United Nations Protocol to Prevent, Suppress and Punish Trafficking in Persons in 2007, the Indonesian government has used it as a basis to prosecute perpetrators of human trafficking. According to the 2017 'Trafficking in persons' report, the anti-trafficking unit of the National Police investigated 110 new cases in 2016 (down from 221 in 2015) and the Supreme Court reported 256 convictions (compared with 119 in 2015), with sentences up to seven years (US Department of State 2017: 209).

There are several factors that make it difficult to investigate and prosecute human trafficking cases. First, institutional constraints in police departments and the judicial system contribute to the low prosecution rates for human trafficking. The police and the judiciary need to be educated on the provisions of the country's anti-trafficking legislation, to prevent them from being influenced by market-driven interests that prioritise the need for 'flexible' employment schemes (Juliawan 2010). The practice of putting the interests of recruitment agencies and investors before the rights of citizens needs to stop.

Second, Law No. 21/2007 on the Elimination of Human Trafficking (the Human Trafficking Law) suffers from problems of drafting and implementation. In particular, the Human Trafficking Law does not refer to Law No. 39/2004 on the Placement and Protection of Indonesian Migrant Workers, a labour law dealing with various aspects of overseas migration. The disconnection of these two laws creates confusion in the judicial system about whether trafficking should be treated as a human rights offence (under the Human Trafficking Law) or as a labour violation (under Law No. 39/2004). Many human trafficking cases are downgraded to administrative disputes using Law No. 39/2004, which has lower penalties. In 2016, for example, an attorney in Kupang said that only four of nineteen human trafficking cases had been prosecuted under the Human Trafficking Law, with the rest proceeding under Law No. 39/2004 (Timor Express 2017). The main problem is that, in interpreting the law, prosecutors focus on exploitation after a person has been trafficked, rather than on exploitation during the recruitment process itself. Thus, the law does not work as a preventative instrument.

Third, there is no administrative mechanism to control human trafficking within Indonesia, and no national body responsible for preventing it. The Anti-Trafficking Taskforce established by Presidential Regulation No. 69/2008 is merely a coordinating body for the relevant national ministries. Its daily operations are led by the Ministry of Women's Empowerment and Child Protection, which lacks both the institutional design and the budget to tackle such a complex issue as human trafficking. All provinces except Papua and West Papua have their own anti-trafficking taskforces, but they lack a firm budget and operational mandate. The existence of similar forums at the district level depends on the initiative of the executive and the legislature in each area.

Finally, there is no integrated database on human trafficking in Indonesia. The official data on human trafficking are scattered across several institutions, including the Ministry of Women's Empowerment and Child Protection, the Ministry of Social Affairs, the Ministry of Manpower and BNP2TKI. Moreover, the data that do exist are problematic, because the context continues to be labour migration to foreign countries (outside Indonesia), even though human trafficking within Indonesia is becoming an increasingly serious problem.

It is therefore often left to media and civil society organisations to collect their own data, and to focus public attention on human trafficking issues. IRGSC estimated that 2,291 people in East Nusa Tenggara had been victims of human trafficking in 2014–16, based on an examination of media reports in three printed newspapers in the capital, Kupang. In 2016, local journalists reported that 23 people from East Nusa Tenggara had died as a result of human trafficking. In the same year, Ampera counted 54 coffins of migrant workers that had arrived at Kupang's El Tari Airport, although it was not clear how many of the deaths were due to human trafficking (Ampera 2016).

THE DYNAMICS OF MIGRATION FROM EAST NUSA TENGGARA

At a time when modern slavery is on the rise, many are reminded of the colonial and pre-colonial periods when slave trading was widespread in eastern Indonesia (Boomgaard 2003; Hägerdal 2010; Ormeling 1957; Parimartha 2002). According to historians, the eastern islands were a source of slaves during the Dutch colonial period, with coastal areas such as Waingapu in Sumba, Ende in Flores and Atapupu in West Timor known as slave trading ports (Hägerdal 2012; Parimartha 2002). The use of slaves from Timor, Sawu and Rote dates back to at least the seventeenth century, with reports of slaves from these areas being taken to Banda to work in nutmeg and mace plantations (Ormeling 1957) and to Batavia (Jakarta) to work as domestic servants (Hägerdal 2010). In 1829 there were 1,200 slaves in Kupang, and a slave port was still found in Flores in 1878 (Ormeling 1957) — that is, after the abolition of slavery by European countries.

Today, migration from East Nusa Tenggara follows the general labour migration trends for Indonesia. The pull factor mostly comes from production areas such as oil palm plantations, and from cities in the case of female domestic servants. The demand for low-skilled labour from East Nusa Tenggara corresponds to the province's position on the Human Development Index; it is placed third from the bottom, ahead of only West Papua and Papua. BPS data indicate that most of East Nusa Tenggara's children drop out of school in their first year of junior secondary school. The province has a high unemployment rate, but the official employment data provided by BPS may actually understate the extent of the problem, since much of the agricultural sector provides work for less than four months of the year.

Most of the victims of human trafficking in East Nusa Tenggara are recruited from the two main islands of Sumba and Timor. Modern mobility combined with the persistence of traditional social systems contributes to the ease with which people are trafficked. Sumba, for instance, has the remnants of a caste system in which the feudal lord controlled most of the resources and the upper echelon of society owned slaves (*ata*). Timor was another of Indonesia's 'slave reservoirs' (Ormeling 1957: 180), and the late adopters of modernity on the island are still the most likely to be the victims of human trafficking.

In the past, the interisland slave traders tended to be Christians associated with the Dutch East India Company or Muslims based in Ende, while those who were traded as slaves were usually non-Christian and non-Muslim (Parimartha 2002). The adoption of Christianity or Islam by the natives was therefore a good strategy to avoid slavery. Hägerdal (2010) highlights the case of a local woman who converted to Christianity in order to get fair treatment from the Dutch community in Kupang after she reported her husband for the rape of a minor in their house in 1679.

Government administrations from the colonial period onward have paid little heed to the development of Timor and nearby islands, chiefly because the region has never made a large economic contribution to the central government (Furnivall 1967; Touwen 2001). In the 1950s, Ormeling (1957: 104) observed that 'until recently the Timorese economy bore all the characteristics of a self-sufficient economy [...] Man produced his own food, just enough to provide a bare living; he wove his own cloth and made his own simple tools'. Although this assessment was made more than 50 years ago, my own observations confirm that similar conditions prevail today. Families in rural areas continue to live subsistence lifestyles, making very little use of cash. In the heavily rural districts of North Central Timor and South Central Timor, for example, the cash income of 45.2 per cent of families is less than Rp 500,000 ($37) per month (Li, Banunaek et al. 2017).

The main barrier preventing rural youth in East Nusa Tenggara from obtaining skilled jobs in the service or government sectors is that they have not completed junior secondary school. IRGSC found that 13.05 per cent of all human trafficking victims in East Nusa Tenggara in 2014–16 were children; 34 children were trafficked in 2014, 87 in 2015 and 97 in 2016. Most children are recruited when they drop out of school, and some children are kidnapped from schools. Most come from the Timor and Sumba hinterlands. The traffickers forge new identities for the children that allow them to be passed off as adults. The criminal networks behind these activities often have close connections with civil registration officers and village heads, who are the officers authorised to release birth certificates (Seo 2016a).

Another push factor for migration is the low salaries domestic workers receive in East Nusa Tenggara itself. Job advertisements in daily newspapers in Kupang indicate that domestic servants can expect to receive Rp 0.5–1 million ($37–73) per month. Thus, when recruiters make false promises of much higher salaries, workers tend to accept their assurances uncritically and leap at what they see as a big opportunity. In fact, however, workers from East Nusa Tenggara are unlikely to obtain well-paying jobs because they are viewed as coming from one of the least talented labour pools in Indonesia. The lack of education and skills in the province can be an impediment even for domestic workers. When interviewed in 2014, for instance, a human trafficking victim from Belu district (on the border between West Timor and Timor Leste) said that she had been rejected to work in Malaysia because she did not meet the 'international standard'. The response of the recruitment agency was to switch the destination to Medan in North Sumatra, where she was enslaved for more than two years (Li, Paul et al. 2017).

Figure 13.1   Number of passengers using East Nusa Tenggara airports, 1984–2016 (million)

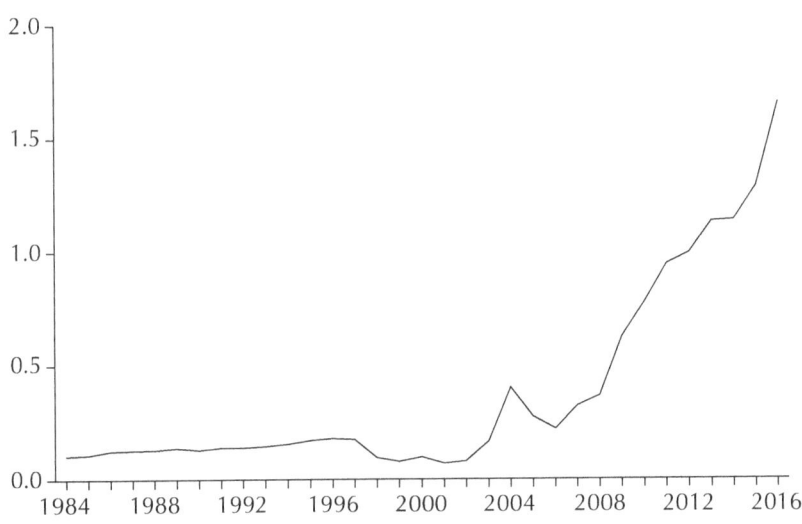

Source: BPS.

Kupang is the main hub and exit point for human trafficking from East Nusa Tenggara. Most victims come from districts in the islands of Timor (Belu, Malaka, North Central Timor, South Central Timor and Kupang), Sumba (West Sumba and Southwest Sumba) and Flores (East Manggarai, Nagekeo, West Manggarai and East Flores). Jakarta and Surabaya are the main transit hubs in Java used by the traffickers. The main hubs to enter Malaysia are Nunukan in Kalimantan, and Batam. They function not only as places of transit, but also as centres of document forgery.

During the Suharto era, East Nusa Tenggara had few and infrequent air services. As Figure 13.1 shows, passenger numbers were flat throughout the New Order period, and for several years afterwards. Since around 2006, however, there has been a huge increase in the number of flights to and within East Nusa Tenggara, and the cost of air travel has fallen sharply. From only 77,000 passengers per year in 1999 (the lowest point of the Asian financial crisis), the number of passengers passing through all airports in East Nusa Tenggara reached more than 1.5 million in 2016.

While the current government continues to promote connectivity within Indonesia, a new, unanticipated problem has arisen: connectivity may actually *facilitate* trafficking by making it easier to transport naïve and uneducated people from one part of the country to another, or overseas. Migrant workers from villages in East Nusa Tenggara have very little education (or may even be illiterate), are not given legal contracts by their recruiters and do not know much about the destination areas. Unfortunately, improved air connections, and better transport and communications technology more generally, have made it easier for brokers to target people living in remote locations, far from the main centres of economic activity. Women, children and poor people are particularly vulnerable. For instance, brokers often exploit the traditional, trust-based *oko mama* community networks in Timor to obtain the consent of poor, rural parents to their daughters being sent abroad or to other provinces (Dethan-Penpada 2017). Those parents have no idea about working conditions in foreign countries and would not be able to imagine that their children might be enslaved or treated as a commodity.

Ideally, better transportation infrastructure would be good news. But in practice globalisation has introduced a predatory element in which brokers and middlemen target vulnerable women and children from small rural villages and poor areas. The commodification of people by brokers is apparent even in the way they advertise those workers' services. In North Sumatra and Bali, for example, female workers from East Nusa Tenggara are advertised as being 'obedient and economical' (*taat dan murah*) — the implication being that they are easily exploited and require very little to live on. In 2016, the East Nusa Tenggara police reported that the price brokers were asking to recruit 20 persons from East Nusa Tenggara was equal to the price of a Xenia (a mid-sized passenger car), namely Rp 190 million, that is, around $700 per person (Seo 2016a).

The decentralisation of central government powers to the provincial and district levels of government has also had consequences for human trafficking. In East Nusa Tenggara, the implementation of decentralisation has meant a return to ethnicity-based forms of organisation based on traditional clan systems — that is, a return to collective corruption or clan corruption. During the Suharto period, clan politics was suppressed in order to elevate the notion of the Indonesian citizen. In the *reformasi* era, transactional democracy has become intertwined with the old clan system, resulting in a notion of citizenship that is based not on the rights of the citizen, but rather on the connections the citizen can tap into. While new elites have emerged within the clan-based system, those who are not represented within the system are very vulnerable to exploitation. Faced with a lack of social status and job opportunities at home, they react passively to exploitation in the destination areas, as if they had no other choice.

Finally, human trafficking is associated with the rise of Indonesia's palm oil industry. Unskilled workers from East Nusa Tenggara are in strong demand from oil palm plantations in Kalimantan, Sulawesi, Papua and Sumatra. Where workers from East Nusa Tenggara, especially East Flores, once used to take jobs in the oil palm plantations of Sabah in

Table 13.1 Palm oil companies that have recruited East Nusa Tenggara workers without following proper procedures, 2014–16

Company	Plantation location	Area (hectares)	No. of recruiters	Origin of recruiters
PT Mulia Agro Permai (multinational)	Central Kalimantan	–	6	Belu
PT Muara Toyu Subur Lestari	East Kalimantan	12,000	28	North Central Timor
PT Minamas Plantation	–	216,911	21	Alor
PT Borneo Sejahtera Marimun	–	–	63	North Central Timor, Belu, Malaka
Fangiono Agro Plantation	East Kalimantan	–	83	Unidentified
PT Buana Hijau Abadi (BHA)	Jakarta	–	20	Unidentified
PT Citra Bina Tenaga Mandiri	Kota Kupang	–	4	South Central Timor
PT Citra Borneo Indah	Central Kalimantan	–	7	Unidentified

Source: Data collected by IRGSC–Ampera based on articles in three Kupang newspapers (Pos Kupang, Timor Express and Victory News) in 2014, 2015 and 2016.

eastern Malaysia (Hugo 1995), today they are more likely take jobs in Indonesian plantations owned by the same Malaysian palm oil companies.

Table 13.1 lists some of the palm oil companies that are alleged to have employed workers illegally recruited from East Nusa Tenggara. The list is based on media reports in three Kupang newspapers in the period 2014–16. According to the provincial police, these companies failed to provide proper contracts for their workers, making them vulnerable to exploitation.

Migration from East Nusa Tenggara to other provinces within Indonesia, and the attendant stories of human trafficking, is not limited to the plantation sector. One of the most brutal cases concerns the enslavement of 26 women from West Timor and Rote for periods of two to four years to work in a bird's nest enterprise in Medan (Li, Paul et al. 2017). The owner was able to reap large profits by selling this delicacy to his Chinese contacts in Hong Kong; at the same time, he enslaved his female workforce and made them take medicine that would prevent menstruation (Lewanmeru 2014). At least two workers are reported to have died while working for this enterprise.

Figure 13.2 Number and type of perpetrators of human trafficking in East Nusa Tenggara, 2014–16

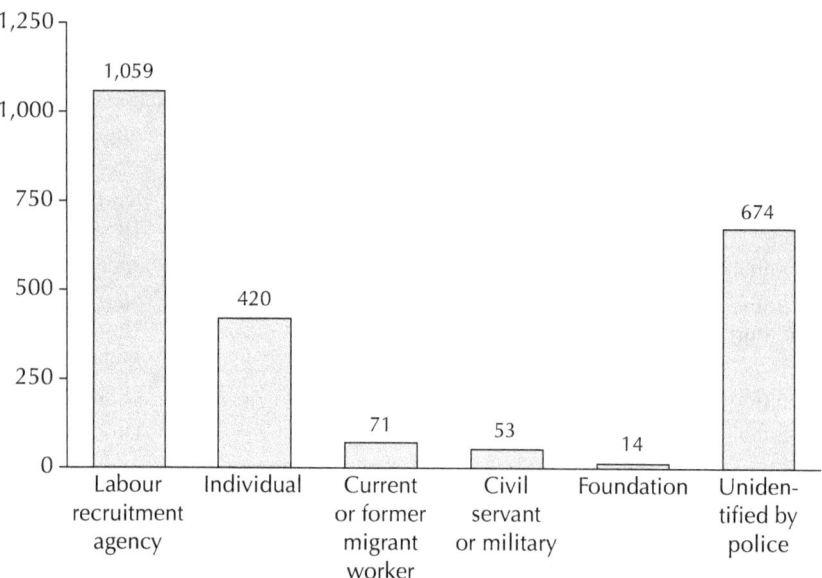

Source: Data collected by IRGSC–Ampera based on articles in three Kupang newspapers (*Pos Kupang*, *Timor Express* and *Victory News*) in 2014, 2015 and 2016.

THE ROLE OF LABOUR AGENCIES IN HUMAN TRAFFICKING

By its nature, a human trafficking network is hard to identify. IRGSC research indicates, however, that the main perpetrators of human trafficking in East Nusa Tenggara are found in recruitment agencies, as shown in Figure 13.2. These agencies are legally registered with the Ministry of Manpower.

Analysis of media reports in three printed newspapers in Kupang shows that the perpetrators of human trafficking can be categorised as follows: (1) recruitment agencies; (2) individuals; (3) current or former migrant workers; (4) civil servants or military; and (5) foundations (the latter usually established by recruitment agencies to camouflage their activities). In some cases it can be difficult to identify the perpetrators of human trafficking, because the police often strike deals with them to keep their identities secret.

Even though IRGSC identified 42 recruitment agencies that were allegedly involved in human trafficking in 2014–16 in East Nusa Tenggara, none has been charged with any wrongdoing. In the case of the women enslaved in the bird's nest industry in Medan, for instance, only one individual recruiter has been punished, despite staff in several recruitment agencies in Kupang and Medan being implicated. The heaviest sanction imposed by the Ministry of Manpower in such cases is to close the recruitment agency.

The lack of appropriate penalties and enforcement is one of the most difficult challenges in dealing with human trafficking cases within Indonesia. Another is that it is not easy to coordinate joint investigations between the police forces of two or more provinces, or to decide whether a trial should be held in the place of recruitment or the destination. In the case of the women enslaved in a bird's nest enterprise in Medan, for example, the pressure to pursue the case has come from Kupang, while the police investigation itself has taken place in Medan. Four years later, the investigation remains bogged down in the Medan police office, amidst allegations that police reports have been manipulated (Maia 2016; Najwa 2014b). Meanwhile, the firm's owner remains free, despite at least two deaths being linked to his factory (Li, Paul et al. 2017).

Clearly the government needs to develop a comprehensive strategy to prevent registered labour recruitment agencies, police and military officers, and bureaucrats from participating in human trafficking. In the absence of strong government action, it is only the cases highlighted by the media and civil society organisations that are properly investigated and prosecuted. In East Nusa Tenggara, for instance, the support of NGOs ensured that the case of the local recruiter involved in the Medan bird's nest case, as well as those related to the deaths of Ance Punuf (Leo 2017) and Dolfina Abuk (Zacharias 2016), was treated seriously by the judicial system.

One particularly sad aspect of human trafficking is that the bodies of the victims may simply be abandoned. In February 2017, for instance, the coffin of a human trafficking victim was left at El Tari Airport for three days, until a Kupang-based newspaper focused public attention on this matter. Part of the problem is that the victims of human trafficking may be working under assumed identities. My own research indicates that it can take days or even weeks to uncover a person's real identity. According to the Ministry of Manpower, 1.9 million of the 4.5 million Indonesians working in foreign countries may not have the proper legal documentation. This makes them more vulnerable to human trafficking.

THE ROLE OF CIVIL SOCIETY ORGANISATIONS AND CITIZENS' MOVEMENTS

In East Nusa Tenggara, where human trafficking is common and state institutions seem to be incapable of preventing it, the fight against labour exploitation is led mainly by civil society organisations. These organisations have formed a broad alliance to demand that the state take action to ensure the welfare of citizens. While most of the debate about labour migration controls concerns state intervention or market orientation, in East Nusa Tenggara, the idea of a civil society movement to prevent labour abuses is flourishing.

When the state apparatus fails to take responsibility, civil society organisations have no choice but to become the frontline organisations to uphold victims' rights and demand greater government accountability. In addition to organising mass rallies calling for better systems to protect vulnerable citizens, the civil society organisations in East Nusa Tenggara assist victims of trafficking, are present in courtrooms to ensure a fair trial and document the stories of victims. The main agenda is to pressure judicial institutions to prosecute perpetrators; this includes monitoring human trafficking cases as they pass through the courts to make sure that victims are treated fairly. Counting the dead bodies arriving each week at El Tari Airport, and publicising the results, is another effective way of raising awareness of the human trafficking issue. Fifty-four coffins arrived in Kupang in 2016, and at least 40 coffins arrived in the provincial capital between January and August 2017 (Ampera 2016; Selan 2017).

Ideally, state institutions, particularly the judiciary, would have good processes for identifying and countering criminal activity. But when the government is determined to give recruitment agencies 'flexibility', and the labour market is treated as an independent entity over which the government has little control, the rights of migrant workers are easily ignored. In practice, the 'right to migrate' is elevated over the 'right not to be sold' and the 'right to have a safe migration'. Indeed, the current treatment of migrant workers shows that the idea of slavery as the commodification of a human being, which has been criticised and banned since the mid-nineteenth century (Boomgaard 2003), has managed to find a back entrance into the modern-day Indonesian labour market (Dillon 2015; Li, Paul et al. 2017; Patty 2015).

Sen (1999: 6) argued that 'the contribution of the market mechanism to economic growth is, of course, important, but this comes only after direct significance of the freedom to interchange—words, goods, gifts—has been acknowledged'. In the context of my criticisms of Indonesian labour market policy, I argue that the civil society movement is important for facilitating the freedom of citizens to 'interchange words' with the private sector and the state apparatus in a situation in which the system is manifestly unfair. This becomes difficult when organised criminal networks have the capability to bribe state officials in the judicial system. But when markets operate outside the law and the law itself has become commodified, this is also the time when a civil society movement is most important.

The emergence of the anti-trafficking movement in East Nusa Tenggara was triggered by the deaths of two local women who had been enslaved in Medan. This became a turning point for the civil society movement, especially after police whistleblower Rudy Soik revealed the involvement of high-ranking provincial police officers in human trafficking networks (Soik 2014). He received support from several organisations to speak on national television about the involvement of the police in human trafficking. The Indonesian police force, however, failed to appreciate this brave initiative.

In 2016, one of the leaders of Ampera was elected head, and the first female leader, of the Timorese evangelical church. Under her leadership the church's anti-trafficking group has focused on addressing some of the push factors for human trafficking. To ensure that poor rural families are not pushed into migration by poverty, for example, the members are introducing better agricultural technology and encouraging the revitalisation of primary education in rural areas.

When the state no longer functions in the best interests of citizens, civil society organisations must take responsibility for defending the ethical line in the public arena so that the notion of sovereignty still has meaning for ordinary citizens and people can be sure that their lives matter. When the agents of state behave in a predatory fashion towards the citizenry — or when the princes become peddlers, as Xiang (2012) expresses it for the case of China — civil society needs to intervene between the state and the market, and offer a better system. In peripheral areas of Indonesia where state authority is weak, such as East Nusa Tenggara, citizens should take direct action to uphold their rights.

CONCLUDING REMARKS

This chapter has described how the dominant role of recruitment agencies and brokers in labour migration has influenced Indonesian labour law, which is insensitive to labour exploitation. Moreover, village, district and provincial bureaucracies, the police and the judiciary, and airports have all been infiltrated by criminal networks. The main problem facing the vulnerable communities that are the targets of human trafficking is that there is no clear line to prevent labour exploitation in recruitment areas. The government therefore needs to develop a new strategy that is specifically directed at preventing human trafficking in the major recruitment areas.

The high number of human trafficking cases in East Nusa Tenggara province is itself an indicator of the underdeveloped state of one of the most marginalised areas in Indonesia. The end of Suharto's corporatist regime has had a disproportionate impact on East Nusa Tenggara because of its subsistence economy and poor human development indicators. Human trafficking networks like to operate in such places where vulnerable groups have limited access to resources and no way to escape the poverty trap.

The response of state institutions to the problem of human trafficking has not been nearly adequate to deal with the organised crime networks; the civil society organisations, for their part, can do little more than offer an emergency response. After a century or more of neglect, including by post-independence governments, much of the population of East Nusa Tenggara remains impoverished and vulnerable to exploitation. Rather than being independent subjects in a post-colonial state, as promised in the constitution, those citizens continue to be the object of the most banal form of capitalism.

The existence of a sovereign state is therefore questionable. The free movement of people is part of globalisation. What was not anticipated by the Indonesian state was the threat globalisation posed to vulnerable citizens – the possibility that human beings would be treated as a commodity in a free-movement framework or in modern laissez-faire economics. In Indonesia human trafficking is considered a crime, but it is not yet treated as an extraordinarily serious crime. With only minimum controls over the labour market in the *reformasi* period, the attitude of the government has contributed to the exploitation of one of the most vulnerable populations in Indonesia.

The efforts of civil society organisations to counter trafficking should remind the state of its responsibility to protect the lives of its citizens, and to prevent the return of slavery-like conditions for vulnerable groups of people, especially poor people in rural areas with low levels of skills and education. The development of transport infrastructure since the early 2000s has improved connectivity for people from all sections of society. However, it has also increased the vulnerability of the poor in rural areas, who are more easily targeted by human traffickers. The state failed to anticipate this aspect of the new migration landscape, leaving civil society to deal with the consequences in peripheral areas such as East Nusa Tenggara.

REFERENCES

Alawi, M.A. (2014a) 'Nakertrans dan Imigrasi NTT diduga terlibat trafficking' [East Nusa Tenggara Offices of Manpower and Immigration allegedly involved in trafficking], *Pos Kupang*, 1 December. http://kupang.tribunnews.com/2014/12/01/nakertrans-dan-imigrasi-ntt-diduga-terlibat-trafficking

Alawi, M.A. (2014b) 'Kompol Cecep: Brigpol DA mengaku dapat Rp 1 juta sekali perjalanan' [Police Commissioner Cecep: Brigadier-General DA admits to Rp

1 million bribe per trip', *Pos Kupang*, 18 December. http://kupang.tribunnews.com/2014/12/18/kompol-cecep-bigpol-da-mengaku-dapat-rp-1-juta-sekali-perjalanan

Alawi, M.A. (2015) 'Satu perwira menengah dan dua bintara diperiksa polda NTT' [One mid-level officer and two non-commissioned officers investigated by East Nusa Tenggara police], *Pos Kupang*, 10 March. http://kupang.tribunnews.com/2015/03/10/satu-perwira-menengah-dan-dua-bintara-diperiksa-polda-ntt

Amjad, R. (1989) 'Economic impact of migration to the Middle East on the major Asian labour sending countries: an overview', in R. Amjad (ed.) *To The Gulf and Back: Studies on the Economic Impact of Asian Labour Migration*, United Nations Development Programme, International Labour Organisation and Asian Employment Programme, New Delhi: 1–27.

Ampera (Aliansi Melawan Perdagangan Orang) (2016) 'Data buruh migran asal NTT yang dipulangkan dalam kondisi meninggal tahun 2016' [Data on migrant workers from East Nusa Tenggara who were sent home in coffins in 2016], unpublished report, Ampera, Kupang.

Amrullah, A. (2017) 'Cabut moratorium TKI, BNP2TKI dinilai langgar aturan' [Remove the moratorium on Indonesian migrant workers, BNP2TKI believes it violates regulations], *Republika.co.id*, 12 September. http://nasional.republika.co.id/berita/nasional/umum/17/09/25/owucb9299-cabut-moratorium-tki-bnp2tki-dinilai-langgar-aturan

Antara (2016) 'Sekda Kupang: proses hukum sekdes terlibat perdagangan orang' [Kupang regional secretary: village secretary's legal process involved human trafficking], *Pos Kupang*, 23 January. http://kupang.tribunnews.com/2017/01/23/sekda-kupang-proses-hukum-sekdes-terlibat-perdagangan-orang

Asia Times (2018) 'Malaysia allows online direct hiring of maids', *Asia Times*, 2 January. http://www.atimes.com/article/malaysia-allows-online-direct-hiring-maids/

Aspinall, E., and M. Sukmajati (eds) (2015) *Politik Uang di Indonesia: Patronase dan Klientelisme pada Pemilu Legislatif* [Money Politics in Indonesia: Patronage and Clientelism in Legislative Elections], PolGov, Yogyakarta.

Boomgaard, P. (2003) 'Human capital, slavery and low rates of economic and population growth in Indonesia, 1600–1910', *Slavery and Abolition* 24(2): 83–96.

Castells, M. (2010) *End of Millennium. The Information Age: Economy, Society, and Culture Volume III*, second edition, Wiley-Blackwell, Chichester.

De Jong, J., and G. Rizvi (eds) (2008) *The State of Access: Success and Failure of Democracies to Create Equal Opportunities*, Brookings Institution Press, Washington DC.

Dethan-Penpada, D. (2017) 'Budaya oko mama dan perdagangan orang di NTT' [*Oko mama* culture and human trafficking in East Nusa Tenggara], in Supriatno (ed.) *Gereja Melawan Human Trafficking* [Churches against Human Trafficking], Mission 21, Bandung: 89–98.

Dillon, P. (2015) 'Over 500 new human trafficking victims identified in Indonesia since Benjina "slave fisheries" exposed', International Organization of Migration (IOM), 3 August. http://weblog.iom.int/over-500-new-human-trafficking-victims-identified-indonesia-benjina-%E2%80%98slave-fisheries%E2%80%99-exposed

Farrell, A., and R. Pfeffer (2014) 'Policing human trafficking: cultural blinders and organizational barriers', *Annals of the American Academy of Political and Social Science* 653(1): 46–64.

Fauzi, M. (2018) 'Indonesia tolak direct hiring Malaysia' [Indonesia rejects direct hiring from Malaysia], *Validnews.co*, 10 January. http://www.validnews.co/Indonesia-Tolak-Skema-Direct-Hiring-Malaysia--kEP

Furnivall, J.S. (1967) *Netherlands India: A Study of Plural Economy*, Cambridge University Press, Cambridge MA.

Hägerdal, H. (2010) 'The slaves of Timor: life and death on the fringes of early colonial society', *Itinerario* 34(2): 19–44.

Hägerdal, H. (2012) *Lords of the Land, Lords of the Sea: Conflict and Adaptation in Early Colonial Timor, 1600–1800*, KITLV Press, Leiden.

Hugo, G. (1995) 'International labor migration and the family: some observations from Indonesia', *Asian and Pacific Migration Journal* 4(2-3): 273–301.

Jones, L., D.W. Engstrom, T. Hilliard and M. Diaz (2007) 'Globalization and human trafficking', *Journal of Sociology and Social Welfare* 34(2): 107–22.

Juliawan, B.H. (2010) 'Extracting labor from its owner: private employment agencies and labor market flexibility in Indonesia', *Critical Asian Studies* 42(1): 25–52.

Leo, N. (2017) 'DPO kasus trafficking TTS Boy Mooy tiba di Kupang' [The wanted trafficker from South Central Timor, Boy Mooy, arrested in Kupang], *Pos Kupang*, 29 December. http://kupang.tribunnews.com/2017/12/29/dpo-kasus-trafficking-tts-boy-mooy-ditangkap-satgas-trafficking-tts-di-liliba-kupang

Lewanmeru, O. (2014) 'Kasus penyekapan TKW di Medan, TKW NTT disuruh minum ramuan agar tidak haid' [The case of female migrant workers in Medan, East Nusa Tenggara workers told to drink potion to prevent menstruation], *Pos Kupang*, 8 August. http://www.tribunnews.com/regional/2014/08/08/kasus-penyekapan-tkw-di-medan-tkw-ntt-disuruh-minum-ramuan-agar-tidak-haid

Li, D.E, R. Banunaek, L.M. Kini and M. Tukan (2017) 'Contemporary risk assessment on children in TTS and TTU district in NTT province', internal document (baseline research) submitted to Plan Indonesia, Institute of Resource Governance and Social Change (IRGSC), Kupang.

Li, D.E, S. Paul, R. Bernadetha and L. Wetangterah (2017) 'Human trafficking and corruption in post Suharto period "within" Indonesian border', IRGSC Working Paper, Institute of Resource Governance and Social Change (IRGSC), Kupang.

Lindquist, J. (2010) 'Labour recruitment, circuits of capital and gendered mobility: reconceptualizing the Indonesian migration industry', *Pacific Affairs* 83(1): 115–32.

Lindquist, J. (2017) 'Brokers, channels, infrastructure: moving migrant labor in the Indonesian–Malaysian oil palm complex', *Mobilities* 12(2): 213–26.

Lindquist, J., B. Xiang and B.S. Yeoh (2012) 'Opening the black box of migration: brokers, the organization of transnational mobility and the changing political economy in Asia', *Pacific Affairs* 85(1): 7–19.

Maia, M.A. (2016) 'Kabar dari Medan' [News from Medan], 18 August. https://www.youtube.com/watch?v=6LypA6I5mYo

Najwa, M. (2014a) 'Brigpol Rudy: walaupun ada beberapa perusahaan, tapi jaringan trafficking satu' [Police Brigadier Rudy: there are many firms but there is only one trafficking network], *Metrotvnews.com*, 19 November. http://video.metrotvnews.com/play/2014/11/19/321072/brigpol-rudy-walaupun-ada-beberapa-perusahaan-tapi-jaringan-trafficking-satu

Najwa, M. (2014b) 'Bisnis manusia 7' [Human trafficking 7], *Metrotvnews.com*, 20 November, https://www.youtube.com/watch?v=RMDtiQqKJKw

Ormeling, F.J. (1957) *The Timor Problem: A Geographical Interpretation of an Underdeveloped Island*, J.B. Walters, Groningen and Jakarta.

Padeng, P. (2017a) 'Terdakwa human trafficiking Diana Aman kabur' [Human trafficking suspect Diana Aman escapes], *Victory News*, 12 April. http://www.victorynews.id/terdakwa-human-trafficiking-diana-aman-kabur/

Padeng, P. (2017b) 'Jaksa yakin bisa tangkap dan eksekusi Diana Aman' [Prosecutors believe they can arrest and execute Diana Aman], *Victory News*, 3 June. http://www.victorynews.id/jaksa-yakin-bisa-tangkap-dan-eksekusi-diana-aman/

Palupi, S., P. Prasetyohadi, C. Pahun, A.S. Kusni, K. Sulang, J. Jenito and D. Warnadi (2015) 'Industri perkebunan sawit dan hak asasi manusia: potret pelaksanaan tanggung jawab pemerintah dan korporasi terhadap hak asasi manusia di Kalimantan Tengah' [The palm oil industry and human rights: a portrait of the implementation of government and corporate responsibility for human rights in Central Kalimantan], Institute for Ecosoc Rights, Jakarta. Published in English as 'Palm oil industry and human rights: a case study on oil palm corporations in Central Kalimantan'. http://www.jus.uio.no/smr/english/about/id/docs/indonesia/report-palm-oil-industry-and-human-rights-2015.pdf.

Parimartha, I.G. (2002) *Perdagangan dan Politik di Nusa Tenggara, 1815–1915* [Trade and Politics in Nusa Tenggara, 1815–1915], KITLV and Penerbit Djambatan, Jakarta.

Patty, R.R. (2015) '347 ABK asing korban perbudakan masih berada di Tual' [347 foreign crew who were victims of slavery are still in Tual], *Kompas.com*, 11 April. http://regional.kompas.com/read/2015/04/11/10234211/347.ABK.Asing.Korban.Perbudakan.Masih.Berada.di.Tual

Patunru, A.A., and R. Uddarojat (2015) 'Reducing the financial burden of Indonesian migrant workers', SEANET Perspectives No. 3, Center for Indonesian Policy Studies (CPIS) and Southeast Asia Network for Development (SEANET), Jakarta, October.

Rambu, B. (2017) 'NTT provinsi "budak"' [East Nusa Tenggara the province of slaves], *Victory News*, 23 April. http://www.victorynews.id/ntt-provinsi-budak/

Selan (2017) 'The numbers of deaths of migrant workers from NTT province in 2016', unpublished report.

Sen, A. (1999) *Development as Freedom*, Oxford University Press, Oxford.

Seo, Y. (2016a) 'Perdagangan manusia di NTT, 20 TKI ditukar sebuah mobil' [Human trafficking in East Nusa Tenggara, 20 Indonesian migrant workers for one car], *Tempo*, 23 August. https://nasional.tempo.co/read/798176/perdagangan-manusia-di-ntt-20-tki-ditukar-sebuah-mobil

Seo, Y. (2016b) 'Staf terlibat human trafficking, bandara El Tari diperketat' [Staff involved in human trafficking, El Tari Airport on high alert], *Tempo*, 26 August. https://nasional.tempo.co/read/799074/staf-terlibat-human-trafficking-bandara-el-tari-diperketat

Soik, R. (2014) Unpublished letter to the Indonesian president alleging corruption within the Indonesian police force, and other supporting documents.

Timor Express (2017) 'Kejati eksekusi Beny Kamarudin' [High Court to execute Beny Kamarudin], *Timor Express*, 26 January. https://timorexpress.fajar.co.id/2017/01/26/kejati-eksekusi-beny-kamarudin/

Touwen, J. (2001) *Extremes in the Archipelago: Trade and Economic Development in the Outer Islands of Indonesia, 1900–1942*, KITLV Press, Leiden.

US Department of State (2017) 'Trafficking in persons report June 2017', US Department of State, Washington DC, June. https://www.state.gov/j/tip/rls/tiprpt/2017/

Widyatmoko, J.D. (2013) *Oligarki dan Korupsi Politik Indonesia: Strategi Memutus Oligarki dan Reproduksi Korupsi Politik* [Oligarchy and Political Corruption in

Indonesia: Strategy to Break the Oligarchy and the Reproduction of Political Corruption], Setara Press, Malang.

Xiang, B. (2012) 'Predatory princes and princely peddlers: the state and international labour migration intermediaries in China', *Pacific Affairs* 85(1): 47–68.

Xiang, B., and J. Lindquist (2014) 'Migration infrastructure', *International Migration Review* 48: S122–48.

Zacharias, V. (2016) 'Polda NTT tetapkan 3 tersangka kasus human trafficking Dolfina Abuk yang meninggal di Malaysia' [East Nusa Tenggara police name three suspects in the human trafficking of Dolfina Abuk who died in Malaysia], *RRI*, 27 June. http://rri.co.id/post/berita/287297/daerah/polda_ntt_tetapkan_3_tersangka_kasus_human_trafficking_dolfina_abuk_yang_meninggal_di_malaysia.html

PART 5

Navigating the new globalisation

14 Indonesia and the global economy: missed opportunities?

*Hal Hill and Deasy Pane**

'Indonesia was born a free trader yet is consistently reluctant to accept globalization.' (Basri 2012: 46)

More open economies generally grow faster than less open economies. But openness needs to be managed. That is, to participate in the global economy, countries need not only to open their economies to trade, investment and technology, but also to make supply-side investments to ensure that the benefits of openness are widely distributed. These investments include making sure that the country's population is equipped with the skills to take advantage of global opportunities, that there are social safety nets in place to manage the volatility that is inevitably associated with globalisation, and that the benefits are spatially dispersed.

Indonesia is an excellent laboratory for exploring these issues. After progressively disengaging from the global economy during the first two decades of independence, Indonesia has created a policy regime that has been broadly open since 1966. There were major and successful reform episodes in the late 1960s and the first half of the 1980s, and the economy and polity recovered surprisingly quickly from the deep economic and political crises of 1997–98. But the quotation above captures the central theme of this chapter: Indonesia continues to experience widespread ambivalence towards globalisation, and, as a result, the country is missing out on some of the opportunities available to more open economies.[1]

---

* The authors are grateful to Arianto Patunru and Indonesia Update Conference participants for helpful comments and suggestions on an earlier draft.
1 The phrase 'missed opportunities' was popularised in the academic literature on Indonesia by Booth (1998).

In this chapter, we illustrate these issues by examining the links between Indonesia's policy environment and its export performance. In particular, as a case study we focus on the three most important footloose manufactured exports for most developing economies: garments, footwear and electronics.

INDONESIA AND GLOBALISATION

An overview

It is a well-established empirical and theoretical proposition that, in times of growing world trade, more open economies generally grow faster than less open ones (Bhagwati 2004). Openness has also been central to East Asian economic success. All the high-growth East Asian economies adopted variants of the export-oriented development strategy, albeit with considerable variation from free-trade Singapore to the heavily managed Korean model of export orientation (Perkins 2013). At least until recently, these economies were able to achieve dramatic export success, in the context of a benign and increasingly open global economy in which the principle of multilateralism by and large held sway.

The East Asian experience demonstrates the nexus between openness, growth and living standards. Milanovic (2016) demonstrates the welfare dimension of globalisation forcefully with his so-called 'elephant curve': based on an estimation of the global income distribution for the period 1988–2008, he concludes that 'the great winners have been the Asian poor and middle classes' (p. 20) in China and other dynamic Asian economies, including Indonesia.[2] Manning and Purnagunawan's (2016) detailed examination of East Asian labour markets complements this analysis. It shows that rapid, labour-intensive growth in the more advanced East Asian economies hastened their transition to and through the Lewis turning point, a threshold not yet generally evident in Indonesia.

Of course, openness has to be managed. Even the strongest advocates of liberal trade policies recognise the case for regulating some international commercial transactions, in particular short-term capital flows (Bhagwati 1998). Moreover, to participate in the global economy, countries need not only to open their economies to trade, investment and technology, but also to invest in infrastructure, skills and health, in order to ensure that the benefits of openness are widely distributed. And to the extent that greater

---

2 The second part of the quote from Milanovic—'the great losers [have been] the lower middle class of the rich world'—reminds us why globalisation is unpopular in many advanced economies.

international exposure increases economic volatility, social safety nets need to be in place to protect vulnerable low-income earners (Rodrik 1998).

In the case of Indonesia, having endured more than three centuries of colonialism and a protracted struggle for independence, it is hardly surprising that the country turned inwards after independence. Much influential Indonesian opinion was (and continues to be) ambivalent about globalisation, and about economic liberalism more generally. In this respect, Indonesia is similar to the other Asian giants, China and India, and also to smaller economies, such as Vietnam, that experienced bitter paths out of colonialism.

But countries are not forever prisoners of their history. More than most of its neighbours, in the post-colonial period Indonesia has had economic and political policies that have ranged across the spectrum, from disengagement and even hostility towards the global economy, to very open trade and investment regimes. In the early 1960s, Indonesia joined the Peking–Pyongyang–Hanoi–Phnom Penh–Jakarta axis of New Emerging Forces, and it withdrew from the United Nations and Bretton Woods institutions. In May 1964, President Sukarno memorably told Western donors they could 'go to hell' with their aid. Economic mismanagement in the first two decades of independence was both a cause and a consequence of this growing economic isolation.

Yet just three years after Sukarno's memorable speech, the policy settings changed dramatically. As a key policy-maker in the early Suharto years would later observe, 'When we started out attracting foreign investment in 1967 everything and everyone was welcome. We did not dare to refuse; we did not even ask for bonafidity of credentials' (Mohammad Sadli, quoted in Palmer 1978: 100). Indonesia has never disengaged from the global economy since then, although the pendulum has swung back and forth (Basri and Hill 2004). There was a resurgence of economic nationalism in the 1970s owing to the oil boom and a perception that liberalisation — always a term with negative connotations in Indonesia — had gone too far. In turn, there were sweeping reforms in the 1980s as commodity prices fell sharply, threatening macroeconomic stability and growth. Consequently, the technocrats were able to persuade Suharto of the urgency of reform, and push through major trade and investment liberalisation packages (Soesastro 1989). Although protectionist pressures and rhetoric have been ever-present, over the past quarter-century these reforms have never fundamentally been overturned, even during the 1997–98 Asian financial crisis, when strong anti-Western sentiment surfaced in the wake of the IMF's mismanagement of the economic rescue package for Indonesia.

As a result, after more than seven decades of independence, Indonesia does not fit neatly into any significant Asian grouping with regard to economic openness. The principal text on the Southeast Asian economies around 1970 divided them into inward- and outward-looking economies, with Indonesia clearly in the former camp at that time (Myint 1972). This was in marked contrast to its neighbours, Singapore, Malaysia and Thailand, which had always been open (in the technical, Sachs–Warner sense). Nor did Indonesia adopt a variant of the Japanese–Korean model, of limited reliance on foreign investment together with a strong commitment to education and an export-oriented, 'guided' (and sometimes heavily interventionist) industrial policy, in spite of the enduring appeal of this approach in many Indonesian policy circles. Unlike China (and Vietnam) it did not adopt a 'state capitalism' model, even though state-owned enterprises have been an ever-present feature of post-independence Indonesia (despite their generally indifferent commercial performance). Perhaps Indonesia has most in common with India, in the sense that the two countries have quite well-defined policy turning points (1966 for Indonesia, 1991 for India), microeconomic reform has proceeded slowly in both, and public opinion remains sceptical about the merits of a liberal economic order. But here too there are major differences, particularly in political systems and structures.

Factors shaping Indonesian policy-making

History, geography, ideology, institutions and key individuals have shaped Indonesia's stance towards globalisation, as they have in most countries. The interplay of these factors has been crucial. For example, economic nationalists and rent-seekers have been natural bedfellows: business groups seeking special privileges from government have been able to mobilise support by appealing to sentimental notions of self-sufficiency (especially in the case of food policy; see Patunru 2017), or to call for protection of infant industries on the basis of contentious economic theories such as strategic trade policy.[3]

We identify and briefly discuss six factors that have shaped policy-making in Indonesia: history, geography, natural resources, ideology, macroeconomic policy and inequality. It is important to emphasise the interactive and cumulative nature of these factors; for example, history and geography obviously interact, as do natural resources and inequality. Moreover, there are clearly issues of causality and endogeneity that are beyond the scope of this discussion.

Historical influences have already been briefly alluded to. The pernicious effects of colonialism are a central strand in the literature on

---

3 The originator of the concept, Paul Krugman, subsequently argued that it was a theoretical construct, not developed as a basis for policy formulation.

Indonesian economic history. A related literature highlighted the dualism that was evident in the colonial economy between the modern European enclaves and the indigenous economies. Commonly associated with the work of J.H. Boeke (1884–1956), this literature attracted international attention (see, for example, Szirmai 2015). The 'non-economic behaviour' and 'backward-sloping supply curves' that Boeke observed were essentially a product of this colonial economic and political structure. A major implication was the failure of an entrepreneurial class to emerge. In the words of Acemoglu and Robinson (2012: 250), drawing on Reid (1993):

> Dutch colonialism fundamentally changed [Southeast Asia's] economic and political development. The people [...] stopped trading, turned inward. [...] In the next two centuries, they would be in no position to take advantage of the innovations that would spring up in the industrial revolution.

Geography has also shaped Indonesian commercial policy in a variety of ways. With its 17,000 islands and proximity to very open Singapore and Malaysia, Indonesia is sometimes characterised as being 'made by God for free trade', as our introductory quote implies. Illegal trade has flourished in the presence of high trade barriers, with a general rule of thumb being that smugglers are in business once tariffs exceed 25 per cent, especially for items with a high value-to-volume ratio.

Another important neighbourhood effect is Indonesia's membership of ASEAN. Indonesia is the largest member of ASEAN, the most durable regional grouping in the developing world. Soesastro (2006) has described the organisation as a case of outward-looking regional economic integration. ASEAN has progressively lowered its tariffs on intra-regional trade, and most of these liberalisations have been multilateralised. This process has been driven both by the general wave of reforms that has swept through the region since the 1970s, and by the administrative impracticality of running two-tier customs arrangements within ASEAN (Hill and Menon 2012). A related neighbourhood effect has been reform in China from 1978 and in India from 1991, triggered by what Mari Pangestu has termed 'competitive liberalisation': the desire to keep up with—and emulate—high-growth neighbours.

A third factor has been Indonesia's bountiful endowment of natural resources. Countries with plentiful natural resources are likely to have greater exchange rate variability than less well-endowed countries, driven by fluctuations in commodity prices. In such countries, the real exchange rate is likely to appreciate as the terms of trade increase, and to depreciate during periods of low commodity prices. A stronger exchange rate squeezes profitability in the non-commodity, tradable sectors (such as manufacturing) through the familiar Dutch disease effects, triggering demands for increased protection. A more general effect operates through the 'resource curse' mechanism, developed analytically by Sachs and Warner (2001). According to this hypothesis, the quality of economic policy-making suffers during periods of resource abundance, resulting in an increased likelihood of protectionism.

This general literature is highly relevant to Indonesia's interaction with the global economy. Indonesia was one of the few energy-rich developing countries outside the Middle East to successfully navigate the 1980s era of low commodity prices and rising third world debt (Gelb and Associates 1987). The country reformed quickly and effectively as oil prices declined sharply, demonstrating the operation of what has become known as Sadli's Law, that bad times make for good policies, and good times often the converse.[4] The implication for Indonesian trade policy is that there has been an inverse relationship between commodity prices and economic openness, a relationship first examined systematically and empirically by Basri (2001). According to this argument, the open-door policies of the late 1960s were overtaken by a much more dirigiste regime in the 1970s as the oil boom effects took hold. There was then a major reversal back to openness during the 1980s in response to declining oil prices. The commodity boom of the past decade had a similar effect in triggering rising economic nationalism, an effect that has only partly been overturned in the last few years as commodity prices have weakened.[5]

The fourth factor influencing commercial and trade policy is ideology. The ambivalence towards globalisation evident in influential Indonesian opinion is reflected in the continuing debate over the interpretation of article 33 of the constitution. It states that 'The economy is to be structured as a common endeavour based on familial principles', and further that 'Production sectors that are vital to the state and that affect the livelihood of a considerable part of the population are to be controlled [*menguasai*] by the state'. As Soesastro, Simandjuntak and Silalahi (1988: 33) observed 30 years ago, in a comment that continues to have poignancy, 'Forty years after the adoption of the Constitution, different interpretations of Article 33 continue to exist'. A key element of the ambiguity concerns the meaning of the word *menguasai*, in particular whether it means to 'own' or to 'regulate'.

---

4   Sadli's Law was of course named after the late Mohammad Sadli, one of Indonesia's most influential policy-makers and intellectuals.
5   Soesastro (1989) is the key reference work on the reforms of the 1980s. The validity of the Sadli Law proposition has been questioned in the post-Suharto democratic era, including by Patunru and Rahardja (2015). A relevant consideration here is the size of the commodity sector. It is now a good deal smaller than it was when the Sadli-Basri-Soesastro conjectures were being formulated, so the influence of resource abundance on policy-making has (probably) also diminished commensurately.

Table 14.1 Attitudes towards globalisation in selected countries, 2014

	Indonesia	United States	China	India	Philippines
Does trade with other countries lead to job creation, job losses or does it not make a difference?					
Job creation	63	20	67	49	56
Job losses	19	50	11	24	10
No difference	18	30	22	27	34
Does trade with other countries lead to an increase in wages of workers?					
Increase	56	17	61	49	41
Decrease	20	45	12	23	14
No difference	24	38	27	28	45
Effect of foreign companies buying domestic companies on country					
Good	41	28	39	56	66
Bad	53	67	50	30	30
No effect	6	5	11	14	4

Source: Pew Research Center (2014).

This ambiguity has had diverse and far-reaching effects. Reformers continue to eschew use of the word 'liberalisation', preferring the more neutral term 'deregulation'. Support for cooperatives, and for the 'weaker economic groups' (*golongan ekonomi lemah*) — referring to indigenous Indonesian (*pribumi*) enterprises — remains popular, even though in practice most experiments with cooperatives as a business model have been problematic. There is continued ambivalence towards foreign and non-*pribumi* (mainly ethnic Chinese) ownership. And the community remains tolerant of the extensive state enterprise sector, in spite of its generally indifferent performance.

Attitudinal surveys suggest that some of the concerns about ideology may be overstated. For example, according to the September 2014 Pew survey results, Indonesians do not hold strong anti-globalisation views (Table 14.1). For what the results are worth — attitudinal surveys have to be interpreted carefully — Indonesians are more likely than the citizens of two other Asian democracies, India and the Philippines, to regard trade as beneficial, but less positive about the effect of foreign takeovers. Indonesians are also more positive than Americans on all three questions listed in the table (see also the results reported by Damuri and Pangestu in Chapter 7 of this book).

The fifth factor is macroeconomic policy and how it is linked to commercial policy, and to attitudes towards globalisation more generally.[6] A very general observation is that macroeconomic crises force governments to respond in some way; in the words of Lal and Myint (1996: 288), synthesising the results of a large cross-country study, 'turning points [in economic policy] are invariably associated with macroeconomic crises'. The question is, which way does policy turn? It depends of course on what form the crisis takes. In the earlier era of fixed exchange rates and loose fiscal policy, a typical crisis took the form of rising inflation, in turn leading to an appreciating real exchange rate that adversely affected competitiveness, triggered a balance of payments crisis and prompted the government to impose import controls. This was the Indonesian experience in the 1950s and early 1960s, which led also to the chaotic system of multiple exchange rates.

Indonesia's traumatic experience with hyperinflation in the mid-1960s has arguably underpinned the country's generally prudent macroeconomic policies ever since. The one exception was the Asian financial crisis in 1997–98, when highly unusual extraneous factors together with policy drift at home resulted in an economic and political crisis that led to a temporary loss of macroeconomic control. Even in this special case, however, Indonesia did not turn inward, for a range of reasons. In fact, as part of its highly controversial Letter of Intent (LOI) with the IMF, the Indonesian government introduced further reforms, albeit not on the scale that was evident in the 1980s. We conclude that — as in Indonesia's mostly prudent Southeast Asian neighbours, but unlike in many other developing countries — macroeconomic crises have generally not been a major factor in shaping commercial policy outcomes in Indonesia.

Sixth, inequality has been a factor behind anti-globalisation sentiment among Indonesians, on the presumption that the two are causally connected. Inequality has always been central to Indonesian policy debate, but in practice it has had a limited effect on the country's commercial policies, except in the peripheral sense that global narratives about inequality do have their local adherents.

The empirical evidence for Indonesia shows no clear correlation between openness and inequality. We illustrate this in Figure 14.1 by comparing the long-term trends in two variables: the Gini ratio and total merchandise trade relative to GDP (the latter being a widely used, albeit crude, proxy for openness). As the figure shows, there is no systematic relationship between the two variables.

In fact, in some respects liberalisation has clearly been good for Indonesia's poor. First, it has accelerated economic growth and therefore

---

6   Little et al. (1993) remains one of the most comprehensive surveys of this issue.

Figure 14.1 Economic openness and inequality in Indonesia, 1976–2015

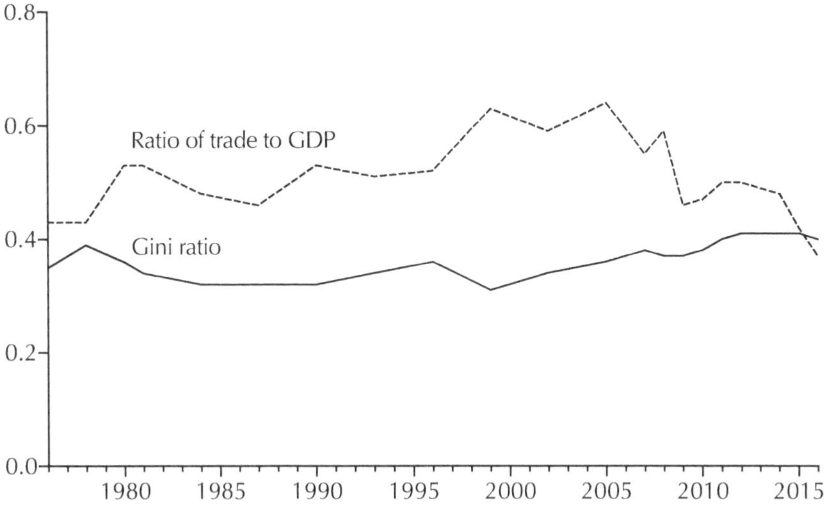

Source: Gini ratio: World Income Inequality Database; trade-to-GDP ratio: BPS.

contributed to a faster reduction in poverty. Second, the 1980s reforms, which have been studied intensively, have been found to have had beneficial effects on inequality. In this case, the major channel was the labour market. The trade reforms unshackled Indonesia's latent comparative advantage in labour-intensive activities. The country shifted towards a more labour-intensive growth trajectory as millions of workers were drawn into the rapidly expanding export-oriented manufacturing industries, which offered better working conditions than those available in the agricultural and informal sectors (Manning 1998). Especially during this period, Indonesia was a good example of Milanovic's observation that those in the lower and middle deciles of the global income distribution, mainly located in developing East Asia, enjoyed faster income growth than all but the very rich.

The evidence that globalisation inevitably leads to a 'race to the bottom' for middle-income developing countries such as Indonesia is therefore unpersuasive. However, consistent with the major theme of this chapter, the policy environment needs to ensure that globalisation works to the benefit of the citizenry. In Indonesia's case, that means a labour-intensive growth path, supply-side reforms to increase efficiency, a tax system that is both robust and progressive, and social safety net programs to protect the poor and near-poor. In all four areas, Indonesia's unfinished reform agenda is substantial.

The political economy framework

These factors are of course mediated by Indonesia's political system and its institutions. The political economy framework that has guided Indonesian policies on the global economy is quite well defined, albeit with significant differences between the Suharto and democratic eras. Ever since the late 1960s, macroeconomic policy has been largely a technocratic domain, in which the political pressures for adventurous fiscal and monetary policies have been contained. In the Suharto era, this took the form of the balanced budget rule (of course with sometimes very large off-budget expenditures). The central bank was subservient to the Ministry of Finance but its monetary policy objectives were supported by the absence of any serious fiscal crisis. Law No. 17/2003 on State Finances and an independent Bank Indonesia have been the guiding principles of the democratic era, again creating a *cordon sanitaire* that has similarly constrained political interference. This pragmatic approach to macroeconomic policy has underpinned the continuity in Indonesian economic policy-making for 50 years. It is of course grounded in the painful lessons learned from the early post-independence years.[7]

Microeconomic policy, on the other hand, has been a contested and political sphere. As noted, Basri (2001) identified the key policy actors in the Suharto era—the nationalists, technocrats, donors, 'technologs' and so on—and showed how, mediated by the president himself, their influence waxed and waned depending on economic circumstances, most of all the international oil price.[8] Consistent with this framework, Soesastro (1989) documented the adroit role played by the key economics ministers in the 1980s reforms. They were able to persuade the president that his commitment to maintaining economic growth necessitated major microeconomic reform. Crucially, they were able to avoid grand ideological debates. The parliament (DPR) was relatively unimportant in this reform episode. The result was a fairly clean trade regime by the early 1990s, with much reduced reliance on non-tariff barriers (NTBs) and a lower (though

---

[7] In addition to the earlier quote from Professor Sadli, the following observation from another influential economist, Professor Sumitro Djojohadikusumo, is illustrative: 'In 1954/55, I was a strong protagonist of foreign exchange controls. [...] Then I saw what happened under Ali Sastroamidjojo and Sukarno. I know how easy it is to smuggle goods, and I know that those who are close to the sources of power will get their hands on the foreign exchange' (Djojohadikusumo 1984: 38).

[8] See also Basri (2012). For a political science approach that is broadly consistent in its views and conclusions, see Mallarangeng (2000).

not insignificant) dispersion of industry assistance across sectors (Fane and Condon 1996).[9]

In the democratic era, Indonesia's trade and commercial policy settings have reflected the interplay of political forces that are evident in most plural polities. The old model of jockeying for influence around the president has now been replaced by a broader and more fluid constellation of factors, including international agreements and other external factors, the constraints of pragmatism, political pressures, and the preferences of the president and the executive. The international factors include WTO commitments and the more substantial ASEAN agreements. Also, as noted, policy-makers are aware of the reality that trade barriers above some threshold invariably induce smuggling. But the growing international dissatisfaction with a liberal capitalist order and, since the global financial crisis, the ever-present threat of beggar-thy-neighbour trade and exchange rate policies also have domestic resonance, reinforcing the push for protectionist measures.

Cabinet appointments and priorities in the democratic era are similar, in some respects, to those of the Suharto era. The Ministry of Finance remains powerful, and its ministers, mostly with strong technical credentials, have generally favoured more open economic policies. The finance minister is also a key policy-maker on tariff levels, but not the levels of NTBs. The line ministries, agriculture and industry, have generally sought to represent these sectors' interests, and the more influential players in them. Agriculture has been consistently (and often blatantly) protectionist, especially in the case of food crops (Patunru 2017). With the departure of Suharto and the loss of his strong personal interest in agriculture, the department has arguably become more interested in self-sufficiency and distributional issues and less interested in productivity and efficiency. The Ministry of Industry continues to be a marginal player in Indonesian economic policy-making, caught between its instinctive preference for greater regulation and protection and the contemporary reality of increasingly globalised manufacturing.

The Ministry of Trade is perhaps the most difficult to characterise, as its ministers have covered virtually the entire spectrum of abilities and predilections. The country's leading international academic economist, Mari Pangestu, was the minister for the longest period (2004–11) but the trade ministers for other periods have included some with close party

---

9 What the data could not show, of course, was the increasingly egregious intrusion of Suharto family business interests into many major sectors of the economy, especially non-tradables, and tradables with a significant regulatory presence.

connections, business-aligned dealmakers and, briefly, one who could be regarded as an ultra-nationalist.[10]

It is of course the president who presides over these competing forces, who appoints the ministers and who ultimately determines major policies. In the post-Suharto era, the first three presidents were mainly concerned with economic recovery and democratic consolidation. Neither of the two presidents since 2004 has had clearly articulated views on globalisation in general and trade policy in particular. President Yudhoyono was of course an internationalist in important respects, but his approach to international economic issues was cautious and at times ambivalent. President Widodo has thus far shown considerably less interest in international affairs unless there is a tangible commercial outcome in prospect.

The above analysis is greatly simplified. We need more case studies examining the workings of the trade and investment regime in order to ascertain how powerful the forces of 'protection for sale' and business lobbying are. Of course, such interventions are invariably dressed up with lofty national motives such as 'self sufficiency', protection for weak economic groups, protection against 'unfair' international competition and so on. But the analysis is at least generally indicative of the sets of forces in play.

Outcomes

How have these various factors played out in the Indonesian policy context, specifically with reference to commercial policy and attitudes towards globalisation? We briefly illustrate the outcomes with reference to three policy areas: trade and investment policy; international trade policy initiatives and negotiations; and industry policy.

First, as noted above, Indonesia's willingness to adopt trade and investment reforms has fluctuated for decades. Indonesia has never fundamentally reversed the global economic engagement that took root in the late 1960s, but in some respects it has remained only precariously open.[11]

---

10 This portfolio has had one of the highest turnovers in the democratic era: seven ministers in total since 2001, and six ministers in just four years if one excludes the long-serving Mari Pangestu. The obvious implication is that there has been a lack of policy continuity, except during the Pangestu era.

11 The two major studies of effective protection conducted in the past quarter-century, by Marks and Rahardja (2012) and Fane and Condon (1996), illustrate the broadly open nature of the trade regime, albeit with pockets of high protection. In passing, it is striking that both studies were sponsored by the World Bank. A not-unreasonable conclusion is that there is limited interest in Indonesian policy circles in this powerful analytical tool, which exposes the beneficiaries (and the losers) from industry assistance.

Table 14.2 Comparative indicators of economic openness

Country	(Exports + imports)/ GDP (%)	Stock FDI/ GDP (%)	Average tariffs (most favoured nation) (%)	2017 Index of Economic Freedom, (score)
Indonesia	42	25.6	6.9	61.9
Malaysia	134	40.0	6.1	73.8
Philippines	63	19.9	6.3	65.6
Thailand	127	44.8	11.0	66.2

Source: Exports, imports, FDI and GDP: BPS; tariffs: UNCTAD Trade Analysis Information System (TRAINS); Index of Economic Freedom: Heritage Foundation.

An appealing intellectual argument for an open economy has remained elusive, export constituencies have generally lacked the political clout evident in the more open ASEAN economies, and both the think-tank and policy communities have remained ambivalent. Only a small handful of established Indonesian academics have consistently argued the case for liberal economic policies. Thus, the periods of trade liberalisation – the late 1960s, the mid-1980s and, in a more halting fashion, the current period – have been triggered by economic adversity, or at least the threat of it. The pendulum swings in foreign investment policy have been even more pronounced. Except for a few years in the late 1960s and early 1970s, Indonesia has adopted a more restrictive policy towards foreign direct investment (FDI) than most of its neighbours, including post-Doi Moi (post-liberalisation) Vietnam. Thus, Indonesia could be characterised at best as a moderately open economy, as the various indicators shown in Table 14.2 reveal.[12] Among major Asian developing economies, the closest parallels would be India and the Philippines.

A second consequence has been Indonesia's 'sitting on the fence' in international trade policy initiatives and negotiations (Basri 2012). This phrase aptly summarises Indonesia's stance towards the global economy, driven by a combination of policy ambivalence and bureaucratic inertia. This is nowhere better illustrated than in Indonesia's regional and global commercial policy engagement. In spite of its size, Indonesia has not been a major actor in global or even most regional trade and related forums.

---

12 The usual caveats need to be mentioned in interpreting these data: trade is typically less important for large countries; fragmentation trade overstates the importance of trade shares for some countries; and variable trade values resulting from fluctuating commodity prices need to be discounted.

Indeed, it is difficult to think of an instance where it has registered globally in this respect, apart from the important 1994 Bogor APEC Declaration.[13]

Indonesia has of course been central to ASEAN. As the dominant country in the grouping, its low-key, consensual approach has been one of the secrets to the association's longevity. Nevertheless, even here it could hardly have been said to be a leader in ASEAN commercial policy negotiations. Of the original five ASEAN countries, Indonesia has favoured the most cautious approach, placing a substantial number of trade items on its 'sensitive list' of items excluded from ASEAN agreements. In services trade and labour mobility it has also been comparatively restrictive (see Chapter 15 by Anas and Narjoko for more discussion).

Another manifestation of this caution—or perhaps more accurately, hesitation—has been Indonesia's limited participation in various international trade agreements. It has not signed the second Information Technology Agreement (ITA II), a puzzling decision given that this WTO-sponsored protocol governs trade in electronics and related goods, which now accounts for more than half of intra-ASEAN and developing East Asian merchandise trade. Indonesia also lags behind its major neighbours in its participation in preferential trade agreements (Pangestu, Rahardja and Ing 2015). While participating in ASEAN trade deals,[14] it has signed only one significant non-ASEAN agreement, with Japan. Moreover, this agreement did not involve any significant trade policy concessions from either side. Of course, sceptics of the efficacy of preferential trade agreements would approve such an outcome. Indeed, at crucial reform junctures in its history, Indonesian policy-makers have, appropriately in our view, pursued unilateral liberalisations.

A third outcome has been a lack of coherence in industry policy. As noted, the Ministry of Industry has been a minor player in Indonesian economic policy. During periods of greater policy influence—that is, when the policy pendulum has swung towards economic nationalism—its favoured approach has been some variant of a state-led industrialisation strategy, including trade protection, subsidised credit, tighter industrial licensing and support for state enterprises. However, the results of such a strategy have generally been disappointing. In a world of global manufacturing, what Indonesian firms need most is an efficient supply-side economy, that

---

13 The history of Indonesia's international commercial diplomacy, and its domestic political economy roots, remains to be written, certainly in English (and probably in Bahasa Indonesia as well). There is nothing comparable, for example, to the brilliant analysis of Indonesia's foreign policy by Wanandi (2012).

14 There has been vocal domestic opposition to some of these agreements, including vigorous opposition in parliament to the ASEAN–China agreement when it took effect in 2010.

is, a reliable and economical power supply, an efficient logistics system, a simpler regulatory system, more secure property rights, a well-trained workforce and so on. Most of these are not within the ministry's purview. Moreover, the Ministry of Industry does not possess the skilled staff needed to effectively implement a strategy of 'picking winners', in the way that, for example, Singapore's Economic Development Board does. Even when the ministry is able to offer regulatory incentives or subsidies, industry is sceptical owing to the frequent changes (or even reversals) in government policy. There is also the continuing problem of corruption at the implementation stage, especially when the interventions are firm-specific and opaque. Not surprisingly, therefore, Basri's (2001) characterisation remains apposite: 'governments may not be good at picking winners, but losers are good at picking governments'. The limited empirical research on this topic confirms such a conclusion.[15]

A CASE STUDY OF INDONESIAN GLOBAL ENGAGEMENT: MANUFACTURING EXPORTS

How have the changes in Indonesia's policy regime influenced its trade outcomes? Is there evidence of missed opportunities? We address these questions with reference to a case study of the country's export performance since the 1980s in three major manufacturing industries: electronics, garments and footwear. These industries have been central to East Asia's economic success. Combined with relatively open global markets and strong domestic investments in infrastructure and human capital, rapid export-oriented industrialisation in the region has had transformative effects on the labour market and poverty reduction.

The three industries

Three features of the electronics, garments and footwear industries deserve mention. First, they are all generally labour-intensive activities, across almost all products in the case of footwear and garments, and for significant segments of electronics. Thus, they are well suited to labour-surplus economies such as Indonesia. For example, garments employs about 14 per cent of the Indonesian workforce in large and medium manufacturing

---

15 See, for example, Hill (1996), who found no persuasive evidence that the industries favoured by subsidies and protection during the Suharto era performed more strongly than the non-favoured industries. Rock (2017) has disputed these findings, arguing that Hill's study underestimated some of the intangible externalities associated with Suharto's interventionist regime.

firms (defined as firms with at least 20 employees), while footwear and electronics absorb about 6 per cent and 4 per cent respectively.

Second, international trade in these industries is relatively unhindered by commercial policy barriers. The export performance of these industries is therefore a good indication of the international competitiveness of economies, and they constitute an excellent case study for comparing efficiency and productivity across countries. The international trade in footwear has always been open. Trade in garments was historically heavily regulated by the Multi Fibre Arrangement (MFA), but the MFA was abolished in January 2005. Trade in electronics, especially parts and components, typically occurs within multinational enterprises and involves production and assembly across many countries. Called 'fragmentation trade' (owing to the geographically dispersed production stages, sliced up according to host countries' comparative advantage), trade in electronics occurs under the umbrella of the ITA. The range of products included in this agreement was expanded in 2015 under ITA II.

Third, while the three industries share common features, there are also significant differences between them. The major international connections in the buyer-driven garments industry occur as much at the marketing stage as at the production stage. This industry has both a mass production segment, in which economies of scale are important, and a smaller, specialised 'fashion-intensive' segment in which design creativity is essential. Footwear tends to be more scale intensive and is dominated by international brand names. Trade in electronics — or at least parts and components — is typically producer-driven and, as noted, dominated by multinational enterprises and their global production networks, geared to the requirements of the final assembly stage. In East Asia, China is increasingly assuming this final role. At the production stage, electronics has the most varied factor intensities, ranging from routine labour-intensive activities through to R&D- and skill-intensive activities. The global production networks therefore range across both high- and low-income economies. Since they involve production sites in several countries, highly efficient, internationally oriented logistics systems are a key requirement for participation in these networks (Athukorala 2014). The Indonesian data on firm ownership, as reported by the central statistics agency (BPS), reflect these differences in foreign ownership intensities: about 40 per cent of electronics firms operating in Indonesia have some level of foreign equity, compared with about 12 per cent and 8 per cent respectively for firms in the garments and footwear industries.

In the analysis that follows, we are interested in Indonesia's performance over time and relative to its neighbours. We want to test whether the various Indonesian reform episodes have been reflected in the country's export performance and, by extension, what the results reveal about the pace of reform in Indonesia compared to its neighbours. Implicit in our analysis is the assumption that rising export shares (at least compared to one's competitors) are a likely outcome—and indicator—of successful reform, while declining export shares are suggestive of the converse.[16] It is important to emphasise that we do not attempt formal econometric estimates of these relationships; that is for another paper. It also needs to be emphasised that other variables are at play, in addition to domestic policy reforms. An obvious one in the case of Indonesia is movements in the real exchange rate, driven by changing terms of trade and international capital flows.

Indonesia's export shares in the three industries

Following Athukorala (2014), we divide trade in electronics into trade in parts and components and trade in final products (Table 14.3).[17] The assembly of final products is dominated by the larger, more technologically advanced economies. Historically Japan was the leader in this field, but its share has shrunk dramatically since 1990, more or less mirroring China's equally dramatic rise. Korea and Singapore play significant secondary roles; the shares of both are now larger than that of Japan. Indonesia's participation in this segment has always been very small. Developing countries usually play a more significant role in parts and components, especially the labour-intensive areas, but here too, Indonesia has only a small and declining presence, about 0.4 per cent of the global total. A key feature of the table is Vietnam's rapid and very recent rise, with an export share now six times that of Indonesia.

Table 14.4 shows global export shares for garments. Here too China's rise has been remarkably rapid, while Japan and Korea are now very minor participants. Reflecting the nature of the industry, the industry has a more diverse set of suppliers, with several significant South Asian exporters, but only minor participation by Malaysia and Singapore. Indonesia's share rose steadily from the 1980s, peaking at 2.6 per cent of the global total in 2000. Again, Vietnam's record is impressive, with a share almost three times that of Indonesia in 2015. Exports from low-income economies such as Bangladesh and Cambodia have also grown rapidly. The latter's

---

16 A word of caution needs to be added. Our focus on exports does not imply that exports are more important than imports, as is implicit in the mercantilist approach to trade. Rather, we select exports because they are less affected by Indonesian trade policy than imports and are therefore a clearer indicator of what Indonesia is good at producing.

17 For details and explanations of the SITC codes used in the calculations, see Athukorala (2014) and the references cited therein.

Table 14.3 Global market shares in electronics, 1990–2015 (%)

Country	1990	1995	2000	2005	2010	2015
Parts & components						
Indonesia	0.04	0.32	0.89	0.69	0.58	0.44
Malaysia	2.93	2.77	5.03	6.16	6.02	5.38
Philippines	–	0.57	3.19	2.2	1.38	1.61
Singapore	5.56	8.55	6.8	6.25	5.41	4.02
Thailand	1.24	1.98	2.06	2.05	2.78	2.45
Vietnam	–	–	0.13	0.21	0.48	3.03
China	–	2.73	5.34	16.29	24.28	32.41
Japan	18.62	16.22	11.57	8.49	6.88	4.74
Korea	2.93	2.77	5.03	6.16	6.02	5.38
Final products						
Indonesia	0.06	0.42	0.53	0.5	0.61	0.45
Malaysia	2.23	4.05	4.49	5.04	3.11	3.06
Philippines	–	0.23	0.85	0.99	0.55	1.20
Singapore	5.30	8.06	6.76	8.01	7.81	7.07
Thailand	0.78	1.67	1.74	1.82	1.77	1.68
Vietnam	–	–	0.01	0.03	0.33	1.68
China	–	2.73	4.74	18.43	29.46	33.53
Japan	25.94	19.16	13.53	8.66	6.79	4.23
Korea	6.05	9.04	5.99	5.78	5.6	7.12

Source: UN Comtrade.

rise is particularly notable given its decades of conflict and isolation; its export share is not far short of Indonesia's even though its population is only about 6 per cent of the latter's.

Broadly similar patterns are evident in the case of footwear (Table 14.5). Korea was the dominant Asian supplier in the 1970s but it has now exited the industry and been replaced by China, which in 2015 had a similar export share to that of Korea 40 years earlier. Vietnam's ascent has been rapid and it now has a global share of 10 per cent. Indonesia's share rose quickly during the 1980s, peaked at around 6 per cent in the mid-1990s, when it was the third-largest Asian exporter after China and Thailand, and has declined since then, to a little over half its peak share.

Table 14.4 Global market shares in garments, 1976–2015 (%)

Country	1976	1985	1990	1995	2000	2005	2010	2015
Cambodia	–	–	–	–	0.53	0.83	0.89	1.35
Indonesia	–	0.86	1.65	2.36	2.60	1.94	2.02	1.74
Philippines	–	0.67	0.67	0.74	1.39	0.87	0.32	0.35
Malaysia	–	0.82	1.3	1.55	1.22	0.93	1.14	1.09
Singapore	–	1.35	1.57	1.00	0.99	0.64	0.32	0.31
Thailand	1.97	1.44	2.79	3.44	2.05	1.56	1.27	0.86
Vietnam	–	–	–	–	0.99	1.77	3.05	4.99
Bangladesh	–	0.42	0.64	1.34	2.25	2.60	4.36	6.06
India	–	2.30	2.50	2.81	3.24	3.29	3.29	4.12
Sri Lanka	–	0.70	0.64	–	1.51	1.08	1.02	1.08
China	–	4.88	9.55	16.52	19.58	27.94	38.02	39.69
Japan	10.12	1.79	0.58	0.37	0.30	0.19	0.16	0.12
Korea	45.35	11.22	7.93	3.4	2.73	0.97	0.47	0.48
Mexico	–	–	0.09	1.87	4.68	2.75	1.28	1.02

Source: UN Comtrade.

Table 14.5 Global market shares in footwear, 1976–2015 (%)

Country	1976	1985	1990	1995	2000	2005	2010	2015
Cambodia	–	–	–	–	0.08	0.07	0.22	0.53
Indonesia	–	0.07	2.08	6.00	4.60	2.51	2.96	3.68
Philippines	–	0.35	0.29	0.46	0.22	0.05	0.01	0.02
Thailand	0.04	0.76	2.75	6.27	2.24	1.63	0.98	0.53
Vietnam	–	–	–	–	4.17	5.66	6.25	10.09
China	–	1.47	7.24	18.85	27.13	34.31	41.07	42.99
India	–	0.37	0.69	1.04	1.11	1.53	1.73	2.07
Japan	5.75	0.52	0.19	0.24	0.10	0.06	0.05	0.04
Korea	46.75	13.8	15.4	3.74	1.25	0.23	0.15	0.13

Source: UN Comtrade.

Discussion

The export shares of the three industries are broadly indicative of the effect of Indonesia's reform episodes on the country's performance, both over time and relative to its neighbours. Prior to 1980 Indonesian manufactured exports were minuscule. The end of the 1970s oil boom triggered a large depreciation in the real exchange rate and far-reaching trade, investment and microeconomic reform (Hill 2000). The supply response was strong and sustained. Not only did Indonesia avoid the debt trap that beset many developing-country commodity exporters, but it also became a significant industrial exporter for the first time. The statistics in Tables 14.3–14.5, especially the data for garments and footwear, demonstrate this clearly. Indonesia's share of the global garments trade almost trebled over the decade 1985–95, while its share of footwear grew even faster, more than doubling in the decade 1990–2000. Initially its garment exports were facilitated by MFA quotas, but the fundamental driver was competitiveness, as illustrated by the fact that, when the industry became constrained by the quotas in the early 1990s, firms resorted to the two main avenues of export growth then available: rising unit values in MFA markets and increased sales to non-MFA markets (Hill 1991). Indonesia also became a significant exporter of a range of other manufactures, mainly resource-based products.

However, success in the last 15 years of the twentieth century was followed by declining revealed competitiveness in the first 15 years of the twenty-first century. Two events occurred more or less simultaneously. First, Indonesia's reform momentum had more or less run its course by the mid-1990s, and the Asian financial crisis followed shortly thereafter. While the financial crisis resulted in a sharp initial depreciation in the real exchange rate, the beneficial effects were nullified by several factors: high inflation (especially in 1998); the struggle to overcome the devastating effects of the crisis; the massive reworking of the country's institutions and political systems; and several new features of the policy landscape, including declining infrastructure investments and restrictive labour regulations.

Second, other countries that were less affected by the Asian financial crisis quickly began to reform their trade regimes. As Tables 14.3–14.5 show, the star Southeast Asian performer this century has been Vietnam, which has performed strongly in all three industries. Bangladesh and Cambodia have also achieved notable export success through reform, particularly in garments. Wage levels are considerably lower in these countries than in Indonesia. At the same time, labour productivity levels in Indonesia have not risen enough to support its higher wages, rendering it less competitive in international markets.

The electronics story differs from these two, given the production specificities of the industry (see Soejachmoen 2012, on which this analysis draws). Indonesia has always been a small player in regional production networks, even during the reform episodes, and in spite of its advantageous location adjacent to the two early major Southeast Asian players, Singapore and Malaysia. As noted, participation in this industry requires an open policy towards FDI and a high-quality, internationally oriented logistics system. Indonesia lags its neighbours in both areas.

Specific factors have also been at work. In the early 1970s two major electronics multinationals, Fairchild and National Semiconductor, set up assembly plants in Indonesia (in 1973 and 1974 respectively). Both plants closed in 1986 due to a worldwide slump in the semiconductor business. However, both companies managed to keep their production bases in Singapore and Malaysia open, with some restructuring and labour shedding in response to the contraction in demand. According to press accounts at the time, in 1985 Fairchild announced a plan to introduce new technology that would have involved some reduction in its Indonesian workforce, but the Ministry of Manpower opposed any retrenchments resulting from automation (Thee and Pangestu 1998).

In 1989 Indonesia's electronics industry received a major boost from a deregulation package that effectively converted Batam Island into a free-trade zone linked to Singapore. This created the opportunity to attract labour-intensive operations that were no longer viable in Singapore. Batam was also included in Singapore's customs zone as part of that country's free trade agreement with the United States. As a result, for a few years around the turn of the century, about half the increment in Indonesian manufactured exports was sourced from Batam. In the words of Hutchinson (2017: 1), this led observers to conclude that 'the island has an unbeatable business proposition [...] ideally placed to absorb investments from its wealthier neighbour'. However, for reasons elaborated by Hutchinson, it has failed to build on this potential. Moreover, as noted, Indonesia's failure to ratify ITA II effectively precludes it from playing a major role in the international electronics industry.

Firm-level insights

Space considerations preclude a detailed analysis of Indonesia's rich firm-level data, but in summary we can observe that they support our thesis concerning missed opportunities. The number of firms in the electronics, garments and footwear industries has fallen during this century, evidently because they were not sufficiently competitive in the changed commercial environment. Productivity in the three industries has stagnated (while remaining significantly higher in electronics, as is usually the case). Export participation among garments and footwear firms has declined significantly compared with the reform era, from about 30 per cent of garments firms and 25 per cent of footwear firms in the early 1990s, to around 15 per cent of firms in both industries in the period since 2000. The export intensities of both industries have also decreased between the two periods, by about 10 percentage points. In electronics, in spite of the generally rapid growth in Asia-centred global production networks, export participation has not changed significantly, and remains at about 30 per cent of firms. The export intensity of Indonesian electronics firms also remains comparatively low: about 30 per cent of their output is exported.

Policy implications[18]

The electronics, garments and footwear industries are internationally mobile — they will gravitate towards countries that are commercially attractive. Therefore, successful participation in these industries depends on a country's international competitiveness, including its exchange rate, its business environment, its political stability and the availability of a well-trained workforce and efficient infrastructure. These in turn affect the ability of countries to attract mobile factors, principally capital, technology and market knowhow, which are often, but not always, bundled into FDI.

How does Indonesia rank on international indicators of efficiency and competitiveness? This is a very large topic on which there is a voluminous literature. We examine this issue briefly with reference to some of the most widely used indicators, noting the usual caveat that their reliability depends on their methodologies and data reliability.

Table 14.6 shows the World Bank's Ease of Doing Business and Logistics Performance Index rankings (where 1 is the top ranking). Indonesia occupies an intermediate position on both indices, improving over time in the former case (at least since 2012) but slipping according to the latter. Its ranking on the Ease of Doing Business Index is similar to that of lower-middle-income ASEAN economies such as the Philippines and Vietnam; it ranks ahead of India but well behind its more advanced neighbours, Malaysia and Thailand. On the Logistics Performance Index, Indonesia ranks about the same as Vietnam, ahead of the Philippines but behind the other countries.

Even though Indonesia has achieved much progress in enrolments and other quantitative indicators of educational performance, it lags behind its neighbours (including lower-income Vietnam) in educational quality, at least as captured by students' performance in maths and science testing (Table 14.7).

---

18 The analysis in this section draws on Aswicahyono and Hill (2018) and other papers in Ing, Hanson and Indrawati (2018).

Table 14.6 Comparative rankings on Ease of Doing Business Index and Logistics Performance Index, 2006–17

Country	Ease of Doing Business Index			Logistics Performance Index		
	2006 (155 countries)	2012 (183 countries)	2017 (190 countries)	2007 (150 countries)	2012 (155 countries)	2016 (160 countries)
Indonesia	115	129	91	43	59	63
Malaysia	21	18	23	27	29	32
Thailand	20	17	46	31	38	45
Philippines	113	136	99	65	52	71
Vietnam	99	98	82	53	53	64
Singapore	2	1	2	1	1	5
China	91	91	78	30	26	27
India	116	132	130	39	46	35

Source: World Bank.

Table 14.7 Comparative performance on PISA maths and science tests, 2003–15 (score)

Country	Maths			Science		
	2003	2012	2015	2006	2012	2015
Indonesia	360	375	386	393	382	403
Malaysia	–	421	446	–	420	443
Singapore	–	573	564	–	551	556
Thailand	417	427	415	421	444	421
Vietnam	–	511	495	–	528	525
Japan	557	536	532	531	547	538

Source: Programme for International Student Assessment (PISA).

Indonesia's ranking on Transparency International's Corruption Perceptions Index, as a proxy for institutional quality, has varied somewhat. In recent years it has been ahead of the Philippines and Vietnam, but behind India and China (Table 14.8).

Table 14.8   Comparative rankings on Corruption Perceptions Index, 2000–16

Country	2000 (90 countries)	2005 (158 countries)	2010 (178 countries)	2016 (176 countries)
Indonesia	85	137	110	90
Malaysia	36	39	56	55
Philippines	69	117	134	101
Singapore	6	5	1	7
Thailand	60	59	78	101
Vietnam	76	107	116	113
China	63	78	78	79
India	69	88	87	79

Source: Transparency International.

CONCLUSION

Perhaps understandably, Indonesia has been ambivalent about globalisation. Our survey of the factors shaping the country's attitudes towards globalisation suggests that this ambivalence is likely to persist. Yet, paradoxically, our empirical analysis clearly shows that, when Indonesia has embraced globalisation through well constructed and implemented policy reform, as in the late 1960s and mid-1980s, there has been a clear policy dividend in terms of stronger export performance, leading to faster employment generation and poverty reduction. When reform has regressed, or not proceeded as fast as in neighbouring countries, Indonesia has missed out on these opportunities. Moreover, although not the subject of this chapter, there is nothing in our analysis to support the proposition that, in periods when Indonesia has been more open to the global economy, it has been at the cost of equity objectives, or has involved some sort of 'race to the bottom' in regulatory standards.

It is important to view these results in perspective. Clearly international competitiveness is but one of a number of complex policy issues with which governments have to wrestle. Our analysis focuses on a small subset of the issues related to Indonesia and globalisation. Given that Indonesia has a larger economy than its Southeast Asian neighbours, it is not surprising that trade is less important for Indonesia. Also, its resource abundance means both that its export specialisation differs from its less well-endowed neighbours and that its export performance in footloose tradable activities (such as manufactures) will be affected by its more variable terms of trade. Most importantly of all, the country had to navigate its way through one of the deepest economic and political crises in recent global history. The fact that it succeeded in managing this process, including the transition from authoritarian to democratic rule and the maintenance of its territorial integrity, is of greater importance than its performance in global manufacturing export markets.

REFERENCES

Acemoglu, D., and J.A. Robinson (2012) *Why Nations Fail: The Origins of Power, Prosperity and Poverty*, Crown, New York NY.

Aswicahyono, H., and H. Hill (2018) 'Indonesian industrialisation and industrial policy: catching up, slowing down, muddling through', in L.Y. Ing, G. Hanson and S.M. Indrawati (eds) *The Indonesian Economy: Trade and Industrial Policies*, Routledge, London.

Athukorala, P.C. (2014) 'Global production sharing and trade patterns in East Asia', in I. Kaur and N. Singh (eds) *Oxford Handbook of the Economics of the Pacific*, Oxford University Press, New York NY: 333–61.

Basri, M.C. (2001) 'The political economy of manufacturing protection in Indonesia, 1975-1995', PhD thesis, Australian National University, Canberra.

Basri, M.C. (2012) 'Indonesia's role in the world economy: sitting on the fence', in A. Reid (ed.) *Indonesia Rising: The Repositioning of Asia's Third Giant*, Institute of Southeast Asian Studies, Singapore: 28–48.

Basri, M.C., and H. Hill (2004) 'Ideas, interests and oil prices: the political economy of trade reform during Soeharto's Indonesia', *World Economy* 27(5): 633–56.

Bhagwati, J. (1998) 'The capital myth: the difference between the trade in widgets and dollars', *Foreign Affairs* 77(3): 7–12.

Bhagwati, J. (2004) *In Defense of Globalization*, Oxford University Press, New York NY.

Booth, A. (1998) *The Indonesian Economy in the Nineteenth and Twentieth Centuries: A History of Missed Opportunities*, Macmillan, London.

Djojohadikusumo, S. (1984) 'Recollections of my career', *Bulletin of Indonesian Economic Studies* 22(3): 27–39.

Fane, G., and T. Condon (1996) 'Trade reform in Indonesia, 1987-1995', *Bulletin of Indonesian Economic Studies* 32(3): 33–54.

Gelb, A., and Associates (1987) *Oil Windfalls: Blessing or Curse?* Oxford University Press, New York NY.

Hill, H. (1991) 'The emperor's clothes can now be made in Indonesia', *Bulletin of Indonesian Economic Studies* 27(3): 89–127.

Hill, H. (1996) 'Indonesia's industrial policy and performance: "orthodoxy" vindicated', *Economic Development and Cultural Change* 45(1): 147–74.

Hill, H. (2000) *The Indonesian Economy*, second edition, Cambridge University Press, Cambridge.

Hill, H., and J. Menon (2012) 'ASEAN economic integration: driven by markets, bureaucrats, or both?', in M. Kreinin and M. Plummer (eds) *The Oxford Handbook of International Commercial Policy*, Oxford University Press, Oxford: 357–86.

Hutchinson, F.E. (2017) 'Rowing against the tide? Batam's economic fortunes in today's Indonesia', Trends in Southeast Asia No. 8, ISEAS – Yusof Ishak Institute, Singapore.

Ing, L.Y., G.H. Hanson and S.M. Indrawati (eds) (2018) *The Indonesian Economy: Trade and Industrial Policies*, Routledge, London.

Lal, D., and H. Myint (1996) *The Political Economy of Poverty, Equity and Growth*, Oxford University Press, Oxford.

Little, I.M.D., R.N. Cooper, W.M. Corden and S. Rajapatirana (1993) *Boom, Crisis, and Adjustment: The Macroeconomic Experience of Developing Countries*, Oxford University Press, New York NY.

Mallarangeng, R. (2000) 'Liberalizing New Order Indonesia: ideas, epistemic community and economic policy change, 1986–1992', PhD thesis, Ohio State University, Columbus OH.

Manning, C. (1998) *Indonesian Labour in Transition: An East Asian Success Story?* Cambridge University Press, Cambridge.

Manning, C., and R.M. Purnagunawan (2016) 'Has Indonesia passed the Lewis turning point and does it matter?', in H. Hill and J. Menon (eds) *Managing Globalization in the Asian Century*, Institute of Southeast Asian Studies, Singapore: 457–84.

Marks, S.V., and S. Rahardja (2012) 'Effective rates of protection revisited for Indonesia', *Bulletin of Indonesian Economic Studies* 48(1): 57–84.

Milanovic, B. (2016) *Global Inequality: A New Approach for the Age of Globalization*, Harvard University Press, Cambridge MA.

Myint, H. (1972) *Southeast Asia's Economy: Development Policies in the 1970s*, Penguin, Harmondsworth.

Palmer, I. (1978) *The Indonesian Economy since 1965: A Case Study of Political Economy*, Frank Cass, London.

Pangestu, M., S. Rahardja and L.Y. Ing (2015) 'Fifty years of trade policy in Indonesia: new world trade, old treatments', *Bulletin of Indonesian Economic Studies* 51(2): 239–61.

Patunru, A.A. (2017) 'On the rice fracas in Indonesia', Indonesia Study Group seminar, Australian National University, Canberra.

Patunru, A.A., and S. Rahardja (2015) 'Trade protectionism in Indonesia: bad times and bad policy', Analysis, Lowy Institute for International Policy, Sydney, 30 July.

Perkins, D.W. (2013) *East Asian Development: Foundations and Strategies*, Harvard University Press, Cambridge MA.

Pew Research Center (2014) 'Faith and skepticism about trade, foreign investment', Pew Research Center, Washington DC, September.

Reid, A. (1993) *Southeast Asia in the Age of Commerce, 1450–1680*, Yale University Press, New Haven CT.

Rock, M.T. (2017) *Dictators, Democrats, and Development in Southeast Asia: Implications for the Rest*, Oxford University Press, New York NY.

Rodrik, D. (1998) 'Why do more open economies have bigger governments?', *Journal of Political Economy* 106(5): 997–1,032.

Sachs, J.D., and A.M. Warner (2001) 'The curse of natural resources', *European Economic Review* 45: 827–38.

Soejachmoen, M. (2012) 'Why is Indonesia left behind in global production networks?', PhD thesis, Australian National University, Canberra.

Soesastro, M.H. (1989) 'The political economy of deregulation in Indonesia', *Asian Survey* 29(9): 853–69.

Soesastro, M.H. (2006) 'Regional integration in East Asia: achievements and future prospects', *Asian Economic Policy Review* 1: 215-34.

Soesastro, M.H., D.S. Simandjuntak and P.R. Silalahi (1988) *Financing Public Sector Development Expenditure in Selected Countries: Indonesia*, Economics Office, Asian Development Bank, Manila.

Szirmai, A. (2015) *The Dynamics of Socio-economic Development*, Cambridge University Press, Cambridge.

Thee, K.W., and M. Pangestu (1998) 'Technological capabilities and Indonesia's manufactured exports', in D. Ernst, T. Ganiatsos and L. Mytelka (eds) *Technological Capabilities and Export Success in Asia*, Routledge, London: 211-65.

Wanandi, J. (2012) *Shades of Grey: A Political Memoir of Modern Indonesia, 1965-1998*, Equinox, Singapore.

15 International cooperation and the management of globalisation: the Indonesian experience

Titik Anas and Dionisius Narjoko*

In this chapter we discuss how international trade cooperation has influenced the process of globalisation in Indonesia. International trade cooperation here refers to the set of rules and institutions, binding and non-binding commitments, and principles and best practices that define the conduct of international trade, including the movement of goods, services, investment and people. We evaluate the role of international trade cooperation in shaping both the reform process in Indonesia and, more generally, Indonesia's response to globalisation. We are interested in how the country has managed to balance the domestic political pressure for protection, on the one hand, against its role in international forums, on the other.

The chapter consists of five sections. In the first section we discuss the experience of Indonesia with globalisation. We then examine the role of international trade arrangements such as the General Agreement on Trade and Tariffs (GATT), the World Trade Organization (WTO), the Association of Southeast Asian Nations (ASEAN) and Asia-Pacific Economic Cooperation (APEC) in shaping that experience. Next, we highlight two cases in which trade facilitation has contributed to Indonesia's global economic integration: logistics and tourism. This is followed by a discussion of the recent trend towards protectionism in Indonesia and its implications for regional trade negotiations. We end with some conclusions and recommendations.

---

* The authors would like to thank Thaliya Wikapuspita of Presisi Indonesia for her excellent research assistance.

THE CASE FOR GLOBALISATION: INDONESIA'S EXPERIENCE

Globalisation has benefited a large number of countries. As one of the East Asian 'miracle' countries, Indonesia achieved high and sustained economic growth, reductions in poverty and improvements in equity during the period 1965–90 by maintaining an open trade and investment policy (World Bank 1993). Many developing countries were able to grow faster than the advanced economies, leading to a narrowing of the gap between the two groups of nations. Baldwin (2016), for instance, shows that the share of developed (G7) economies in world GDP has declined sharply since 1990, while that of six fast-growing industrialising countries (China, Korea, India, Indonesia, Poland and Thailand) has risen.

The literature on the impact of trade and investment liberalisation on productivity and investment has identified a number of channels through which globalisation benefits countries. The main ones are lower prices and higher-quality goods for consumers, and improved productivity and innovation among firms as a result of increased competition and knowledge spillovers from foreign direct investment (FDI). Using Indonesian manufacturing census data for the period 1991–2001, for example, Amiti and Konings (2007: 1,611) showed that a 10 percentage point fall in input tariffs led to a productivity gain of 12 per cent for firms that imported their inputs, 'at least twice as high as any gains from reducing output tariffs'. Similarly, using product- and plant-level data for manufacturing firms in Indonesia's apparel industry, Hayakawa, Matsuura and Takii (2017) found that a reduction in input tariffs generally boosted product quality upgrading.

Whether or not technology spillovers are successful depends on the absorptive capacity of local firms or workers. Narjoko (2009) found that the skill levels of workers mattered for exporters in Indonesia. This suggested the importance of investing in human capital to ensure successful technology spillovers and reap the full benefits of globalisation.

Given the benefits of globalisation, it is not surprising that Indonesia has generally been receptive towards openness and willing (for the most part) to undertake the necessary policy reforms. These reforms have been shaped by the context in which they arose, including the evolution of cooperative international trade arrangements.

INTERNATIONAL TRADE COOPERATION AND INDONESIA

In the 1990s, Indonesia undertook a series of reforms in order to meet its WTO commitments and (after the Asian financial crisis in 1997–98) to comply with the Letter of Intent (LOI) describing the policies Indonesia intended to implement in exchange for financial assistance from the IMF.

Figure 15.1   MFN and applied tariff rates in Indonesia, 1989–2016 (%)

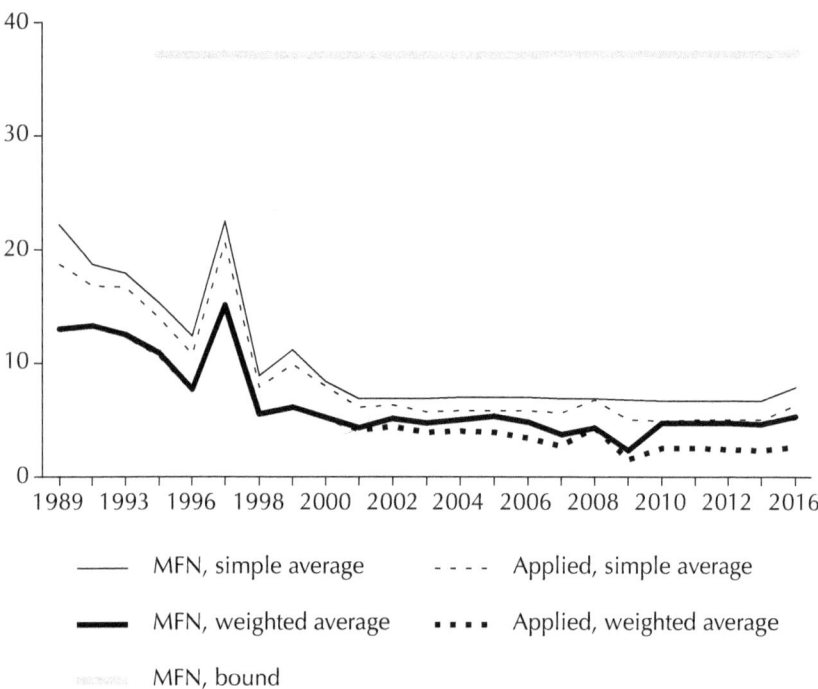

Source: World Integrated Trade Solution (WITS) database.

Figure 15.1 shows that both most-favoured-nation (MFN) tariffs (the tariffs that Indonesia has agreed to impose on imports from other WTO members) and applied tariffs (the rates that Indonesia actually applies in practice—that is, the lowest available rates) declined between 1989 and 2016 as Indonesia made progress in meeting its WTO, IMF and other (for example, ASEAN) commitments. The average MFN tariff declined from 22.2 per cent in 1989 to 7.9 per cent in 2016. However, the average bound MFN tariff remained high at 37.3 per cent, with some agricultural products having even higher bound rates.[1]

Studies of industry performance show that lower import tariffs have benefited Indonesia. Using Indonesian manufacturing census data for

---

1   A bound rate is the maximum tariff that a country can impose for a given commodity line under its WTO commitments, and can be much higher than the applied rate that is actually imposed.

Figure 15.2   Relationship between value of trade and applied tariff rates in Indonesia, 1989–2016

[Figure: Line chart showing Imports, Exports, Trade (left axis, $ billion, 0–400) and Applied tariff (right axis, %, 0–25) from 1989 to 2016. Trade rises from about $38 billion in 1989 to a peak around 2012 then declines to about $280 billion in 2016. Applied tariff declines over the period.]

Source: World Integrated Trade Solution (WITS) database.

the period 2000–13, for instance, Narjoko, Anas and Herdiyanto (2018) demonstrated that there had been robust development of intermediate input sectors such as parts and components even without trade protection. The authors concluded that the recent shift in government policy towards an import substitution strategy for intermediate inputs would retard the growth and development of the industry and was therefore misguided. Moreover, firms that imported their inputs would become worse off and might exit the market.

Studies also show that the Indonesian economy has grown strongly since the mid-1980s, fuelled by trade expansion. Blalock and Gertler (2004: 400–401) found that trade liberalisation in Indonesia in the 1980s led to a doubling in the number of Indonesian-owned exporting firms between 1990 and 1996, as exporters succeeded in increasing their market share in existing markets or expanding into new markets. Figure 15.2 shows that Indonesia's total trade increased from just $38 billion in 1989 to $280 billion in 2016. The country's stellar performance can be attributed in part to the multilateral and regional commitments that have shaped and disciplined Indonesian policy-making, leading to tariff reductions and other trade reforms. We discuss Indonesia's participation in some of these international economic arrangements next.

Multilateral commitments

Since coming into effect in 1948 and 1995 respectively, GATT and the WTO have imposed disciplines and commitments on Indonesia's trade policy. At the request of the United States, for example, Indonesia signed the GATT Code on Subsidies and Countervailing Duties in 1985 and removed the implicit export subsidy in its export certificate program in 1986. Under the new duty drawback system, which is still in effect today, exporters can claim refunds on the duties and taxes paid for the inputs used in their products (Pangestu and Boediono 1986; Pangestu 1996).

As a member of the WTO, Indonesia is obliged to meet its WTO commitments to bind or reduce tariffs, and faces international discipline if it succumbs to political pressure to introduce protectionist policies. Thus, the national car policy Indonesia introduced in 1996 quickly became the subject of a WTO complaint. The company that had been given the exclusive right to produce the national car—a joint venture between a Korean car company and President Suharto's son—was exempted from import duties and Indonesia's high local content requirements, despite importing fully built-up cars. The WTO Dispute Settlement Panel decided that Indonesia's national car policy violated the most basic principle of non-discrimination (article I.1 of the GATT on MFN treatment) and that the local content requirements violated, in particular, the Trade-Related Investment Measures (TRIMs) Agreement (WTO 1998). As a result, Indonesia was forced to withdraw its discriminatory national car policy.

A more recent example concerns a complaint lodged in 2015 by New Zealand and the United States about 18 measures in Indonesia's import-licensing regime for horticultural products, animals and animal products. In November 2017 the WTO's Appellate Body ruled that Indonesia must bring these measures into conformity with WTO agreements (WTO 2017). Marks (2017: Table 5) estimated that, in 2015, a large number of products subject to Indonesia's non-transparent licensing regime had very high effective rates of protection (ERPs): 116.5 per cent for beef, 27 per cent for fruits and 21.8 per cent for vegetables, for instance. As a result, Indonesian food-processing firms faced a high cost of inputs, reducing their competitiveness and increasing consumer prices. In other words, far from working as intended, the government's protectionist policies actually led to higher prices for a number of commodities in the domestic market.

Indonesia became more active in the WTO during the Doha Round of trade negotiations, which began in 2001. Together with like-minded countries, Indonesia played an active role in advocating for special and differential treatment for developing countries—that is, for less stringent commitments for developing countries, longer deadlines for developing countries to meet those commitments and, more recently, a more coherent strategy for aid to promote trade and capacity building in developing countries. The Doha negotiations made some progress only when WTO members approved the Trade Facilitation Agreement at the WTO Ministerial Conference in Bali in 2013. However, progress has generally been slow, and the stalled negotiations meant that Indonesia searched for other options, chiefly through bilateral and regional trade agreements. We examine some of these agreements and other options next.

Asia-Pacific Economic Cooperation (APEC)

We start with the APEC forum, which was established in 1989. Although not a regional trade agreement, APEC contributed significantly to Indonesia's efforts to open up, especially in the period before the Asian financial crisis. As a regional forum to promote, but not enforce, free trade among Asia-Pacific countries, APEC helped members build the capacity and confidence to undertake unilateral trade and investment reforms, based on either WTO or agreed-upon, non-binding principles. In fact, in the early 1990s APEC became a 'cheerleader' for the completion of the Uruguay Round of trade negotiations and the creation of the WTO, and continues to support efforts to multilateralise trade reforms and frameworks.

As the chair of APEC in 1994, Indonesia played a crucial role in setting the pattern for host countries to champion unilateral reforms in the year in which they chaired the organisation. Marking an important turning point in the way Indonesia's political leadership viewed globalisation, in that year President Suharto delivered his famous statement to the Indonesian public that 'Whether we like it or not, whether we are ready or not, we have to participate in globalisation' (quoted in Pangestu 2012: 6).

In 1994, Indonesia's economic technocrats were able to use the country's position as the chair of APEC to convince the political leadership to undertake a significant unilateral reform: the removal of foreign investment restrictions. More importantly, Indonesia was able to secure agreement for the Bogor Goals, a set of targets to realise free trade and investment in the Asia-Pacific by 2010 for industrialised APEC economies and by 2020 for developing APEC economies. Indonesia also contributed to the thinking on the way in which APEC accounted for the different levels of development among member economies, resulting in different deadlines (that is, special and differential treatment) for developing countries to achieve the Bogor Goals, and in a mechanism to provide capacity building for less developed countries.

Although the Bogor Goals and other APEC principles are non-binding, APEC played an important role, especially in the 1990s, in persuading member countries to remove trade and investment impediments and to adopt the principles and best practices (such as national treatment and transparency) that form the backbone of national reforms. Regular evaluations of members' progress towards achieving the Bogor Goals also exerted peer pressure on members to achieve the recommended reforms (see, for example, Kuriyama, Yuhua and Hew 2014).

Regional trade agreements: ASEAN and beyond

ASEAN has been a cornerstone of Indonesia's globalisation strategy since it joined as a founding member in 1967. Initially, political–security considerations were the main focus of cooperation among members; trade agreements came into the picture in the 1970s but were too limited to have a liberalising effect. It was only in 1991, after Indonesia had undertaken its own trade liberalisation and other reforms in response to a decline in oil prices, that a comprehensive free trade agreement (FTA) among ASEAN member states became possible. An important argument made at the time was that ASEAN could provide a training ground for member countries to open up and experience competition, prior to opening up more widely. Thus, the ASEAN Free Trade Agreement signed in 1992 originally aimed to reduce tariffs on intra-ASEAN trade to zero within 15 years (by 2007), but this was later accelerated to 10 years (by 2002).

In 2003, under Indonesia's leadership as the chair of ASEAN, member countries agreed to create an even broader ASEAN Community with three pillars: the ASEAN Economic Community, the ASEAN Political–Security Community and the ASEAN Socio-Cultural Community. Regional economic integration took a further step forward with the formal establishment of the ASEAN Economic Community in 2015. Successive blueprints have provided clear targets and timelines for each aspect of the ASEAN Economic Community, both to exert peer pressure on member countries to meet the targets and to provide a measure of progress (Soesastro 2008; ASEAN 2015). The blueprints have helped shape unilateral reforms in Indonesia, not just to reduce trade barriers but also to implement trade facilitation measures such as the National Single Window (see the case study in the next section).

The outcome of these processes has been to reduce intra-ASEAN tariffs to zero for the majority of ASEAN members under the ASEAN Trade in Goods Agreement (ATIGA), compared with an average MFN tariff of 8.8 per cent (Figure 15.3). Pangestu and Ing (2016) find that ASEAN has also been trade creating for its members, including Indonesia. In the case of the services sector as well, Indonesia's commitments under the ASEAN Framework Agreement on Services (AFAS) are more advanced than its commitments under the WTO's General Agreement on Trade in Services (GATS). Indonesia has agreed to liberalise 97 service sectors under the ninth AFAS liberalisation package (AFAS 9), but only 61 under GATS (Thanh and Bartlett 2006; Anas and Panjaitan 2018). Moreover, the

Figure 15.3 Average tariff rates under Indonesia's MFN and FTA commitments, 2017 (%)

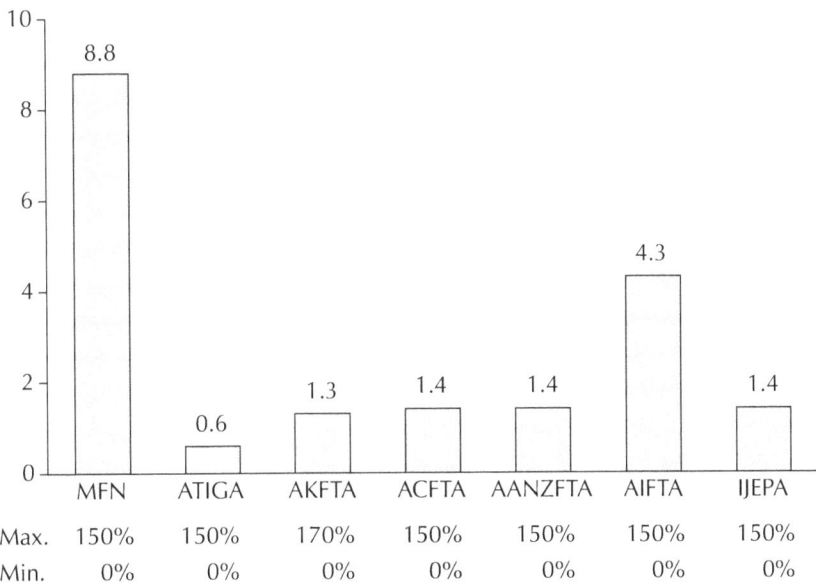

MFN = most favoured nation; ATIGA = ASEAN Trade in Goods Agreement; AKFTA = ASEAN–Korea Free Trade Agreement; ACFTA = ASEAN–China Free Trade Agreement; AANZFTA = ASEAN–Australia–New Zealand Free Trade Agreement; AIFTA = ASEAN–India Free Trade Agreement; IJEPA = Indonesia–Japan Economic Partnership Agreement.
Source: Authors' calculation based on Indonesia's MFN and FTA tariff commitments.

allowable level of foreign equity in domestic firms is higher under AFAS than under GATS—as high as 70 per cent for ASEAN investors in some sectors. ASEAN has also adopted a liberal interpretation of an ASEAN investor to include both businesses that originate in an ASEAN country and those that have a substantial presence in ASEAN. All these measures should help ASEAN achieve the objective of the ASEAN Economic Community to establish a single market and production base for the entire region within the next few years.

Since the early 2000s, ASEAN has concluded a series of ASEAN+1 free trade agreements with its trading partners: China in 2005, Korea in 2007, Japan in 2008, India in 2010 and Australia and New Zealand in 2010. The tariff rates set by these regional agreements are well below Indonesia's MFN rates and, with the exception of the FTA with India, are zero for more than 90 per cent of tariff lines.

The evolution of these ASEAN+1 FTAs shows how ASEAN has managed globalisation, the different approaches it has taken to its partnerships with other countries and the complexity of the issues at hand. In the case of the FTAs with China and Korea, the agreement was implemented in stages, with an early harvest component (that is, the liberalisation of certain goods in advance of the FTA) as an enticement or confidence-building measure, followed by the liberalisation of goods, then services and investment. This was in line with the way ASEAN economic integration itself had proceeded. The pattern for Japan, meanwhile, was to start with bilateral agreements with most of the major ASEAN countries that incorporated goods, services and investment (and also, in the case of the Indonesia–Japan agreement, capacity building and movements of people). The emphasis on 'partnership' from around this time to stress the importance of capacity building when the signatories to an agreement—the 'partners'—were at different levels of development set the pattern for all future bilateral and regional trade agreements. The ASEAN–Australia–New Zealand Free Trade Agreement was the most comprehensive FTA that ASEAN had engaged in, covering not only goods, services and investment but also new areas such as environment and labour. The section of the agreement on trade in goods covered 99 per cent of tariff lines, compared with around 90 per cent for most other ASEAN+1 FTAs, and only 80 per cent for the least open FTA, that between ASEAN and India.

However, despite zero or very low tariffs for intra-ASEAN trade and trade between ASEAN and its FTA partners, the utilisation rate of the FTA concession is low. Figure 15.4 shows that the share of Indonesian exports using the FTA concession—indicated by the proportion of exports using certificates of origin (COO or, in Indonesian, SKA)—was around 40 per cent of the country's total exports in 2015.[2] The largest numbers of SKA were issued for goods claiming the ASEAN concession (Form D) and those claiming the concession under the ASEAN–China Free Trade Agreement (Form E). Both the number of SKA issued and the value of exports using the SKA increased in 2015, except in the case of the ASEAN–Australia–New Zealand Free Trade Agreement.

The share of Indonesian imports using the FTA concession is also small. Figure 15.5 shows the share of Indonesian imports using the FTA concession plotted against the margin of preference, that is, the difference between the MFN and FTA rates. The agreement covering trade in goods within ASEAN, ATIGA, has the highest margin of preference because of its preferential rates of zero. The utilisation rate of the ATIGA concession

---

2 The Surat Keterangan Asal (SKA) is a certificate showing the country of origin of an exported product, and therefore whether the product is eligible for a preferential tariff rate under an FTA between Indonesia and another country. Note that the utilisation rate as measured by the import data of a trading partner may be lower than the rate based on exports, because a trading partner may reject the certificate of origin issued by an exporting country.

Figure 15.4   Indonesian exports using the FTA concession, 2013–15

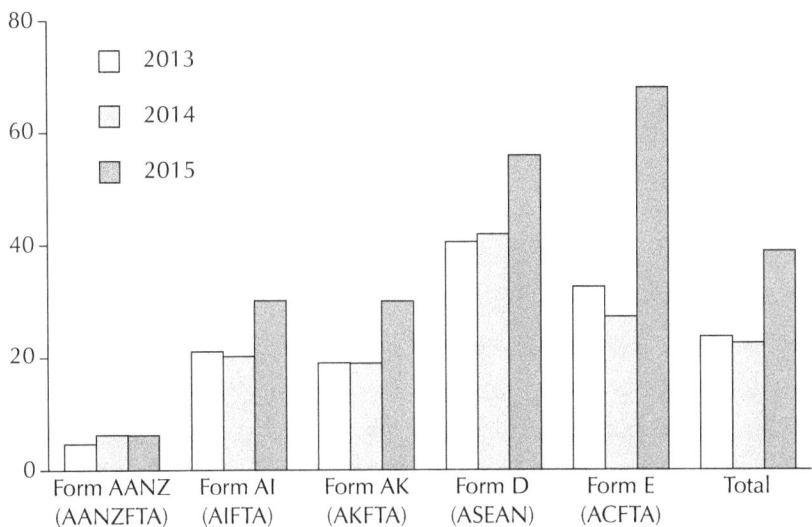

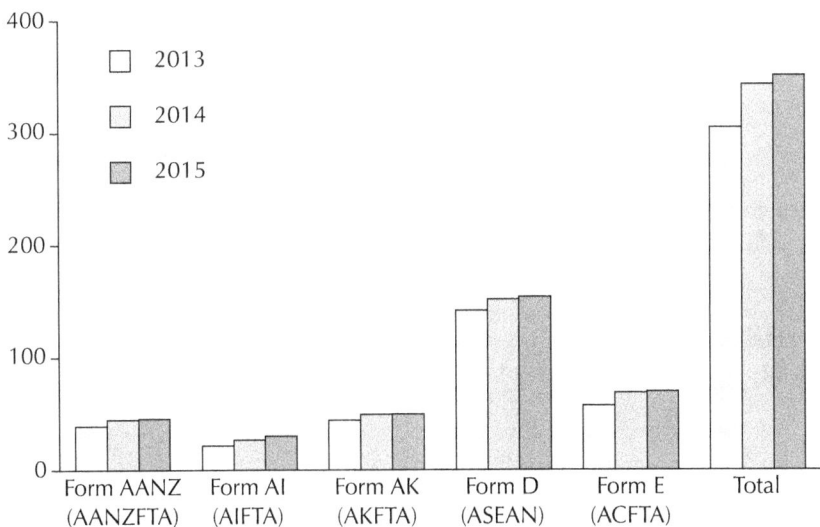

SKA = Surat Keterangan Asal; AANZFTA = ASEAN–Australia–New Zealand Free Trade Agreement; AIFTA = ASEAN–India Free Trade Agreement; AKFTA = ASEAN–Korea Free Trade Agreement; ASEAN = Association of Southeast Asian Nations; ACFTA = ASEAN–China Free Trade Agreement; IJEPA = Indonesia–Japan Economic Partnership Agreement.

Source: Calculated based on Pambagyo (2017) and World Integrated Trade Solution (WITS) database.

Figure 15.5   Indonesian imports using the FTA concession, 2016 (%)

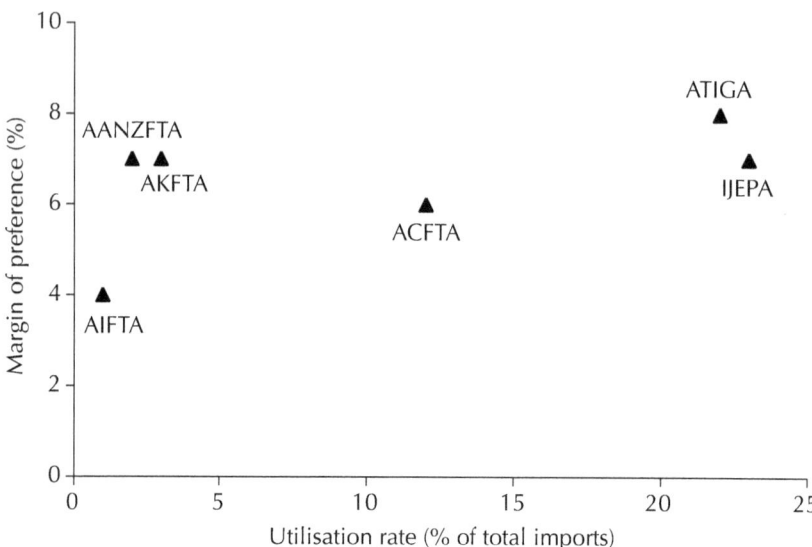

AANZFTA = ASEAN–Australia–New Zealand Free Trade Agreement; ACFTA = ASEAN–China Free Trade Agreement; AIFTA = ASEAN–India Free Trade Agreement; AKFTA = ASEAN–Korea Free Trade Agreement; ATIGA = ASEAN Trade in Goods Agreement; IJEPA = Indonesia–Japan Economic Partnership Agreement.

Note: Does not include split HS products (219 products), 3706.10.90.00 and 3706.90.90.00. Margin of preference = MFN rate minus FTA rate.

Source: Authors' calculation based on BPS data.

is the second highest after the Indonesia–Japan Economic Partnership Agreement (IJEPA) if automotive products are included in the list.[3]

Researchers have come up with several possible explanations for the low rates of utilisation of the FTA concession, including trade-restricting rules of origin of the FTA. Ing and Cadot (2016) calculated that the average tariff ad valorem equivalent (AVE) of ASEAN's rules of origin was 3.4 per cent across all instruments and sectors. The highly traded goods had

---

[3] The authors examined the utilisation rate of the FTA concession among Indonesian importers by product line at the two-digit HS level. The results suggested that the automotive sector made most use of the concession available under Indonesia's bilateral agreement with Japan (IJEPA). Indonesian manufacturers made least use of the concession available under the ASEAN–India FTA (AIFTA), as one would expect given that this agreement offers the lowest level of concessions (and thus has the lowest margins of preference) of all ASEAN+1 FTAs. The results of the estimations for individual product lines are available from the authors upon request.

less restrictive rules of origin, resulting in a lower trade-weighted average of 2.09 per cent. The authors also found fairly high AVEs in sectors such as leather, textiles and apparel, footwear and automobiles. The AVE of ASEAN's rules of origin in textiles stood out as being relatively more trade inhibiting than other sectors.

Lack of knowledge during the initial period of FTA implementation has been identified as the primary reason for the low utilisation of the FTA concession (CSIS 2013a; Wigjoseptina, Yunita and Sofiyandi 2015; Pangestu and Ing 2016). Later on, low export quantities, small benefit margins (the difference between the margin of preference and the cost of applying for an FTA concession) and inability to fulfil the rule-of-origin requirements also become important (Pangestu and Ing 2016; Anas, Mangunsong and Panjaitan 2017: 107). The increase in utilisation of the FTA concession by Indonesian exporters observed in 2015 (Figure 15.4) can be attributed both to an improved understanding about how to apply for the concession and to improved administrative procedures, which were simplified with the implementation of electronic certificates of origin (e-SKA).

It is also important to note that the margins of preference for individual product lines at the two-digit Harmonised System (HS) level tend to lie within the 0–10 per cent range, with most having a margin of around 5 per cent. Thus, one could argue that the margins of preference of the current FTAs are not large enough to lead to significant reductions in prices. If one adds an AVE of dealing with rules of origin of 3–4 per cent, then the net preferential effect becomes lower still, making it even less worthwhile to apply for the preferential rate compared with paying the regular MFN rate on imports. This is indicative of the influence of regional agreements on unilateral reforms to reduce barriers to trade on an MFN basis.

Concerns about the 'spaghetti bowl' of overlapping agreements and schedules (Bhagwati 2008) motivated Indonesia as the chair of ASEAN in 2011 to propose consolidating all of ASEAN's FTAs into a single body. To be called the Regional Comprehensive Economic Partnership (RCEP), the new body would comprise the 10 ASEAN members plus China, Korea, Japan, India, Australia and New Zealand. The objective was to achieve a modern and comprehensive FTA between ASEAN and its trading partners that would include capacity building and e-commerce, that could be ratcheted up over time to achieve best practice and that would be flexible enough to allow other countries that did not have an FTA with ASEAN to join later. Negotiations began in 2012 but progress has been slow, partly because the global climate has become less supportive of openness since the global financial crisis, but also because of a lack of leadership, including from Indonesia, to complete the negotiations in a timely way. In 2017, ASEAN leaders made strong calls for the finalisation of the negotiations in 2018.

Meanwhile, the United States, four members of ASEAN (Brunei, Malaysia, Singapore and Vietnam) and a few other Asia-Pacific countries had launched talks for another comprehensive trade agreement, the Trans-Pacific Partnership (TPP). The TPP gained clout when Japan joined in 2013, and the negotiations were completed in 2015 under the Obama administration. However, the ratification process in Congress had not been completed before the change in administration, and one of President Trump's first acts upon coming to office was to withdraw the United States from the TPP. Despite this setback, the other 11 members decided to forge ahead with the agreement without the participation of the United States. The revised TPP, the Comprehensive and Progressive Agreement for Trans-Pacific Partnership (CPTPP), was signed in early 2018 and could be ratified and implemented in the next few years.

These two competing trade negotiations and architecture — the RCEP and the TPP — split ASEAN during the 2013–16 period. While Malaysia, Singapore and Vietnam were active negotiating parties to the TPP, Indonesia originally stated that it had no intention of joining (Radja 2011). This was mainly because the TPP was perceived as being too liberal, driven too much by the interests of the United States and requiring too many legal and institutional changes. Indonesia was concerned, for instance, about the TPP's investor–state dispute settlement mechanism and about its regulations on government procurement and state-owned enterprises, which would have been difficult for Indonesia to meet. More generally, the last two years of Susilo Bambang Yudhoyono's administration and the first year of Joko Widodo's administration were a time of more inward-looking trade policies in Indonesia.

Given this background, President Widodo surprised many when he announced during his first state visit to the United States in October 2015 that Indonesia intended to join the TPP (Yong 2015). The underlying reason for this shift in position appeared to be the concern of Indonesian manufactured exporters, especially furniture, footwear, and textiles and garments exporters, that they would lose market share to their main competitors, Vietnam and Malaysia, which were parties to the TPP. The president's announcement galvanised the whole government into action and focused attention on the areas that were in need of reform. However, following President Trump's decision to leave the TPP in early 2017, Indonesia shelved its efforts to join the TPP and intensified its efforts to finalise the RCEP and key bilateral FTAs, such as those with Australia and Europe.

BEYOND TRADE LIBERALISATION: TWO CASE STUDIES

International trade cooperation extends beyond trade liberalisation to areas such as trade facilitation and economic cooperation. In this section we discuss two examples of such arrangements that have contributed positively to Indonesia's global economic integration.

Trade facilitation and the ASEAN Single Window

Trade facilitation measures, including the simplification of paperwork, the modernisation of procedures and the harmonisation of customs requirements, can reduce the cost and time needed to import and export goods and contribute positively to trade and growth. The WTO has estimated, for example, that over the period 2015–30, full implementation of the WTO Trade Facilitation Agreement will reduce global trade costs by an average of 14.3 per cent, add 2.7 per cent to world export growth and boost world GDP growth by more than 0.5 per cent (WTO 2015: 73).

Promoting the free flow of goods within ASEAN by integrating customs procedures — that is, by establishing a 'single window' for all ASEAN countries — was an important element of the plan to establish an ASEAN Economic Community by 2015. The Economic Research Institute for ASEAN and East Asia (ERIA) estimated that a 1 per cent improvement in customs and logistics performance would increase intra-ASEAN trade by 1.5 per cent (cited in Intal 2015: 4). Several other studies also concluded that improved trade facilitation among ASEAN member states would significantly boost economic growth (Wilson, Mann and Otsuki 2003; Otsuki 2011; Itakura 2013).

The ASEAN Single Window for customs clearance integrates the various National Single Windows of ASEAN members through the synchronised, electronic exchange of cargo clearance data. The National Single Windows allow traders to provide information just once for all government agencies involved in customs clearance, thus vastly simplifying and speeding up procedures. The initial target was to establish an ASEAN Single Window for the original six ASEAN economies by 2008 at the latest, and for the rest of ASEAN by no later than 2012. Although the 2008 target was not met, a pilot project began in 2011 and the full rollout of the ASEAN Single Window (covering five member states) started in 2016.

Intal (2015) finds that there have been significant improvements in trade facilitation in ASEAN, although significant challenges remain. According to the indicators in the World Bank's Logistics Performance Index, ASEAN member states exhibited remarkable reductions in the time required to import and export goods between 2007 and 2015 (Intal 2015: Table 1a). An ERIA survey on private sector perceptions of customs procedures in ASEAN also found improvements in 2009–11, especially in the submission of forms for clearance, the inspection and release of goods, and tariff classification (cited in Intal 2015: Figure 3).

The goal to establish an ASEAN Single Window by 2008 led to a concerted effort by ASEAN countries to integrate the many different export

Figure 15.6 Indonesia's score on the Logistics Performance Index, 2010–16

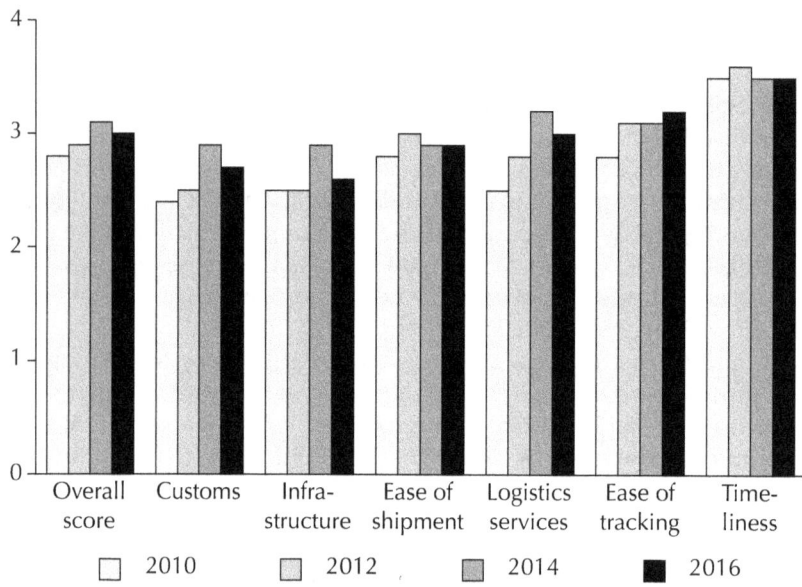

Source: World Bank.

and import procedures under different ministries into National Single Windows before the deadline. Implementation was not always smooth (CSIS 2013b), but port handling in general improved. Although Indonesia continues to lag behind its regional peers, its score on the Logistics Performance Index has improved since 2010 for all indicators except timeliness (Figure 15.6).

Visa-free travel within ASEAN

In 2006, ASEAN agreed to provide visa exemptions for ASEAN citizens travelling to other ASEAN countries for a maximum stay of 14 days, provided the stay was not for any other purpose than a visit. The original six ASEAN countries were the first to implement this visa-free policy, followed in stages by the other countries. The last country to allow visa-free entry was Myanmar — in 2013, when it was the chair of ASEAN. The numbers of intra-ASEAN (and also extra-ASEAN) visitor arrivals have increased sharply since the policy was introduced in 2006, including in Indonesia (Figure 15.7).

Intra-ASEAN visitor arrivals account for close to 50 per cent of total ASEAN arrivals, driven by geographical proximity, familiarity and the

Figure 15.7 Intra-ASEAN and extra-ASEAN visitor arrivals in the ASEAN region and Indonesia, 1995–2015

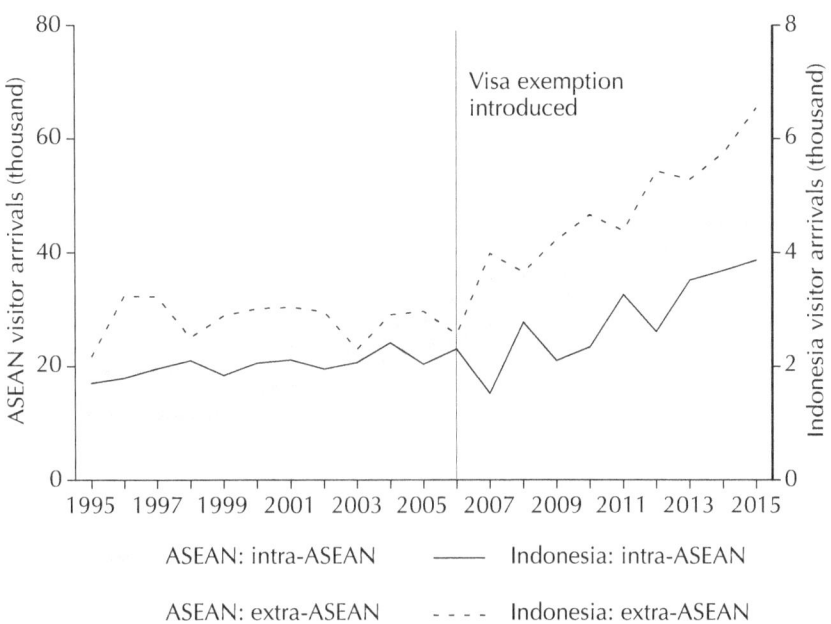

Source: ASEAN Secretariat.

growth of budget airlines. This has contributed to the growth of tourism services in Indonesia, which in turn has highlighted the importance of the economic contribution of tourism. The current administration has prioritised tourism as a leading sector, and has extended the ASEAN visa exemption to 165 other countries in an effort to boost tourism arrivals. This is in line with the finding that Indonesians view foreign visitors more positively than they do other attributes of globalisation, as Damuri and Pangestu point out in Chapter 7 of this volume.

PROTECTIONISM AND INDONESIA'S DECLINING ROLE IN INTERNATIONAL ENGAGEMENT

The past few years have witnessed growing protectionism in Indonesia. The government has enacted new laws on mining, agriculture and horticulture that contain trade-restricting elements. In 2013, the government banned exports of raw minerals to comply with the Mining Law and to promote domestic processing. The country's new industrial and trade laws embody the same spirit of protectionism. More and more imported products require permits and non-automatic licensing. During the period 2015–17, the government increased MFN tariffs on selected commodities, presumably to 'harmonise' tariffs. The new trend increased not only Indonesia's average MFN tariff rates but also non-tariff barriers, resulting in higher rates of protection. Marks (2017: Table 4) has estimated that the nominal rate of protection increased from 1.1 per cent in 2008 to 3.7 per cent in 2015, while the effective rate of protection increased from 4.8 per cent to 12.1 per cent. The increase in protection has resulted in a higher cost of living and a higher poverty incidence (see Chapter 8 of this volume by Yusuf and Warr).

Patunru and Rahardja (2015) argue that the trend towards protectionism can be attributed to several factors, including exchange rate appreciation, anti-foreign sentiment and a more active industrial policy. From around 2012, Indonesia pulled back from active participation in cooperative international arrangements, halting negotiations for free trade agreements, rejecting the TPP and standing in the way of productive RCEP negotiations. In 2015, however, amid concerns about a slowdown in investment flows and the economy, the government reversed its position. In September, President Widodo announced a major economic deregulation package to reduce the costs of doing business, remove bottlenecks and increase investment (Chilkoti and Hidayat 2015). The following month, he announced that Indonesia intended to join the TPP. Since then, the government has announced a further 16 deregulation and reform packages.

Despite the switch in position, Indonesia remains ambivalent towards openness and international cooperation. On the one hand, it has increased protection by imposing a large number of trade restrictions, including on imports of agricultural products such as salt and sugar. On the other hand, after a freeze in negotiations beginning in 2012, it has begun to reactivate regional and bilateral negotiations since the last quarter of 2015. Some of those negotiations have not been concluded despite years of talks, partly due to the three-year hiatus and partly due to the difficulty of resolving issues affecting certain sectors, particularly the services sector.

The agreements currently being negotiated include a number of bilateral preferential trade agreements, free trade agreements and economic partnership agreements with major trading partners such as the European Union, neighbouring countries such as Australia, and Latin American and African countries such as Chile, Peru, Kenya and Nigeria. Indonesia is also showing signs of a stronger commitment to finalise the RCEP negotiations. It is in Indonesia's interest to complete these negotiations given the size of the RCEP market and the fact that the CPTPP has now been signed. Expressed in terms of GDP, in 2016 the RCEP represented close to one-third of global GDP and was nearly 10 times the size of all ASEAN

Table 15.1 GDP by country group, 2016

Country group	GDP ($ billion)	Trade with Indonesia	
		Value ($ billion)	Relative to Indonesia's total trade (%)
WTO	72,873.7	271.1	97
APEC	44,578.8	199.8	71
RCEP	23,757.6	167.0	60
ACFTA	13,753.8	115.5	41
AJFTA	7,494.1	97.0	35
AIFTA	4,818.2	80.9	29
AKFTA	3,965.9	81.6	29
AANZFTA	3,944.3	77.4	28
ASEAN	2,554.7	67.9	24
World	75,871.7	280.0	100
Indonesia	932.3		

WTO = World Trade Organization; APEC = Asia-Pacific Economic Cooperation; RCEP = Regional Comprehensive Economic Partnership; ACFTA = ASEAN–China Free Trade Agreement; AJFTA = ASEAN–Japan Free Trade Agreement; AIFTA = ASEAN–India Free Trade Agreement; AKFTA = ASEAN–Korea Free Trade Agreement; AANZFTA = ASEAN–Australia–New Zealand Free Trade Agreement; ASEAN = Association of Southeast Asian Nations.

Note: Data for WTO members includes only 159 members. Data for APEC do not include Chinese Taipei.

Source: GDP: World Development Indicators; trade data: World Integrated Trade Solution (WITS) database.

economies combined (Table 15.1). Indonesia's trade with RCEP countries amounted to $167 billion, equivalent to 60 per cent of Indonesia's trade with the world.

Even though it was the chair of ASEAN when the RCEP was conceptualised in 2011, Indonesia did not take a strong leadership role in the subsequent negotiations and in fact did not offer many concessions during the negotiations. Indonesia has also had more difficulty than other ASEAN countries in meeting the RCEP requirement to reduce tariffs to zero on at least 92 per cent of tariff lines. Thus, President Widodo's instruction to his negotiators to complete the RCEP negotiations in 2018 marked a welcome change in direction. This was reinforced by RCEP leaders at the ASEAN Summit in the Philippines in November 2017 and by ASEAN leaders at the ASEAN–Australia Special Summit in March

2018. The parties to the negotiations will have to resolve various difficulties, including ensuring a balance between the ambition, scope and capacity of developed and developing members to provide commitments, and securing agreement between parties to the RCEP that do not currently have FTAs with each other.

It is important for Indonesia to play a leadership role in completing the RCEP negotiations in order to signal its commitment to openness in the context of the uncertainties in the trading system, and to reducing what Bhagwati (2008) has called the 'spaghetti bowl' of overlapping agreements, schedules and rules. If past experience is a guide, then this process should help to strengthen Indonesia's stance on openness and drive trade and investment reform.

CONCLUSIONS AND RECOMMENDATIONS

International cooperation has benefited Indonesia in a number of ways — helping to reduce barriers to trade, provide policy discipline to withstand rent-seeking activities, facilitate engagement with the global economy and frame policy reforms. The benefits of these reforms in a conducive external environment have included higher growth, accelerated development and reductions in poverty. Swayed by political pressure, however, the country has shifted towards a more protectionist stance in the past few years. This is reflected in higher MFN tariff rates, increased use of non-tariff measures such as licensing and quotas, and ambivalence towards international cooperation.

Since 2015, President Widodo has repeatedly emphasised the importance of making Indonesia more competitive and set a clear direction for Indonesia's global engagement, particularly through trade agreements. His instruction to his trade negotiators to aim to complete the RCEP negotiations in 2018 should push Indonesian policy-making in the direction of globalisation and openness and send an important signal that Indonesia supports the consolidation of regional trade agreements. Moreover, given the influence of international cooperation in the past, we believe that Indonesia's participation in the RCEP negotiations and other international forums will be important in shaping Indonesia's own reform agenda.

Of course, there is an important caveat: the completion of the RCEP negotiations will depend on whether the political will at the top translates into implementation at the technical level and whether the appetite for reform can be sustained during the period leading up to the presidential elections in 2019. Moreover, in Indonesia as elsewhere, it will be important to construct a narrative that can build public and political support for openness, and to institute effective policies that can ensure broad distribution of the benefits of globalisation.

REFERENCES

Amiti, M., and J. Konings (2007) 'Trade liberalization, intermediate inputs, and productivity: evidence from Indonesia', *American Economic Review* 97(5): 1,611–38.

Anas, T., C. Mangunsong and N.A. Panjaitan (2017) 'Indonesian SME participation in ASEAN economic integration', *Journal of Southeast Asian Economies* 34(1): 77–117.

Anas, T., and N.A. Panjaitan (2017) 'Reforming Indonesia's logistics sector', in T.S. Yean and S.B. Das (eds) *Services Liberalization in ASEAN: Foreign Direct Investment in Logistics*, ISEAS – Yusof Ishak Institute, Singapore: 42–76.

ASEAN (Association of Southeast Asian Nations) (2015) 'ASEAN Economic Community Blueprint 2025', ASEAN Secretariat, Jakarta. http://www.asean.org/wp-content/uploads/images/2015/November/aec-page/AEC-Blueprint-2025-FINAL.pdf

Baldwin, R. (2016) *The Great Convergence*, Harvard University Press, Cambridge MA.

Bhagwati, J. (2008) *Termites in the Trading System: How Preferential Agreements Undermine Free Trade*, Oxford University Press, Oxford.

Blalock, G., and P.J. Gertler (2004) 'Learning from exporting revisited in a less developed setting', *Journal of Development Economics* 75: 397–416.

Chilkoti, A., and T. Hidayat (2015) 'Lacklustre Indonesia tries to boost economy with reforms', *Financial Times*, 10 September.

CSIS (Centre for Strategic and International Studies) (2013a) 'Impacts of FTAs in Indonesia: study and business perspective survey results 2013', CSIS, Jakarta. https://media.neliti.com/media/publications/217-EN-impacts-of-ftas-in-indonesia-study-and-business-perspective-survey-results-2013.pdf

CSIS (Centre for Strategic and International Studies) (2013b) 'Towards informed regulatory conversations and improved regulatory regime in Indonesia: logistics sector and trade facilitation', CSIS, Jakarta.

Hayakawa, K., T. Matsuura and S. Takii (2017) 'Does trade liberalization boost quality upgrading? Evidence from Indonesian plant-product-level data', *Developing Economies* 55(3): 171–88.

Ing, L.Y., and O. Cadot (2016) 'How restrictive are ASEAN's rules of origin?', *Asian Economic Papers* 15(3): 115–34.

Intal, P.J. (2015) 'AEC Blueprint implementation performance and challenges: trade facilitation', ERIA Discussion Paper Series No. ERIA-DP-2015-41, Economic Research Institute for ASEAN and East Asia (ERIA), Jakarta, May.

Itakura, K. (2013) 'Impact of liberalization and improved connectivity and facilitation in ASEAN for the ASEAN Economic Community', ERIA Discussion Paper Series No. ERIA-DP-2013-01, Economic Research Institute for ASEAN and East Asia (ERIA), Jakarta.

Kuriyama, C.A., B.Z. Yuhua and D. Hew (2014) 'APEC's Bogor Goals progress report', Asia-Pacific Economic Cooperation Policy Support Unit, Asia-Pacific Economic Cooperation Secretariat, Singapore, August. http://www.apec.org/~/media/Files/AboutUs/AchievementsBenefits/20120822_APECsBogorGoalsProgressReport.pdf

Marks, S.V. (2017) 'Non-tariff trade regulations in Indonesia: nominal and effective rates of protection', *Bulletin of Indonesian Economic Studies* 53(3): 333–57.

Narjoko, D. (2009) 'Foreign presence spillovers and firms' export response: evidence from the Indonesian manufacturing', ERIA Discussion Paper Series No. ERIA-DP-2009-23, Economic Research Institute for ASEAN and East Asia (ERIA), Jakarta, December.

Narjoko, D., T. Anas and R. Herdiyanto (2018) 'The elusive pursuit of import substitution in 21st century Indonesia', *Asian Economic Papers* 17(1): 73–93.

Otsuki, T. (2011) 'Quantifying the benefits of trade facilitation in ASEAN', OSIPP Discussion Paper No. DP-2011-E-006, Osaka School of International Public Policy (OSIPP), Osaka University, Osaka.

Pambagyo, I. (2017) 'PTA/FTA/CEPA dan Indonesia' [PTA/FTA/CEPA and Indonesia], Dirjen Perundingan Perdagangan Internasional, Ministry of Trade, Jakarta.

Pangestu, M. (1996) *Economic Reform, Deregulation, and Privatization: The Indonesian Experience*, Centre for Strategic and International Studies (CSIS), Jakarta.

Pangestu, M. (2012) 'Globalisation and its discontents: an Indonesian perspective. Heinz W. Arndt Memorial Lecture, Canberra, 1 September 2011', *Asian-Pacific Economic Literature* 26(1): 1–17.

Pangestu, M., and Boediono (1986) 'Indonesia: the structure and causes of manufacturing sector protection', in C. Findlay and R. Garnaut (eds) *The Political Economy of Manufacturing Protection: Experiences of ASEAN and Australia*, Allen & Unwin, Sydney: 1–47.

Pangestu, M., and L.Y. Ing (2016) 'ASEAN: regional integration and reforms', *Asian Economic Papers* 15(2): 44–60.

Patunru, A.A., and S. Rahardja (2015) 'Trade protectionism in Indonesia: bad times and bad policy', Lowy Institute for International Policy, Sydney, July.

Radja, A.M. (2011) 'Indonesia not in a hurry to join TPP: president', *Antaranews.com*, 19 November. https://en.antaranews.com/news/77762/indonesia-not-in-a-hurry-to-join-tpp-president

Soesastro, H. (2008) 'Implementing the ASEAN Economic Community (AEC) Blueprint', in H. Soesastro (ed.) *Deepening Economic Integration in East Asia: The ASEAN Economic Community and Beyond*, Economic Research Institute for ASEAN and East Asia (ERIA), Jakarta: 47–59. http://www.eria.org/RPR-2007-1-2.pdf

Thanh, V.T., and P. Bartlett (2006) 'Ten years of ASEAN Framework Agreement on Services (AFAS): an assessment', REPSF Project No. 05/004, ASEAN Secretariat and Regional Economic Policy Support Facility (REPSF), Jakarta, July. http://aadcp2.org/file/05-004-FinalReport.pdf

Wigjoseptina, C., L. Yunita and Y. Sofiyandi (2015) 'Survey on the utilisation of free trade agreements in Indonesia', in L.Y. Ing and S. Urata (eds) *The Use of FTAs in ASEAN: Survey-based Analysis*, Economic Research Institute for ASEAN and East Asia (ERIA), Jakarta: 77–102.

Wilson, J.S., C.L. Mann and T. Otsuki (2003) 'Trade facilitation and economic development: measuring the impact', Policy Research Working Paper No. 2988, World Bank, Washington DC.

World Bank (1993) 'The East Asian miracle: economic growth and public policy: main report (English)', Oxford University Press, New York. http://documents.worldbank.org/curated/en/975081468244550798/Main-report

WTO (World Trade Organization) (1998) 'Indonesia: certain measures affecting the automobile industry. Report of the panel', WTO, Geneva, 2 July. http://www.worldtradelaw.net/reports/wtopanelsfull/indonesia-autos(panel)(full).pdf.download

WTO (World Trade Organization) (2015) 'World trade report 2015. Speeding up trade: benefits and challenges of implementing the WTO Trade Facilitation Agreement', WTO, Geneva. https://www.wto.org/english/res_e/booksp_e/world_trade_report15_e.pdf

WTO (World Trade Organization) (2017) 'Indonesia: importation of horticultural products, animals and animal products. Report of the Appellate Body', WTO, Geneva, 9 November. https://www.wto.org/english/tratop_e/dispu_e/477_478r_e.pdf

Yong, J.A. (2015) 'Indonesia intends to join TPP, says President Jokowi', *Straits Times*, 27 October.

Index

A
Aceh, 19, 21, 23, 24, 25
　Aceh–Dutch war, 23–5
ADB, 4
AFAS
　see ASEAN Agreement on Services
Africa, 46, 193, 310
agriculture
　banks, 191
　cash crops, 19, 93
　employment, 162, 163, 164, 167, 203, 204, 206, 226, 251
　food crops, 81, 83, 139, 143, 206, 277
　import ban, 5, 40, 46
　industrial, 83
　mono-crops, 83
　productivity, 226
　protectionism, 4, 5, 40, 110, 139, 143, 277, 309, 310
　subsidies, 80
　technology, 259
　Widodo policy, 81
　see also corn; rice
AIIB
　see Asian Infrastructure Investment Bank
AKAN
　see International Labour Placement Program
Alibaba, 212
Alliance Against Human Trafficking (Ampera), 244, 250, 258
Ambon, 182
Ampera
　see Alliance Against Human Trafficking

Anglo-Dutch Treaty, 21–2, 22–3, 27
ANI
　see Indonesian Nickel Association
Antam
　see PT Aneka Tambang
anti-globalisation
　see globalisation, unpopularity/ action against
Anti-Trafficking Taskforce, 250
ANZ, 185
Apkasi
　see Association of Indonesian District Governments
APEC
　see Asia-Pacific Economic Cooperation
army
　see military; *see also* Indonesian National Army (TNI)
Asahi, 194
ASEAN, 3, 7, 12, 53, 54, 57, 58, 64–5, 220, 243, 248, 271, 277, 294, 296, 311
　communique on South China Sea dispute, 60–61
　criticism of effectiveness, 62, 64
　Charter, 60
　formation, 32, 60
　Free Trade Area (FTA), 32, 300–301
　GDP, 311
　indicators of openness, 113
　Indonesia cautious approach, 280
　Information Technology Agreement (ITA II), 280, 287
　Ministerial Meeting on Transnational Crime, 247
　rules of origin, 302–5

317

Single Window for customs
    clearance, 307-8
  tariffs, 300
  trade agreements, 280, 300-306
  visa-free travel, 308-9
ASEAN Agreement on Services
    (AFAS), 300-301
ASEAN Economic Community, 300,
    301
ASEAN Political-Security
    Community, 300
ASEAN Socio-Cultural Community,
    300
ASEAN Trade in Goods Agreement
    (ATIGA), 300, 302
ASEAN+1 free trade agreements,
    301-6
Asian financial crisis, 3, 9, 11, 35, 40,
    104, 133, 134, 135, 152, 153, 176,
    181, 187, 188, 189, 190, 196, 201,
    203, 204, 212, 221, 253, 269, 286,
    295, 299
Asian Infrastructure Investment Bank
    (AIIB), 4
Asian-African Summit, 4
Asia-Pacific Economic Cooperation
    (APEC), 12, 294, 299-300, 311
  CEO Summit, 3
  Indonesia as chair, 299, 311
  Bogor Goals, 280, 299-300
Association of Indonesian District
    Governments (Apkasi), 95
Astra, 184, 190
Asuransi Bintang, 182
ATIGA
  see ASEAN Trade in Goods
    Agreement
Australia, 35, 39, 47, 48, 52, 64, 310
  ASEAN Special Summit, 312
  ban on export of live cattle, 80
  and New Zealand ASEAN Free
    Trade Agreement (AANZFTA),
    301, 302, 303, 304, 311
  policy on turning back boats
    carrying refugees, 57n
  statement on freedom of
    navigation, 63
  visit of President Widodo, 63
autarchy theories, 6, 27

B
Bangkok Bank, 185

Bangladesh, 283, 285, 287
bangsa (nation), 8, 73, 77-81, 85, 86
Bank Bali, 185
Bank Buana, 191
Bank Bumi Daya, 183, 185, 191
Bank Bumiputera (Asuransi
    Bumiputera Group), 186
Bank Central Asia, 185, 186, 190, 192
Bank Dagang Negara, 183, 185, 191
Bank Danamon, 185, 191, 192
Bank Duta, 185
Bank Ekspor Impor Indonesia, 183,
    185, 191
Bank for International Settlements,
    187
Bank Indonesia, 183, 185, 187, 188,
    191, 192-3, 276
Bank Indonesia Regulation No. 14/8/
    PBI/2012 on the Ownership of
    Shares in Commercial Banks, 191
Bank Internasional Indonesia (Sinar
    Mas Group), 186, 191
Bank Mandiri, 101, 191, 192
Bank Negara Indonesia (BNI), 101,
    183, 185, 191, 192
Bank Niaga, 182, 185, 186, 191
Bank NISP, 191
Bank Nusa Nasional (Bakrie Group),
    186
Bank of Tokyo, 185
Bank Permata, 191
Bank Rakyat Indonesia (BRI), 101, 183,
    185, 191, 192
Bank Summa (Soeryadjaya family),
    186
Bank Tabungan Negara, 183, 185, 191
Bank Tabungan Pensiunan Nasional,
    191, 192
Bank Tunggal, 183, 185
Bank Umum Nasional, 185
banks and banking sector, 185-8, 190,
    191-3, 196
  automation and digital technology,
    186, 193
  banking crisis, 188, 191, 192
  banking licences, 185, 186, 190
  commercial, 186, 191-2
  competition, 192, 196
  e-commerce, 190, 193
  electronic banking, 186
  electronic payments, 193, 194
  foreign, 185, 186, 188, 190, 191

Go-Pay, 194
government guarantee for deposits, 188
improved strength, 193
loan currency, 188, 192
mergers, 191
nationalisation, 183
National Payments Gateway, 193
non-performing loans, 192
number of branches, 186, 192, 193
private, 185, 186, 188, 191
regulation, 186–7, 191, 192–3
state-owned, 183, 185, 188, 191–2
see also Asian financial crisis; global financial crisis; name of bank
Banser, 43
Banten, 19–20
Bapindo, 183, 185, 191
Bappenas
see National Development Planning Agency
Basri, Chatib, 95
Batam Island, 287
Batavia, 20, 21, 22, 23, 25, 26, 251
bauxite, 92, 94n, 95, 96, 97, 98, 99, 139
beef, 80, 83, 84, 298
Belgium, 22
bird's nest enterprises, 245, 246, 255, 256, 257
Bishop, Julie, 63
BNP2TKI
see National Agency for the Placement and Protection of Indonesia Migrant Workers
BPS, 141, 142, 209, 226, 227, 251, 282
Brazil, 103, 160, 194
Bretton Woods, 269
Brexit, 1–2, 109
Britain, Great, 21–5
Brunei, 53
Bukit Asam, 99
Bulog, 79

C
Cambodia, 60, 248, 283, 285, 287
Carrefour, 209
Central Java, 225, 234, 238
Centre for Strategic and International Studies (CSIS), survey, 111, 114–29
CGE model, 140, 141–2
see also INDONESIA-E3 model

Chase Manhattan Bank, 185
Chen-hsun, Chang, 24
children and youth
cost of raising, 160, 168
education, 8, 251, 252
human trafficking, 244, 249, 252, 254
labour, 161
marriage, 227
malnutrition, 74
Chile, 310
China, 2, 4, 7, 37, 48, 64, 182, 194, 205, 259, 269, 270, 271, 289, 290
anti-Chinese sentiment, 30, 273
attitude towards globalisation, 273
ASEAN–China Joint Working Group, 61
ASEAN Free Trade Agreement (ACFTA), 280n, 301–4, 311
business-to-business e-commerce, 212
demand for resources, 90, 92, 190
exports, 283, 284, 285
fishing vessels in Natuna waters, 7, 53, 55–7, 63
growth, 190, 290
hangar space on artificial islands in South China Sea, 62
illegal workers in Indonesia, 123
investment in Indonesia, 60, 97
labour market, state intervention, 246–7
reaction to naming of North Natuna Sea, 59
territorial claims in South China Sea, 54, 58
trade deficit with United States, 109
UN arbitration ruling on South China Sea dispute with Philippines, 56, 60
China Minzhong Food Corporation, 194
Chinatrust Bank, 185
Christianity, 182, 251
CIMB, 191
Citibank, 185, 186, 192
civil society organisations, 11, 237, 246, 250, 257–60
coal, 92, 99, 203, 206
Coen, Jan Pieterszoon, 20

colonialism, 5, 6, 25, 26, 27, 40, 41, 42, 77, 180, 181, 182, 183, 184, 195, 251, 252, 260, 269, 270–271
commodities
    booms, 3, 5, 7, 40, 90, 91, 92, 190, 201, 203
    prices, 90, 91, 98, 113, 190, 269, 271, 272
Commonwealth Bank, 185
Companhia Mineira de Açúcar e Álcool Participações, 194
compensation mechanisms, 2, 13, 111
competition/competitiveness, 5, 10, 40, 84, 92, 121n, 157–61, 176, 180, 192, 194, 196, 202, 274, 282, 286, 288, 290, 295, 298, 300, 306, 312
    rankings on Ease of Doing Business Index and Logistics Performance Index, 289
Comprehensive and Progressive Agreement for Trans-Pacific Partnership (CPTPP), 306, 310
    see also Trans-Pacific Partnership
conglomerates, 190, 192
Constitution of the Republic of Indonesia, 94, 226, 272
construction sector, 114, 164, 166, 179, 204n, 216, 228
Convention on the Elimination of All Forms of Discrimination against Women, 27
copper, 92, 94n, 95, 96, 97, 101, 139
copra, 29
corn, 80, 81
corruption, 2, 4, 84, 245, 246, 248, 248–9, 252, 254, 258, 281
    Transparency International's Corruption Perceptions Index, 289, 290
Corruption Eradication Commission (KPK), 4, 47
CPTPP
    see Comprehensive and Progressive Agreement for Trans-Pacific Partnership
crime
    financial and banking fraud, 2
    narcotics, 38, 44, 46
    organised, 11, 260
    see also corruption; human trafficking

Criminal Investigation Agency (Bareskrim), 248
CSIS
    see Centre for Strategic and International Studies
currency
    exchange rate, 5, 186, 203, 205, 272, 274, 286, 310
    loans funded in rupiah, 188, 192
    rupiah appreciation, 5
    rupiah devaluation, 3, 188
    Thai baht, 188

D

Darul Islam Islamic-state movement, 182
DBS Bank, 185
decentralisation, 133, 189, 233, 234, 241, 254
democratisation, 36, 47, 48, 104, 133, 188, 276, 277, 278, 291
Desbumi
    see Village of Care for Migrant Workers
developing countries, 142, 181, 201, 212, 213, 219n, 272, 274, 275, 283, 286, 295
developmentalism, 8, 13, 91, 92, 93, 102–3
Dharmala, 182
Directorate General of Labour Force Placement and Expansion of Employment Opportunities (Binapenta), 226
Djarum, 184, 190
Djohan, Robby, 186
Domestic Workers Convention, 229
    ratifying countries, 229n
DPD
    see Regional Representative Council
DPR
    see parliament
Dutch East India Company, 202, 251
    see also United East India Company
Duterte, Rodrigo, 1

E

East Java, 225, 234, 238
East Nusa Tenggara, 11, 225, 232, 234, 238, 244

corruption, 254
decentralisation, 54
El Tari Airport, 250, 157, 258
human trafficking, 244, 250, 251–9
Kupang, 244, 250–53, 257, 258
migration, 251–6
police, 245, 249, 254, 255, 257, 259
Sumba, 251, 252
Timor, 251, 252, 253
underdevelopment, 251, 259–60
East Timor, 39
e-commerce, 190, 193, 201–2, 212, 214, 305
economy
deregulation, 3, 273, 287, 310
development, 53, 60, 63, 82, 104, 237
growth, 35, 98, 104, 135, 189, 192, 194, 203, 229, 258, 274, 276, 295, 297, 307
inflation, 83, 183, 274, 286
see also GDP
education, 8, 119–20, 123, 126, 160, 162, 179, 181, 195, 207, 207n, 209n, 209–10, 254, 259, 270
children, 251, 252
comparative performance on PISA mathematics and science tests, 288, 289
low levels, 49, 160, 225, 252, 253–4, 260
sector, 208, 208n
elections
see politics
electronics industry
case study, 280, 281–2, 283–91
global market shares by country, 283, 284
multinationals, 287
employment
agriculture, 162, 163, 164, 167, 203, 204, 206, 226, 251
effect of new technology, 216–19, 221, 287
female, 165–77
future, 10, 202
industry, 203–9
informal, 206, 206n, 207, 208, 221
labour force participation by sector, 163
labour-intensive, 203, 205, 209, 214, 215–16, 268, 275, 281–3, 287

male, 9, 158, 159, 160, 161, 162, 164, 167, 169, 176, 177, 227, 228
manufacturing, 163, 203–5, 212, 219n, 221
retrenchments, opposed by Ministry of Manpower, 287
services sector, 163, 203, 204, 206–9, 221
structure, 158, 159, 160, 203, 204
temporary, 218, 219, 221
see also labour; labour markets; women
English East India Company, 21
environmental issues, 82–3, 187, 190
deforestation, 181, 187, 190
pollution, 181, 190
Erdoğan (President), 2
ethnic minorities, 36, 47, 182, 189
Europe, 18, 214
European Asian Bank, 185
European Union, 109, 189, 311
exclusive economic zone, 4, 7, 53, 54, 55, 56, 58
export orientation, 12, 281
export-oriented firms, 169, 203, 204, 209, 211, 221, 275, 297
export performance, 12
case study, 281–90
exports, 5, 7, 19, 29, 31, 77, 113, 190, 203–6, 221
FTA concession, 302, 303, 304, 304n
manufacturing, case study, 281–91
refunds on duties paid on inputs, 298
sectors, 169, 179
see also mineral export ban

F

Fairchild, 287
Financial Services Authority (OJK), 192
food, 73–86
accessibility, 8, 73, 75, 76, 77, 78, 79, 80, 81, 84, 86
corporatisation of global regime, 77
estates, 82–3
Food Law of 2012, 79, 80
global crisis, 79, 80, 83, 84
malnutrition, 8, 74–5, 79, 86
prices, 80, 84, 298
protectionism, 139, 149–50, 298

security, 5, 8, 73, 74, 75–6, 77, 83
self-sufficiency, 5, 8, 12, 19, 38, 75, 77, 79, 80, 81, 83, 110, 270, 277
sovereignty, 6, 7–8, 73–86
state control over system, 8, 81
World Food Summit, 75
see also agriculture; *kedaulatan pangan* (food sovereignty)
footwear industry
case study, 281-3, 284–91
global market shares, 284, 285
see also textiles, clothing and footwear industry
foreign aid, 48, 182, 269
foreign direct investment (FDI), 113, 114, 279, 287, 288, 295
negative investment list, 114
net inflows, 113
foreign interference/influence, 2, 7, 30, 35, 39, 44–5, 45–6, 47, 100
foreign investment, 3–4, 6, 8, 26, 27, 40, 42, 60, 114, 121, 184–5, 194, 201, 202, 205, 209, 269, 270, 279
Chinese, 30, 182
Japanese, 184
public opinion on, 112–29
foreign policy, 7, 52–3, 60, 62, 64, 112
Archipelagic Outlook, 52
France, 23, 26

G

G20 countries, 109
trade restrictions, 138
G20 Summit, 3–4
garment industry, case study, 281–2, 283–91
global market shares, 283, 285
MFA quotas, 286
see also textiles, clothing and footwear industry
gas, 101–2
gas, and oil sector, 59, 99, 101, 103, 114
GATT
see General Agreement on Trade and Tariffs
GDP
agricultural, 81
country group, 311
current account, 113
growth, 189
growth per capita, 9, 26, 133, 135, 152

impact of commodity boom, 92
net inflows of FDI, 113
trade, 112, 113
world, 1, 137–8, 189, 295, 310, 311
General Agreement on Trade and Tariffs (GATT), 294, 298
GATT Code on Subsidies and Countervailing Duties, 298
geography of Indonesia, 12, 17–32, 271
Germany, 23
global financial crisis of 2007-08, 1, 3, 10, 109, 137, 189, 192, 201, 277, 305
Global Slavery Index, 229
globalisation, 133–56, 180–96
attitude towards, in selected countries, 273
benefits, 1, 10, 181, 187, 194, 202, 211, 221, 295, 312
costs, 10, 181, 221
driver of technology innovation, 212
response of Indonesian companies, 10, 193–4
impact on labour markets, 201–22
impact on openness, 112–14, 195, 267–91
public opinion surveys, 8, 114–29, 273
unpopularity/action against, 1–2, 8, 9, 76, 109, 117, 133–4, 153
see also human trafficking; welfare of households, study using INDONESIA-E3 model
Gobel, Rachmat, 4
Go-Jek, 194, 202, 212, 214, 215, 219–20, 221
gold, 95, 96, 99, 101, 102
Golkar, 183
Go-Pay, 194
Government Regulation No. 1/2017 on the Fourth Change to Government Regulation No. 23/2010 on the Implementation of Mining Company Activities for Mineral and Coal Mining, 97
Grab, 194, 220
Green Revolution, 226
Grotius doctrine of free trade, 18–19
Guided Democracy, 30, 41
Gunung Sewu, 182
Gusman, Irman, 84

H

Habibie, B.J., 188, 231
Hartarto, Airlangga, 5
Heckscher–Ohlin model of comparative advantage, 111
HeidelbergCement, 190
Hock, Chin, 29
Holland
    see Netherlands
Hong Kong, 21, 185, 190, 246, 247, 255
hotels and restaurants sector, 144, 146, 166, 179, 206, 207, 208, 215, 216
HSBC, 185
Human Development Index, 251
human rights, 39, 240, 245, 250
    violations of migrant workers, 225, 227, 229, 230, 231, 233, 234, 250
human trafficking, 2, 10, 11, 225, 227, 232, 243–60
    civil society organisations, role in prevention, 257–9
    corruption, 245, 246, 248, 252, 253, 257, 258
    criminal networks, 43, 244, 246, 252, 258, 259, 260
    deaths, 250, 255, 257, 258, 259
    definition, 244
    East Nusa Tenggara, 251–9
    global report, 245
    human trafficking/migrant worker laws disconnection, 250
    involvement of state institutions, 245, 260
    lack of database, 250
    lack of penalties/enforcement, 257
    law, 249–50
    mechanisms for controlling, 250, 260
    minors, 244, 249, 252, 254
    number of cases investigated and reported, 249
    number of victims, East Nusa Tenggara, 250
    palm oil industry, 254–5
    perpetrators, 246, 256
    prosecutions, 248
    Sumba, 251
    Timor, 51
    transport services, 253–4
    vulnerability, 254, 257, 259–60
    within Indonesia, 249–51
    see also migrant workers; slavery

Hungary, 37
Husin, Saleh, 5

I

IMF, 4, 40, 188, 269, 296
    Letter of Intent, 188, 274, 295
import licences/licensing, 4, 30, 79, 84, 182, 298
import restrictions, 3, 4, 38, 40, 46, 79, 84–5, 110, 113, 149
    agriculture, 5, 40
import substitution, 3, 182, 184, 297
imports, 19, 77, 296–7
    anti-foreign sentiment, 8, 112–29
    food, 83, 84, 139, 298
    FTA concession, 302, 304
income disparity, 10, 195
    see also inequality
India, 21, 37, 64, 182, 269, 270, 271, 273, 288, 289, 290, 295
    ASEAN Free Trade Agreement (AIFTA), 301, 303, 304, 304n, 311
    call centres, 213
    demand for resources, 92
    exports, 285
    openness/globalisation view, 273, 279
    textile imports, 19, 20
Indian Ocean Rim Association, 63
Indocement, 190
Indofood, 190, 193–4
Indomart, 209
INDONESIA-E3 model
    analysis of welfare of households, 140–53
    definition, 140
    description of SAM database, 141–2
Indonesian Communist Party, 42
Indonesian Democracy Party (PDI), 183
Indonesian Democratic Party of Struggle (PDIP), 101
Indonesian National Army (TNI), 43, 47
Indonesian Nickel Association (ANI), 95
Indonesian Peasants Union (SPI), 76, 85
Indonesian Smelter and Minerals Processing Association, 97
Indosat, 190

industry
    capital-intensive, 83, 110, 184, 205
    employment, 203–9
    labour-intensive, 203, 205, 209, 214, 215–16, 268, 275, 281–3, 287
    policy, 280–81
inequality, 1, 9, 10, 48, 86, 92
    gender, 158–60
    Gini coefficient, 1976–2016, 136
    globalisation effect, 201, 202, 274–5
    income, 10, 195
    see also welfare of households, study using INDONESIA-E3 model
infrastructure, 123, 184, 190–91, 205, 219, 232, 268, 281, 286, 288, 308
    energy, 96n, 222
    investment, 60
    irrigation, 81
    mobile phone, 193
    rural, 79
    transport, 253–4, 260
INPEX, 101
Institute of Resource Governance and Social Change (IRGSC), 244, 250, 251, 256
International Convention on the Protection of the Rights of All Migrant Workers and Members of Their Families, 233, 241
International Court of Justice, 39
International Labour Office, 229
International Labour Placement Program (AKAN), 226
IRGSC
    see Institute of Resource Governance and Social Change
Ishaaq, Luthfi Hasan, 84
Islam, 18, 36, 42, 43, 45, 182, 251
    political parties, 183

J

Japan, 194, 270
    ASEAN Free Trade Agreement (AJFTA), 301, 311
    banks, 185–6, 191
    exports, 283, 284, 285
    Indonesia–Japan Economic Partnership Agreement (IJEPA), 301, 302, 304
    joint venture companies in Indonesia, 190

    student protests against Japanese investment, 184
    TPP membership, 306
    visit of prime minister Kakuei Tanaka to Indonesia, 184
    war-time, 27, 28
Jardines, 190
Java, 20, 21, 22, 23, 25, 181

K

Kalimantan, 8, 90, 96n, 187, 54
    forest fires, 82
    west, 21, 26
Karimun Island, 27–8, 31
kedaulatan pangan (food sovereignty), 7–8, 12, 73–86
    definition, 76
    co-optation as political construct, 85–6
    policy interventions contributing to poverty, 82–3
ketahanan pangan (food security), 73, 80–81
Kenya, 310
Khazanah Nasional, 191
Komnas Perempuan, 227
Konfrontasi, 31, 42
Koninklijke Paketvaart Maatschappij (KPM), 25–6, 28
    seizure of offices, 28–9
Korea, 268, 270, 295, 298
    ASEAN Free Trade Agreement (AKFTA), 301, 303, 304, 311
    banks, 185
    exports, 283, 284, 285
Korea Exchange Bank, 185
Korea–US Free Trade Agreement (KORUS), 109
KPK
    see Corruption Eradication Commission
KPM
    see Koninklijke Paketvaart Maatschappij

L

La Via Campesina, 76, 85
labour
    child, 161
    exploitation, 11, 48, 225, 226, 227–41, 243, 244, 245–6, 254, 255, 257–8, 259

female intensity of labour force, 10, 165–79
foreign, 8, 13, 112–29, 220, 247
internal migrant, 246
migrant, 10–11, 13, 227–41, 247–9, 251–9
outflows, 46, 48
unskilled, 10, 148, 202, 213, 218, 219, 220, 221, 222, 225, 254, 260
see also employment; women
labour markets, 92, 157–79, 258
digital technology effect, 212–20
exporting firms, 209–10
flexibility, 13, 219, 249, 258
gender segregation, 158–60, 161, 164
globalisation impacts, 201–22, 260
labour force participation rate, 162
recruitment agencies, 45, 226, 231, 235, 240, 245, 247, 248, 249, 252, 254, 256, 256–7, 258
trade liberalisation effect on female participation, 157–79
wages, 209–11, 213, 252, 286
see also employment; migrant workers
Laos, 103, 245, 248
Latin America, 194
Law No. 17/2003 on State Finances, 276
Law No. 39/2004 on the Placement and Protection of Indonesian Migrant Workers, 225, 233, 231, 249
Law No. 25/2007 on Capital Investment, 114
Law No. 4/2009 on Mineral and Coal Mining, 90, 92
Law No. 6/2012 on the Ratification of the International Convention on the Protection of the Rights of All Migrant Workers and Members of Their Families, 231, 233
Law No. 18/2012 on Food, 79
Law No. 6/2014 on Villages, 226, 228, 235
Law No. 18/2017 on the Protection of Indonesian Migrant Workers, 233, 240, 241
Law No. 21/2007, 249 on the Elimination of Human Trafficking, 249

Leaders Summit of the Indian Ocean Rim Association, 3
Lembong, Thomas, 4
Lippo Bank (Lippo Group), 186, 191
Lukita, Enggartiasto, 4

M

Macau, 247
Mahakam, 101, 102
Malari affair, 184
Malaya, 24, 27, 28
Malayan Banking Berhad (Maybank), 185, 191
Malaysia, 6, 31, 32, 39, 42, 45, 46, 48, 52, 53, 187, 190, 191, 221, 270, 271, 279, 287, 288, 289, 290
banks, 185, 191
'Crush Malaysia' campaign, 39, 41, 43
cultural dispute, 40–41, 49
exports, 283, 284, 285
human trafficking, 247, 248, 249, 254–5
multinational oil palm companies, 246
territorial dispute, 39, 41
TPP membership, 306
trade ban, 31
Maluku, 19, 74, 182, 245
Manila, 21, 61
manufacturing sector, 110–11, 184, 185, 187, 190, 295
Asia-centred global production networks, 282, 288
automation and technology, 212, 214–16, 221, 287
employment, 163, 203–4, 204–5, 212, 219n, 221
wages, 210–11, 221
Marsudi, Retno, 53
Master Plan for the Acceleration and Expansion of Indonesia's Economic Development (MP3EI), 82, 83
Mastercard, 93
Mecca, 24
Medan, 24, 25, 29, 245, 252, 255, 256, 257, 259
media and media reports, 35, 41, 44, 49, 55, 63, 84, 94, 97, 100, 101, 102, 111, 250, 255, 256, 257
impact on public attitude towards openness, 9, 119, 121–5

reporting of human trafficking, 244–5
Melaka, 18, 22
Merauke Integrated Food and Energy Estate (MIFEE), 82, 83
metals and machinery sector, 169, 205
Mexico, 159, 160, 285
Middle East, 17, 193, 194, 221, 229, 230, 231, 247, 272
MIFEE
   see Merauke Integrated Food and Energy Estate
Migrant CARE, 11, 225, 228, 230
migrant workers, 2, 10–11, 225–41
   brokers, 11, 227, 230, 232, 235, 239, 240, 246, 254, 259
   domestic workers, 226, 228, 229, 247, 251, 252
   East Nusa Tenggara, 251–9
   false identities, 248–9, 252, 257
   government protection programs, 230–32
   human trafficking, 232, 245–9, 258
   human trafficking/migrant worker laws disconnection, 250
   human rights violations, 225, 227, 229, 230, 231, 233, 234, 250
   identity check for applicants, 248–9
   number, 228
   share by gender, 228
   villages, 230–33
   vulnerability, 229–30, 253–4, 259
   wages, 247, 252
   see also Village of Care for Migrant Workers (Desbumi); slavery
migration, international, 10, 11, 201, 221, 243
migration policies, 229, 231
military, 6, 27, 29, 30, 31, 42, 45, 47, 48, 58, 59, 257
   exercises in Natuna waters, 7, 63
   memorandum of understanding with Ministry of Energy and Mineral Resources, 59
   occupation of East Timor, 39
   Suharto era, 183–4
   village level, 81
mineral export ban, 8, 90–105, 114, 309
   downstream mineral-processing facilities, 91, 92, 93, 94, 96
   export permits, 97, 98
   selective application of ban on export of minerals, 95–6
   value adding prior to export, 8, 90, 92–4
mining, 9, 90–105, 187
   contribution to total export revenue, 97
   divestment obligations, 99–100, 104, 105, 114
   employment, 9, 164, 206
   foreign-owned companies, 99, 100, 102
   global boom, 8, 90
   Mining Law of 2009, 90, 92–3, 94, 99, 309
   see also commodities; mineral export ban; resources sector
Minister of Energy and Mineral Resources Regulation No. 1/2014, 90
Minister of Home Affairs Regulation No. 290/2010 on Guidelines for the Monitoring of Foreigners and Foreign Organisations in the Regions, 45
Minister of Manpower Regulation No. 4/1970, 226
Ministerial Regulation No. 1/2014 on Improving the Value-added of Minerals through Mineral Processing and Purification Activities, 95
Ministerial Regulation No. 7/2012 on Improving the Value-added of Minerals through Mineral Processing and Purification Activities, 95
Ministerial Regulation No. 11/2012, 95
Ministry of Agriculture, 4
Ministry of Energy and Mineral Resources, 59, 93, 95, 97, 98–9
Ministry of Finance, 96, 193, 276, 277
Ministry of Foreign Affairs, 57
Ministry of Home Affairs, 45, 189
Ministry of Industry, 4, 277, 280–81
Ministry of Justice and Human Rights, 45
Ministry of Manpower, 222, 226, 250, 256, 257, 287
Ministry of Marine Affairs and Fisheries, 55, 56

Ministry of Maritime Affairs, Coordinating, 58, 59
Ministry of Social Affairs, 245, 250
Ministry of Trade, 4, 113, 277
Ministry of Women's Empowerment and Child Protection, 245, 250
Mizuho Bank, 185
Modern Bank (Modern Group), 186
Moeldoko, General, 43, 57
motor vehicle services sector, 214, 216
MP3EI
    see Master Plan for the Acceleration and Expansion of Indonesia's Economic Development
Mulyani, Sri, 99
Muslims, 26, 122, 182, 202, 247, 251
Myanmar, 248, 308

N
Nahdlatul Ulama, 43
National Agency for the Placement and Protection of Indonesia Migrant Workers (BNP2TKI), 228, 247, 250
national car policy, 298
National Development Planning Agency (Bappenas), 60
National Medium-Term Development Plan for 2015-19, 241
National Police, 184, 248, 249
National Semiconductor, 287
National Socio-Economic Survey (Susenas), 74n, 141, 164, 227
nationalism, 2, 3, 35-49, 85-6, 90-105, 110
    cultural, 40-41
    economic, 2-6, 40, 104, 269, 272, 280
    global trend, 37
    history, 41-4
    Jokowi policy, 3, 6, 38-41
    national dignity, 7, 36, 45-6
    national identity, 36-7, 182
    resource, 8, 13, 40, 90-91, 97, 102-3, 104, 114
    territorial, 39, 80
Natuna Islands, 4, 7, 53, 54
    Chinese acknowledgement of Indonesian sovereignty, 55
    Chinese fishing vessels' illegal operations, 55-7
    increased defences, 58, 63
    renaming of sea to the north, 59, 62, 64
    territorial dispute, 57-8
natural resources
    see resources sector; see also mining
Nederlandsch-Indisch Stoomvaart Maatschappij (NISM), 23, 24, 25
Netherlands, The, 18-26, 64
    Amsterdam, 20
    decline of naval power, 21
    Netherlands Trading Society (NHM), 23
    trade balance with Indonesia, 26
    see also United East India Company
New Emerging Forces (NEFOs), 42, 43, 269
New Order, 2, 3, 38, 42, 101, 103, 104, 180, 184, 185, 187, 202, 205, 253
New Zealand, 298
    Australia and, ASEAN Free Trade Agreement (AANZFTA), 301, 302, 303, 304, 311
Newmont, 96
    Batu Hijau mine, 101, 102, 103
nickel, 92, 94n, 95, 96, 97, 98, 99, 139
    smelting capacity, 96-7
Nigeria, 310
NISM
    see Nederlandsch-Indisch Stoomvaart Maatschappij
Nitisastro, Widjojo, 3
non-government organisations
    see civil society organisations
North American Free Trade Agreement (NAFTA), 109, 159, 160, 189
North Natuna Sea, 59, 64
    see also South China Sea dispute
Nurmantyo, General Gatot, 44

O
OCBC Bank, 191
oil booms, 3, 269, 272, 286
oil price, 3, 276, 291, 300
oil sector, 59, 99, 101, 103, 114, 185
OJK
    see Financial Services Authority
Old Established Forces (OLDEFOs), 43
Ooredoo, 190

openness, 3, 9, 21, 195, 305, 310, 312
    comparative indicators, 279
    need in globalised economy, 267, 295
    public opinion survey, 114–29
openness, study of public perceptions, 114–29
    demographic characteristics and political perceptions of participants, 118–19
    estimation results, 119–22
    independent variables and expected signs, 120
    robustness test of study, 122, 126–9
    selected indicators (% of GDP), 113
    statistically significant variables, 121
    summary, 122–5
opium, 19, 21, 22, 23, 24
ORANI-G model, 141

P

palm oil, 82, 83, 184, 187, 206
    daily workers, 247
    human trafficking, 254–5
    migrant workers, 251
Pancasila ideology, 44
Panigoro, Arifin, 101
Panin Bank, 185
Panjaitan, Luhut, 59
Papua, 39, 41, 250, 251, 254
    Grasberg mine, 99–100, 102
    West, 82, 250, 251
parliament (DPR), 249, 276
PDI
    see Indonesian Democracy Party
PDIP
    see Indonesian Democratic Party of Struggle
Pelni, 29
Penang, 22, 23, 24, 25
people smuggling, 244
Pertamina, 101, 185
Peru, 310
Philippines, 1, 21, 32, 53, 60, 112, 229n, 273, 279, 288, 289, 290
    call centres, 213
    exports, 284, 285
    openness/globalisation view, 273, 279
    South China Sea dispute arbitration, 56

pilgrims, 24, 25
piracy, 18, 26
PKS
    see Prosperous Justice Party
Poland, 295
police, 184, 245, 249, 254, 255, 257, 259
politics, 276–8
    elections, 2, 9, 80, 100, 189, 312
    political economy, 86, 122, 276–8, 280n
    political parties, 183, 188, 189
    populist, 1, 2, 5–6, 109
population, 73
    middle class proportion, 192
    world, 75
Portugal, 18, 19
poverty, 1, 5, 7, 11, 46, 82, 83, 226
    incidence, 48, 74n, 84, 134–5, 142, 145, 149, 151, 153, 155–6, 310
    rate of reduction/alleviation, 9, 40, 79, 92, 133, 152, 153, 161, 275, 295
    rural, 135, 143, 226, 243, 252, 254, 259
    rural vs urban comparison, 141–52
    urban, 84, 135
    women, 225, 226
    see also inequality; welfare of households, study using INDONESIA-E3 model
PPP
    see United Development Party
Presidential Decree No. 10/1959, 30
Presidential Instruction No. 10/2016 on the Prevention and Eradication of Corruption, 4
Presidential Regulation No. 69/2008 on the Anti-Trafficking Taskforce, 250
pribumi (indigenous) businesses, 30, 182, 273
primary industries, 205–6
private sector, 94, 99, 102, 103, 104, 104n, 180–96, 203, 226
productivity, 1, 10, 124, 194, 209–14, 277, 287, 295
    improvement through digital technology, 213, 221
Prosperous Justice Party (PKS), 84
protectionism, 1, 2, 3, 5, 9, 10, 80, 83, 104, 110, 189, 195, 269, 271, 298, 309–12

effective rates of protection (ERPs), 138–9, 298, 310
global, 43–6, 152, 153
impact on poverty and inequality, 133–56
response to globalisation, 138, 180
Widodo policy, 4, 5, 110n
see also welfare of households, study using INDONESIA-E3 model
PT Aneka Tambang (Antam), 8, 91, 98–100
PT Freeport Indonesia, 91, 96, 99, 100, 101, 102
Grasberg mine, 99, 100
share divestment, 99, 100
PT Inalum, 99, 100, 102
PT Medco Energi Internasional, 101, 103
public opinion survey, economic openness, 8, 111, 114–29
Pudjiastuti, Susi, 60
Putin (President), 2

Q
Qatar, 190

R
Raffles, Thomas Stamford, 22
Rajasa, Hatta, 94
RCEP
see Regional Comprehensive Economic Partnership
recession, global, 3
reformasi, 10, 80, 180, 188–93, 195, 245, 254, 260
Regional Comprehensive Economic Partnership (RCEP), 12, 13, 305, 306, 310–11
date for completion of negotiations, 305, 310, 311, 312
value of Indonesia's trade with, 311
Regional Representative Council (DPD), 84
rent-seeking, 6, 12, 32, 40, 84, 94n, 110, 270
resources sector, 8, 38, 91–2, 93, 101, 102–5, 184, 190, 227, 90
foreign exploitation, 8, 38, 40, 44, 48, 91, 100–101
memorandum of understanding between military and Ministry of Energy and Mineral Resources, 59
see also nationalism, resource
retail sector, 214
employment, 167, 209
Riau, 21, 26, 27, 31, 54, 244
Ricardo–Viner model, 112
rice, 5, 38, 40, 77–8, 79, 81
imports, 38, 40, 83–4
Mega Rice Project, 82
price, 79, 81, 83, 84
productivity, 226
regulation of imports, 79
Sukarno influence, 77–8, 85, 86
world market, 5, 80
rubber, 28, 29, 146, 169, 179, 206
rupiah
see currency
Russia, 2, 94n, 229n
Ryacudu, Ryamizard, 63

S
Sadli's Law, 272, 272n
Said, Sudirman, 100, 100
Salim Group, 184, 190, 193
Samudera Indonesia, 182
Saudi Arabia, 194, 229, 247
services sector, 144, 164, 202, 206–9, 300, 310
employment, 163, 203, 204, 206–9, 221
jobs in selected industries, 208
major subsectors, 207
Shell, 101
Simbolon, Colonel Maludin, 29
Sinar Mas, 182
Singapore, 6, 22, 27, 32, 48, 187, 247, 268, 270, 271, 287, 289, 290
banks, 185, 191
Economic Development Board, 281
exports, 31, 283, 284, 285
free port, 22
Temasek Holdings, 190, 191
TPP membership, 306
trade, 21, 22–6, 28
trade ban, 31
trade balance with Indonesia, 28, 29
SKA
see trade, certificates of origin

slavery, 227, 227n, 229, 243, 247, 251, 251-2, 255, 258
smuggling, 18, 26, 27-8, 29, 31, 271, 276n, 277
military, 29
social media, 2, 40, 43, 189
Soemarno, Rini, 98, 99
Soik, Rudy, 245, 249, 259
South China Sea dispute, 4, 7, 52-65
ASEAN-China hotline, 61
China's nine-dash line, 54, 58
Declaration on the Conduct of Parties in the South China Sea, 54, 61, 62
informal workshops to manage conflicts, 53-4
naming of North Natuna Sea, 59, 62, 64
role of ASEAN, 60-63
sovereignty, 45
early Indonesian government years, 28, 29, 30
economic, 94, 121n
food, 12-13, 73-86
geographic, 24, 25, 52-65
Widodo policy, 38
Soviet Union collapse, 42
SPI
see Indonesian Peasants Union
Spice Islands, 19
spices, 17, 19, 20, 21
Sri Lanka, 285
Standard Chartered Bank, 185, 191
state-owned enterprises (SOEs), 91, 98-9, 100, 101, 102, 103, 182, 184, 190, 270, 273
banks, 183, 185, 191-2
Stolper-Samuelson theorem, 111, 112
Straits Settlements, 22, 23, 24, 26
students
demonstrations against Suharto, 188
protests against Japanese investment, 184
Subianto, General Prabowo, 4, 38, 40, 44, 82, 100
Suharto, President, 2, 3, 6, 7, 10, 31, 36, 38, 39, 42, 47, 52, 79, 86, 104, 104, 180, 182, 231, 245, 254, 259, 269, 276, 277, 277n, 281n
fall, 188

reopening to globalisation, 183-8, 195, 202, 299
Sukarno, President, 2, 3, 6, 7, 10, 31, 38, 41, 42, 43, 47, 52, 77-8, 79, 86, 180, 184, 202, 231, 269
economic openness, 181-3, 184, 195
fall, 183
Sukarnoputri, Megawati, 231
Sulaiman, Amran, 5
Sulawesi, 8, 29, 43, 90, 254
north, 26, 29
Permesta rebellion 1958, 29, 182
south, 26
Sumatra, 8, 21, 22, 27, 28, 29, 90, 181, 187, 254
east, 21
north, 21, 24, 246, 252
PRRI rebellion 1958, 29, 31, 182
Sumitomo Mitsui Banking Corporation, 185-6, 191
surveys
countries most admired, 49
private sector perceptions of customs procedures in ASEAN, 307
public opinion, on economic openness, 8, 111, 114-29
World Values Survey, 37
Susenas
see National Socio-Economic Survey
Sustainable Development Goals, 229, 233

T

Taiwan, 185, 247
technology
advanced, 10, 159, 194, 195, 209
ASEAN National Single Windows, 307
automation, 186, 212, 214
banking sector, 186, 196
computer use, 212, 213-14
digital, 189-90, 193, 195, 202, 203, 212-13
e-commerce, 190, 201-2, 212, 214
e-KTP ('smart' card), 249
effect on labour market, 10, 159, 201-22, 287
Information Technology Agreement (ITA II) (ASEAN), 280, 287

internet use by firms, 214–15
spillovers, 295
use by criminals, 2
telecommunications, 190
mobile phones, 190, 193, 194, 203, 212, 213, 219
Telekom Malaysia, 190
Telkomsel, 190
Temasek Holdings, 190, 194
textiles
British cloth, 21, 22
imported, 3
Indian, 19, 20
textiles, clothing and footwear industry, 146, 203, 204, 205, 210, 214, 215, 216
female employment, 158, 159
see also footwear industry, case study; garment industry, case study
Thailand, 32, 246, 248, 270, 279, 288, 289, 290, 295
exports, 284, 285
Timah, 99
tin, 31, 95, 96, 99, 139
TNI
see Indonesian National Army
tourism, 8, 116, 308–9
number of visitor arrivals, 309
public perception of foreign visitors, 8, 116, 123, 309
TPP
see Trans-Pacific Partnership
trade
certificates of origin (SKA), 302–3
comparative advantage, 111–12, 159, 161, 275, 282
development of state monopoly, 6, 17–18
factors of production, 111–12, 140, 144, 145, 147, 148, 150
free, 3, 21–2, 111–12
historical trade routes, 17–18
liberalisation, 3, 9, 104, 157–79, 212, 269, 271, 273, 279, 297
Logistics Performance Index, 307, 308
most favoured nation (MFN) tariffs, 296, 298, 301, 302, 305, 310, 312
non-tariff barriers (NTBs), 4, 5, 113, 113n, 177, 276, 277

openness, 3, 9, 10, 11, 21, 109–29, 160, 195, 279, 295
reforms and gendered labour market effects, 158–60
restrictions, 79, 84, 110, 133, 138, 139, 310
tariffs, 3, 4, 9, 22–3, 109, 143, 159, 160–61, 165, 167, 176, 177, 189, 271, 279, 295, 296, 297, 311
total value, 297
trade-to-GDP ratio, 138
value with RCEP countries, 311
world growth, 1, 109, 113, 136–8, 201, 307
see also globalisation; imports; exports; protectionism
trade agreements, 294–312
ASEAN, 280, 300–306
bilateral, 12, 13, 299, 310
Japan, 280
multilateral, 298–9
regional, 13, 301, 305, 310
'spaghetti bowl', 305, 312
trade restricting rules of origin, 304–5
trade policy, 1, 3, 4, 5, 110, 111–12, 122–4, 270, 272, 278–9
international, 279–80
international cooperation, 294–312
trade unions, 28, 202
Trans-Pacific Partnership (TPP), 4, 109, 306, 310
Comprehensive and Progressive Agreement for Trans-Pacific Partnership (CPTPP), 306, 310
membership, 306
withdrawal of United States, 12, 306
transport sector, 139, 144, 146, 164, 166, 179, 194, 202, 206, 207, 208, 214, 215, 216, 219–20
Trump, Donald, 2, 5, 109, 189, 201
Turkey, 2, 194

U
Uber, 194, 215, 219
unemployment, 204, 206, 226, 247, 251
Unicef, 227
United Development Party (PPP), 183
United East India Company (VOC), 6, 18–20, 21, 23
bankruptcy, 21

governor-general, 20
spice monopolies, 19, 20
United Kingdom, 64, 190, 191
   Brexit, 1–2, 109, 189
United Nations, 39, 227, 229, 269
   Food and Agriculture Organization, 75
   South China Sea dispute, 54–5, 59
United Nations Convention on the Law of the Sea, 52, 54, 57
   arbitral tribunal constituted under Annex VII, 56
United Nations Protocol to Prevent, Suppress and Punish Trafficking in Persons Especially Women and Children, 244, 249
United Overseas Bank (UOB), 185, 191
United States of America, 2, 4, 37, 42, 48, 109, 110, 112, 159, 214, 298
   attitude towards globalisation, 273
   election of Donald Trump, 2, 109
   historical naval trade, 21, 23
   manufacturing, 213
   ties with Indonesia, 63–4
   trade restrictions, 109, 201
   withdrawal from TPP, 12, 109

V

van Heutsz, J.B., 25
Vietnam, 53, 60, 205, 269, 270, 279, 288, 289, 290
   exports, 283, 284, 285, 286
   TPP membership, 306
Village of Care for Migrant Workers (Desbumi), 10–11, 225, 228, 234–41
   challenges, 235
   funding, 235
   programs operating, 235–7
   progress summary of projects, 239–40
   project location and funding, 238
   role, 234
   three pillars, 235, 236–7
   see also human trafficking; migrant workers
violence
   against women, 227
   clashes between different religious and ethnic groups, 189
   student protests against Japanese investment, 184
Visa, 193

visitors, foreign
   see tourism
VOC
   see United East India Company

W

Wacik, Jero, 95
Wahid, Abdurrahman, 231
welfare of households, study using INDONESIA-E3 model, 140–53
   impact of global protectionism on real expenditure per capita, 144
   impact of global protectionism on real return to factors of production, 145
   impact of global protectionism on output by sector, 146
   impact of Indonesia's protectionism in the food and mineral sectors on real expenditure per capita, 152
   impact of Indonesia's protectionism in the food sector on real expenditure per capita, 148
   impact of Indonesia's protectionism in the mineral sector on real expenditure per capita, 151
   impact of Indonesia's protectionism on inequality, 150
   impact of Indonesia's protectionism on nominal return to factors of production, 148
   impact of Indonesia's protectionism on poverty incidence, 149
   measurement of inequality (Gini coefficient), 155–6
   measurement of poverty incidence, 155
   model structure, 141–3
   summary, 152–3
   urban v. rural comparison, 143, 144, 145, 147, 149, 150, 151, 152
West Java, 225, 234, 238
West Nusa Tenggara, 225, 231, 234, 238
Widodo, Joko, 3–4, 6, 60, 221, 229, 306
   deregulation, 310
   economic openness, 120, 122, 124, 278
   election (2014), 9, 38, 58, 100, 119, 124, 189

food policy, 78, 81, 82
infrastructure, 190–91
maritime issues, 60, 63
migration policies, 229
mining policy, 91, 97, 98, 99–100, 101, 102
nationalism, 3, 6, 8, 100–102, 103
Natuna Islands cabinet meeting on warship, 4, 7, 58
Natuna Islands development and defences, 63
Nawacita, 81, 84, 233, 241
protectionism, 4, 5, 110n
RCEP support, 311
South China Sea dispute, 58, 63
visit to Australia, 63
visit to United States, 306
women
abuse of domestic workers, 2, 221, 228–9, 252
child marriage, 227
discrimination against, 158, 159, 227
effect of international trade on female employment, 165–77
employment in export-oriented sectors, 169–71, 179, 275
employment in import-oriented sectors, 172–6
employment opportunities, 9–10, 157–79, 204, 209, 213, 214, 221
female intensity of labour force, 10, 165–79
labour force participation, 157, 161–7
labour force participation by age, 163
labour force participation by sector, 163
migrant workers, 11, 221, 225–41, 247, 255
poor, 11, 225, 226, 247, 254
trade reform effects on employment, 160–61
violence against, 227
wages, 158, 159, 160, 221
wood and wood products, 83, 139, 146, 179, 184, 205, 209, 210, 215, 216
Woori Bank, 185
workforce, 206, 222, 281, 288
female, 9, 158, 161–79, 209

manufacturing, 281–1
participation rates, 162
retrenchments opposed by Ministry of Manpower, 287
see also employment; labour; labour markets
World Bank, 4, 81
Logistics Performance Index, 307
World Trade Organization (WTO), 12, 13, 109, 113, 277, 280, 294, 295, 296, 298–9, 299, 311
appeal by United States and New Zealand on import licensing, 298
Dispute Settlement Panel, 298
Doha Round, 5, 298–9
General Agreement on Trade and Tariffs (GATT), 294, 298
General Agreement on Trade in Services (GATS), 300–301
Trade Facilitation Agreement, 299, 307
Trade-Related Investment Measures (TRIMs) Agreement, 298
Uruguay Round, 299
World Values Survey, 37

X

Xi (President), 2
XL, 190

Y

Yudhoyono, Susilo Bambang, 3, 8, 40, 80, 82, 83, 90, 94, 96, 98, 99, 201, 231, 278, 306

Z

Zaini, Air Commodore Fahru, 57

INDONESIA UPDATE SERIES

1989
Indonesia Assessment 1988 (Regional Development)
Edited by Hal Hill and Jamie Mackie

1990
Indonesia Assessment 1990 (Ownership)
Edited by Hal Hill and Terry Hull

1991
Indonesia Assessment 1991 (Education)
Edited by Hal Hill

1992
Indonesia Assessment 1992: Political Perspectives on the 1990s
Edited by Harold A. Crouch and Hal Hill

1993
Indonesia Assessment 1993: Labour: Sharing in the Benefits of Growth?
Edited by Chris Manning and Joan Hardjono

1994
Indonesia Assessment 1994: Finance as a Key Sector in Indonesia's Development
Edited by Ross McLeod

1996
Indonesia Assessment 1995: Development in Eastern Indonesia
Edited by Colin Barlow and Joan Hardjono

1997
Indonesia Assessment: Population and Human Resources
Edited by Gavin W. Jones and Terence H. Hull

1998
Indonesia's Technological Challenge
Edited by Hal Hill and Thee Kian Wie

1999
Post-Soeharto Indonesia: Renewal or Chaos?
Edited by Geoff Forrester

2000
Indonesia in Transition: Social Aspects of Reformasi and Crisis
Edited by Chris Manning and Peter van Diermen

2001
Indonesia Today: Challenges of History
Edited by Grayson J. Lloyd and Shannon L. Smith

2002
Women in Indonesia: Gender, Equity and Development
Edited by Kathryn Robinson and Sharon Bessell

2003
Local Power and Politics in Indonesia: Decentralisation and Democratisation
Edited by Edward Aspinall and Greg Fealy

2004
Business in Indonesia: New Challenges, Old Problems
Edited by M. Chatib Basri and Pierre van der Eng

2005
The Politics and Economics of Indonesia's Natural Resources
Edited by Budy P. Resosudarmo

2006
Different Societies, Shared Futures: Australia, Indonesia and the Region
Edited by John Monfries

2007
Indonesia: Democracy and the Promise of Good Governance
Edited by Ross H. McLeod and Andrew MacIntyre

2008
Expressing Islam: Religious Life and Politics in Indonesia
Edited by Greg Fealy and Sally White

2009
Indonesia beyond the Water's Edge: Managing an Archipelagic State
Edited by Robert Cribb and Michele Ford

2010
Problems of Democratisation in Indonesia: Elections, Institutions and Society
Edited by Edward Aspinall and Marcus Mietzner

2011
Employment, Living Standards and Poverty in Contemporary Indonesia
Edited by Chris Manning and Sudarno Sumarto

2012
Indonesia Rising: The Repositioning of Asia's Third Giant
Edited by Anthony Reid

2013
Education in Indonesia
Edited by Daniel Suryadarma and Gavin W. Jones

2014
Regional Dynamics in a Decentralized Indonesia
Edited by Hal Hill

2015
The Yudhoyono Presidency: Indonesia's Decade of Stability and Stagnation
Edited by Edward Aspinall, Marcus Mietzner and Dirk Tomsa

2016
Land and Development in Indonesia: Searching for the People's Sovereignty
Edited by John F. McCarthy and Kathryn Robinson

2017
Digital Indonesia: Connectivity and Divergence
Edited by Edwin Jurriëns and Ross Tapsell

2018
Indonesia in the New World: Globalisation, Nationalism and Sovereignty
Edited by Arianto A. Patunru, Mari Pangestu and M. Chatib Basri